KT-367-349

Ōdd bins
DICTIONARY OF WINE

General Editor
SIMON COLLIN

BLOOMSBURY

www.bloomsbury.com

First published in Great Britain 2004

Bloomsbury Publishing Plc
38 Soho Square, London, W1D 3HB

British Library Cataloguing in Publication Data

A catalogue entry for this book is available from the British Library

ISBN: 0 7475 6641 0

Text computer typeset by Hewer Text Ltd, Edinburgh
Printed and bound in Italy by Legoprint

All papers used by Bloomsbury Publishing are natural, recyclable
products made from wood grown in well-managed forests. The
manufacturing processes conform to the environmental regulations
of the country of origin.

CONTENTS

General Editor
SIMON COLLIN

Special thanks to:
Laurie Webster, Dan Wilkinson, Corinna Thompson, Lynne
Coyle and all the managers of Oddbins branches, past and
present, whose knowledge and passion for wine have been the
inspiration for this book.

Editors
Lesley Brown, Gordon Kerr

Pronunciations
Dinah Jackson

Adviser
John Beeston
Author of *Concise History of Australian Wine*
and *Wine Regions of Australia*

Maps
bounford.com

Text production and Proofreading
Katy McAdam, Daisy Jackson, Joel Adams,
Sarah Lusznat, Charlotte Regan,
Emma Harris, Ruth Hillmore

BLOOMSBURY REFERENCE

| *Dictionaries Publisher* | *Executive Editor* | *Production Editor* |
| Faye Carney | Susan Jellis | Nicky Thompson |

PREFACE
Matthew Jukes

Over the years I have often found myself both amazed and impressed by the level of wine knowledge and honesty of UK wine drinkers in discussing the taste of wine. Interestingly, the same cannot be said for our friends around the world. In fact, wine-producing countries, in my experience, often have the least well-informed citizens. I have puzzled over why this might be. Perhaps they are too close to the subject and, as they inevitably drink wine regularly, often every lunch and dinner, they don't tend to think much about what's in the glass. Also, they rarely drink wine from outside their own locale. We are lucky in this respect. Wine drinking is our number one social hobby!

With a few notable exceptions, we don't make much wine over here, and coupled to the fact that we have long been seafarers and merchants and are therefore connoisseurs of wares from overseas, we have learned to appreciate wine at a much faster rate than other nations. Wasn't it the Brits whose palates changed the style of Champagne from sweet to the dry style it is today? Also, over the centuries, the British were responsible, to a greater or lesser degree, for the production of other great wine styles like Bordeaux, port and Madeira. These days, with easier, faster transport and more wanderlust, even historically introspective regions like Burgundy are teeming with winemakers who have worked all over the world, experiencing and enjoying the cooking, culture and wines from the New World as well as their own beloved Old World creations. This may be true about the winemakers, but it is far from accurate when it comes down to the everyday Burgundians' diet. I imagine they don't often drink anything other than their own local stuff. Would any of them have ever seen a bottle of Aussie Shiraz or Chilean Carmenère? Sadly, I very much doubt it. We, in the UK, are the consumers who inhabit the global driving seat, and we continue to set the pace. Even the Americans are playing catch-up with us as regards Australia, New Zealand and South Africa.

So do we make the most of this fortunate position? On the whole, yes. A London cabbie the other day swore blind that he hadn't touched a drop of wine until four or five years ago (he was exclusively a beer man), and now he is partial to Chilean Merlots, Chianti and Côte du Rhônes, and he even went as far as saying he couldn't get his head around South African Pinotage. For me this was a remarkably astute rundown of his exact wine needs. This core knowledge is creeping into society every day. I particularly liked his point about Pinotage, which was, admittedly, accurate in my opinion! We tend to take our knowledge levels, no matter how small, for granted, because wine is becoming ingrained in our foodie culture. But we must all congratulate ourselves for coming so far so fast. Even you, for picking up (and hopefully buying) this book, would be considered an aficionado, whether you feel it is warranted or not.

As a wine writer, I am delighted about this desire for wine knowledge because we have never had it so good – there has never in history been as wide a range of global wine sold in the UK as there is today. More choice, more enthusiasm, more chance to try anything and everything. But hang on. If we are so good at it then why do we need a brand new dictionary?

We are fortunate enough to have a very active wine market and some cracking buyers in the UK. But it has to be said everyone's knowledge could always be tweaked even more.

I travel around the country hosting tastings and have met thousands of people of all ages and backgrounds. Gosh, some of the studious sorts blind me with their knowledge of Bordeaux blends, down to the exact percentage, others talk about malo-lactic fermentation and Brettanomyces until they are blue in the face. I find this exciting and encouraging, as this means that there are people out there who are as bonkers about this massive and continuously evolving subject as I am. These people I call the 'haves', and they are all very welcome. But I also adore talking to the 'have nots'. Now before you think me rude, I am referring to those who 'have' been well and truly bitten by the wine bug and those who 'have not'. The 'have nots' are an equally fascinating Venn diagram of people. This contented band of keen gluggers is happy to bumble along buying whatever seems to work, drinking hits one night and misses the next.

To find out whether you are a have or a have not, did you understand the malo and Brett sentence a few lines back? If no, this doesn't make any difference to me, as you are the proud possessor of something the 'haves' haven't got. You know exactly what you like and why you like it. The 'haves' pretend to like and understand everything, which by the way is impossible. They deliberate over choosing a bottle in the shop for hours, wasting valuable drinking time (I am one, I should know). You 'have nots' are a wonderful lot. You may be bemused amateurs and enthusiastic drinkers, but on the occasion that you do absorb a fact you'll never let it go. To you, finding out that Marlborough in New Zealand and Sancerre in France share a common grape variety (Sauvignon Blanc links them) is nothing short of a revelation. This fact may not have bothered you before, as you have always enjoyed both styles of wine, but when the penny drops, it is an unexpected and welcome bonus and this book can give you a boost like that every day.

Now I have read this book and, despite classing myself in the 'have' category, have learned a ton from these pages. This is not surprising, as wine is a monstrous subject never knowingly tamed by any one individual, and I suppose that is part of its charm. Remember you can never truly be an expert – only the wine can be that.

So for all of you 'have nots' who want to make that leap, and even for those of you who often can't be bothered but would like to find quickly the answer to a tricky expression, seemingly convoluted tasting notes or high falutin' wine words, this is the book for you. And for all of you 'haves' who think they know it all but have barely scratched the surface, this is also the book that will make your lives much easier.

This is a dictionary, you don't have to read it cover to cover. All you have to do is refer to it whenever you are stuck – grab it, locate the page, read and smugly nod – quick, in and out, like an SAS raid. No matter who you are or what your level of knowledge, this book will open the subject up for you, and hopefully answer some of those nagging questions. Happy browsing, glass in hand.

Matthew Jukes is the author of the UK's best-selling wine guide, *The Wine List*, and *www.expertwine.com*

PRONUNCIATION GUIDE

Symbol	Example	Symbol	Example
a	**a**t	n, nn	**n**ot, fu**nn**y
aa	f**a**ther	ng	so**ng**
aw	**a**ll	o	**o**dd
ay	d**a**y	ō	**o**pen
air	h**air**	ŏŏ	g**oo**d
b, bb	**b**ut, ri**bb**on	oo	sch**oo**l
ch	**ch**in	ow	**ow**l
d, dd	**d**o, la**dd**er	oy	**oi**l
ə	**a**bout, edibl**e**, it**e**m,	p, pp	**p**en, ha**pp**y
	comm**o**n, circ**u**s	r, rr	**r**oad, ca**rr**y, ha**r**d
e	**e**gg	s, ss	**s**ay, le**ss**on
ee	**ee**l	sh	**sh**eep
f, ff	**f**ond, di**ff**er	th	**th**in
g, gg	**g**o, gi**gg**le	<u>th</u>	**th**is
h	**h**ot	t, tt	**t**ell, bu**tt**er
hw	**wh**en	u	**u**p
i	**i**t, happ**y**, med**i**um	ur	**ur**ge
ī	**i**ce	v, vv	**v**ery sa**vv**y
j, jj	**j**uice, pi**g**eon	w	**w**et
k	**k**ey, thi**ck**	y	**y**es
l, ll	**l**et, si**ll**y	z, zz	**z**oo, bli**zz**ard
m, mm	**m**other, ha**mm**er	<u>zh</u>	vi**s**ion

Foreign pronunciations
/<u>kh</u>/ as in German ba**ck**, Spanish **Gij**on
/N/ to show nasalisation of the preceeding vowel as in the French pronunciation of **un bon vin** blanc /öN boN vaN blaaN/
/ö/ as in French b**oeuf**, German sch**ö**n
/ü/ as in French r**ue**, German gem**ü**tlich

Stress
´ over a vowel indicates the syllable that has the main stress, or the syllable before this that has the second most important stress.
' before /l/, /m/, or /n/ shows that the consonant is pronounced as a whole syllable

Symbols
♀ named grape variety   ◊ named wine   ♀ tasting term

A WINEMAKER'S VIEW

Chester D'Arenberg Osborn
D'Arenberg
Australia

It was a very easy decision to become a winemaker. I was born into it! My mother carried me around the winery at the age of two telling me how I was going to be an inventive, great winemaker. At the age of about six, Len Evans, a well-known Australian wine judge and writer, asked me 'What sort of wine are you going to make when you grow up'. I said 'a yummy one'. The point is he didn't ask me if I was going to be a winemaker – it was a given.

A piece of art

Nowadays, I get caught with mainly flavours, spending six hours a day tasting grapes during vintage, followed by hours tasting ferments. Outside of vintage, it's judging or tasting my wines amongst the consumers and listening to their opinions, or most importantly, tasting each barrel blind, deciphering why it tastes as it does, as environment and management of grapes and the wine influence the wine. Then I decide which wine blend each barrel will go into.

Getting so intimately involved with each parcel of vines, and in turn each batch of wine followed by each blend, means that I get very attached to each as if they were my children, making it difficult to choose between them.

Wine and grape flavours and aromas are like sight to me. Once you taste the wine, a whole myriad of things are seen: how and where the grapes were grown, the season, the winemaking method, the individual characters, the balance, type and intensity of each different taste character. There is an amazing amount of detail that you can find in a wine – it's a real buzz.

These reasons, and the fact that it is an expression of one's self, a piece of art, is why I make wine. There are also all the great people and perks that go with the job but they are secondary.

Boutique winemaking on a big scale

I doubt whether there is another winery of d'Arenberg's size basket-pressing whites and reds. Included in this are hundreds of 4.5 to 5 tonne batches from individual parts of vineyards being kept separate in headed-down (submerged cap) open fermenters and foot-trod. Pumping over or plunging is not used. Over half of the production finishes ferment in small oak – much of which remains on lees for over a year. No fining or real filtering of the wine is done. Hence, we have small, specialist, 'boutique' winemaking undertaken on a big scale.

Extreme viticulture is also a motto at d'Arenberg. If a winery has had to trim the vines during the growing season, they have failed as the vines are too vigorous. In 2003, the average yield was 1.3 tonne/acre and in 2004, the average yield was 1.5 tonne/acre. Intense fruit.

The Australian winemaking scene

Gradually winemakers are focusing more on the fruit in the vineyard as well as making less oaked wines. The structures of many are still too open and fat without long, gritty fruit tannins that lengthen the palate and give the wine great ageability. It is this more fragrant, lengthy wine with great expression of terroir that I aim to achieve using extreme viticulture practices and very gentle winemaking. Some winemakers are into major manipulation of the wine in the processing. I don't like to over-process the wine.

The future

My goals are to make great wine that I like to drink. I won't be able to grow the business much more as I won't be able to keep on top of all of the tastings required for each vineyard and barrel. I would like to think that d'Arenberg would become one of the greatest wineries in the world, rolling off anyone's tongue when asked the name of a great winery.

I am very interested in varieties new to McLaren Vale and new blends. Who knows whether there is an even more well-suited grape to McLaren Vale than Shiraz, Grenache or Mourvèdre. We have now all the white Rhones and Tempranillo, Souzão and Tinta Cão, and possibly Petit Manseng in the future.

Randall Grahm
Bonny Doon Vineyard
California

You explain your actions to yourself retrospectively, but if I were to try to reconstruct my thought process at the time, my motivation for becoming a winemaker would have gone something like this: having worked briefly in the retail trade and been given the unique opportunity to taste the most extraordinary wines in the world, I had become thoroughly smitten with the aesthetic of wine. Maybe I was a closet synesthete all along, but I imagined that I saw and heard organoleptic and textural counterpoint. Tasting '71 Scharzhofberger Auslese Goldkapsel was about the most hallucinatory experience I enjoyed in the early 70s. I had nothing more than the intuition that the craft of winemaking could be something like a mandala, a way of finding a sort of balance in life, of creating a structured harmony, but in fact, my experience of life as a winemaker has largely brought me that – on good days. What continues to motivate me to make wine is that it appears that I have some proficiency in the craft and that I continue to find meaning in what I do. The craft of winemaking seems to be sufficiently metaphoric to nourish my minimum daily requirement for art/drama/beauty/sensuality/otherworldliness.

Satisfy and delight consumers
We try really, really hard and we continuously experiment and iterate in the development of new grape varieties, new viticultural regions and wine styles. There is a certain Faustian dimension to all of this. I have personally tried to surgically excise the systemic pretentiousness of the wine business in all of what we do. We really do try to make wines that satisfy and delight the mind, spirit and body of our consumers.

The Californian winemaking scene
Wineries are getting a lot more cynical and regressed, i.e. deciding that what they personally want to achieve doesn't really matter, but they feel that they must produce wines in a certain style to, most importantly, please the important wine media, secondarily, the wine public – to the extent that the wine public understands what it wants itself. On the other hand, there are a few winemakers who are agonising about how they can truly produce distinctive wines and a few of them are actually taking the notion of terroir

seriously. I am heartened that there does appear to be a growing interest in alternative grape varieties. Tempranillo is often bandied about, but I don't as yet see a lot of interest in the real warm-climate grapes of southern Italy and Greece, i.e. grapes that do not come with a snooty, pedigreed calling card.

Short and long-term goals

I would really like to make wines that are far more distinctive and interesting than the ones that we are currently producing, indeed wines that are necessary, wines that make the world more interesting. It would also be exceptionally cool if indeed we could produce a wine, or wines, that was truly capable of expressing terroir. In the near term, my immediate goal is to attempt to persuade our growers to make the transition from conventional to organic farming and ideally to biodynamie, if they can make that imaginative leap. It is my intention to exclusively produce wines made from organic grapes within the next few years, but there is a tremendous amount of work that needs to be done to make that occur.

The future

I can't speak for the rest of the world, but I would ultimately, after some significant machination, like to get to a place of extreme simplicity, where as a winemaker I am working with grapes that arrive in the winery already programmed for success, i.e. balanced, sufficiently concentrated, expressive, such that I do not have to move heaven and earth to contrive an interesting wine from them. It would be great if somehow I could offer a wine that was simply a wine rather than a wine 'brand'.

Kent Rasmussen
Kent Rasmussen Winery
California

It's a rare winemaker who wakes up one day in his youth and says 'I am going to be a winemaker'. Instead, winemaking is a calling that one arrives at later in life, having experienced other vocations along the path. Why develop a passion for wine-making versus widget-making? Hard to say, but after having been a winemaker for over 25 years now, I can see that it requires a certain type of soul. A scientist? An artist? I have read that people are either goal-oriented or process-oriented. A winemaker's work is the epitome of process-orientation, without it they could never survive!

My route to winemaking was as different as most others in the profession. I was headed down the dusty halls of librarianship, another noble *and* very process-oriented profession, but found that I didn't take well to the constraints of four walls and a pay-slip. Winemaking had been a passion for me since my teenage years. I think the thing that appealed, and still does, to me most about winemaking is (as economists say) the 'vertical integration' of the profession. After all, if you are process-oriented, isn't it better that the process be a long one? The old adage that 'winemaking starts in the vineyard' doesn't begin to go back far enough.

Winemaking starts with finding the land and a trip to the bank, then planting the vineyard and building the winery (to the bank again!), purchasing all that equipment, then grapes (a milestone!) and harvest, then the fermentation (with its one million non-quantifiable choices of how to turn the aforementioned grapes into wine) and at last: *The Wine*. But then you are only halfway through! From there, the process continues: cellaring, package design, bottling, ageing and God-help-us, every-winemaker's-nightmare, a goal-oriented activity: *Marketing*. But is that the end? No! Then there are critics, reviews, corked bottles, fame, fortune (we all hope) and, oh yes, the goal: someone, somewhere enjoys a good bottle of wine. But, in the meantime, the winemaker has many more vintages in process. What a life! *It is a great life!*

The attraction of two varieties

While over the years I have worked with many varieties of grapes, and made many a wonderful wine out of most of them, my true focus and interest has lain with just two varieties that are as different as different can be: Pinot Noir and Petite Sirah. In my mind Pinot Noir is the world's greatest grape, and Petite Sirah is the world's most Californian grape. Thus, my attraction to them is clear – I am a Californian winemaker!

Pinot Noir's evolution in California has largely occurred over just the last 25 years, with the quality of the variety going from bluntly appalling in the 1970s to world-class in recent vintages. Some of this improvement can be attributed to the increase in wine quality worldwide, using scientific knowledge instead of the 'this-is-the-way-we-have-always-done-it' approach. California's Pinot Noir has improved more by the focus that winemakers have given to the issues of grape-growing: climate (particularly the discovery of cool growing regions like Carneros), trellising, clonal selection and maturity, although changes in cellar practice, maturation and finishing procedures have helped also. Pinot Noir is every winemaker's challenge. For me, making any wine is fun, but making a mind-boggling Pinot Noir is seventh heaven.

Petite Sirah is another story altogether. Major European varieties were introduced into California in the mid-1800s, and many of the best wines through California's history have been made from Petite Sirah grapes. Although almost unknown elsewhere, it is a variety that shines under the California sun. Rich, dark, astringent and overwhelmingly fruity, it is the masculine antithesis of our delicate, sophisticated Pinot Noir, and yet it is also a wonderful wine. In its youth, Petite Sirah (farmers call it 'Pets' or 'Petty Sarah') has a vast and irresistible sensory presence in both mouth and nose, with oodles of fruit and masses of tannin. As it ages it develops much of the character of a fine Cabernet, and it can live a long, long time! I have been making Petite Sirah now for almost 25 years, and have never once been disappointed in the outcome. Each year I become more convinced that Pets will have a much larger place in the future's history than it has at present.

The Californian winemaking scene
Throughout my years as a winemaker in California, each vintage has brought new ideas and innovations that make our wines better. Twenty-five years ago, California was leading the world into a new era of winemaking, merging modern science into the age-old art. Now many, if not most, of the world's major wine-growing areas are cognisant of, even if not economically able to use, these methods. California is still a major centre for trial and innovation in the industry, both in primary research on the academic level, and also, due to the economic health of the industry, on the artistic level in vineyard and the cellar. Here wine-growing has achieved the longevity that allows re-evaluation and the major theme these days is to look again at the ideas of the last few decades regarding grape growing, particularly at the ultra-premium end of the spectrum, in terms of matching varieties to micro-appellations.

The future
There is ongoing interest in the many new 'tools' that modern technology has given us, for example non-invasive alcohol reduction. In sales and marketing, we are re-evaluating what

consumers want and deserve. Many winemakers want an end of corks as a closure method because of the seemingly unsolvable problem of corkiness.

Like all successful businesses, we re-evaluate continually to change with the times, rather like when we first decided to become winemakers. And like all great artists, our style matures, but doesn't really change. Like a fine wine?

Aurelio Montes
Montes
Chile

Somehow I always knew I would be a winemaker. From very early on I loved nature sea, soil and space and, even when a teenager, was fascinated by wine, vines and climate. The motivation was strong, starting with tasting the top world wines, especially those that have been highly rated by respected wine writers, inspecting and working on the vines and vineyards, testing the soil to detect which grapes were the best match for it. The challenge is always to do better than the model, which, in turn, was a super wine acquired abroad.

Working with small plots

My approach is to investigate different varieties in new territories, searching for the best fit and then, eventually, achieving the best terroir for that particular grape. I insist on vinifying in small plots of two hectares at the largest, separating the total vineyard into small plots, vinifying each plot separately to discover exactly where the best wines in barrels have come from. If a plot is consistently above the rest in quality, we test how much better it is. Our Montes Alpha 'M' (a Bordeaux blend) and Montes Folly (100% Syrah), were the result of this slow search, both the best of Chile in their categories.

The South American winemaking scene

A revolution! Chile has evolved from an uninspiring producer of supermarket wines to competing with the best in the world in 15 short years! It has come from almost the Stone Age to state-of-the-art facilities. Chilean wines witness to it and ours in particular, as we were the first to aim for premium wines. Now we also have ultra-premiums!

Argentina has also quickly evolved and I have started my own winery there, named 'Kaiken'.

The future

My goal is to produce distinct wines that are equal to or better than the best elsewhere.

I am now busy with our first super-high-tech winery for our premium Montes Alpha red wines and our two super wines, Montes Alpha 'M' and Montes Folly, and we have concentrated our efforts in our two estates, 'La Finca de Apalta' (a whole mountain, with vineyards in up to 45° slopes, in the Apalta Valley, considered to be the best for reds in Chile today, and from where our 'M' and Folly are sourced), and 'El Arcangel' (in Marchigüe, closer to the coast), both in the Colchagua Valley. I expect wonders from these two estates and was the pioneer in both.

As far as the future of the 'world of wine' goes, it is very difficult to see. The only professed indicator is that everyone seems bent on quality – some genuinely, others just claiming so. Only a few will make history and I would bet on the New World as there are so many new regions to explore. I see the greatest enthusiasm in the New World and Old World big names seem to have received the message. In Chile alone, France has the largest foreign investment in wines and they are all top names you would recognise. Overall, due to the ever-increasing interest in wines and their increasing prestige as healthy beverages, premium wines are certainly the future. Ten years from now the standard will have greatly increased. I foresee a superb future for premium wines from every wine region in the world as consumers become more knowledgeable and have the disposable income to support their curiosity.

Marcelo Papa
Concha y Toro
Chile

When I was studying agronomy at University, I had the chance to do a winemaking course, which I took just for fun. I never thought of working as a winemaker, but once I started, I never wanted to stop.

If I could start again with my life for sure I would decide to enjoy and work again as a winemaker. The opportunities that this job offers are so special, working with weather conditions and nature's other elements. So we are at one with nature and our contact with it is so strong. We feel it. That is very unusual these days. We also get strong feedback from consumers and wine writers about our wines, so we know directly how we are progressing.

The Chilean winemaking scene

For a long time we got great wines from France, and Bordeaux in particular, from 1860 to 1990. I think that at this time there were not too many changes in style. However, during the 1990s, the big revolution in technology in all wineries began. Now I think what is going on is that during the last 15 years a lot of people have come from the USA, Italy, Australia, and other places as well as France to help share experiences in style, winemaking, origins and many other things. So now in Chile we are an old country with long experience of making wine but with a lot of new people, full of energy to make changes that we never previously imagined. We are now producing wines from many different grape varieties across many valleys. Not only concentrating on great wines from Cabernet Sauvignon, Sauvignon Blanc and Carmenère, but also from grapes like Syrah, Viognier and Pinot Noir.

Long-term goals

My biggest goal is to enter and play in a very strong and serious way in terms of quality and value at all prices. I believe we are continuing to raise winemaking standards in Chile and that we have started to produce benchmark wines. We are producing wonderful wines. Chile is amazing and my feeling is that we are in a very good position to realise our great potential for great wines.

I am very focussed on expression. I want my wines, at every single level, to express the character of our country and culture. I don't want to copy other styles. At Concha y Toro we have found our own way: very Chilean and very modern.

Dr. George Tsantalis
Tsantali Vineyards and Wineries
Greece

I was born to a family of winemakers. My grandfather, father and uncle tended their own vines and made wine and tsipouro for themselves and this hobby then became their main occupation. As far back as when I was nine years old, I was in the vineyards helping with the harvest and then joining in the pressing of the grapes with our bare feet.

My family founded the company out of deep respect for the beauty of the land and a strong commitment to quality. The spirit and tradition of nurturing the vines to yield the most precious grapes and of a proud winemaking heritage has continued to evolve through the passage of time.

Today, the third generation of our family shows the same dedication to the values of our grandparents, continuing to create exceptional wines and taking pride in their constant commitment to only the finest vineyards and winemaking skills.

Tradition therefore definitely plays a significant role and influences not just our work philosophy, but our life philosophy too. Although in the meantime the winery has greatly expanded, our way of thinking is closer to that of a winegrower than that of a businessman.

Organic terroir

In 1971, in the middle of a storm, my uncle Evangelos Tsantalis sought refuge among the monks at the domain of Chromitsa. There he saw a vineyard that the monks did not tend any more. Tsantalis offered his help in tending the unique vineyard, if he was also allowed to make wine for himself. The monks agreed to this historic step and Mount Athos wine thus came to the 'outside world'. The winemaking tradition that has lasted throughout the centuries and made Mount Athos wine renowned is kept alive today at the Tsantali Mount Athos Vineyards project.

The vineyards of the Metoxi (Domain) of Chromitsa, property of the St. Panteleimon Monastery, extend across an area of 80 hectares. The benevolent climatic and geographic parameters enable organic growing without problems, as the relatively dry climate and the sandy soil and strict isolation of the vineyards from other cultivations offer an excellent basis for organic growing. The yields of grapes are lower per hectare, making for more concentrated, complex wines. The careful choice of varieties optimally accentuates the characteristics of the terroir.

The Greek winemaking scene

Dramatic changes have taken place in the Greek 'winescape', with an emphasis on quality and respect for regional varieties. In the vineyards, new canopy management techniques produce a striking acidity never before attained, while the intensity and ripeness of fruit is unbelievable. Modern winemaking practices result in vibrant, fruitier, riper wines and the wine is finished in new wood, something unheard of until the last decade.

It would have been a lot easier for Greek producers to plant Chardonnay, Syrah and Merlot, the wines of which have won awards all over the world, but they grow Greek varieties and experiment with different styles of wine. Three years ago, if you gave a Limnio to an 'outsider' they would have stared at you in astonishment, but every year the opposition is smaller. Wine consumers are becoming more adventurous with their choices.

If you are looking for excellent quality and uniqueness at a good price, then you must shy away from preconceptions and let the taste buds discover the wonderful diversity offered by indigenous Greek varieties. With Greek wines, you know that you are in the Old World, but the wines have ripe modern fruit.

Long-term goals

At Tsantali we are trying to achieve a harmony between the traditional image of Greece – as a land of life, happiness and sunshine – and the new image of a higher standard of quality.

The Tsantali mission is to deliver consumer-oriented, quality-driven wines, based on a value-for-money rationale. The aim of our family is to consistently offer the wine lover quality wines from naturally cultivated vineyards, with respect to each region's microclimates and local traditions. We want to supply outstanding wines and distillates, with a fair price/performance ratio, utilising equipment of the latest technology, as well as highly developed vinification methods.

We also hope to convey Tsantali's commitment to a relaxed and sophisticated lifestyle through a comprehensive marketing, educational and cultural programme. To this aim, we would like to place more emphasis on winery tours, wine seminars, tastings, PR, advertising campaigns and events.

In terms of our work in the vineyards, we have been trying for many years, with our cooperating viticulturists, to reduce the irrational and unrestrained usage of plant protection products in the vineyard, as we are very sensitive both towards quality issues and environmental protection, and also because of our great viticultural activity.

With the vine growers of each viticultural area, value is placed on a long-lasting collaboration, which develops on a qualitative, not a quantitative basis. The constant controls and courses for the associate vine growers serve as a guideline for Quality Assurance in the vineyard.

Tsantali also organises seminars and meetings on topics, such as wine-grape cultivation, terroir selection, nutritional methods, environmentally conscious organic or integrated vineyard farming, harvest time etc.

Through constant supervision of the vineyard workers and smooth information exchange, our goal is to optimally exploit synergy effects, so that the best is gained from the vineyards.

The future

A lack of knowledge and classification of the Greek varieties inhibits their spread into other countries. I do believe though that in the future the road for the wider propagation of Greek varieties will clear, as happened in antiquity with the spread of Greek grape varieties (Grecanico, Greco di Tufo, Aglianico etc.) to southern Italy.

It is just a process that will take some time. Winemakers from Spain have shown interest in the Xinomavro grape. Let's not forget that most Californian and Australian winemakers, despite their Italian ancestry, initially turned to the consumer-friendlier 'international' varieties and only recently have begun to return to their roots, experimenting with Italian varieties such as Sangiovese.

Perhaps it is not too late to hope that there will be progress regarding the systematic recording of the varietal wealth of the Greek vineyard, giving real impetus to the fertile local traditions, and that this entire effort will be combined with the best that clonal selection has to offer.

I am a strong believer that the future will bid well for the preservation of wine diversity, for wines that have something to say. We must not forget that wines tell a story, about people and places and about the complex relationship between man and nature.

It is logical that, after a certain degree of homogenisation has prevailed in the world of wine, the consumer will tire and turn once again to what is genuine and authentic. I believe in the use of indigenous varieties in the wines of each area, even in the use of local wood for the ageing of these wines. This will safeguard the uniqueness of local traditions and will keep the interest of the ever more demanding consumer alive.

Maddalena Pasqua di Bisceglie
Musella
Italy

My motivations for making wine come very much from my family. My grandfather set up a wine business in 1925, therefore for us wine has always been a family affair, but in the last 10 years, with the purchase of the Musella estate, it has become a great passion and a way of living.

We are working hard in the vineyards and in the cellar in order to achieve the quality we are aiming for and for us it's crucial to find the right balance between nature and technology, the soil and the wine, our traditions and the market.

Working with nature

Our main motivation is to work with nature itself, to exploit the beauty and uniqueness of the estate and try to project it into the wines we produce. Musella is a unique place, a wonderful walled estate which dates back 500 years. It is spread over 350 hectares, of which 28 are vineyards, rich in ancient forest, rivers and canals, hills and lots of history.

The future

So what we expect for the future is to produce a wine that you will easily recognise as a Musella product. Our aim is to give a specific identity to each wine we produce, always respecting the nature we have the pleasure of living with every day and the tradition of our wine region Valpolicella.

The future for Italian wines could be to retain a strong Italian identity, which we can easily achieve with our indigenous unique grape varieties and our unique land and soil. This is something the Italian authorities and wine institutions understand, so there are now incentives offered for planting more indigenous grapes rather than Cabernet or Chardonnay, which until now was thought to be the right thing to do. From Sicily to Veneto we are trying to rediscover the wonder of lost grape varieties, such as Oseleta in Verona or Sussumaniello in Puglia.

Luigi Rubino
Piane del Sole
Italy

I guess what attracted me to winemaking was wine itself. We started planting vineyards about 15 years ago and vinification came later once the vineyards matured. In 1999 we bottled our first product, in our brand-new state-of-the-art winery. The key for our winery is viticulture and the uniqueness of our grape varieties. We also treasure our collaboration with Riccardo Cotarella, who has been our wine consultant since the beginning and who made us implement techniques and methods of production in order to achieve modern-style wines in a region rich in tradition.

Ancient and modern
And this is perhaps our strength: we produce modern-style wines with ancient varieties, giving the wines unique characteristics. We have planted only indigenous grapes on the 160 hectares of vineyards all directly controlled and owned by us. Primitivo, Negroamaro, Malvasia Nera are the red stars of Puglia, producing very intense and warm wines. We are also rediscovering Sussumaniello, an ancient grape with wonderful characteristics.

The future
The rediscovery of indigenous grapes is a trend that is happening all over Italy, and in my opinion it is the right direction to take. In my wine vision, Italy will represent the best valid alternative to the Cabernet and Chardonnay of the world. So my aim is to achieve wines that best reflect the characteristics of the variety written on the label.

Alex Dale
Radford Dale
South Africa

I really didn't choose wine; it kidnapped me. Having worked my first vintage at 15, in Burgundy whilst taking a month off school, I fell completely in love with wine and its wonderful way of life. It simply took over my existence. Ever since, I have done nothing else – and wouldn't wish to.

I enjoy the excitement and the stimulation of creation. The satisfaction of turning an abstract idea into a living reality. An elusive and imperfect reality, but one made from my own mind and hands. Wine is what makes me tick. It is a combination of a love for nature and the gratification of a certain accomplishment and the fuel of a dream lifestyle.

Each crop brings a completely new and unpredictable set of events, circumstances and experiences, which means that life is eternally challenging, unpredictable and magnificently varied. Every step is a thrill. An adventure lived differently with each season. This is not a job, but a passion.

Individual and confident

We aim above all to be individual, both in terms of our wine philosophy and our approach to how we conduct our business. We aim to produce wines that we enjoy to drink ourselves, in the styles that we prefer. We are sufficiently confident in what we do to grant ourselves this luxury. But above all, we never forget to enjoy ourselves. That is the great privilege of working in wine.

Today, it is so important to consider the requirements of the market. Without a customer, we have no future. It is necessary to strike a balance between doing what you want and doing what you are able to profitably find a market for. When we started out, we designed the type of wines and business we wanted to put together. Everything has been deliberate. We have focused on making premium wines, for example, from some of the best vineyards in the Cape, leaving the cut-throat volume or commodity wines to others. We are infinitely more motivated to produce 250 cases of beautiful Shiraz than 250,000 cases of branded syrup.

We also do not let our wine styles be dictated to by influential journalists. Our wines are not 'in your face', but more subtle and thoughtful. Such wines can be considerably more difficult to find a market niche for in the early years, but in the long term can develop a very loyal and passionate following. Consequently, we do not seek medals, trophies or other subjective 'accolades' – which usually reward what I call 'steroid wines', with boosted sugar, oak etc. We prefer to evolve our reputation by word of mouth, dedicated retailers, top sommeliers and so on. Again, this is a question of confidence and determination. We are different in that we know what we want to achieve. We understand the complexity and fickle nature of the market and we are prepared to take the hard route to get to our objectives, consistently.

We are different in that for every level that we produce wines at, we are determined to offer good value. What is a wine worth? I suppose whatever somebody will pay for it. But what is a good value wine? A wine of better quality than the price suggests, and one which people will thus give preference and allegiance to. Dependably and willingly.

Finally, we are different in that we always live by the maxim 'Work hard, play hard'. A distinction that has opened up many friendships around the planet and that ensures a constant flow of wine and good times wherever we go – as well as good business.

The South African winemaking scene

The South African wine industry is undergoing a great deal of structural change. It never feels like it's going quickly enough when you're immersed in it, but when you take a step back and see how far we've come since democracy in 1994, it's really remarkable. Certain conservative die-hards as well as spirit-dominated groups continue to dominate the domestic market. However, as with the former political régime, international influences will cause renewal and progress.

What's really interesting at the moment is the surfacing of the second phase of the new generation of South African wine-makers. Not the best of the first phase, who steered South African wines out of isolation into the new era, but the younger more travelled and passionate winemakers who cut their teeth during South Africa's re-emergence, making wine for others, and who are now starting to release their own wines. Wines with greater character and individuality, bursting with passion. That's where we see ourselves – and most of our friends.

Long-term goals

Having brought several South African wine interests together under one roof, which we have named The Winery, we have set ourselves an ambitious goal: to become a leader in South Africa. Not only by making some of the most interesting wines, but by forging an innovative team with a unique ethic. Our team has expanded to include two Frenchmen, an Australian, an English-man (with another about to join), and five South Africans – all women. We have set out to prove that idealism doesn't need to be limited to the content of our bottle. The lives and experiences of our entire team are as important to our journey as the wines we make, and by focusing on both, we're certain that what we do can only be better and more intriguing. There is not one person from the vineyard to the bottling who is not passionate about what we do. Over time, that will make a huge difference and will always underpin our point of difference.

We are planning to introduce two new ranges into our wines; one from the exciting and emerging viticultural area just inland from the West Coast of the Cape, the other from a cooler region with greater altitude. We believe that the character and styles of wines from these new areas will suit a number of varieties that we would like to produce, whether as blends or as single vineyard wines (and will fully complement what we already do in Stellenbosch). By focusing on the greatest strengths of each region we work in, we aim to constitute an overall highly diverse and yet specialised range, something which is quite a unique concept in the Cape. Our goal is to be *the* source of a variety of South Africa's most interesting wines, from its most promising wine regions – both established and emerging.

The future

There are currently too many wines and too many producers for the existing markets. In most of the major markets consolidation is well under way – in all aspects of supply, from retailers back to importers, and back again to the production base. Globalisation is beginning to make deep inroads into the wine industry and gone are the days of simple tradition and 'who you know'. With everyone having to fight for space more and more competitively, with quality around the world equalling up progressively, a crunch has to come. The unavoidable conclusion therefore is that you need to be absolutely sure that you have quality wines, good distribution and a loyal consumer base. And in our view, we can achieve this by being notable and individual in everything we do. Wines, styles, packaging, work ethic, value. These are the pillars of our future.

As we secure our place, we'll start to play around more and experiment with some quirky projects. In fact, we're already beginning that phase . . .

Life is too short to drink bad wine.   Gray Monk

abboccato
Italian used to describe wines with a little residual sugar, ranging from medium sweet to medium dry (*pronounced* ábbō kaátō)

Abfüller
German printed on labels of wines from Germany to show who bottled the wine (*pronounced* áb fŏŏlər, *literally* 'bottler', *plural* **Abfüller**)

Abfüllung
German printed on labels of wines from Germany to show who bottled the wine (*pronounced* áb fŏŏlŏŏng, *literally* 'bottling')
See also **Erzeugerabfüllung**; **Gutsabfüllung**; **Originalabfüllung**

Ablan *another name for* **Palomino**

abocado
Spanish medium sweet (*pronounced* ábbō kaádō)

Abruzzo, Abruzzi
Italy a mountainous wine-producing region on the eastern coast of Italy, growing mostly the Trebbiano grape variety for white wines and the Montepulciano grape variety for red wines (*pronounced* ə broótsō *or* ə broótsi)
See also **Montepulciano d'Abruzzo DOC**

abv *abbreviation* alcohol by volume

AC *abbreviation*
1. *French* Appellation Contrôlée
2. *Portuguese* adega cooperativa

acacia honey
(*tasting term*) a sweet taste or floral aroma associated with white wines made from the Marsanne grape variety

acerbic
(*tasting term*) used to describe a wine that is assertive and acidic

♀ **acescence**
(*tasting term*) an excess of acetic acid in a wine, giving it a sweet-and-sour or vinegary smell and taste. As little as 0.1% per unit volume of acetic acid will make a wine undrinkable.

acetaldehyde
a colourless, volatile, natural chemical compound that exists in tiny quantities in good table wine and in large quantities in oxidised, spoiled wines. This chemical is in the group of compounds called aldehydes. It is produced when alcohol reacts with air during oxidation. Although in some cases this chemical can add complexity to a wine such as fino sherry, its pungent smell is normally noticed on spoiled wine.

♀ **acetic**
(*tasting term*) used to describe a wine that has turned sour and vinegary through overexposure to air

acetic acid
a chemical that is produced as a by-product during the wine-making process. Its quantity needs to be controlled to prevent the wine from tasting vinegary.

acetification
the chemical process of wine turning into vinegar either because of spoilage by oxidation or as a result of bacteria converting the alcohol content to acetic acid

Acetobacter
bacteria that produce acetic acid in wine that has come into contact with oxygen

♀ **acetone**
(*tasting term*) a sharp but sweet and fruity smell that is normally caused by esters

acid¹
a chemical that is present in grapes and is produced during the fermentation process. Grapes from cooler regions or seasons have higher acid levels, while grapes from warmer climates have lower acid levels. In wine the acids provide the sharpness and definition to the taste of the wine. The three main acids that occur naturally in a wine are tartaric, malic and citric acids. Each has a different function: tartaric acid provides the sharpness of a wine and ensures that the ageing process enhances the

complexity of the wine, while malic acid is often responsible for the fruity smell and taste of a wine. The most dominant acid in a wine is tartaric, but the levels of all acids are measured (in a process called titration) to produce the total acid content, written as a percentage of total acids per litre of wine. Dry wines have a total acid content of around 0.7%, while sweet wines have one around 0.8%. In a well-balanced wine, the acid content should enhance the taste and should not be a noticeable element – during assemblage, the winemaker can alter the acid levels by blending wines from different batches of grapes or grapes picked at different times. Those left on the vine longer have higher levels of sugar and lower acid levels.

♀ **acid²**
(*tasting term*) used to describe a wine that tastes very sharp or sour due to an excess of acid

acid adjustment *same as* **acidification**

♀ **acidic** *same as* **acid²**

acidification
the process of adding an acid, usually a natural grape acid, to a wine during the fermentation process to help balance the taste of the wine. It is often used when grapes are overripe and have become too sweet. Some grape-producing countries and regions with a warm climate allow it, while others don't.
Also called **acid adjustment**; **acidulation**

acidity
♀ **1.** (*tasting term*) one of the key elements of any wine, providing a sharpness and definition to the taste
2. the level of acid found in soil. Acidity and alkalinity are shown according to the pH scale on which pH7 is neutral, numbers above 7 indicate alkalinity, and those below 7 indicate acidity.

acid soil
soil that has a pH value of 6 or less. Most crops will not grow well if the soil is very acid. This can be cured by applying one of the materials commonly used for adding lime, e.g. ground chalk or limestone.

acidulation *same as* **acidification**

acre
a unit of measurement of land area, equal to 0.4047 hectares, or
4,840 square yards

adamado
Portuguese sweet (*pronounced* áddə maádō)

adega
Portuguese a wine estate or wine cellar (*pronounced* a dáygə)

adega cooperativa
Portuguese a wine cooperative (*pronounced* a dáygə kō opərə
teévə, *plural* **adegas cooperativas**)

Adelaide Hills, Adelaide
Australia an important wine-producing region of South Australia 15 km to the east of the city of Adelaide, about 400–500
metres in altitude and one of the cooler areas of South Australia,
producing excellent Chardonnay and good Sauvignon Blanc
and also well-known for good Pinot Noir

aerate
1. to expose wine to air during fermentation to activate the yeast
2. to allow a wine to 'breathe' before drinking it

aeration
1. the process of deliberately exposing wine to air. During
winemaking, oxygen is required as part of the fermentation
process to activate the yeast, but too much will result in
unwanted oxidation.
2. the process of allowing a wine to 'breathe' before drinking it.
This can help break down and reduce the harsh tannins in a
young wine, but can also alter the balance of a fine older wine.

aestivalis *see* **Vitis aestivalis**

Affentaler Spätburgunder Rotwein
a red wine made in the Baden region of Germany from Pinot
Noir (Spätburgunder) grapes. It can vary from dry to sweet.
(*pronounced* áffən taalər shpáyt bur gőondər rőt vīn)

aftertaste
(*tasting term*) the taste that lingers in your mouth after wine has
been tasted and either swallowed or spat out. It is often the best
indicator of the quality of a wine.
See also **finish**

ageing
the storing of wine in order to improve its taste. Wine that is wood-aged in oak barrels or casks takes on some of the flavours of the wood, and ageing often softens the wine and increases the depth of flavours as a little of the water content evaporates through the wood. Ageing wines in bottles develops further depth to the character and flavour of the wine, though during the first few weeks after being bottled, wine can suffer from bottle sickness. Light wines do not normally improve with bottle-ageing, but many other wines continue to develop character and complexity during the ageing process.

♀ aggressive
(*tasting term*) used to describe a wine that has a harsh and unpleasant taste or texture, usually because of high levels of tannin or acid

♦ Aghiorghitiko, Agioritiko
a red-wine grape variety native to Greece, and the second most planted grape there (*pronounced* agyori teʹekō)

♦ Aglianico
a red-wine grape variety grown in southern Italy. The best-known producers of pure Aglianico wine are the Aglianico del Vulture DOC and Taurasi DOC regions. The best wines made from this grape can be aged for up to ten years. (*pronounced* a lyaʹanikō)

Aglianico del Vulture DOC
Italy a DOC region in southern Italy that produces amabile and spumante wines, but is best-known for its still red wine made from the Aglianico grape variety, which, although high in acid and tannins, matures well to produce good, balanced wine (*pronounced* a lyaʹanikō del voʹol toʹor ay)

♦ Agliano *another name for* **Aleatico** (*pronounced* a lyaʹanō)

agrafe
a small metal clip for holding the cork in place during the bottle fermentation stage when making sparkling wine by the méthode champenoise. This device is now rarely used and has been replaced by a crown cap.

Ahr
Germany a small, very old wine-growing region in northwestern Germany that is one of the most northerly in the world. It grows

the Pinot Noir (Spätburgunder) and Portugieser red grape varieties as well as the Riesling and Müller-Thurgau white grape varieties, which are all tolerant of the cold climate. (*pronounced* aar)

♀ **aigre**
French (*tasting term*) having a sour taste (*pronounced* aýgrə)

♀ **aimable**
French (*tasting term*) used to describe a well-balanced wine (*pronounced* ay maáblə)

Aïn Merane *see* **Algeria**

♡ **Airén**
a white-wine grape variety that is the world's most commonly planted. It is widely grown in Spain and is used to make light dry wines. (*pronounced* ī rén)

Aix *see* **Coteaux d'Aix-en-Provence AOC**

Ajaccio AOC
France an appellation on the western coast of Corsica that grows the Sciacarello grape to make red and rosé wines and grows Vermentino and Trebbiano grapes to make white wines (*pronounced* a jáksi ō)

Alba
Italy a town in the Piedmont wine-producing region south of Turin that lends its name to a number of well-known red-wine producing DOCs, including Barbera d'Alba and Dolcetto d'Alba, and to some DOCGs, including Barolo and Barbaresco (*pronounced* álbə)

♡ **Albana**
a white-wine grape variety predominantly grown in northern Italy, rarely producing great wine. The grape is used to produce a range of wine styles including still, dry, medium sweet, sparkling and sweet. The best-known DOCG is Albana di Romagna. (*pronounced* al baánə)
Also called **Biancame**; **Greco**; **Greco di Ancona**

Albana di Romagna DOCG
Italy a DOCG wine-producing zone in the Emilia-Romagna region of northern Italy with a history dating from Roman times. It produces a white wine made from the Albana grape variety. This fine wine has a golden colour and can be sweet

(dolce or amabile) or dry (secco). It has a DOCG rating, Italy's highest official classification. There is also a spumante sparkling wine from the region, but it only carries the lower-class DOC rating. (*pronounced* al baánə dee rō mánnyə)

Albany
Australia a wine-producing area in Western Australia, a sub-region of the Great Southern region

☼ Albariño
a white grape grown in the Galicia region of northwestern Spain. The grape's skin is very thick and only a small amount of juice can be squeezed from it, producing crisp, refreshing and light-bodied wines with hints of citrus and peach. (*pronounced* álbə reényō)
Also called **Alvarinho**

albariza
white, chalky soil that is characteristic of Spain's Jerez de la Frontera sherry region (*pronounced* álbə reéthə)

☼ Albarola
a white-wine grape variety that is the most widely planted grape in Liguria, Italy, and is used with the Bosco grape in some examples of Liguria's most famous wine, Cinqueterre (*pronounced* álbə róllə)

albumin
a water-soluble protein found in egg white, used in fining to clarify red wines after barrel-ageing to help remove excessive tannins

Alcamo DOC
Italy a wine-producing region in the west of Sicily that grows mostly the Catarratto grape to produce crisp white wines (*pronounced* al kaámō)

☼ Alcanol *another name for* **Macabeo** (*pronounced* álkə nól)

☼ Alcayata *another name for* **Monastrell** (*pronounced* álkə yaátə)

alcohol
the chemical compounds that are the result of the chemical process of fermentation when sugars from the grape juice are processed by yeast. Alcohol is a tasteless and colourless liquid and in wine it mostly consists of ethyl alcohol. It provides much

of the body and balance of a wine. The alcohol content is usually shown on the label on the bottle. It normally varies between 8 and 14% by volume and content for wine. The alcohol content of sherry is normally 17 to 20% by volume and for port it is 18 to 20% by volume.

alcohol by volume
a measure of the amount of alcohol per unit volume of wine, expressed as a percentage and normally shown on the label. *Abbreviation* **abv**

♀ **alcoholic**
(*tasting term*) used to describe a wine that is out of balance because it contains too much alcohol

alcoholic content, alcoholic strength
the amount of alcohol in a wine, usually shown on the label of the bottle as a percentage of a unit volume of the wine, e.g. a wine with an alcoholic content of 10% contains a relatively low amount of alcohol, whereas a wine with an alcoholic content of 14% is very strong – you can probably even taste or smell the alcohol on such wine. For comparison, spirits such as vodka have an alcoholic content of between 35 and 45% and beer has an alcoholic content per unit volume of between 4 and 6%, although alcohol in beer is usually expressed in terms of specific gravity.

alcoholic fermentation *same as* **primary fermentation**

alcoholic strength *see* **alcoholic content**

alcool
French, Italian alcohol (*pronounced* alkō ól)

☿ **Aleatico**
a red grape that is a member of the Muscat family of grapes and is grown in Italy and California, USA. It is usually used for sweet dessert wines such as some Italian vin santos. Fortified wine made from the Aleatico grape, called 'liquoroso', is similar in style to port. (*pronounced* álli áttikō)
Also called **Agliano**; **Allianico**; **Moscatello**; **Muscateller**

Alella DO
Spain a DO zone in the northeast of Spain in the Catalonia region near Barcelona that grows mainly the Xarel-lo (called Pansá Blanca locally) and Grenache Blanc (Garnacha Blanca)

grape varieties to produce dry and medium sweet white wines. A little red and rosé wine is produced from the Tempranillo and Grenache (Garnacha) grape varieties. (*pronounced* a lélya)

Alentejo
Portugal a huge wine-producing region in southern Portugal growing Roupeiro grapes for white wines and Periquita grapes for full-bodied red wines (*pronounced* állən táyzhō)

Alexander Valley AVA
USA a wine-growing region on the western coast of the USA, north of San Francisco in Sonoma County that grows a wide range of grape varieties including Cabernet Sauvignon, Chardonnay, Merlot, Riesling, Sauvignon Blanc and Zinfandel

◊ Alfrocheiro Preto
a Portuguese red-wine grape variety that is grown especially in the Dão DOC, but also in Alentejo, Bairrada and Ribatejo. It has a strong colour and for this reason is often used in blends. (*pronounced* alfro sháyrō préttō)

Algeria
a country that was a major wine producer when it was a French colony but since independence there has been a significant lack of investment. It now has few wine-growing regions and little production. The French set up a VDQS system of 12 recognised wine-growing regions, which has now dwindled to seven, with the best regions Aïn Merane, Mazouna and Tanghrite. The vines usually grown are Alicante Bouschet, Carignan, Cinsault, Grenache, Syrah and Trebbiano grape varieties, but there is now some planting of Cabernet Sauvignon, Merlot, Syrah and Chardonnay. Production and sales of wine are heavily centralised.

◊ Alicante Bouschet
a red grape that has red skin and red flesh. This variety was developed in France in the late 1880s by Henri Bouschet and is a hybrid of Grenache. Alicante Bouschet is widely grown in southern France and North Africa and is grown in limited quantities in California, USA. This grape variety produces lower-quality wines and is often used to add depth of colour to wines made from other grape varieties. (*pronounced* ali kánti boó shay)

Alicante DO
Spain a DO zone in the southeast of Spain in Alicante province that grows mostly Monastrell and Grenache (Garnacha) grape

varieties to produce full-bodied red wines and the Merseguera grape variety to produce dry white wines. It also produces a sweet white wine from Muscat grapes and the high-alcohol Fondillon wine from the Monastrell grape variety. (*pronounced* álli kánti)

〇 **Alicante Ganzin**

a red grape variety that was one of the varieties used in breeding Rubired in California (*pronounced* álli kánti gán theen)

〇 **Aligoté**

a white grape variety used in blends in many countries and best known for its light-to-medium-bodied, crisp, dry white wines produced in the Burgundy region of France and in eastern European countries. (*pronounced* álli go táy)
Also called **Blanc de Cabernet Sauvignon**; **Chaudenet Gris**; **Plant Gris**

alkalinity

the level of alkali found in soil. Alkalinity and acidity are shown according to the pH scale on which pH7 is neutral, numbers above 7 indicate alkalinity and those below 7 indicate acidity.

allergies

Wine has been found to cause allergies in some people, not usually caused by the grape or the alcohol, but arising from the other constituents of wine including sulphur dioxide which is used as a preservative, yeast cultures, fining agents and histamines, which are more prevalent in red wine than white

〇 **Allianico** *another name for* **Aleatico** (*pronounced* a lyaánikō)

Allied Domecq *see* **Domecq**

Allier

France a département in central France where oak forests produce the wood for the oak barrels used by many winemakers (*pronounced* álli ay)

Almansa DO

Spain a DO zone in central Spain that mostly produces red wine from the Monastrell, Tempranillo and Grenache (Garnacha) grape varieties (*pronounced* al mánssə)

♀ **almond**

(*tasting term*) a taste or aroma associated with Italian wines, especially dry white wines such as Soave and Prosecco, but also with red Valpolicella

Aloxe-Corton
France an area in the Côte de Beaune region in Burgundy
producing red and white wines, including two grands crus,
Corton AOC (producing red wine) and Corton-Charlemagne
AOC (producing white wine) (*pronounced* aa loss kawr tóN)

Alpine Valleys
Australia a wine-producing region in northeastern Victoria

Alsace AOC
France a wine-producing region on the French border with
Germany that produces distinctive white wines that are, in
the main, varietal. The main grape is Riesling and the wines
are dry and rich in aroma. White wines from Alsace are usually
bottled in a distinctive tall, slim green bottle. The town of
Colmar is the commercial hub of the region. Alsace Grand
Cru is a distinct appellation that includes over 50 of the top
vineyards in the region producing wines made only from
Gewürztraminer, Muscat, Pinot Gris or Riesling grape varieties.
A number of wine styles are produced, in the main based on a
single grape variety. Riesling is recognised as Alsace's noblest
grape and produces its best wine. It is very different from its
German equivalent: gunflint and steel are often used to describe
its complex aromas and fruity flavours. Gewürztraminer with its
distinctive, fruity, lychee aroma, is dry, low in acidity and big in
body. Pinot Blanc, known locally as Klevner, makes creamy,
medium-bodied wines. Alsace's Muscat is a blend of two varieties, Muscat à Petits Grains and Muscat Ottonel. The result is a
crisp, dry, aromatic wine. Pinot Gris, formerly known in Alsace
as Tokay, is smoky and concentrated. Sylvaner is aromatic and
flavoursome. Edelzwicker is a blend of grape varieties and is
generally inexpensive, quaffing wine. Pinot Noir is Alsace's only
red variety, producing light wine, and Crémant d'Alsace is a
sparkling wine most often made using Pinot Blanc. (*pronounced*
al záss)

Alsace Vendange Tardive
a late-harvest wine from the Alsace AOC region of France that
uses very ripe grapes with high sugar levels that produce rich, very
dry wine. The other late-harvest wine from this region is called
Sélection de Grains Nobles and uses grapes infected with *Botrytis
cinerea* to produce a very sweet wine. Both wines can only be
made from Gewürztraminer, Muscat, Pinot Gris or Riesling
grape varieties. (*pronounced* al záss vaaN dáa<u>zh</u> taar déev)

○ Altesse, Altesse Vert

a white-wine grape variety that is grown in the Savoie region of eastern France to produce good quality, full-bodied white wines. The majority of the Altesse grapes grown in this region are used to produce a sparkling white wine, Seyssel Mousseux. (*pronounced* al téss *or* al téss váir)
Also called **Mâconnais**; **Roussette**

altitude

height above sea level. This can affect climate in many ways: the temperature drops about 0.5°C for every 90 metre rise above sea level. Every 15 metre rise in height usually shortens the growing season by two days and may check the rate of growth during the year. High land is likely to receive more rain than lowland areas.

Alto Adige DOC

Italy a mountainous DOC zone in the northeast of Italy, the northern part of the Trentino-Alto Adige region, on the border with Austria, that grows all of the premium European grapes, in addition to native varieties. Schiava is the predominant grape of the area, producing medium-bodied red wines. Other red varieties found are Lagrein and Pinot Noir. Pinot Gris (Pinot Grigio), Chardonnay and Pinot Blanc (Pinot Bianco) are amongst the white-wine varieties. Modern methods have raised the area's quality in the last 20 years. (*pronounced* áltō a deé gay)

Altus

USA a town in western Arkansas, USA, where wine has been produced since the 1800s

○ Alvarinho

a white-wine grape variety grown in the Vinho Verde region of Portugal. The grapes have very thick skins so produce only a little juice that makes good and expensive rich and creamy white wines. (*pronounced* álvə reényō)
Also called **Albariño**

amabile

Italian medium sweet (*pronounced* ə maábi lay)

Amador County

USA an important wine-producing region in California within the Sierra Foothills AVA, east of the Napa Valley, that was one of the first regions of the USA to have been planted with vines. The main grape varieties are Zinfandel and Sauvignon Blanc.

amaro
Italian used to describe a wine that has a bitter taste or is very dry (*pronounced* a maárō)

♀ **amarognolo**
Italian (*tasting term*) a bitter almond flavour in a wine (*pronounced* ámmə rónnyəlō)

amarone
Italian a very dry wine (*pronounced* ámmə rố nay, *plural* **amaroni**)

◊ **Amarone della Valpolicella**
a variety of Valpolicella wine from Veneto, Italy that uses grapes partly dried in the sun to increase the flavours and alcohol content, resulting in a sweeter wine with a high alcohol content. This style of wine can be drunk with cheese or as an after-dinner drink as well as with main course dishes. The best style is normally termed 'classico'. (*pronounced* ámmə rố nay delə vál poli chéllə)
Also called **Recioto della Valpolicella Amarone**

ambra
Italian amber (*pronounced* ámbrə)
See also **Marsala DOC**

amelioration
techniques used to improve a wine, including adding sugar, water or acid to help balance the taste

American hybrid
any one of the varieties of grape that have been selectively bred in the USA, usually the result of a cross between a common American grape variety and a traditional European variety

� **Americano** *another name for* **Isabella**

American oak
oak used to make barrels in which wines are aged, giving the wines a distinctive vanilla and cedar flavour as well as an oak flavour

American Viticultural Area
USA any one of the delimited geographical grape-growing areas in the USA that have been given appellation status by the main Federal Bureau of Alcohol, Tobacco and Firearms in a system established in 1970 and loosely modelled on the original French

AOC system. The main difference is that an AVA is defined only by geographical region, whereas an AOC has extra, complex rules governing the types of grapes, how they are grown and how wine is made in the region. AVAs include the well-known Napa Valley, which itself includes smaller AVAs such as Stags Leap District and Sonoma Valley.
Abbreviation **AVA**

American wine
wine blended from grapes grown in an unspecified state of the USA

amontillado
full-bodied sherry from Spain. Aged in barrels and with more body, colour and flavour than fino sherry, it can be dry or sweet. (*pronounced* ə mónti lyaádō, *plural* **amontillados**)
See also **sherry**

amoroso
a dark and sweet type of oloroso sherry. (*pronounced* ámmə rôssō, *plural* **amorosos**)
Also called **East India sherry**

ampelography
the study and identification of the species, varieties and clones of grapevine, particularly by their physical characteristics

Ampurdán-Costa Brava DO
Spain a DO zone in the Catalonia region of Spain, north of Girona and next to the border with France, that grows mostly Grenache (Garnacha) and Carignan (Cariñena) grape varieties for red and rosé wines, and a smaller quantity of Macabeo and Xarel-lo for rosé and white wines. It formerly produced much of the rancio style of wine, and then concentrated on rosé wine for local consumption, but is now looking to better-quality wines and wider markets. (*pronounced* ámpoor dán kostə braávə)

Amtliche Prüfungsnummer
German a number printed on German wine labels to show that the wine has been officially tested and has passed a range of chemical tests. (*pronounced* ámtlikhə proófoŏngz noŏmər, *literally* 'official testing number')
Abbreviation **A.P.Nr**

amyl acetate
an aromatic chemical compound (an ester) that is present in newly bottled wine and that can give it a noticeable aroma

Anbaugebiet
German any one of 13 wine-producing regions in Germany that are recognised under German wine laws (*pronounced* án bow gə beet, *plural* **Anbaugebiete**)

Andalucía, Andalusia
Spain the southern region of Spain running across the country from coast to coast. It includes eight provinces, which have five DO regions (Condado de Huelva, Jerez-Xérès-Sherry, Manzanilla Sanlúcar de Barrameda, Malaga and Montilla-Morilés), traditionally producing wines high in alcohol, which are mostly fortified.

Anderson Valley
USA a long, narrow wine-producing region between mountains in Mendocino County, on the western coast of California. It is known for its sparkling wines from Chardonnay and Pinot Noir grape varieties as well as still wines using Riesling and Gewürztraminer grapes.

añejado por
Spanish aged by (*pronounced* án ye haádō páwr)

añejo
Spanish old or aged (*pronounced* a nyéhō)

angelica
a sweet fortified wine, associated with California, traditionally produced for use as Communion wine in church. It was formerly made from Mission or Muscat grapes and fortified with brandy, but is now made from almost any type and blend of wine, producing a wine that lacks any distinctive flavour.

♀ angular
(*tasting term*) used to describe a wine that has dominant, sharp flavours. The characteristic is most commonly found in young, dry wines.

Anjou
France a wine-growing area in the western Loire region of France that produces mainly white wine made from the Chenin Blanc grape variety and a smaller quantity of rosé and red wine. The

rosé wines are the best known, and include the undistinguished and often sweetish Rosé d'Anjou AOC and the higher-quality Cabernet d'Anjou AOC. Good red wine is produced in the Anjou-Villages AOC, and light reds, especially from the Gamay grape, are made elsewhere in the area. (*pronounced* aáN zhoo)

Anjou Mousseux AOC

France an appellation in the Anjou area in the western Loire region of France that produces sparkling white and rosé wines using the méthode champenoise (*pronounced* aáN zhoo moo só)

Anjou-Villages AOC

France an appellation in the Anjou area in the western Loire region of France that produces good-quality red wine from the Cabernet Franc and Cabernet Sauvignon grape varieties (*pronounced* aáN zhoo vee laázh)

annata

Italian vintage year (*pronounced* a naátə)

année

French year (*pronounced* a náy)
See also **vin de l'année**

año

Spanish year (*pronounced* ánnyō, *plural* **años**)

Ansonica *another name for* **Inzolia** (*pronounced* an sónnikə)

anthocyanin

a colour pigment that provides the red colour of red wine

Antinori, Marchese Piero

an influential winemaker in Tuscany and Umbria, Italy, who produces some of the best Chianti wines of the country (*pronounced* ánti náwri)

antioxidant

a chemical added to wine during the winemaking process to reduce the spoiling effects of oxygen, e.g. ascorbic acid

Antonopoulos

Greece a Greek wine company with vineyards in the Patras region of the northern Peloponnese in southern Greece but also in Corfu and elsewhere in the country (*pronounced* antə nóppəllǝss)

AOC *abbreviation French* Appellation d'Origine Contrôlée

Aosta *see* **Valle d'Aosta DOC**

apéritif, aperitif
an alcoholic drink served before dinner, traditionally to stimulate the appetite

apéritif wine
a wine served before a meal. In France this category includes kir and vermouths or other similar wines flavoured with herbs and spices.

aphid
a small insect of the Hemiptera order that sucks sap from new shoots of plants and can multiply very rapidly, e.g. blackfly or greenfly. Aphids can carry virus diseases from infected plants to clean ones.

A.P.Nr *abbreviation German* Amtliche Prüfungsnummer

♀ **appearance**
(*tasting term*) the look of a wine, rather than the colour, defined in terms of being brilliant (crystal clear), cloudy or containing sediment

appellation
a designated wine-producing area together with a set of rules enforced by the country's government that covers a range of criteria for growing and producing wine in the region to help produce consistent, reliable, quality wine. The main countries using appellations are France (split into areas given the name Appellation d'Origine Contrôlée), Italy (areas given the name Denominazione di Origine Controllata), Portugal (areas given the name Denominação de Origem Controlada), Spain (areas given the name Denominación de Origen), Australia (geographically defined into Geographical Indications) and the USA (geographically defined into American Viticultural Areas).

Appellation Contrôlée *see* **Appellation d'Origine Contrôlée** (*plural* **Appellations Contrôlées**) *abbreviation French* **AC**

Appellation d'Origine Contrôlée
French a system of laws and rules devised in France in 1935 to regulate French wine production and quality and define its origins. The rules are administered by the Institut National des Appellations d'Origine (INAO) and cover almost every aspect of wine production, from which varieties of grape can

be planted in different appellations and which production methods can be used to make the wines to vine-planting density and expected yields. The rules govern every part of the process, including the area in which the grapes can be grown, the varieties used, the ripeness of the grapes when picked, the alcoholic strength of the wine produced and even the vineyard yields. Wines with this label are normally produced in state-controlled wineries to produce a consistent, reasonable-quality wine; this type of wine represents the top quarter of all French wines. Wine producers who have not earnt AOC status can be classed (in descending order of quality) as Vin Délimité de Qualité Supérieure (VDQS), Vin de Pays, then Vin de Table. (*pronounced* áppə lássyoN dori <u>zh</u>eén koN trō láy, *plural* **Appellations d'Origine Contrôlées**)
Abbreviation **AOC**

Appellation of Origin of Superior Quality
an official category for dry quality wines under Greek wine laws. These wines are sold with a pink seal over the cork.
Abbreviation **OPAP**

♀ **apple, appley**
(*tasting term*) a smell usually associated with young Chardonnay wine, German Riesling and some Chenin Blanc wines. If the smell is of bitter apples, it can also be a signal that the wine has been oxidised and spoilt or has an excess malic acid content.

♀ **apricot**
(*tasting term*) a smell normally associated with Sémillons, Muscats, and some sweet Riesling wines

Apulia
Italy a wine-producing region in the extreme southeastern corner of Italy with a large number of DOC areas, including eight in the 'heel' of Italy, the Salento peninsula, where the region's best wines are produced. Apulia makes large quantities of wine, especially red wine, and grows a wide range of grape varieties, dominated by Primitivo and Negroamaro. Primitivo from Apulia is generally considered the original source of the Zinfandel grape variety that is used so much in California, USA. (*pronounced* a poólyə)

Aquileia DOC
Italy a DOC zone in the Friuli region of northeastern Italy that grows a number of different grape varieties to produce a range

of wines, most of which are light- or medium-bodied and few of which are exported (*pronounced* ákwi láy ə)

Aragón
Spain a wine-producing area in the Rioja region of northern Spain that produces dark red wines from Grenache (Garnacha) grapes (*pronounced* árrə gón *or* árrəgən)

Aragonez *another name for* **Tempranillo** (*used in* Portugal)

Aramon
a red-wine grape variety used in producing a hybrid rootstock that was widely used in California from the 1950s until attacked by a new strain of phylloxera root aphid in the late 1980s. Aramon is grown for wine in the Languedoc-Roussillon region of southern France. It is a high-yielding vine and produces a weak, pale red wine. (*pronounced* árrə mon)
Also called **Ugni Noir**

Arbois
France a white-wine grape variety that is grown in the Loire district of France and is one of the grapes permitted in wines labelled as from the Touraine AOC (*pronounced* aar bwaá)

Arbois AOC
France an appellation in the Jura region of eastern France that is known especially for its vin jaune. Arbois produces mostly white wine from Chardonnay and Savagnin grapes, including a sparkling white wine, Arbois Mousseux, made from Chardonnay grapes using the méthode champenoise, but also some rosé and light red wines from Pinot Noir, Poulsard (a local variety) and Trousseau grapes. (*pronounced* aar bwaá)

Arbois Mousseux
a sparkling wine made by the méthode champenoise in the Arbois AOC in the Jura region of eastern France (*pronounced* aar bwaá moo só)

Ardèche
France a wine-producing region of central southern France producing red, white and rosé wines and covering a number of AOCs including Côtes du Rhône and Côtes du Vivarais (*pronounced* aar désh)

are
a unit of metric land measurement, equal to 100 square metres

arenaceous soil
soil that has a high proportion of sand particles

Aretini *see* **Chianti DOCG** (*pronounced* arə teénee)

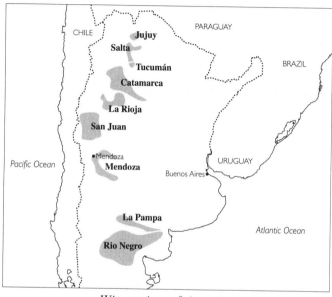

Wine regions of Argentina

Argentina
the world's fifth largest wine-producing country and potentially one of the most exciting and dynamic. Traditionally most of its wine has been consumed locally rather than exported, but recent investment in vineyards and technology has enabled Argentine wine to more than hold its own internationally. Foreign investors have been attracted by the opportunity to produce wine of high quality at very attractive prices. Crucially, foreign consultants and winemakers such as the French oenologist Michel Rolland and the Lurton family have become involved, and their expertise has begun to create a vibrant modern wine industry hungry for exports. The main wine-producing region, Mendoza province, produces the majority of the best-quality wines from Argentina. Traditionally the most popular grape varieties grown have been Mission (Criolla) and Malbec, both

producing full-bodied red wines. The drive for export markets, however, is leading to the production of more international varietal styles. Syrah and Cabernet Sauvignon have been added to Argentina's rich array of red wines, and Chardonnay is proving very successful.

argillaceous soil
soil that has a high proportion of clay particles

argol
crystals of a natural tartar that accumulate during fermentation on the sides and bottoms of wine vats and sometimes in bottles, where they are attached to the bottom of the cork

arid
1. used to describe soil that is very dry
2. used to describe an area of land that has very little rain

Arinto
a white-wine grape variety, grown mostly in Portugal, that produces fresh, crisp white wines with a high acidic content. (*pronounced* ǝ ríntō)
Also called **Pederanão**

arm
one of the woody parts of a vine that grow out of the cordon. Vines can be trained with the arms in different positions.

Armagnac
France a district in Gascony in southwestern France that is best-known for distilling wine into brandy. There are three sub-regions within Armagnac: Bas-Armagnac, Ténarèze and Haut-Armagnac. Armagnac can be sold younger than Cognac, though it is slower maturing, so cheaper Armagnacs often suffer in comparison. It is produced in a very similar way to Cognac, but uses some different grapes (including Folle Blanche and Colombard) and is only distilled once, giving it a lower alcoholic content (normally around 53% compared to 70% for Cognac) and a different style. The district also uses its grapes for crisp white table wines. (*pronounced* áarmǝ nyak)

Armillaria
a soil fungus that kills vines (*pronounced* áarmǝ láiriǝ)

Arneis
a white-wine grape variety grown in the Piedmont region of Italy (*pronounced* aar náy eess)

Arneis di Roero *see* **Roero DOC**

Arneis DOC

Italy a DOC wine-producing region in Piedmont, Italy. It produces dry white wines that smell of apples and pears from Arneis grapes. (*pronounced* aar náy eess)

aroma

(*tasting term*) the smell of a wine, normally the smell of the grapes within the wine or the effects of fermentation of a wine. Sometimes, aroma and bouquet are used interchangeably, but strictly the bouquet represents the smells due to the effects of the wine maturing.

aroma compound

one of the chemical compounds responsible for the various individual characteristics of a wine's taste, flavour and smell. These compounds are formed during fermentation and vary with different varieties of grape and methods of fermentation.

aromatic

(*tasting term*) used to describe a wine with a very strong or particular smell, e.g. the smell from the Riesling grape

aromatic compound

one of the chemical substances found in wine that give the wine its flavour and smell

aromatised wine

a drink created from a wine base to which alcohol, sugar and herbs are added. Perhaps the best-known is vermouth.

aroma wheel

a circular graphic designed by Professor Ann Noble at the University of California, Davis, USA, who organised the types of taste and aroma and flavour found in wines into groups, giving a basic structure to the process of tasting wines

arresting of fermentation

the stopping of fermentation and preservation of any remaining sugar in the wine. This can be achieved in a number of ways including cooling the wine until the yeast is no longer active and using a centrifugal spinning machine to separate out the yeast cells.

arroba

Spanish a measure of grapes and the amount of wine this produces, equal to approximately 10 kg of grapes (*pronounced* ə róbə)

Arroyo Grande AVA
USA a subregion of San Luis Obispo, the wine-growing region on the western coast of California that grows mostly Chardonnay and Pinot Noir grape varieties (*pronounced* ə róyō grándi)

Arroyo Seco AVA
USA a wine-growing area, a smaller part of the Monterey AVA, in Monterey County, California, that grows mostly Chardonnay and Riesling grape varieties (*pronounced* ə róyō sékō)

asciutto
Italian very dry (*pronounced* əs choótō)

ascorbic acid
a chemical sometimes added to wine during the winemaking process to reduce the spoiling effects of oxygen

♀ asparagus
(*tasting term*) an aroma associated with wines made from Sauvignon Blanc grapes, especially Pouilly-Fumé and Sancerre

assemblage
the process in which the winemaker evaluates the wines from different lots to decide which will be used in the final product. This usually takes place three to six months after the harvest, though it can be later. In France in Bordeaux vineyards, the process identifies which lots will be used for the top wine carrying the vineyard's name, which will be sold as its second wine and which will be sold under a wider regional designation. In vineyards in other regions, assemblage identifies the exact blend to go forward to bottling or further ageing. In Champagne, assemblage is important in producing a consistent house style that does not vary year-on-year.
See also **blending**

♀ assertive
(*tasting term*) used to describe a wine that has a full, distinctive taste, probably with high levels of tannins or acidity

◊ Assyrtiko
a high-quality white-wine grape variety grown in Greece that is able to produce wine with good acidity even in a hot climate (*pronounced* ə seérti kō)

Asti DOCG
Italy a DOCG zone near the town of Asti in the Piedmont

region of Italy which produces the sparkling white wines Asti Spumante and Moscato d'Asti (*pronounced* ásti)

◊ **Asti Spumante DOCG**
a blended semi-dry sparkling white wine produced in large quantities in the Asti DOCG in the Piedmont region of Italy. It is made from a Muscat grape variety using a version of the Charmat or bulk process. (*pronounced* ásti spyoo mán tay)

♀ **astringent**
(*tasting term*) used to describe a bitter, dry sensation in the mouth when tasting red wines, and a few white wines, that have too much tannin present

asztali bor
Hungarian table wine (*pronounced* aás taali baa)

aszú
Hungarian botrytised (*pronounced* aa soó)

♡ **Athiri**
a white grape variety grown mainly on the Aegean islands and parts of mainland Greece and used to produce white still and, on Rhodes, sparkling wine (*pronounced* ə theéri)

ATM *abbreviation* atmosphere **2**

atmosphere
1. the condition of the air around a plant. If the atmosphere is too damp, diseases such as blights and moulds spread rapidly; if the atmosphere is too dry, buds fall off and leaves shrivel.
2. a unit of measure of pressure, equal to 14.7 pounds per square inch, used to measure the pressure inside a bottle of sparkling wine or Champagne. Most commercial sparkling wines such as Champagne or Cava contain between four and six atmospheres of carbon dioxide gas at room temperature.
Abbreviation **ATM**

♀ **attack**
(*tasting term*) the initial taste of a wine

♀ **attenuated**
(*tasting term*) used to describe a wine that is past its best and is beginning to lose the flavour of the fruit as it ages

Attica
Greece a wine-producing region in the southeast of Greece that grows local varieties of grapes to produce retsina. It has participated little in the recent revolutions in Greek wine-making.

Auckland
New Zealand a wine-producing region in the north of the North Island of New Zealand growing especially the Cabernet Sauvignon grape variety for red wines and Chardonnay for white wines

♢ Aurore, Aurora
a hybrid grape variety originally developed in the 19th century in France that is still used in sparkling wine production, especially on the eastern coast of the USA (*pronounced* aw ráwr *or* aw ráwrə)

Ausbruch
German the second level of quality Austrian wines, below Trockenbeerenauslese, made from grapes infected with the fungus *Botrytis cinerea* and then allowed to dry naturally to produce concentrated juice that has both a very high sugar content and balancing acid. Ausbruch is associated especially with the town of Rust. (*pronounced* ówss bro͝okh)

Auslese
German the class of white wine that is the third-best within the Qualitätswein mit Prädikat system under German wine laws. It is defined as wine from grape bunches harvested when riper than those harvested for the Spätlese class of wine. (*pronounced* ówss layzə, *literally* 'selected harvest', *plural* **Auslesen**)

Ausone, Château
France a tiny estate in the Saint-Émilion region of Bordeaux, France, producing some of the best red wines of the region and graded in the top two premiers grands crus classés in the classification of Saint-Émilion wines in 1955 (*pronounced* aw són)

♀ austere
(*tasting term*) used to describe a wine taste that is strong and dry, normally with high acid levels and high levels of tannin. It can indicate wines that lack depth and roundness, but also describes the finest wines from Pauillac and Saint-Julien that will mature with age.

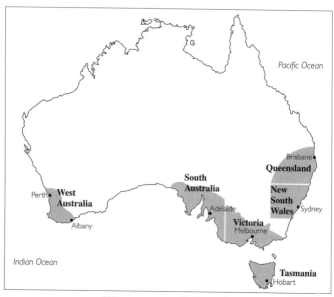

Wine regions of Australia

Australia

a country that is the sixth-largest wine producer in the world and certainly one of the most influential. Australia has had vineyards since the 18th century, winemaking started in earnest in the 1860s and by the 1980s its wine was being exported around the world. Wine is now one of Australia's major industries, exports having risen from A$13 million in the early 1980s to more than A$2 billion in 2001–02, which, in itself, was double the figure for 1999. It is the world's fourth-largest exporter of wine, behind France, Italy and Spain. Although only 15% of the wine consumed in the UK is Australian, it is claimed that in the vital £4–£6 price range Australian wine is responsible for some 50% of UK sales. The success of Australian wines in recent times can be attributed to the remarkable value for money it offers as well as for its consistency and strongly defined varietal flavours. A number of factors enable Australian winemakers to produce just about every style of wine that there is, from hearty, full-bodied red wines, through fruit-driven, buttery Chardonnays to delicate sparkling wines and complex fortified wines. Geographically, the wine-growing areas lie within ideal latitudes for viticulture, and the temperature is moderated by the surrounding oceans. A variety of climates, soil conditions and topography provides ample opportunity for a proliferation of wine styles in the 56 wine-growing regions. These, in the main, cling to the coast across the cooler southern part of the country, mainly concentrated in the southeast and southwest of the continent. The main regions are in South Australia, New South Wales, Victoria, Queensland, West Australia and Tasmania. The most commonly grown grape varieties are Syrah (Shiraz), Cabernet Sauvignon and Merlot for red wine production. Chardonnay, Sémillon and Riesling are the main grape varieties grown for white wine production. Australian wine labels can show a single grape variety only if the wine contains at least 85% of this grape. Blends are common and grape varieties are listed in descending order, e.g. Cabernet-Shiraz, a wine predominantly made from Cabernet Sauvignon grapes with a smaller quantity of Syrah (Shiraz). Australian influence on winemaking around the world has been immense in the last decade. Young Australians, known as flying winemakers, have taken the Australian wine-making philosophy both to other New World countries and to the Old World, producing stunning wines in all kinds of conditions. Their influence can be seen in recent developments in a number of Old World winemaking countries, as they hunger for the kind of success that Australian wine has achieved and try to match the expectations that Australian wines have created in British wine consumers.

Australian Wine and Brandy Corporation
the organisation that administers the Australian system of Geographic Indication.
Abbreviation **AWBC**

Austria
a country whose wines are often grouped together with German wines in style, but which has a warmer climate that ensures that the grapes ripen more, providing more sugar and a stronger wine. Austrian wine laws are now very strict, with 11 categories of quality: Tafelwein, Landwein, Qualitätswein and Kabinett and 7 wines classed as Prädikatswein: Spätlese, Auslese, Strohwein, Eiswein, Beerenauslese, Ausbruch and Trockenbeerenauslese. The majority of Austrian wine is white, made mostly from Grüner Veltliner, Gewürztraminer, Muscat, Pinot Blanc and Riesling grape varieties.

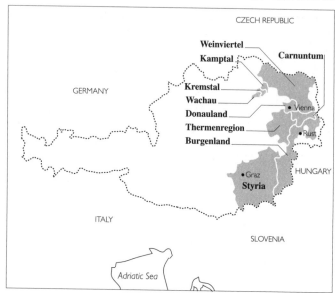

Wine regions of Austria

autoclave
a sealed container used to produce sparkling wines using the Charmat or bulk process, e.g. Asti Spumante

autolysis
decomposition of dead yeast cells after fermentation. If wine is left with its lees, this process can add complex and subtle flavours to a wine. It can last from months to several years, according to the winemaker.

Auvergne *see* **Côtes d'Auvergne VDQS**

Auxerre *see* **Côtes d'Auxerre**

Auxerrois *another name for* **Malbec** (*pronounced* ố sair waá, *used in* Cahors, France)

Auxerrois Blanc (*pronounced* ố sair waá blaáN)
I. a white-wine grape variety grown in the Alsace region of France
2. *another name for* **Chardonnay**

○ **Auxerrois Gris** *another name for* **Pinot Gris** (*pronounced* ố
sair waá greé)

Auxey-Duresses AOC
France a village appellation in the Burgundy region of France
that includes several premier cru vineyards and grows Pinot
Noir grapes to produce good red wines and Chardonnay grapes
to produce good whites. Much of its wine is sold under the Côte
de Beaune-Villages AOC, though the village appellation is
becoming better known in its own right. (*pronounced* ốk say
doŏ réss)

AVA *abbreviation USA* American Viticultural Area

○ **Avesso**
a white grape variety grown in Portugal, where it is used to
produce Vinho Verde wines (*pronounced* ə véssō)

AWBC *abbreviation* Australian Wine and Brandy Corporation

♀ **awkward**
(*tasting term*) used to describe a wine that has poor structure or
is not correctly balanced

azienda
Italian a wine-producing estate. The word's presence on a wine
label indicates that the grapes were grown and the wine produced on the estate in question. (*pronounced* a tsyéndə, *plural*
aziende)

B

They are not long, the days of wine and roses.

Ernest Dowson, 1986

BA *abbreviation German* Beerenauslese

◊ **Bacchus**
1. an early-ripening white-wine grape variety, the result of a cross between Müller-Thurgau and a Sylvaner-Riesling hybrid, that produces wine with low acidity but with good body that is often used in Germany in blends with Müller-Thurgau. The grape is also grown in England.
2. the Roman god of wine.
Compare **Dionysus**

back blending
the adding of grape juice to a wine to sweeten the final wine

♀ **backbone**
(*tasting term*) the quality of red wines that are full-bodied, well-structured and well-balanced with the correct level of acidity

♀ **backward**
(*tasting term*) used to describe a wine that tastes less developed than its age and retains youthful characteristics despite considerable ageing

◊ **Baco Blanc**
a white grape variety grown mostly in the Armagnac region of France and widely used to produce brandy (*pronounced* bákō blaáN)

◊ **Baco Noir**
a grape variety developed in France and used primarily in the eastern USA to make light, dry and fruity red table wines (*pronounced* bákō nwaár)

bacteria
microorganisms that help in the decomposition of organic matter but can cause disease and spoil wine. The main bacter-

ium causing problems in winemaking is Acetobacter, which converts alcohol to acetic acid in the presence of oxygen.
See also **malolactic fermentation**

♀ **bacterial**
(*tasting term*) used to describe wines with unpleasant odours or flavours

Badacsonyi
Hungary a wine-producing region in western Hungary, on the volcanic slopes at the southwestern end of Lake Balaton, growing mostly Pinot Gris grapes but also a little Kéknyelü (*pronounced* búddə chonyi)

Baden
Germany a major German wine-producing region stretching from the border with Franken (Franconia) to Switzerland in the south. It is one of the 13 Anbaugebiete (quality wine-producing regions), with 8 Bereiche (districts) that have varying geographical conditions and grow mainly Müller-Thurgau, Pinot Gris and Riesling grape varieties for white wine, but also some Pinot Noir for red wine. Its warm climate produces wines with higher levels of alcohol but less acidity than other German regions. (*pronounced* baád'n)

♡ **Baga**
the most popular red-wine grape variety grown in Portugal's Bairrada DOC region, producing richly coloured red wine with high levels of tannin. It is also planted in the Dão and Douro regions. (*pronounced* baágə)

bag-in-box
a method of selling wine inside a vacuum-sealed plastic bag that has a small tap moulded into the bottom corner. The bag is fitted inside a cardboard box for protection and provides a cheap, airtight and convenient container for low-price wines.

Bairrada DOC
Portugal a DOC wine-producing region in northern Portugal that produces mainly red wine from the Baga grape variety. The wines have high levels of tannin and acid due to the traditional process of leaving the wine in contact with the skins and stalks during fermentation, but recently producers have been seeking ways to make softer wines. Some sparkling white wine without DOC status is also made in Bairrada. (*pronounced* bī raádə)

♀ **baked**
1. (*tasting term*) used to describe a wine that tastes noticeably of alcohol or that has a high alcoholic content
2. (*tasting term*) used to describe a burnt taste in wine from grapes grown in hot climates

baking *same as* **estufagem**

♀ **balance**
(*tasting term*) the quality in wine in which each element contributes to the overall experience with no one element dominating. The key elements include sweetness, acidity, tannin, alcohol and fruit. The balance of these elements in a wine will change as the wine ages, so a fine wine might start out of balance and gradually change into a perfectly balanced, great wine.

balanced wine
a well-made wine in which no one element of the wine dominates

Balbi (*pronounced* bálbi)
◊ **1.** *another name for* **Prosecco**
2. *Argentina* a well-known winery in the Mendoza region of Argentina, now owned by Allied Domecq

balthazar
an oversize bottle that can hold 12 litres, equivalent to 16 standard 750 ml bottles

♀ **banana**
(*tasting term*) the smell of some very young wines due to the amyl acetate found in newly bottled wine, which diminishes with age

Bandol AOC
France a small wine-producing appellation by the sea in Provence, southern France, east of Marseilles, that grows especially the Mourvèdre grape variety to produce good-quality red and rosé wines. Very little white wine is produced. (*pronounced* baáN dol)

Banyuls AOC
France a small wine-producing appellation in the Languedoc region of southern France with terraced vineyards above the Mediterranean Sea near the border with Spain and the small

village from which it takes its name. It is best-known for its vin doux naturel, a sweet white wine produced from late-harvest and sometimes shrivelled Grenache grapes that, by law, must contain at least 15% alcohol. Various styles are made, including a dark-coloured rancio produced by partly oxidising the wine. Red wines produced from the same vineyards are labelled Collioure AOC. (*pronounced* baáN yoolss)

Barbaresco DOCG
Italy a small DOCG zone in the Piedmont region of north-western Italy. It grows Nebbiolo grapes and the wine is aged for at least two years, one of which must be in wooden barrels (three years for the riserva variety). Barbaresco shares its elegant, spicy but dry style with Barolo, though the wines do not usually have the body and intensity of flavour of the best Barolos. (*pronounced* baárbə réskō, *plural* **Barbarescos**)

☿ Barbera
a red-wine grape variety, native to Piedmont, Italy, that ripens late and produces wines with deep colour, high acidity, low tannin levels and lots of fruity aroma. It is one of the most widely planted varieties in Italy and is also used in California, USA, and Argentina. It is used for a wide range of wines, from cheap blended wines, as in California, to high-quality aged wines in Italy. (*pronounced* baar báirə)

Barbera d'Alba DOC
Italy a DOC area of the Piedmont region of northwestern Italy that grows the Barbera grape variety to produce high-quality red wines. It neighbours the Barbera d'Asti DOC. (*pronounced* baar báirə dálbə)

Barbera d'Asti DOC
Italy a DOC area of the Piedmont region of northwestern Italy that grows the Barbera grape variety to produce red wines that are lighter than those from neighbouring Barbera d'Alba (*pronounced* baar báirə dásti)

Bardolino DOC
Italy a DOC area in the Veneto region of northeastern Italy producing light red and rosé wines blended from several grape varieties including Corvina and Rondinella. The name appears on labels in various compounds: Bardolino Chiaretto is a rosé wine, made in still and sparkling styles; Bardolino Classico uses

the better-quality grapes from around the town of Bardolino; Bardolino Superiore must be aged a year before release and has a higher alcohol content; Bardolino Novello is a light, fruity wine that should be drunk when young. (*pronounced* baárdə leénō, *plural* **Bardolinos**)

♀ **barnyard**
USA (*tasting term*) *same as* **farmyard**

Barolo DOCG
Italy a small DOCG wine-producing area within the Piedmont region of northwestern Italy. It grows Nebbiolo grapes, and the wines are aged for at least three years (four years for the riserva variety) to produce some of Italy's best red wines that are dark red, with high levels of tannin and alcohol and can be aged for between 10 and 30 years. (*pronounced* bə rólō, *plural* **Barolos**)

Barossa Valley
Australia an important wine-producing region in South Australia, producing good-quality table wines and growing mostly Riesling, Sémillon and Chardonnay for white wines and Syrah (Shiraz), Grenache and Cabernet Sauvignon for red wines. With the adjoining Eden Valley it forms the Barossa Wine Zone. (*pronounced* bə róssə válli)

barrel
a wooden, normally oak, container used to store wine for a period of time to add flavour and age the wine, A standard French barrel, typically used in the Bordeaux region, is called a barrique and contains 225 litres of wine.
Compare **butt; cask; pièce**

barrel ageing *see* **ageing**

barrel fermenting
the fermenting of wine, usually white wine, in wooden barrels rather than stainless steel tanks. This adds a layer of complexity, texture and flavour to the wine and can dramatically change the taste of the wine. Red wine is never totally fermented in wooden barrels because red wines must be fermented in contact with their grape skins and it is very difficult to push grape skins in and out of a barrel through the small bung-hole.

barrelling down
the pouring of wine into wooden barrels for ageing

barrel inserts
oak slats or oak chips put into wine, as a cheap way of adding oak flavour

barrel maturation
the maturing of wine in the traditional way by filling new oak or older oak barrels with the new wine

barrica
Spanish a wooden barrel similar to a barrique (*pronounced* ba reeka)

barrique
French a wooden oak barrel with a capacity of around 225 litres, equivalent to a quarter of a tonneau or 25 cases of wine. The term is usual in the Bordeaux region; in Burgundy the similar barrel is called a pièce. (*pronounced* ba reek)

barro
Spanish the clay soil in the wine-producing DO regions of Jerez-Xérès-Sherry and Manzanilla Sanlúcar de Barrameda (*pronounced* bárrō)

Barsac AOC
France a small commune of Sauternes in the Bordeaux region of western France, known for sweet white wines made from botrytised Sémillon and Sauvignon Blanc grapes. Producers may use either 'Barsac' or 'Sauternes' on the label. (*pronounced* baár sak)

Bas-Armagnac
France one of the three subregions of Armagnac in southwestern France, in the west, producing the best brandy of the region (*pronounced* baa ármə nyak)

base wine
each of the wines in a blend

basket press
a traditional wooden wine press in which the grapes are squeezed by a horizontal disc fitting into a cylindrical basket of staves bound with hoops

Bas-Médoc
France the lower and more northerly part of the Médoc AOC wine-producing region of France, north of Bordeaux (*pronounced* baá may dók)

Bâtard-Montrachet AOC

France a small grand cru vineyard in the Côte de Beaune area of the Burgundy region of France that grows Chardonnay grapes to produce outstanding white wines. (*pronounced* ba taár moN ra sháy)

See also **Bienvenues-Bâtard-Montrachet AOC**

BATF

a USA Federal Government agency that collects alcohol taxes and administers wine regulations and the AVA scheme.

Full form **Bureau of Alcohol, Tobacco and Firearms**

batonnage *French same as* **lees stirring** (*pronounced* bá to naázh)

Baumé scale

a system used in much of Europe for indicating the sugar content of a liquid such as grape juice by its density or specific gravity. This scale is similar to the Brix system used in the USA but 1 degree on the Baumé scale is approximately equal to 1.8 degrees on the Brix system. The Baumé scale directly correlates to the final alcohol per unit volume for a wine with one degree equal to 1% alcohol. (*pronounced* bố may skayl)

bead

a bubble that floats on top of a fermenting wine or on top of a sparkling wine in a glass.

See also **mousse**

Béarn AOC

France an appellation in southwestern France that grows Cabernet Sauvignon and Cabernet Franc grapes to produce red and rosé wines and grows the Gros Manseng grape variety for white wines (*pronounced* bay aárn)

Beaujolais AOC

France a famous wine-producing area in the southern Burgundy region of western France that grows Gamay grapes, rather than Pinot Noir as in the rest of Burgundy. It produces almost exclusively red wines using the carbonic maceration method. The best-known style of its richly coloured, light and fruity red wines is Beaujolais Nouveau. The wine-producing area is split into several sections: to the south near Lyons the wines produced are labelled Beaujolais AOC wines; in the north towards Mâcon, there are two styles of red wine, Beaujolais-Villages and the higher-quality single cru produced in ten villages (Brouilly,

Chénas, Chiroubles, Côte de Brouilly, Fleurie, Juliénas, Morgon, Moulin-à-Vent, Régnié and Saint-Amour). The majority of Beaujolais is blended, bottled and sold by négociants, who buy wine from the 4,000 individual growers and 19 cooperatives that make up Beaujolais. There are around 30 négociants, the best known of whom are Georges Duboeuf, Bouchard Père et Fils and Louis Jadot. (*pronounced* bốzhə lay, *plural* **Beaujolais**)

◊ **Beaujolais Nouveau**
a red wine produced in the Beaujolais AOC region of France that is released on the third Thursday of November after the harvest. It is a light and fruity red wine that often improves if aged for six to eight months. (*pronounced* bốzhə lay noo vố, *plural* **Beaujolais Nouveaux**)

◊ **Beaujolais Supérieur**
a red wine produced within the Beaujolais AOC region of France that has a lower yield permitted per hectare and at least 1% more alcohol content than basic Beaujolais AOC wine (*pronounced* bốzhə lay soo páyri úr, *plural* **Beaujolais Supérieurs**)

Beaumes-de-Venise
France a village in the southern Rhône region of France best-known for its sweet white wine, Muscat de Beaumes-de-Venise, made from Muscat grapes. It also grows Grenache and Cinsault grape varieties for red wines. (*pronounced* bốm də və neéz)

Beaune AOC
France an appellation in the Burgundy region of France, with the town of Beaune considered the wine centre of the region. This appellation grows mostly Pinot Noir grapes to produce soft red wines with low levels of tannin. (*pronounced* bōn)

◊ **Beaunois** *another name for* **Chardonnay** (*pronounced* bō nwaá)

Beechworth
Australia a wine-producing region in northeastern Victoria

Beerenauslese
German a German quality rating for wine produced from grapes that have been individually selected from a bunch, ensuring that the winemaker can use the grapes that have reached optimum ripeness, expressed numerically as grapes with at least 110 degrees sugar on the Oechsle scale. This quality rating is just

above the middle level of the six categories that make up the Qualitätswein mit Prädikat system in Germany. It normally refers to sweet, rich, golden white wines, made mostly from botrytised grapes. Not every vintage produces wines that meet this specification. Beerenauslese is also an official category of Prädikatswein in Austria. (*pronounced* báirən ówss layzə, *literally* 'berry selection', *plural* **Beerenauslesen**)
Abbreviation **BA**

beeswing
a thin shiny sediment that forms in port and some other wines when they are kept for a long time after bottling

Beiras
Portugal a wine-producing region of Portugal that covers the same area as the Dão and Bairrada DOCs and produces Vinhos Regionales and lesser wines (*pronounced* báyrəsh)

Beli Pinot *another name for* **Pinot Blanc**

Belle Epoque *see* **Perrier-Jouet**

Bellet AOC
France a small appellation in the French Riviera region in the south of France, growing Cinsault and Grenache grapes for red and rosé wines and local varieties for white wines (*pronounced* bel láy)

bench graft
a form of graft used for vines in which the two parts have matching notches, rather like two jigsaw pieces, so that they can be pressed together, ensuring that they are in tight contact to help them grow together. In a graft, one part is the rootstock from a phylloxera-resistant vine and the other is a cutting from a plant that produces the type of grape required.

Bendigo
Australia a wine region in central Victoria that produces very good red wines from the Syrah (Shiraz) grape variety

Benmore Valley AVA
USA a small viticultural area that is one of three AVAs in Lake County, California

bentonite
a type of clay that is used in fining to clarify wines, usually white wines. The clay is stirred into a wine, and as it settles to the

bottom it absorbs any suspended particles and excess yeast that could otherwise cloud the wine. The clay is then filtered or racked off, taking the yeast protein with it.
See also **fining agent**

Bereich
German a wine-producing region within an Anbaugebiet (quality wine-producing region). There are 43 Bereiche in the 13 Anbaugebiete. The term usually refers to a rather broad area including a number of neighbouring villages and vineyards and is, therefore, no indicator of quality. (*pronounced* bə rĭkh, *plural* **Bereiche**)

Bergerac AC
France a large appellation on the Dordogne river near Bordeaux in the west of France growing Cabernet Sauvignon, Cabernet Franc and Merlot grape varieties for its red wines and Muscadelle and Sauvignon Blanc for its white wines. Within this appellation there are several smaller appellations, e.g. the Monbazillac AOC producing sweet white wines. Dry white wines sell as Bergerac Sec AOC. Wines from the Côtes de Bergerac AOC are of a better quality than basic Bergerac and have a slightly higher alcohol content. (*pronounced* báirzhə rak)

Beringer Vineyards
USA an old-established vineyard in the Napa Valley region of California producing a range of very good red and white wines from its vast vineyards in the surrounding region. It grows Cabernet Sauvignon, Merlot, Chardonnay, Gewürztraminer, Zinfandel and Sauvignon Blanc grape varieties.

♀ berry
1. a small fleshy seed-bearing fruit such as a grape. There are usually many seeds in the same fruit, and the seeds are enclosed in a pulp.
2. (*tasting term*) a sweet fruity taste characteristic of blackberries, raspberries or cherries

berry size
a factor determining the depth of colour in red wines. Small berries have a larger skin area to juice content, which results in more colour extraction and more concentration of flavour.

♂ Biancame *another name for* Albana (*pronounced* byang kaámay)

bianco
Italian white (*pronounced* byángkō)
See also **vino bianco**

Bianco di Custoza DOC
Italy a DOC wine-producing area in the Veneto region of northeastern Italy, best-known for its dry white wine and sparkling white wine (*pronounced* byángkō dee koo stŏtsə)

Bienvenues-Bâtard-Montrachet AOC
France a small grand cru appellation in the village of Puligny-Montrachet in the Burgundy region of France that grows Chardonnay grapes to produce outstanding white wines. (*pronounced* byáN və nyoo ba taár moN ra sháy)
See also **Bâtard-Montrachet AOC**

♀ **big**
(*tasting term*) used to describe a wine with a full, rich flavour, normally as a good point but sometimes implying that the wine is not elegant. When describing red wines, it normally refers to wine with high levels of tannin and alcohol, e.g. Barolo or Châteauneuf-du-Pape. When describing white wines it normally refers to wines with high levels of alcohol or glycerol.
Compare **full**

♢ **Bigney** *another name for* **Merlot** (*pronounced* beényi)

Billecart-Salmon
a Champagne house in Mareuil-sur-Ay in the Champagne region of France that is one of the few still under its original family ownership. It produces Champagne of elegance and quality. (*pronounced* beéyə kaart sal móN)

bin
a set of racks or shelves with compartments for storing bottles of wine in a cellar

bin end
one of the last bottles remaining from a single production of wine, often sold at a reduced price

binning
the storing of newly bottled wine or Champagne in bins for further bottle ageing

biodynamic viticulture
a holistic approach to growing vines, derived from the work of

Austrian philosopher Rudolph Steiner, that takes into consideration all of nature's forces that affect the health and growth of the plants. Planting, harvesting and bottling are timed to coincide with certain positions of the planets, and only natural preparations may be used to nurture the soil and vines. Biodynamie, as it is known in France, is growing in popularity in almost every wine-producing region of the world.

biologique
French organic (*pronounced* beé olo zheék)

♀ **biscuity**
(*tasting term*) used to describe a wine with a sweetish, yeasty or slightly burnt taste, especially Champagne

bisulphite, bisulfite *see* **sodium bisulphite**

♀ **bite**
(*tasting term*) the quality of wine with a noticeable level of acid or tannin. In full-bodied red wines this can be good, giving the wine's finish a sharp tang.

♀ **bitter**
(*tasting term*) one of the four basic tastes sensed by taste buds along the sides and very back of the tongue. It can indicate high levels of tannin, which has a bitter taste, or wine that has not yet matured; a dominant bitter taste indicates a fault with the wine, whereas in sweet wines a trace of bitterness can balance the wine. The other three tastes are salty, sour and sweet.

♀ **blackberry**
(*tasting term*) a taste or aroma associated with dark-coloured, full-bodied red wines such as those made from the Malbec, Tannat, Zinfandel or Mourvèdre grape varieties

♀ **black cherry**
(*tasting term*) a flavour associated with red wines made from the Pinot Noir or Zinfandel grape varieties

♀ **blackcurrant**
(*tasting term*) an aroma normally associated with the Cabernet Sauvignon grape variety or, in a more subtle way, with the Sauvignon Blanc grape.
Compare **cassis**

black goo *USA same as* **black rot**

⟁ **Black Muscat** *another name for* **Muscat Hamburg**

black rot
a disease caused by the fungus *Guignardia bidwellii* that attacks vines and shrivels grapes.
Also called USA **black goo**

bladder press
a wine press that uses a perforated cylinder with an airbag that expands to squeeze the pomace against its inner wall

Blagny AOC
France a village appellation in the Côte de Beaune district of the Burgundy region of France, producing good red and white wines (*pronounced* blaa nyeé)

blanc
French white (*pronounced* blaaN)
See also **vin blanc**

blanc de blancs
French a white wine made from white grape varieties. The term can be used to describe any such wine, but is normally used for Champagne made solely with the Chardonnay grape. (*pronounced* blaáN də blaáN, *plural* **blancs de blancs**)

⟁ **Blanc de Cabernet Sauvignon** *another name for* **Aligoté** (*pronounced* blaáN də kábbər nay số vee nyóN)

blanc de noirs
French a white wine made from black or red grape varieties. Once pressed, the juice is separated from the skins as quickly as possible to prevent colouring. This term can be used to describe any such white wine, but is normally used for Champagne made solely from the Pinot Noir or Meunier grape varieties. (*pronounced* blaáN de nwaár, *plural* **blancs de noirs**)

⟁ **Blanc Fumé** *another name for* **Sauvignon Blanc** (*pronounced* blaáN fyoó may)

blanco
Spanish white (*pronounced* blángkō)
See also **vino blanco**; **Málaga DO**

⟁ **Blanquette**
(*pronounced* blaaN két)
1. *another name for* **Clairette Blanc**
2. *another name for* **Mauzac**

Blanquette de Limoux AOC
France an appellation in southern France producing sparkling wines from the Mauzac (Blanquette) grape variety using the méthode champenoise (*pronounced* blaaN két də lee moó)

blau
German used to describe black or red grapes (*pronounced* blow, *literally* 'blue')

Blauburgunder, Blauer Klevner *another name for* Pinot Noir (*pronounced* blów bur góondər *or* blów ər klévnər, *used in* Germany)

Blauer Limburger *another name for* Blaufränkisch (*pronounced* blów ər lím burger)

Blauer Spätburgunder *another name for* Pinot Noir (*pronounced* blów ər shpáyt bur góondər, *used in* Germany)

Blaufränkisch
a red grape variety grown mostly in Austria and producing a light red wine with high acidity (*pronounced* blow frénkish)
Also called Blauer Limburger; Kékfrankos

Blaye AOC
France one of three appellations surrounding the town of Blaye in the Haut-Médoc district of Bordeaux, western France. It grows mostly Sémillon and Sauvignon Blanc grapes to produce basic white wine. The neighbouring Côte de Blaye AOC produces similar white wines from the same grapes, whereas Première Côte de Blaye AOC grows Merlot and Cabernet Sauvignon to produce average-quality red wines. (*pronounced* blay)

blend
a mixture of different wines or grape varieties intended to result in a more balanced wine or a particular style of wine

blending
the mixing together of different wines to help balance the wine that is the end product. Almost all wine is, in some way, blended – even classic wine-growers might mix wines from different parts of their estate or wines from grapes picked at different times, and so with different sugar and acid levels, to produce a particular style.
See also assemblage

blight

any one of several diseases of grapevines, usually one caused by fungi or bacteria. The destruction caused by the phylloxera root aphid is sometimes called blight.

blind tasting

a tasting and judging of a selection of wines that are simply numbered and have no label or other indication of origin or style

bloom

1. a flower on a vine.
Also called **blossom**
2. the period of time when a vine is in flower
3. a measure of how rigid a sheet of gelatin is when used in fining to clarify wine
4. a grey powdery coating that can cover grapes and is caused by dust and wax

blue fining

a fining process to clarify a wine by adding a solution of potassium ferrocyanide, which removes excess iron or copper from the wine. This process is no longer used in most countries because it can easily create a very toxic wine.

blunt

(*tasting term*) used to describe a wine that has a strong flavour, often with a high level of alcohol and no interesting aromas or finish

blush

a style of pale pink wine that is sweeter and has a more fruity flavour than a rosé. The most common grape source is the red Zinfandel, but some blush wines are made from black grapes such as Pinot Noir or Cabernet Sauvignon. The juice is left in contact with the grape skins for only a short period of time.

Boal, Bual (*pronounced* boo aál)

1. a white-wine grape variety traditionally grown on the island of Madeira
2. a dark, rich style of a medium sweet white wine produced on the island of Madeira, traditionally with Boal grapes. After the vineyards were devastated by phylloxera in the 1870s the Negra Mole grape was often substituted, but Boal is again being planted to meet European Union specifications.

Bobal

a red-wine grape grown widely in Spain and often used to add colour to red-wine blends (*pronounced* bo baál)

Boca DOC

Italy a DOC region in the Piedmont area of northwestern Italy that grows Nebbiolo and Croatina (Bonarda) grapes to make red wines (*pronounced* bókə)

Bocksbeutel

German a short, wide bottle used for good-quality wines from some regions in Germany (*pronounced* bóks boyt'l, *plural* **Bocksbeutel**)

bodega

Spanish a winery, wine producer or wine cellar (*pronounced* bō dáygə)

body

(*tasting term*) the style and weight of a wine when tasted, determined by such factors as the level of alcohol, sugar and extract present. A light-bodied wine often has a less intense colour, is less alcoholic, lighter on the palate and easier to drink; a full-bodied wine has a higher level of alcohol and is much heavier on the palate; a medium-bodied wine is neither light nor heavy and tends to have around 12 degrees of alcohol.

Bohemia

Czech Republic a western province of the Czech Republic that produces a small amount of wine of modest quality. The other region in the country is Moravia.

Bollinger

one of the best-known producers of Champagne in the Champagne region of France, producing blanc de noirs wines from Pinot Noir grapes. It owns large vineyards in the region and is unusual in fermenting some wine in oak barrels. It has a range of qualities of Champagne, from ordinary non-vintage wine through a very good vintage (Bollinger Tradition RD) to a great and rare wine (Vieilles Vignes Françaises). (*pronounced* bóllinjər)

Bolzano

Italy a town in the south Trentino-Alto Adige region of northern Italy, location of a number of wineries (*pronounced* bol tsaánō)

↻ **Bombino Bianco, Bombino**
a white-wine grape variety mostly grown in southeastern Italy to produce basic white wines and often used to blend with other varieties. (*pronounced* bom beénō byángkō *or* bom beénō)
Also called **Trebbiano Abruzzo**

↻ **Bombino Nero**
a relatively rare and ancient red-wine grape variety grown in Apulia in southeastern Italy (*pronounced* bom beénō náirō)
Also called **Cesanese**

↻ **Bonarda**
(*pronounced* bo naárdə)
I. *another name for* **Bonarda Piemontese**
2. *another name for* **Croatina** (*used especially in* Argentina)

↻ **Bonarda Piemontese**
a red-wine grape variety traditionally grown in the Piedmont region of northwestern Italy (*pronounced* bo naárdə pyay mon táy zay)
Also called **Bonarda**

bonded cellar
a wine cellar or storage area in a winery where wines can be stored without paying excise duty. Before the wine can be drunk it must be moved out of a bonded cellar and the excise duty paid. Wine stored in a bonded cellar is often said to be 'in bond'.
Compare **ex cellar**

bonded warehouse
a storage warehouse that is allowed to hold wine in a country before it passes through customs, and where the wine has not yet been subject to excise duty or VAT. A private buyer can store wine in a bonded warehouse and buy from imports or from stock held in the warehouse without paying excise duty or VAT, both of which are only payable when the wine is removed from the warehouse for sale or consumption in the country (if the wine is exported, no duty is payable).

♀ **bone dry**
(*tasting term*) used to describe the driest types of white, rosé and sparkling wines and some very dry fortified wines

Bonnes Mares AOC
France a renowned appellation in the Burgundy region produ-

cing powerful red wines of excellent quality made of Pinot Noir. It is a grand cru of Chambolle-Musigny and Morey Saint-Denis. (*pronounced* bón maár)

Bonnezeaux AOC
France an appellation in the Loire valley in western France growing Chenin Blanc grapes to produce a grand cru sweet white wine (*pronounced* bónnə ző)

Bonny Doon Vineyard
USA a winery founded in 1981 by innovative winemaker Randall Grahm in the Santa Cruz mountain region south of San Francisco in California, USA, that produces a range of unusual but very good red wines, including its best-known wine Le Cigare Volant, a full-bodied red wine made from Grenache, Mourvèdre and Syrah grapes, together with white wines and a range of eaux de vie
See also **A Winemaker's View**

Bonvino *another name for* **Bombino Bianco** (*pronounced* bon véénō, *used in* the Lazio region of Italy)

bor
Hungarian wine (*pronounced* bawr)

Bordeaux AOC
France the largest wine-producing region of France, taking its name from an important city and port and accounting for one quarter of all wine produced in appellations within France. The region produces a very wide range of styles and qualities of wine from ordinary Bordeaux AOC wines to the great crus classés; both red and white wines are produced, but the red wines predominate. The red wines from the area are mostly produced from Cabernet Sauvignon, Merlot, Cabernet Franc, Malbec and Petit Verdot grape varieties, while the white wines are produced from Sémillon, Sauvignon Blanc and Muscadelle grape varieties. The region is divided by the Dordogne river to produce two distinct areas, the right bank (with regions such as Saint-Émilion and Pomerol, growing more Merlot grapes) and the left bank. The best red wines tend to be produced in the north of the region, towards the Médoc and in Graves, Pomerol and Saint-Émilion. (*pronounced* bawr dő)

Bordeaux mixture
a combination of copper sulphate, slaked lime and water that is sprayed onto vines in the growing season to treat or prevent fungal diseases such as downy mildew forming on them

☉ **Bordo** *another name for* **Cabernet Franc** (*pronounced* báwrdō)

☉ **Bosco**
a white-wine grape that is mainly grown in Liguria, Italy. It is the main constituent of Liguria's most famous wine, Cinqueterre. (*pronounced* bóskō)

bota
Spanish a wooden barrel, similar in size to a butt (*pronounced* bóttə)

Botrytis cinerea
a fungus that attacks grapes and causes them to rot and shrivel up. If a white grape is attacked by this fungus, it has the effect of concentrating the grape's flavour and sweetness and, if carefully controlled, can be used to enhance the sweetness and flavours of sweet white wines. When this fungus attacks red grapes, the rot simply ruins the grape. When it attacks white grapes, it is also known as noble rot or noble mould (in English), pourriture noble (in French), Edelfäule (in German) and muffa nobile (in Italian).

botrytise
to allow white grapes to be attacked by the fungus *Botrytis cinerea* to concentrate their flavour and sweetness and to enhance the sweetness and flavours of the sweet white wine produced from them

bottle *see* **wine bottle**

bottle-ageing
the process of allowing wine to continue to mature in the bottle

bottled by
a phrase printed on a label indicating that the named winery simply bottled the wine but is unlikely to have had any part in making it
See also **cellared by**

bottle fermentation
a second fermentation that occurs in a sealed bottle, particularly in making sparkling wine using the méthode champenoise

bottle sickness, bottle shock
a temporary state that can affect wines immediately after bottling and gives the impression of poor quality or disjointed flavours. No one is sure why this happens, but it is presumed to

be caused by the sudden temporary exposure to oxygen during bottling. The effects only last a few days and then disappear totally.

bottle size
Glass bottles have traditionally been used for storing wine. There are a number of standard sizes for the bottles, regardless of the country of origin. The standard size bottle holds 750 ml and other sizes are multiples of this basic size, from quarter-size bottles up to many times the size.
See **wine bottle**

bottle variation
the differences seen in aged wine from bottle to bottle. It is often said that there is no good aged wine, only good bottles.

Bouchard Père et Fils
France the biggest domaine in the Burgundy region of France and also one of the best-known négociants in the area whose vineyards encompass a great range of premiers crus and grands crus (*pronounced* boo shaár páir ay feéss)

♢ **Bouchet** *another name for* **Cabernet Franc** (*pronounced* boo sháy, *used in* the Bordeaux region of France)

♀ **bouquet**
(*tasting term*) part of the overall smell of a wine that derives from the fermentation process but, mostly, evolves as the wine ages. Sometimes aroma and bouquet are used interchangeably, but generally the aroma represents the subtle smells from the grape fruit whereas bouquet refers to the smells due to the effects of the wine maturing.

♢ **Bourboulenc**
a white grape variety that is mostly grown in the south of France where it is one of the 13 grape varieties permitted to be used in making Châteauneuf-du-Pape red wine (*pronounced* boór boo lángk)

Bourg *see* **Côtes de Bourg**

bourgeois *see* **cru bourgeois**

Bourgogne Aligoté AOC
France an appellation within Bourgogne AOC that uses the Aligoté white grape variety to produce ordinary white wine (*pronounced* boor gónnyə álli go táy)

Bourgogne AOC
France a wide-ranging appellation that covers all the wines produced in the Burgundy region of France. There are a number of different requirements within this appellation: red Bourgogne Rouge wine must be made from Pinot Noir, but Beaujolais, also from the Burgundy region, is made from Gamay grapes; white Bourgogne Blanc is usually made from the Chardonnay grape. (*pronounced* boor gónnyə)
See also **Burgundy**

Bourgogne Passe-Tout-Grains AOC
France an appellation within the general Bourgogne AOC that requires the wines to be made from at least one-third Pinot Noir and the remainder Gamay grapes (*pronounced* boor gónnyə pass too gráN)

Bourgueil AOC
France an appellation in the Loire valley of France that is best-known for its light and fruity red wines made from Cabernet Franc grapes (*pronounced* boor gố ee)

bourru
French gruff (*pronounced* boo rố)
See also **vin bourru**

Boutari Group
Greece a Greek wine company based in Naoussa in northern Greece but also with vineyards on the islands of Crete and Santorini and with interests elsewhere in the country

boutique winery
a winery with only a small amount of land planted with vines but producing its own unique wines

Bouzeron AOC
France a village appellation in the Côte Chalonnaise district of the Burgundy region of France that produces white wine solely from the Aligoté grape variety (*pronounced* boo zə róN)

Bouzy
France a village in the Champagne region of France that grows Pinot Noir grapes to produce some of the best Champagne in France (*pronounced* boo zéé)

Bramaterra DOC
Italy a DOC region in the Piedmont area of northwestern Italy that grows Nebbiolo grapes to produce dry red wine, requiring

at least two years' ageing. A riserva style requires three years'
ageing. (*pronounced* brámmə térrə)

♀ **bramble, brambly**
(*tasting term*) a taste or aroma associated with red wines made
from the Cabernet Sauvignon grape variety

branco
Portuguese white (*pronounced* brángkō)

brandy
an alcoholic liquid that is the result of distilling wine and ageing
it in wood barrels. Brandy can be made wherever grapevines are
grown, but the greatest quantities are produced in France and
Spain. The finest French brandies, Cognac and Armagnac, bear
their own names rather than the generic term 'brandy'. Any fruit
can be distilled to form a brandy, but non-grape versions are
normally referred to by their own names, e.g. Calvados is
brandy from apple juice.

♀ **brawny**
(*tasting term*) used to describe a young red wine that has hard,
tannic flavours

Brazil
a country that, in relation to its size and population, produces
little wine. Its wine is mostly produced from US-derived hybrid
vines.

♀ **bread**
(*tasting term*) an aroma of freshly baked bread associated with
Champagne

breathe
to open a bottle of wine (usually red wine) and allow it to stand
for an hour or two before serving. This practice is supposed to
improve the flavour of the wine and reduce the effects of the
tannin, but since the amount of wine in contact with air is so
tiny in the neck of the bottle, this has very little effect. It is
better to decant the wine into a decanter, where it has more
contact with oxygen; this can help balance an older red wine or
young white wine. Wine exposed to air can, however, lose some
of its flavour.
See also **decant**

breed
I. the elegant quality of wines made from good-quality, noble, grapes
2. the good quality that is the result of a good vineyard, soil, grape and winemaker

Breganze DOC
Italy a DOC area in the Veneto region in northeastern Italy that produces red, rosso and white wines from a range of grape varieties including Cabernet Franc, Cabernet Sauvignon, Pinot Blanc, Pinot Gris and Pinot Noir (*pronounced* brə gánzə)

Brenton *another name for* **Cabernet Franc** (*pronounced* braáN toN)

Brettanomyces
a yeast that grows on harvested grapes and in wineries that will spoil any wine. In tiny quantities it can give a wine a musty taste and aroma.

briary
(*tasting term*) used to describe a young wine that has a peppery, earthy taste

brick red
(*tasting term*) a dark red colour of wine, not quite brown, that usually indicates that a wine has reached maturity

bright
(*tasting term*) used to describe a fresh young wine with zest and well-defined flavour

brilliant
(*tasting term*) used to describe a wine that has a perfectly clear appearance, with no trace of cloudiness or sediment. It can indicate a wine that has been highly filtered and so has lost some of its flavour.

Brindisi DOC
a wine-producing DOC area in the Apulia region of the south-eastern tip of Italy that grows mostly Negroamaro grapes to produce dry red and rosé (rosato) wines (*pronounced* brín deezi)

brioche
(*tasting term*) an aroma associated with Champagne

Britain *see* **United Kingdom**

Brix scale
a density scale used in the USA to measure the specific gravity of a liquid. In winemaking it is used to check the sugar levels in grape juice and so estimate the ripeness of grapes and predict the eventual alcohol content of a wine produced from those grapes.

BRL Hardy
Australia a major wine company in Australia with over a dozen estates and brands including the Hardys brand, now part of Constellation, the biggest wine company in the world

Brouilly AOC
France a large appellation in the Beaujolais region of France, producing fruity wines from Gamay grapes. (*pronounced* broó yee)
See also **Côte de Brouilly AOC**

♀ **browning**
(*tasting term*) a change in colour of red wine that can indicate maturity in a great wine or spoilage in other wines

Brown Muscat *another name for* **Muscat à Petits Grains**

brown scale insect
a flat brown insect (*Parthenolecanium corni*) that causes stunted growth and leaf defoliation on vines

bruise
to harm the flesh of a grape under the skin, usually by hitting it

Brunello *another name for* **Sangiovese** (*pronounced* broo néllō)

Brunello di Montalcino DOCG
Italy a famous wine-producing area of Tuscany that produces rich wines with lots of depth, tannin and structure from Sangiovese (Brunello) grapes (*pronounced* broo néllō dee món tal cheénō)

brut
French used to describe dry sparkling wines, particularly Champagne. Although dry, the brut style of wine can have up to 15 g of sugar added per litre of wine to improve the balance. Brut Champagne is drier than sec, demi-sec and extra dry styles of wine. (*pronounced* broot)

Bual *see* **Boal**

♀ **bubblegum**
(*tasting term*) an aroma associated with Beaujolais Nouveau and red wines made from the Pinotage grape variety

bubbly
sparkling wine, especially Champagne (*informal*)

Buçaco, Bussaco
Portugal a town in west-central Portugal, famous for its Palace Hotel, which blends its own wines for its guests. They are among Portugal's best table wines. (*pronounced* bŏŏ saákō)

Bucelas DOC
a small DOC area near Lisbon, Portugal, producing dry white wine from Arinto and local varieties of grape (*pronounced* bŏŏ kéləsh)

bud
1. a very young shoot on a plant, which may be dormant, that will later become a leaf or flower
2. to propagate plants by grafting a piece of stem with a bud from one plant into the stem of another plant

bud break, bud burst
the swelling and beginning of new growth that takes place in buds in the spring

budding, bud grafting
a way of propagating plants, in which a bud from one plant is grafted into the stem of another

bud wood
a stem of a vine that has buds and is suitable for grafting

Bugey, Vin du *see* **Vin du Bugey AOC**

Bulgaria
a country in eastern Europe that is said to be the first place in the world in which vines were planted and wine was made. In the 1980s Bulgarian wine was exposed to western markets by the state-owned wine company, with great export success; the wines were inexpensive varietals, Cabernet Sauvignon being the most popular. The fall of the Communist government left the Bulgarian wine industry in some disarray through the 1990s, as land was returned to its original owners and wineries were privatised, a process which has been slow and is still ongoing. It has now introduced authorised growing regions, Declared Geographical Origins (DGOs) as well as higher-quality wine-

producing regions called Controlirans. It has also embraced modern winemaking technology and planted popular grape varieties such as Cabernet Sauvignon and Merlot, thus providing much of the popular table wine for sale in Europe.

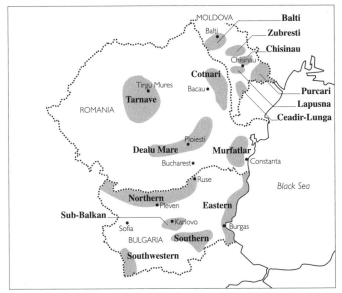

Wine regions of Bulgaria, Romania and Moldova

bulk
1. wine that has not yet been bottled
2. wine sold by the tanker-load and transported by lorry between wineries

bulk process
a method of producing sparkling wines quickly and cheaply by causing secondary fermentation in a large sealed tank rather than by the classic méthode champenoise of secondary fermentation within the original small glass bottle. In the USA wines made in this way must state it on the label. The method is widely used to produce spumante sparkling wine in Italy. For example, the Asti Spumante wine is made using a version of the bulk process in which the grape must is stored at a very low temperature in sealed tanks so that fermentation cannot begin.

The must is warmed gently and yeast is introduced to start fermentation. The carbon dioxide produced during fermentation is retained in the sealed tanks. Once the wine has the correct sugar and alcohol levels, it is rapidly chilled to stop fermentation, then filtered, bottled and corked ready to be sold.
Also called **Charmat process**; **tank method**

Bull's Blood
a well-known brand of robust Hungarian red wine, called Egri Bikavér ('Eger Bull's Blood') in Hungary

bunch
a cluster of grape berries

bung
a stopper used to seal the small opening in a barrel through which the barrel is filled and emptied. Made of hardwood or rubber, the bung prevents the wine from oxidising.

bung-hole
a hole in the side of a barrel through which the barrel is filled and emptied

bung stave
one of the vertical strips that make up a wooden barrel into which the bung-hole is drilled. This stave is the widest in the barrel to ensure that it does not split when making the hole.

Bureau of Alcohol, Tobacco and Firearms
a USA Federal Government agency that collects alcohol taxes and administers wine regulations and the AVA scheme.
Abbreviation **BATF**

Burger *another name for* **Elbling**

Burgundy
France a major wine-producing region in eastern France that grows a limited number of varieties of grape, mainly Pinot Noir for red wines and Chardonnay for white wines, but produces a wide range of styles as well as some of the world's best wines. It consists of four main regions: Chablis, Côte Chalonnaise, Côte d'Or and Macônnais. (Beaujolais is sometimes included, but it possesses its own viticultural identity and is better treated separately.) Burgundy has a large number of small properties, and négociants (wine merchants) often buy and blend wine from many different growers. The quality ratings within the AOC are relatively straightforward, with lowest-quality wines labelled as

general Bourgogne AOC; one up in quality are the region-specific AOCs such as Chablis AOC and Beaujolais AOC; above this are village-specific appellations such as Givry, Meursault and Pommard; above this are premier cru (first-growth) vineyards that label wine with the name of the village and the vineyard; the best-quality wines are graded grand cru and labelled with just the name of the vineyard.

See also **Bourgogne AOC**

burnt
1. (*tasting term*) used to describe a wine that has a smoky or toasted taste

2. used to describe overripe grapes

bush vine
Australia, South Africa a vine trained and pruned to resemble a bush and growing without a trellis. The term can imply a vine of considerable age and therefore quality, but these vines are now often being replaced by vines with a trellis system.

Bussaco *see* **Buçaco**

butt
a large wine barrel that can contain around 29 litres, or 130 gallons, of wine and is normally used to store sherry.

Compare **barrel**; **cask**

buttery
(*tasting term*) used to describe a rich taste and colour that is similar to butter, usually found in a mature or oak-aged Chardonnay

butyric acid
an acid that occurs in spoiled wine, giving it an unpleasant smell of sour milk or rancid butter

Buzet AOC
France an appellation in Gascony in southwestern France, that produces mostly red wine. The area grows Cabernet Sauvignon, Cabernet Franc and Merlot for red and rosé wines and Sémillon and Sauvignon Blanc for white wines. (*pronounced* bŏo záy)

BYO
an unlicensed or sometimes a licensed restaurant that welcomes customers who wish to bring their own wine, for which a fee (corkage) is usually charged for opening the bottle (*an abbreviation of 'bring your own', plural* **BYOs**)

C

A cask of wine works more miracles than a church full of saints.

Italian Proverb

Cab *abbreviation* Cabernet Sauvignon

Cabardes AOC
France an appellation in Languedoc-Roussillon, north of Carcassonne, that grows Bordeaux grape varieties to produce red and rosé wines (*pronounced* ka baárd)

Cabernet *another name for* **Cabernet Sauvignon**

Cabernet Blanc, Cabernet Blush
a white wine made from red Cabernet Sauvignon grapes. (*pronounced* kábbər nay blaáN)
Also called **Blanc de Cabernet Sauvignon**

Cabernet d'Anjou AOC
France an appellation in Anjou in the western Loire region of France that specialises in rosé wine made with the Cabernet Franc grape (*pronounced* kábbər nay daaN zhoó)

Cabernet de Saumur
a light rosé wine made in the Saumur AOC in the Loire region of France (*pronounced* kábbər nay də sō moór)

Cabernet Franc
a red-wine grape variety similar to Cabernet Sauvignon that grows well in cooler areas and produces wines with a taste of blackcurrants that are often used in blends. It is grown in France, particularly in the Loire valley and Bordeaux, and in Italy, California and South Africa. It produces wine with lower levels of tannin and acid than Cabernet Sauvignon. (*pronounced* kábbər nay fraáN)
Also called **Bordo**; **Bouchet**; **Brenton**; **Carmenet**; **Trouchet Noir**

Cabernet Sauvignon
a red-wine grape variety that is now one of the most frequently grown and best known grape varieties in the world. It is drunk as a varietal and also used in blends. It is the main ingredient of

French Médoc and Graves wines as well as of many of California's great wines. In Europe its planting outside France is increasing. It can also be found in Australia, where it is often blended with Syrah (Shiraz), and in South America. The grape is a hardy plant with thick-skinned grapes that allow it to survive cold and be resistant to disease while providing a strong wine with plenty of tannin. It is sometimes referred to as the king of red grapes. The wine at its best is complex and fruity, with good structure. (*pronounced* kábbər nay só vee nyoN)
Also called **Sauvignon Rouge**

Cabrières
France a wine-producing area in the Coteaux du Languedoc region of France, best-known for its light red wines and for stronger Syrah-based red wines (*pronounced* kábbri áir)

Cadillac AOC
France a small appellation in the Bordeaux region of France growing Sémillon, Sauvignon Blanc and Muscadelle grapes to produce sweet or medium sweet white wine (*pronounced* káddi yak)

Cahors AOC
France an appellation in southwestern France near Bordeaux producing dark-coloured red wines with high levels of tannin, made from the Malbec grape variety (*pronounced* kaa áwr)

○ Calabrese
another name for **Sangiovese** (*pronounced* kállə bráyzi)

Calabria
Italy a large wine-producing area in the very tip of the southwestern corner of Italy encompassing a number of DOC regions (*pronounced* kə lábbri ə)

calcium bead
a hard, inert bead that contains yeast, used in making sparkling wine according to the méthode champenoise. The beads roll into the neck of the bottle and are easily removed during disgorgement, eliminating the need for riddling.

California
USA a state in the extreme west of the USA that is the major wine-producing area of North America and is divided into a number of geographical AVAs. Wine production was started in the late 1700s by Franciscan monks, and has waxed and waned over the years but

has now developed to cover many thousands of hectares under vine. The people involved in making wine in California are an eccentric bunch, often people who have dropped out of other professions, coupled with a sprinkling of retirees and hippies. The most widely grown grape is Chardonnay, the state's premier white-wine variety that is almost synonymous with California wine-making; Pinot Blanc, Pinot Gris, Riesling and Sauvignon Blanc are also grown. In the reds, Cabernet Sauvignon is the greatest success story. The rich, distinctive Napa Cabernet is a true classic. Merlot has provided a fashionable and less tannic alternative to Cabernet of late, and there is some fine Pinot Noir, especially in the Carneros and Russian River Valley AVAs. Cabernet is the most widely found red grape variety, though until fairly recently the native Zinfandel occupied that position. The best Zinfandels are fruity, jammy and irresistible.

Caluso Passito DOC
Italy a DOC area in the northern Piedmont region of Italy that is best-known for its sweet white wine made from the Erbaluce grape variety. The grapes are dried in the sun to concentrate the sugar levels and aged for at least five years. (*pronounced* ka loósso pa seétō)

Caluso Passito Liquoroso
a wine from the Caluso Passito DOC region that has been fortified with grape alcohol (*pronounced* ka loósso pa seétō likə róssō)

calyx
a part of a flower shaped like a cup, made up of the green sepals that cover the flower when it is in bud

cambium
a layer of living cell tissue under the bark of a plant that has a woody stem such as a vine

Campania
Italy a large wine-producing area on the eastern coast of Italy that includes a number of DOC zones (*pronounced* kam pánnyə)

Campo de Borja DO
Spain a small DO region in northern Spain that grows the Grenache (Garnacha) grape and produces ordinary red wine with high levels of alcohol, often used to blend with other wines (*pronounced* kámpō day báwrhə)

Campo Viejo

Spain a large wine producer (bodega) in the Rioja DOCa area of northern Spain producing a range of red wines from Tempranillo and some Grenache (Garnacha) grapes and a little white wine from Macabeo (Viura) grapes (*pronounced* kámpō vyéhō)

Canada

a country that consumes more wine than it grows, with most of the wine-producing regions located on the western coast in the provinces of Ontario and British Columbia

☼ Canaiolo Nero, Canaiolo

a red grape variety grown in northern Italy, especially in Tuscany and Umbria. It is used in small proportions in Chianti wines. (*pronounced* kánnī ōlō náirō)

canary

a sweet wine from the Canary Islands, similar to Madeira

Canberra District

Australia a wine region in New South Wales and the Australian Capital Territory about 600 metres in altitude producing excellent red and white table wines from Cabernet Sauvignon, Syrah (Shiraz), Chardonnay and Riesling grapes

cane

a mature shoot of a vine. Mature shoots are brown, new shoots are green.

☼ Cannonau *another name for* Grenache (*pronounced* ká no nō, *used in* Sardinia, Italy)

Canon-Fronsac AOC

France a small appellation in the Bordeaux region of France producing red wine from the Merlot and Cabernet Franc grape varieties (*pronounced* kán oN froN sák)

canopy

the spread of branches and leaves on a vine

canopy management

the technique of trimming and training branches and leaves on a vine in order to change the way the sun reaches the leaves and grapes. Good canopy management improves the quality and yield of grapes and reduces the possibility of disease through lack of air circulation.

Canterbury

New Zealand a wine-producing region in the South Island of

New Zealand, south of Marlborough, growing especially the Chardonnay, Riesling and Pinot Noir grape varieties

cantina
Italian a wine cellar or winery (*pronounced* kan te̒enə, *plural* **cantine**)

cantina sociale
Italian a wine cooperative (*pronounced* kan te̒enə so cha̒ali, *plural* **cantine sociale**)

cap
the mass of skin, pips and fragments of stalks that rises to the top of the liquid during the fermentation process of red wine

capacity
quantity, as opposed to quality, of the total crop produced by a vine

Cape Riesling *another name for* Crouchen (*used in* South Africa)

Capri DOC
Italy a DOC area on the island of Capri growing Piedirosso grapes to produce red wine and Greco and other local grapes for white wine

cap stem
a small piece of stem that connects each individual grape to the bunch

capsule
a metal, traditionally lead, or plastic wrapper that covers the cork and top of the neck of a wine bottle. The capsule helps protect the cork from drying out, which would allow air into the bottle.

carafe
a glass container shaped like a bottle with a wide neck and opening, used to serve ordinary house wine in a restaurant or sometimes used as a container when decanting wine

carafe wine
ordinary house wine served in a restaurant or café.
Also called **vin de carafe**

caramel, caramelly
(*tasting term*) a burnt-sugar aroma and taste, e.g. in Madeira wine or in some oak-aged Chardonnays

carbonation
a method of creating sparkling wine by forcing carbon dioxide gas into the liquid stored in a sealed container. This type of sparkling wine has larger bubbles that quickly disappear compared to traditionally produced sparkling wine.

carbon dioxide
a colourless, odourless gas that occurs naturally in air and is a by-product of fermentation. In still wines the wine is fermented in an open container to allow the carbon dioxide to disperse; in sparkling wines the wine is fermented in a sealed container to force the carbon dioxide into the liquid. Carbon dioxide is also sometimes used at other stages of winemaking to displace oxygen and reduce oxidation. Some winemakers now also bottle white wines with some dissolved carbon dioxide to improve freshness and fruitiness.
Symbol CO_2

carbonic maceration
a method of making wine used mainly in the Beaujolais and Loire regions of France to produce light, fruity red wine that is designed to be drunk when young. In this method, whole grapes, with their stalks and without having been crushed, are fermented in a closed container to produce wine that is full-flavoured with a deep red colour and lots of fruit but that is low in tannin. In the usual method of making wine, the stalks are removed from the bunches of grapes and the grapes are then crushed and fermented without the stalks.

carbon:nitrogen ratio *full form of* C:N ratio

carboy
a large container with a narrow neck used as container for secondary fermentation

Carcavelos DOC
Portugal a small DOC area on the western coast of Portugal, mainly known for its sweet white fortified wine made from local grape varieties (*pronounced* kaárkə váy lōsh)

Carema DOC
Italy a little-known DOC area in the Piedmont region of Italy, north of Turin, that produces red wine from the Nebbiolo grape variety (*pronounced* kar áyma)

Carignan

a red-wine grape variety, widely grown in southern France and around the Mediterranean, and also in California, USA, that yields a lot of fruit from each vine. It produces strong wines with a deep purple colour and a peppery taste similar to that of Syrah, which are often used in blends. (*pronounced* kárri nyaaN) *Also called* **Cariñena**; **Mazuelo**; **Monestel**

Carignan Rosos *another name for* Grenache (*pronounced* kárri nyaaN rőz oss)

Cariñena *another name for* Carignan (*pronounced* kárri nyáynə, *used in* Spain)

Cariñena DO

Spain a DO wine-producing region in northern Spain growing mostly Grenache (Garnacha), Tempranillo and Carignan (Cariñena) grape varieties to produce large quantities of red and rosé wines with high levels of alcohol. Some white wine is produced from Macabeo and Grenache (Garnacha Blanca) Blanc grapes. (*pronounced* kárri nyáynə)

Carmel Valley AVA

USA a small viticultural area in Monterey County, California

Carmenère

a red-wine grape variety that produces deep-coloured full-bodied wines. It was once widely grown in France but was abandoned because of its low yields and susceptibility to disease; it is now showing some signs of revival in the New World, e.g. in Chile. (*pronounced* kaarmə náir)

Carmenet *another name for* Cabernet Franc (*pronounced* kaarmə náy)

Carmignano DOCG

Italy a DOCG area in the Chianti region of Tuscany, in northern Italy, growing Sangiovese, Cabernet Sauvignon and some other grapes that are blended to produce red wines similar to the wines from Chianti (which are made without the Cabernet Sauvignon). This area also produces sweet vin santo and rosé (rosato) wines – both have the lower DOC status. (*pronounced* kaármi nyaánō)

Carnelian

a red-wine grape hybrid derived from Grenache and Cabernet

Sauvignon, developed and grown in California, USA, and producing light red wine

Carneros AVA
USA a region across Sonoma and Napa counties, California, at the top of San Francisco Bay, known for wines made from Chardonnay and Pinot Noir grape varieties (*pronounced* kaar náir oss)
Also called **Los Carneros**

Casablanca
Chile a wine-producing region to the northwest of Santiago in Chile, best-known for its white Chardonnay-based wines

casa vinicola
Italian a company that buys in its grapes to produce wine (*pronounced* kaássə vi neékələ, *plural* **case vinicole**)

case
a standard quantity for selling wine in a cardboard or wooden box containing 12 bottles or 24 half-bottles or 6 magnums

casein
a protein derived from milk that is used in fining to clarify wine

cask
a wooden barrel or other container used for ageing or storing wine, normally made of oak. Casks can also be used to store spirits.
Compare **barrel**; **butt**

♀ casky
(*tasting term*) used to describe the smell or, occasionally, the flavour of a wine that spent too long stored in a wooden barrel or has been stored in a contaminated barrel

casse
cloudiness in a wine due to a chemical imbalance. Formerly copper casse and iron casse were caused by traces of copper and iron from brass or steel fittings and tanks; these problems have been cured by the use of modern stainless steel tanks and equipment. (*pronounced* kass)

♀ cassis
(*tasting term*) *French* blackcurrant (*pronounced* ka seéss)

Cassis AOC
France an appellation in the Provence region in the south of

France. The area is best-known for its white wines made from Sauvignon Blanc, Marsanne and Trebbiano (Ugni Blanc) grape varieties; red and rosé wines are also produced from Grenache and Cinsault grape varieties. (*pronounced* ka seé)

Castelão, Castelão Frances *another name for* Periquita
(*pronounced* kástel yów fran sáyss)

Castel del Monte DOC
Italy a DOC area in the Apulia region of Italy, producing red, white and rosé wines mainly from local grape varieties (*pronounced* kástel del mónt ay)

castello
Italian a description of a vineyard that can only be used on labels of DOC or DOCG status Italian wines (*pronounced* ka stéllō, *literally* 'castle', *plural* **castelli**)

Castilla-La Mancha
Spain a large wine-producing area in central Spain, to the south of Madrid, that includes the La Mancha and Valdepeñas DOs. It is separated by mountains from Castilla-León. (*pronounced* ka stíllyə la mánchə)

Castilla-León
Spain a large wine-producing region of north-central Spain that includes the Ribera del Duero DO. It is separated by mountains from Castilla-La Mancha. (*pronounced* ka stíllyə lay ón)

Castillon *see* Côtes de Castillon AOC

Catalonia, Catalunya
Spain a large Spanish province in the northeast of the country that contains many wine-producing areas including the Cava, Penedès, Priorat and Tarragona DOs

Catarratto
a white grape variety native to the island of Sicily, Italy, which is mostly used for blending in table wines, in the wines of Alcamo DOC and in making the fortified Marsala wine (*pronounced* káttə ráttō)

Catawba
a red hybrid grape developed in the USA and grown in the wine regions of the eastern USA. It is used to make sparkling wines, rosés and very fruity white wines. (*pronounced* kə táwbə)

♀ **cat's pee**
(*tasting term*) an aroma associated with white wines made from the Sauvignon Blanc and Müller-Thurgau grape varieties

◊ **Cava**
a Spanish sparkling wine produced by the méthode champenoise. Cava is best drunk young. (*pronounced* ka᷄avə, *literally* 'cellar', originally in Catalonia)

Cava DO
Spain a large DO region in Spain producing sparkling wines, mostly using Macabeo or Parellada grapes, although the better wines use Chardonnay or Pinot Noir grapes (*pronounced* ka᷄avə)

cave
French a cellar, or any building where wine is stored or sold (*pronounced* kaav)

cave coopérative
French a wine cooperative (*pronounced* ka᷄av ko᷄ óppərə te᷄ev, *plural* **caves coopératives**)

♢ **Cayuga White**
a hybrid grape variety developed and grown in the eastern USA wine regions, which produces delicate white table wines (*pronounced* kī yoógə wīt)

CB *abbreviation* château-bottled

♀ **cedar**
(*tasting term*) an aroma associated with fine French Bordeaux wines and those made from Cabernet Sauvignon grapes or in wine that has been stored or matured in a strongly scented oak barrel

cellar *see* **wine cellar**

cellared by
stored, but not produced, at a winery until it is ready to sell. *See also* **bottled by**

cellaring
1. the processes that a winemaker must undertake to produce wine, including clarification, filtration, blending and bottling
2. the storing of wine in a wine cellar or at a winery

cellar-master
a person who is in charge of the cellars at a wine-producing estate, supervising especially the ageing of wines.
Compare **maître de chai**

Celsius
a scale of temperature in which the freezing point of water is 0° and its boiling point is 100°

♥ **Cencibel** *another name for* **Tempranillo** (*pronounced* then thee bél, *used especially in* the Valdepeñas and La Mancha regions of Spain)

Central Coast AVA
USA a large wine-producing area on the coast of California, stretching from San Francisco to Los Angeles. The name refers primarily to Monterey, San Luis Obispo and Santa Barbara counties, although parts of Alameda, San Benito, Santa Clara and Santa Cruz counties are included.

Central Otago
New Zealand a wine-producing region in the southeast of the South Island of New Zealand growing especially the Riesling and Pinot Noir grape varieties. It is the world's southernmost wine-producing region.

Central Valley
USA a large wine-growing region of California including the Sacramento and San Joaquin Valleys that supplies many of the ordinary blended wines popular in the USA

Central Victoria
Australia a wine-producing zone in Victoria, to the northwest and north of Melbourne

centrifuge filtration
a method of filtering wine by spinning a container very fast in a centrifuge, which separates any solids from the liquid

♥ **Centurion**
a red-wine grape variety which is a hybrid of Cabernet Sauvignon, Grenache and Carignan. It is not widely planted, being grown mostly in the hotter Central Valley region of California, USA.

cepa
Spanish (*pronounced* tháypa)
1. a vine, or the root of a vine
2. a variety of grapevine

cépage
French a variety of grapevine (*pronounced* say paáz̲h̲)

cépages nobles
French the group of great grape varieties used in winemaking in France (*pronounced* sáy paaz̲h̲ nóblə)

Cérons AOC
France a small appellation near the city of Bordeaux that produces sweet white wine using Muscadelle, Sémillon and Sauvignon Blanc grapes. It also produces a dry white wine sold under the Graves AOC. (*pronounced* say róN)

certified planting material
plants certified to be of the variety required and free from disease that will be used in planting or replanting areas for vine cultivation

Cerveteri DOC
Italy a DOC area in the Lazio region of Italy growing Sangiovese and Montepulciano and other grape varieties to produce red wines and mostly Trebbiano grapes to produce whites (*pronounced* cháirvə táiri)

○ **Cesanese** *another name for* **Bombino Nero** (*pronounced* sáy sa náysay)

Chablais
Switzerland a wine-producing area in the Vaud canton of Switzerland in the Rhône valley, growing Chasselas grapes to produce white wine (*pronounced* sháb lay)

◊ **Chablis**
(*pronounced* shábbli, *plural* **Chablis**)
1. *France* a wine-producing area in northern Burgundy, roughly in the middle of France. The area centres on the town of Chablis and has four main appellations, Chablis Grand Cru AOC, Chablis Premier Cru AOC, Chablis AOC and Petit Chablis AOC. These all make variations of dry, full-flavoured white wine from Chardonnay grapes, often with overtones of grass and flint or mineral tastes. The wines are often made without any contact with oak barrels. The grand cru wines can be among the best white wines in the world, and can sustain considerable ageing.
2. *South Africa, USA* very ordinary blended dry white wine

chai
French a building used to store wine before it is bottled (*pronounced* shay)

chalk
fine white sedimentary rock formed of calcium carbonate from animal organisms, widely found in many parts of northern Europe

Chalk Hill AVA
USA a wine-producing area in Sonoma County, California, that grows mainly Chardonnay and Sauvignon Blanc grapes to produce white wines

chalky
used to describe soil that is above a chalk layer and contains chalk

Chalon *see* Château-Chalon AOC

Chalone AVA
USA an appellation in Monterey County, California, with one winery that grows mainly Chardonnay grapes for white wines and Pinot Noir grapes for red

Chambertin AOC
France a grand cru vineyard in Gevrey-Chambertin in the Côte de Nuits district of the Burgundy region growing Pinot Noir grapes to produce highly prized red wines (*pronounced* shómbər taN)

Chambertin Clos de Bèze AOC
France a grand cru vineyard in Gevrey-Chambertin in the Côte de Nuits district of the Burgundy region growing Pinot Noir grapes to produce high-quality red wines (*pronounced* shómbər taN klō də béz)

Chambéry
a light aromatic vermouth made in the French Alps (*pronounced* sham bay reé)

Chambolle-Musigny AOC
France a village appellation in the Côte de Nuits district of the Burgundy region of France that grows Pinot Noir grapes to produce high-quality red wines (*pronounced* shóm bol moo see nyeé)

◯ **Chambourcin**
a red-wine grape variety widely grown in the eastern USA to produce table wines (*pronounced* shóm boor sáN)

Champagne AOC
France a famous winemaking region in northeastern France, centred on the two towns of Reims and Épernay. The region has a chalky soil and, as the most northerly AOC, a relatively cool climate. The most famous wine of the region is the sparkling wine Champagne, though some still wines are also made. The sparkling wine is made using the Chardonnay, Pinot Noir or Pinot Meunier grape varieties; blanc de noirs Champagne is produced entirely from red Pinot Noir or Pinot Meunier grapes, or a mixture of both, while blanc de blancs Champagne is made entirely from white Chardonnay grapes. Rosé Champagne is also made, usually by adding a little red wine to the basic blended Champagne (called the 'cuvée'). The grapes for Champagne are fermented once in a large vat, usually using a specially developed yeast strain, and then fermented a second time in the bottle. This second fermentation produces carbon dioxide that is forced into the wine within the closed bottle. This method of producing wine is often termed the 'méthode champenoise' and is used to produce other sparkling wines, but under European Union laws only wines produced within the Champagne region can be labelled Champagne. Most Champagnes are non-vintage blends made to a consistent style, the house style of the producer (the best of which are unofficially termed 'grandes marques'). Vintage Champagne is made from the best grapes of the harvest in a year when the winemaker considers the harvest to be particularly good. Vintage Champagnes must then be aged for three years. The sugar level of Champagne is described on the label as 'brut' for very dry Champagne with less than 1.5% sugar, 'extra sec' for slightly sweet wine, 'demi-sec' for sweet wine or 'doux' for very sweet wine.

Champagne cork *see* **cork**

Champagne method *same as* **méthode champenoise**

Champenois *see* **Coteaux Champenois AOC**

champenoise *see* **méthode champenoise**

champers
Champagne (*informal*)

Chancellor

a hybrid grape variety grown in the eastern USA and in Canada, producing a fruity, medium-bodied red wine

chapeau

French the mass of skin, pips and fragments of stalks that rises to the top of the liquid during the fermentation process of red wine (*pronounced* sháppō)

Chapoutier

one of the most respected growers in the northern Rhône region of France producing a range of excellent red and white wines around Hermitage and Châteauneuf-du-Pape (*pronounced* sha poo tyáy)

chaptalisation

the process of adding sugar to grape must in order to increase the alcoholic strength of the wine. Adding sugar at this fermentation stage of the winemaking does not increase the sweetness of the wine. Although this process is necessary and legal in cold climates where the lack of sun does not produce enough sugar in the grape, the process is often illegal and unnecessary in countries with hot climates.

Also called **sugaring**

character

(*tasting term*) a distinctive and good style and personality of a wine derived from each element of the winemaking process, reflecting the soil, grape variety and method of production

Charbono

a red-wine grape variety grown mostly in California, USA to produce wines that are full-bodied, dark red in colour and high in tannin and acid levels (*pronounced* shaar bṓnō)

Chardonel

a hybrid grape variety bred in the USA from Chardonnay and Seyval Blanc

Chardonnay

one of the most popular white grape varieties that is grown around the world. It is often synonymous with popular dry white wines, but it can produce a wide range of wines from crisp mineral-flavoured Chablis through rich buttery wines to sparkling Champagne.

Also called **Auxerrois Blanc**; **Beaunois**; **Pinot Blanc**; **Pinot Chardonnay**

Charles Heidsieck

a well-respected grande marque Champagne house based in Reims, in the Champagne region of France and producing a range of Champagne styles (*pronounced* hı́d sek)

Charmat process

a method of producing sparkling wines quickly and cheaply by causing secondary fermentation in a large sealed tank rather than by the classic méthode champenoise of secondary fermentation within the original glass bottle. In the USA wines made in this way must state it on the label. The method is widely used to produce spumante sparkling wine in Italy. For example, Asti Spumante wine is made using a version of the Charmat process in which the grape must is stored at a very low temperature in sealed tanks so that fermentation cannot begin. The must is warmed gently and yeast is introduced to start fermentation – the carbon dioxide produced during fermentation is retained in the sealed tanks. Once the wine has the correct sugar and alcohol levels, it is rapidly chilled to stop fermentation, then filtered, bottled and corked ready to be sold. (*pronounced* shár maá)

Also called **bulk process**; **tank method**

Charmes-Chambertin AOC

France a grand cru vineyard in Gevrey-Chambertin in the Côte de Nuits district of the Burgundy region of France that grows Pinot Noir grapes to produce high quality red wines (*pronounced* shaárm shómbər táN)

♀ charming

(*tasting term*) used to describe a wine that is elegant and immediately appealing

Chassagne-Montrachet AOC

France a well-known appellation in the Burgundy region of France that is best-known for its white wine produced from Chardonnay grapes grown in premier cru and grand cru vineyards. It is rated amongst the best in the world, though less expensive than the similar wines from the famous neighbouring village of Puligny-Montrachet. It also produces red wine from Pinot Noir grapes in almost equal quantities to the white, but the red is unable to rise to a comparable quality. (*pronounced* sha sánnyə moN ra sháy)

○ Chasselas
a white-wine grape variety commonly grown in Switzerland and many other regions of Europe and in Argentina, Australia and California, USA. It produces ordinary white table wine, with low acid levels. (*pronounced* shássə laa)
Also called **Fendant**; **Gutedel**

château
a vineyard or single estate where grapes are grown and wine is produced. The word traditionally referred to a product from the fine-wine producers of the Bordeaux region of France, but it can be used on a label of French wine from any authentic vineyard that traditionally used the term. The property referred to may or may not have a fine residence that might justify the name 'château' (castle or stately home). Spelt chateau, without the circumflex accent, the term is also used in the USA in the names of some wineries. (*pronounced* sháttō, *plural* **châteaux**)

Château
See also below

château-bottled
used to describe wine that has been made from grapes grown exclusively on the château's vineyard and also bottled at the château.
Abbreviation **CB**

Château-Chalon AOC
France an appellation in the Jura region of eastern France producing vin jaune made exclusively from the Savagnin grape variety (*pronounced* sháttō sha lóN)

Château-Grillet AOC
France a small vineyard and appellation in the northern part of the Rhône region of France growing only Viognier grapes to produce some of the best and most expensive dry white wines made from this grape (*pronounced* sháttō gree yáy)

Châteauneuf-du-Pape AOC
France an appellation in the Rhône valley, southern France, near Avignon. This area produces very high-quality red wines that rely mainly on the Grenache grape variety, but, unusually, the rules for the appellation allow another 12 grape varieties to be grown and used within the AOC. The region also produces a small quantity of white wine from the Grenache Blanc, Bourboulenc and Clairette Blanc grapes. Estate-bottled wines display

the coat of arms of the Pope on the label of the bottle (the name means 'the Pope's new castle'). In the 1920s the area was the first to implement a set of rules to regulate the wine production process. These rules were then used as the basis of the Appellation d'Origine Contrôlée system implemented across France. (*pronounced* sháttō nőf dỏo páp)

◊ **Chauche Gris** *another name for* **Trousseau Gris** (*pronounced* shősh greé)

◊ **Chaudenet Gris** *another name for* **Aligoté** (*pronounced* shő dənay greé)

◊ **Chaunac**
a hybrid red grape variety grown in the eastern USA and Canada and producing fruity wines. (*pronounced* shō nák)
Also called **de Chaunac**; **Seibel 9549**

Chave *see* **Domaine B. Chave**

Chave, Jean-Louis
a well-known wine producer in the northern Rhône region of southern France (*pronounced* shaav)

◊ **Chelois**
a hybrid red grape variety grown in the eastern USA and producing light and fruity red or rosé wines.
Also called **Seibel 10878**

Chénas AOC
France a small cru (village and surrounding area) in the Beaujolais region of France producing high-quality red wine from Gamay grapes (*pronounced* sháy naa)

◊ **Chenin Blanc**
a white grape variety that is used to produce a range of wine styles in the Loire region of France, including the sweet Vouvray wines and dry Anjou wines. It is also used in blends in California, Australia and South Africa. South Africa and the USA now both grow more Chenin Blanc than does France. When used to produce sweet white wine the grape can be infected with *Botrytis cinerea* to concentrate sugar levels and flavour. (*pronounced* shə naN blaáN)
Also called **Steen**

♀ **cherry**
(*tasting term*) a flavour and aroma associated with wine made from Pinot Noir or Zinfandel grapes

♀ **chestnut** *same as* **roast chestnut**

Cheval Blanc, Château
France a famous château in the Saint-Émilion district of Bordeaux, France, that makes good red wines from Cabernet Franc, Merlot and a small proportion of Malbec grapes. It was graded in the top two premiers grands crus classés in the classification of Saint-Émilion wines in 1955. (*pronounced* shə val blaáN)

Chevalier *see* Domaine de Chevalier

Chevalier Montrachet AOC
France a famous appellation in the Côte de Beaune district of Burgundy producing grand cru white wine from the Chardonnay grape variety (*pronounced* shə val yáy moN ra sháy)

Cheverny VDQS
France a VDQS area in the Loire region of France, growing mostly Gamay and Cabernet Franc grape varieties to produce red and rosé wines and growing Chardonnay, Chenin Blanc and Sauvignon Blanc to produce white wines (*pronounced* shə vair née)

♀ **chewy**
(*tasting term*) used to describe a rich, full-bodied wine that has a high tannin content and well-balanced acid levels

Chianti DOCG
Italy a large wine-producing area in Tuscany in central Italy that is best-known for its range of dry, medium- to full-bodied fruity red wines produced from a blend of four grape varieties (Sangiovese dominates, then Canaiolo Nero, Malvasia and Trebbiano). The DOCG is divided into seven smaller zones: Chianti Aretini, Chianti Classico, Chianti Colli Fiorentini, Chianti Colli Senesi, Chianti Colline Pisane, Chianti Montalbano and Chianti Rufina. Chianti Classico also produces some of the best-quality wines in this area, and is also the oldest defined area – it was delimited as far back as 1716. Wines labelled 'riserva' have been cask-aged for at least three years and will continue to mature and develop in the bottle. (*pronounced* ki ánti)

chiaretto
Italian light red (*pronounced* keer éttō)

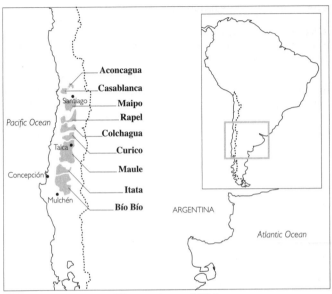

Wine regions of Chile

Chile

a South American country that is the tenth-largest wine-producing country in the world and the fifth largest exporter of wine. The narrow 5,000 kilometre-long strip of land that is Chile is ideal for growing grapes for wine. Everything conspires in its favour: the climate, the volcanic soil and the unusual fact that Chilean vines have never been infected with the phylloxera root aphid and so have some of the only vineyards growing original rootstocks rather than vines produced by the more usual grafting process onto phylloxera-resistant rootstock that is required in other parts of the world. Vines have been grown in Chile since Spanish settlers arrived in the middle of the 16th century, but the modern Chilean wine industry grew out of the travels of the Chilean well-to-do, who, enjoying the fine wines of Europe, brought home new vines to make better wine than that made predominantly from the Pais grape. Foreign winemakers were brought in, early examples of the modern flying winemakers. Chilean wine flourished, especially as the rest of the winemaking world suffered the twin scourges of phylloxera and mildew. In more recent times resistance to Chilean wine was created by a dislike of the prevailing political situation, but the resolution of this situation in the 1980s encouraged further growth and investment. Modern winemaking technology was introduced and Chile's wine exports soared. Chilean wines are notable for their clean, fruity varietal nature. Cabernet Sauvignon is the most successful variety, but Chilean Merlots, Pinot Noirs and Syrahs also do well. Chardonnay and Sauvignon from the Casablanca area are particularly notable. The majority of Chile's wine production takes place from Aconcagua, north of Santiago, to Maule, where the majority of Chile's bulk wines are produced. The Casablanca, Maipo and Rapel areas provide good quality wines from cool-climate vineyards.

Chinon AOC
France an appellation in the Loire region of France that grows mostly the Cabernet Franc grape variety to produce a light, fruity red wine as well as smaller amounts of rosé and grows Chenin Blanc grapes to produce white wines (*pronounced* sheé noN)

Chiroubles AOC
France a small cru (village and surrounding area) in the Beaujolais region of France producing from the Gamay grape variety a high-quality red wine which is very light even by Beaujolais standards (*pronounced* shi roóblǝ)

♀ chocolate
(*tasting term*) an aroma associated particularly with red wines made from Cabernet Sauvignon grapes

Chorey-les-Beaune AOC
France an appellation in the Burgundy region of France that grows mostly Pinot Noir grapes to produce good-quality red wines without cru status (*pronounced* sháw ray lay bốn)

Cigales
Spain a wine-growing zone in northern Spain that grows mainly Tempranillo and Grenache (Garnacha) grapes to produce rosé and red wines (*pronounced* thee gaá less)

♀ cigar box
(*tasting term*) a cedarwood aroma on some wines, notably red wines made with Cabernet Sauvignon grapes

Cinqueterre DOC
Italy a DOC area on the Ligurian coast in northwestern Italy that grows mostly Bosco and Albarola grape varieties to make small quantities of good-quality wine as well as ordinary table wines (*pronounced* chīng kway té ray)

cinquième cru
French used in the classification of 1855 to signify the lowest category of crus classés in the Médoc district. (*pronounced* saN kyem krŏo, *literally* 'fifth growth', *plural* **cinquièmes crus**)
See also **classification of 1855**

♀ Cinsault
a red grape variety most commonly grown in southern France (Provence and the Midi areas) and also in South Africa, producing a very light wine that is often blended with other wines. It is one of the grapes allowed in Châteauneuf-du-Pape wines. South African wine-growers crossed this grape, known locally as Hermitage, with Pinot Noir to produce the Pinotage variety. (*pronounced* saN sŏ)
Also called **Espagne**; **Malaga**; **Prunella**

Cirò DOC
Italy a DOC area in Calabria in southern Italy with a long history of wine production that goes back to the ancient Greeks. It grows mostly Gaglioppo, Trebbiano and Greco grapes to make red, rosé and white wines. (*pronounced* chi rŏ)

♀ citrus, citric
(*tasting term*) used to describe the smell of lemon, lime or grapefruit in the bouquet and as an aftertaste of red or white wine

CIVC *abbreviation French* Comité Interprofessionnel du Vin de Champagne

♀ Clairette Blanc, Clairette
a white-wine grape variety grown in southern France, Australia and South Africa to produce wine that has high levels of alcohol and low acid levels and that tends to maderise (*pronounced* klair rét blaáN)

Clairette de Die AOC
France an appellation in the Rhône region of France that is best-known for its sparkling white wines made from Muscat

or Clairette Blanc grapes and produced using the traditional méthode champenoise (*pronounced* klair rét də deé)

◇ **Clairette Ronde, Clairette Rosé** *another name for* **Trebbiano** (*pronounced* klair rét róNd *or* klair rét rō záy, *used in* France)

◇ **Clare Riesling** *another name for* **Crouchen** (*used in* Australia)

◊ **claret**
an English term for a red wine produced in the Bordeaux region of France. Originally it referred to light red wines, but now it is often used as a generic label for a full-bodied red wine made in the style of the Bordeaux region.

clarete
Spanish used to describe light-red wine. (*pronounced* kla ráy tay)
See also **Valdepeñas DO**

claret jug
a decanter with a handle and a lip for pouring the wine, without a stopper

Clare Valley
Australia a wine-producing region in South Australia, 140 km north of Adelaide, that produces very fine Rieslings as well as excellent Sémillon white wines and excellent red wines made from the Syrah (Shiraz) and Cabernet Sauvignon grape varieties

clarify
to remove unwanted solid matter such as grape skins, pips and stalks together with yeast from wine as a stage in the wine-making process. The wine can be clarified at three points during the winemaking process: before fermentation, the grape juice (the must) can be clarified using a filter or by centrifugal force; during or after fermentation the wine can be racked; lastly, before bottling, the wine can be filtered or fined to produce a clear, bright liquid.

♀ **clarity**
(*tasting term*) the condition of wine that has no dullness or cloudiness

Clarksburg AVA
USA a viticultural area in the Sacramento Delta of California that produces very good white wines from the Chenin Blanc grape variety

classed growth
a literal translation of 'cru classé'
See also **classified growth**

♀ **classic**
(*tasting term*) used to describe wine that is characteristic of the
region or grape variety

Classic
used on labels of German wine to indicate a dry white wine from
a single region and made with a traditional grape variety of that
region.
Compare **Selection**

classico
used as a classification of wine from the smaller region of a
DOC-classified wine-producing region in Italy that is divided up
into smaller regions, with the oldest vines and tradition of
winemaking and normally also the best wine. For example,
the Bardolino Classico DOC area is a smaller area within the
Bardolino DOC region. (*pronounced* klássikō)

classification of 1855
a widely influential system introduced in France in 1855 to
identify which vineyards produced the best-quality wines, to
allow the judges of the prestigious Paris Exhibition to select
which wines should be exhibited. The classification system was
only applied to two areas from the Bordeaux region, Médoc and
Sauternes, with all other wine-producing regions in Bordeaux
and the rest of France considered inferior. The classification
originally included five levels for red wine and two levels for
white wine; these levels were called crus classés (classed growths)
and were ranked numerically with premier cru (first growth) as
the best, then deuxième cru, troisième cru, quatrième cru and
finally cinquième cru. Originally there were 60 châteaux in the
entire classification and just four in the premier cru class of red
wine; in 1973 Château Mouton-Rothschild was promoted to
premier cru, making five. Only two of the originally classed red
wines remain in the same hands. In the white-wine category,
only 24 châteaux were included; the famous Château d'Yquem
was placed in a class of its own, called premier grand cru classé.
This classification system has been widely criticised, but it
remains in place. Its oddities include the fact that the classification is linked to the ownership of the château, not the specific

vineyard, so a vineyard can change ranking overnight if it is sold to a different château in a different class.

classified growth
a literal translation of 'cru classé'
See also **classed growth**

clay
particles in soils smaller than two microns (0.002 mm) in diameter

clay soil
soil with more than 35% clay-size material. Clay soils are sticky when wet and can hold more water than most other types of soil. They lie wet in the winter, and are liable to become muddy under foot; they are slow to warm in springtime. In long periods of dry weather, clay soils become hard and wide cracks may form. They have poor workability.

♀ **clean**
(*tasting term*) used to describe a wine with a fresh taste that has no obvious defects or problems with its aroma, appearance or flavour. It does not necessarily mean a good-quality wine.

Clear Lake AVA
USA a large wine-producing region in California, north of Napa Valley

climat
French the particular combination of soil, aspect and climate of an individual vineyard site (*pronounced* klee maa)

climate
the general weather of a particular place

climatic regions
in California, USA, regions are categorised according to a system of measuring the amount of heat received from the sun during a growing season. The measurement is then used to help identify the suitability of the region for a particular type of grape and wine production. The units of heat from the sun are measured in 'degree days' on the Fahrenheit scale that allow the region to be classed into one of five regions: Region I has up to 2,500 degree days of heat per year, Region II has between 2,501 and 3,000 degree days of heat per year, Region III has between 3,001 and 3,500 degree days of heat per year, Region IV has

between 3,501 and 4,000 degree days of heat per year and Region V has above 4,000 degree days of heat per year. Most wine production is found in areas in Regions I, II and III, but the optimum region varies according to the variety of grape.

clonal selection
selection for desirable improvements within an existing grape variety by assessing the yield, quality and other characteristics of plants grown from grafted cuttings of the original plant. *Compare* **mass selection**

clone
a vine propagated by grafting or budding from one original vine to produce a group of vines with a particularly desirable characteristic of the original vine, e.g. resistance to disease, a particular flavour, or adaptation to different climatic or geological conditions.
See also **cross; hybrid**

clos
French a vineyard in Burgundy. The term can only be used on a label if the vineyard produces and bottles the wine. (*pronounced* klō, *literally* 'walled or enclosed vineyard', *plural* **clos**)

Clos de Bèze AOC *see* Chambertin Clos de Bèze AOC

Clos de la Roche AOC *see* Morey Saint-Denis (*pronounced* klố də la rósh)

Clos de Tart AOC *see* Morey Saint-Denis (*pronounced* klố də taár)

Clos de Vougeot
France a grand cru vineyard in the Côte de Nuits district of the Burgundy region of France that produces red wine from the Pinot Noir grape variety (*pronounced* klố də voo zhố)

♀ **closed**
(*tasting term*) used to describe a young, undeveloped wine that has not yet revealed its character, aroma or flavour but should develop with age.
Compare **dumb**

closed-top tank
a fermentation tank that has a fitted lid that cannot be removed, although there are vents and doors to allow cleaning

Clos Saint Denis AOC *see* **Morey Saint-Denis** (*pronounced* klố saN də neế)

Clos Sainte-Hune (*pronounced* klố saNt ŏon) *see* **Trimbach**

♀ **cloudy**
(*tasting term*) used to describe the appearance of wine that is the opposite of clear or brilliant and is due to a haze visible in the wine. In old wines this can be due to sediment being disturbed, but in younger wines it can be a sign of spoiling through unwanted fermentation or yeast protein remaining in the wine.

Cloudy Bay
New Zealand a vineyard in the province of Marlborough famous for its white wine made with the Sauvignon Blanc grape variety

♀ **clove**
(*tasting term*) an aroma associated with red wines made from the Cabernet Sauvignon or Merlot grape varieties and with some southern Italian wines

♀ **cloying**
(*tasting term*) used to describe a wine that is not very enjoyable because it is very sweet or sugary, unbalanced by acid, alcohol or intense flavour

cluster
a bunch of grapes

C:N ratio
the ratio between relative quantities of carbon and nitrogen in soils or organisms. Both carbon and nitrogen are needed in large quantities as plant nutrients, but if the balance between the two is not right problems will occur. If plant material with a high carbon content such as straw is added to soil, extra nitrogen must be added at the same time to maintain the balance.
Full form **carbon:nitrogen ratio**

CO$_2$ *see* **carbon dioxide**

Coal River
Australia a wine-producing area north of Hobart on the Australian island of Tasmania

♀ **coarse**
(*tasting term*) used to describe a rough or crude wine that has body but a harsh flavour and texture

Codorníu
Spain a wine-producing company based in northeastern Spain that is one of the biggest producers of sparkling wines in the world, including its range of wines from the Cava DO area. It also owns the Rondel brand of sparkling wines and a number of vineyards producing good-quality still wines. (*pronounced* ko dáwr nyoo)

♀ coffee, coffee beans
(*tasting term*) an aroma associated with oak-aged red wines made from the Pinot Noir or Carmenère grape varieties

Cognac
the finest and best-known of the brandies from the wine-producing region in the Charente and Charente-Maritime départements in western France, centred on the town of Cognac. Cognac is normally made from Trebbiano grapes. If the Cognac is labelled fine Champagne, most of the grapes will have been grown in the Champagne region. Once the grapes have fermented, the liquid is double-distilled in a copper pot still as soon as possible, ideally during the winter. This 'raw' Cognac is then oak-aged to soften it and enhance the aroma and taste for at least three years. The producer can control the style of the final product by such factors as the choice of grapes, the age of the oak barrels, the length of ageing and the use of legal additives such as caramel and sugar syrup. Cognac labels usually carry stars to suggest quality, but there is no official scale – more stars merely indicates a longer period of ageing than for the same wine with fewer stars. Labels can also carry the abbreviations VS (very superior), VSOP (very superior old pale) or VVSOP (very, very superior old pale). If the Cognac is labelled extra or reserve, it is the best quality from this producer.

Colares DOC
Portugal a tiny DOC wine-growing area northwest of Lisbon, Portugal, producing chiefly red wines. Its vines are planted on sand dunes on clifftops. Because of the sandy soils, the vines have never been attacked by phylloxera and grow on their own roots. As they must be planted deep in the clay below the sand, replanting involves a great effort that is decreasingly made. (*pronounced* kə laáresh)

cold
used to describe a wine that is served at such a low temperature that its aroma and flavour are hardly noticeable

cold climate
a climate that is colder than that of a Region I climatic region (with less than 2,000 degree days of heat per year) or a winter that is so cold that vines suffer damage from freezing. *Compare* **cool climate**

♀ cold cream
(*tasting term*) an aroma associated with white wines made from the Gewürztraminer grape variety

cold fermentation
a method of fermenting grape juice into wine at a lower-than-normal temperature (around 13°C or 55°F). This helps conserve fruit and character in the wine.

cold maceration *see* maceration

cold stabilisation
a process for clarifying wine by storing the wine at a low temperature (around 0°C) that causes tartrate and other unwanted solids to precipitate into crystals

cold-stabilised
clarified by being stored at a low temperature (around 0°C)

cold stable
used to describe a wine that can be stored in a cold domestic refrigerator without forming a sediment or crystals

Coldstream Hills
Australia an estate in the Yarra Valley, Victoria, producing very good red and white wines from Pinot Noir and Chardonnay grapes respectively

colheita
Portuguese vintage (*pronounced* kol yáytə)

Colli Albani DOC
Italy a white-wine-producing DOC near Rome in Italy that grows Malvasia Nera and Trebbiano grape varieties to produce a range of styles of white wine, dry, sweet and sparkling. It is best-known as the local wine for the Pope's summer villa in the same area. (*pronounced* kólli al baáni)

Colli Fiorentini, Colline Pisane *see* Chianti DOCG (*pronounced* kólli fyáwrən teéni *or* ko leé nay pi saá nay)

Collioure AOC
France an appellation in the Languedoc region of southern France, growing mostly Grenache and Carignan grape varieties to produce dry, full-bodied red wine (*pronounced* kólli oór)

Colli Senesi *see* **Chianti DOCG** (*pronounced* kólli sə náyssi)

⟡ **Colombard**
a white-wine grape variety that is widely grown in California, USA and in France and South Africa, producing white wines with high acidity and good flavour. Some Colombard is also used in making Armagnac. (*pronounced* kólləm baard)
Also called **French Colombard**

Colombo, Jean-Luc
a well-known wine producer based in the Cornas AOC in the northern Rhône region of southern France

colour
I. the classification of a wine as red, white or rosé
♀ **2.** (*tasting term*) the hue and intensity of a wine. The colour of a wine changes with age, and red wines fade and turn brick-red while white wines darken to a rich amber colour.

Columbia Valley AVA
USA a viticultural area in eastern Washington State, USA, that includes the Yakima Valley and Walla Walla Valley AVAs

Comité Interprofessionnel du Vin de Champagne
an organisation that represents the grape-growers and Champagne houses in the Champagne region of France. (*pronounced* kómmee tay áN tair pro féssi ə nél dŏo váN də shom pánnyə)
Abbreviation **CIVC**

◊ **Commandaria**
a dessert wine made in Cyprus from partially dried grapes (*pronounced* kómman daáriə)

commodity wine
a relatively inexpensive wine bought for its general style along with other provisions for everyday consumption

commune
a small administrative area with a village or town and vineyards

Compañia Vinicola del Norte de España *see* **Cune** (*pronounced* kompa nyeé ə vini kólə del náwr tay day es pánnyə)

♀ **complete**
(*tasting term*) used to describe a mature wine that provides good follow-through and aftertaste

♀ **complex**
(*tasting term*) used to describe a wine that has many aspects of flavour and aroma all perfectly balanced with the correct combination of acid, alcohol and tannin

compound bud
a bud that appears at each node along a vine shoot and contains three separate semi-developed shoots. The middle one grows first, the outside two shoots only growing if the primary bud is damaged.

Comtes de Champagne *see* **Taittinger**

concentrate *same as* **grape concentrate**

♀ **concentrated**
(*tasting term*) used to describe a wine with an intense, especially fruity flavour or aroma

Concha y Toro
Chile one of the oldest wineries in the central valley of Chile. The vineyards cover a large area and grow classic French grape varieties including Cabernet Sauvignon, Chardonnay and Merlot to produce a range of red and white wines. It has the distinction of being one of the most popular brands of wine imported into the USA. (*pronounced* kónchə ee táwrō)
See also **A Winemaker's View**

♡ **Concord**
a red-wine grape variety that is native to the USA but is only rarely used for producing wine

Condado de Huelva DO
Spain a DOC wine-producing area in Andalucía, southern Spain, between Jerez and the border with Portugal. It produces mainly fortified wines for local consumption. (*pronounced* kon daádo day hwélvə)

Condrieu AOC
France an appellation in the Rhône region of France that grows the Viognier grape variety to produce good and expensive intense dry, flowery white wines (*pronounced* kóNdree ŏ)

congener
a complex organic molecule that develops in wine and spirits

during the fermentation and ageing processes, thought to be implicated in causing hangovers

Cono Sur
Chile a winery in Chile with an extensive range of vineyards in many of the valleys of Chile, producing a wide range of red and white wines from Merlot, Cabernet Sauvignon, Pinot Noir and Gewürztraminer grape varieties (*pronounced* kónnō soór)

Constantia
South Africa a wine-producing region on the eastern slopes of Table Mountain in Cape Province, South Africa, producing superb Sauvignon Blanc and Sémillon wines. It contains the famous estates Groot Constantia and Klein Constantia. Historically Constantia produced sweet dessert wines that were considered some of the finest in the world. (*pronounced* kon stánti ə)

consumption
the amount of wine drunk on average by the population of an area or country

Conterno, Aldo
a famous wine producer in the Barolo region of Piedmont, Italy. His vineyards are in the Monteforte district of Barolo and produce a range of red and white wines, including a renowned single-vineyard Barolo made from the Nebbiolo grape. (*pronounced* kon táirnō)

continental climate
a climate with greater extremes of heat in summer and cold in winter than a maritime climate, where seasonal temperatures are more even

Controliran
a strictly controlled category of quality wines under Bulgarian wine laws, equivalent to Appellation d'Origine Contrôlée

Controlled Appellation of Origin
an official category for sweet quality wines under Greek wine laws. These wines are sold with a blue seal over the cork. *Abbreviation* **OPE**

♀ **cooked**
(*tasting term*) used to describe a wine that has a sweet, burnt smell or flavour, usually owing to an excessively high temperature during production or to an excess of sugar

cooking wine
a wine that is inferior to normal drinking wine and should only be used for cooking – however, the food would probably taste a lot better if cooked with wine that is good enough to drink!

cool climate
a climate that is cooler than that of a Region I climatic region and has less than 2,500 degree days of heat per year.
Compare **cold climate**

cooler
1. a domestic appliance designed to chill wine
2. a piece of refrigerating machinery used in a winery to chill wine and grape must at various points during winemaking

cooling sleeve
a cylindrical covering for a bottle that can be chilled in a freezer or fridge and then placed over a bottle to chill it or keep it cool

Coonawarra
Australia a very important wine-producing region in the south-east of South Australia, noted especially for its red wines made with the Cabernet Sauvignon grape variety and for the 'terra rossa' soils on which the vines are grown. Coonawarra's first vines were planted in the late 19th century, but it was only when Wynns and Penfolds bought land in the 1950s that it began to establish its reputation.
See also **Wynns Coonawarra Estate**

cooper
a person who makes or repairs barrels, casks or wooden tanks

cooperage
containers used for ageing or storing wine, including barrels, casks and tanks

cooperative
a winery that is owned and run by a group of small-scale producers to help reduce the cost of equipment and marketing expenses. Without cooperatives it would be prohibitively expensive for many thousands of small-scale producers to produce wine from their grapes. Cooperatives can also access European Union subsidies that the individual producer would not be eligible for. The French term for cooperative is 'cave coopérative', the German 'Weingärtnergenossenschaft', the Italian 'cantina sociale' and the Portuguese 'adega cooperativa'.

Copertino DOC
Italy a wine-producing DOC in Apulia in southeastern Italy that produces robust red wines primarily from the Negroamaro grape variety (*pronounced* ko pair teˊenō)

copita
a style of stemmed glass that narrows towards the top and is traditionally used to taste sherry (*pronounced* ko peˊetə)

Corbières AOC
France one of the most highly regarded appellations of the Languedoc region of southern France that grows mostly Carignan and Syrah grape varieties to produce full-bodied red wines, made primarily by cooperatives. Smaller, individual producers can be worth searching out. (*pronounced* káwr byáir)

cordon
a permanent, usually horizontal, branch of a vine from which the fruiting shoots grow

Cordon Rouge
a popular label of non-vintage Champagne produced by the Mumm Champagne house (*pronounced* káwr doN roˊo<u>zh</u>)

cordon training
the training of vines so that fruiting shoots grow at intervals along a usually horizontal cordon allowing light and air to reach the developing grape clusters

cork
material used to seal the end of a bottle, traditionally made from a round plug cut from the bark of a cork oak. Newer plastic materials are more efficient and less likely to include faults that can lead to a corked wine but look and feel different and do not generally appeal to consumers. An alternative is to use a screw-cap, but, again, this does not appeal to consumers particularly of fine wine. Corks for still wines are cylindrical and fit into the neck of the bottle, but those for sparkling wines (popularly known as Champagne corks) are wider and driven into the neck of the bottle so that they develop a mushroom shape. Champagne corks are usually twisted out by hand rather than pulled using a corkscrew.

corkage
a charge made by a restaurant if customers want to bring and drink their own wine

♀ **corked, corky**
(*tasting term*) used to describe wine that has been spoiled by a
faulty or contaminated cork, resulting in a musty smell and a
wine that can range from the slightly unpleasant to the undrinkable. This contamination is now thought to be largely
caused by a chemical compound called trichloranisole (TCA),
which is produced when microorganisms in the cork combine
with chemicals used in the production process, e.g. the strong
chlorine solution in which corks are usually bleached before
use. Trichloranisole can be smelt even in minute quantities.
Corked wine can also result if the cork does not provide an
airtight seal or if the cork has a growth of mould on the base
nearest the wine, when it will also smell musty. Faulty corks
occur in new bottles of wine, but if a bottle of wine is stored
upright for many years even a good cork can dry out and
shrink slightly, breaking the airtight seal and leading to a
corked wine. This is why wine should be stored horizontally
or at an angle to ensure that the cork remains in contact with
the wine and so does not dry out.

cork oak
a species of oak, *Quercus suber*, with a thick bark that can be
stripped off without damaging the tree. The bark is used to
make corks for wine bottles.
Also called **cork tree**

corkscrew
a mechanical device used to remove the cork from the top of a
bottle. A common model has a large screw or spiral that is
twisted into the cork and then pulled out either using two lever
handles or by another mechanical device.

cork tree *same as* **cork oak**

♀ **corky** *see* **corked**

Cornas AOC
France a wine-producing appellation in the northern Rhône
region of France that produces good-quality full-bodied red
wine from Syrah grapes (*pronounced* káwr naá)

corriente
Spanish ordinary (*pronounced* kori én tay)
See also **vino corriente**

Corsica
France a French island in the Mediterranean producing red, white and rosé wines

◊ **Cortese**
a white-wine grape variety mostly found in the Piedmont and Lombardy regions of Italy, producing a crisp, fruity and well-balanced wine (*pronounced* kawr táyzi)

Corton AOC
France a famous grand cru wine-producing district in the Côte de Beaune area of the Burgundy region of France, best-known for its red wines made from Pinot Noir and white wines from Chardonnay, Pinot Blanc and Pinot Gris grapes (*pronounced* kawr tóN)

Corton-Charlemagne AOC
France a famous grand cru white-wine-producing district in the Côte de Beaune area of the Burgundy region of France, known for its very good and expensive full-bodied white wines made from Chardonnay grapes (*pronounced* kawr tóN shaarlə mánnyə)

◊ **Corvina**
a red-wine grape variety grown mostly in Italy and used in Valpolicella and other light, fruity wines from Italy (*pronounced* kawr veénə)

Cos d'Estournel, Château
France a famous chateau in the Saint-Estèphe AOC in Bordeaux, graded deuxième cru (second growth) in the classification of 1855. It produces the best wines of the appellation that are full-bodied, dark and tannic and that develop into wines that rival those from neighbouring Pauillac. They are made from Cabernet Sauvignon, Merlot and a tiny amount of Cabernet Franc grapes. (*pronounced* kő dess toor nél)

cosecha
Spanish vintage (*pronounced* ko sáychə)

Cosme Palacio
a well-known wine producer (bodega) in the Rioja DOCa region of Spain, producing good, dark red wines from the classic Tempranillo grape (*pronounced* kózmay paa láthyo)

Costers del Segre DO
Spain a small wine-producing area in Catalonia, northeastern Spain that is dominated by the Raimat estate (*pronounced* koss táirss del sáy gray)

Costières du Nîmes AOC
France an appellation in the Languedoc region of southern France producing mostly red table wine from Carignan, Cinsault and Grenache grapes (*pronounced* kósti air dŏo neém)

⚘ **Cot** *another name for* **Malbec** (*pronounced* kōt)

côte
French a slope, especially a slope covered by vineyards. The term is usually used to describe a large region. In the Burgundy region, the Côte d'Or includes the Côte de Nuits in the north and Côte de Beaune in the south. (*pronounced* kōt)

Côte, La *see* La Côte

Coteaux Champenois AOC
France an appellation in the Champagne region of France that produces still red, white and rosé wines (*pronounced* kóttō shom pen waá)

Coteaux d'Aix-en-Provence AOC
France an appellation near the city of Aix-en-Provence in southern France growing Cabernet Sauvignon, Cinsault, Grenache and Syrah grapes for red and rosé wines and growing Clairette Blanc, Grenache Blanc and Sauvignon Blanc grapes for white wines (*pronounced* kóttō deks aaN pro vaáNss)

Coteaux d'Ancenis VDQS
France a VDQS wine-producing area in the Loire region of France, growing Gamay and Cabernet Franc grapes for red and rosé wines and Chenin Blanc and Malvasia grapes for white wines (*pronounced* kóttō daáN say neé)

Coteaux de la Mejanelle
France a wine-producing area that is part of the Coteaux du Languedoc AOC, situated near Montpellier in southern France. It produces red wines from Cinsault, Mourvèdre and Syrah grape varieties, white wines from a range of grape varieties and rosé wines from Grenache grapes. (*pronounced* kóttō də la mezhə nél)

Coteaux de l'Aubance AOC
France an appellation in the centre of the Loire valley in France, growing Chenin Blanc grapes to produce white wine (*pronounced* kóttō də lō baáNss)

Coteaux de Layon AOC
France an appellation in the Anjou area of the Loire region of

France, growing Chenin Blanc grapes to produce sweet or medium sweet white wines (*pronounced* kóttō də lay yóN)

Coteaux du Languedoc AOC
France a large appellation in the Languedoc region of southern France, growing Carignan, Cinsault and Grenache grapes to produce red and rosé wines (*pronounced* kóttō dŏo laáNgə dok)

Coteaux du Loir AOC
France a modest appellation in the Loire region of France, on the Loir (NB not the Loire) river that produces red, white and rosé wines (*pronounced* kóttō dŏo lwaâr)

Coteaux du Lyonnais AOC
France an appellation in the south of the Burgundy region of France, growing Gamay grapes to produce red wines (*pronounced* kóttō dŏo leé on náy)

Côte Chalonnaise
France a wine-producing area in the Saône-et-Loire département of the Burgundy region of France. It includes the Givry, Mercurey, Montagny and Rully AOCs. (*pronounced* kót sha lon náyz)

Côte de Beaune
France a famous wine-producing district in the south of the Côte d'Or area of the Burgundy region of France, taking its name from the town of Beaune. Beaune itself is the home of many well-known négociants (wine merchants rather than growers), but they are prevented from dominating the wine trade by the fact that the surrounding area contains many of the grand cru and premier cru vineyards of Burgundy. The area grows mostly Pinot Noir grapes for red wine and Chardonnay grapes for its world-famous white wines from the grands crus of Montrachet. There is also a Côte de Beaune AOC that includes a few vineyards that are not classified with higher status. (*pronounced* kót də bő́n)

Côte de Blaye AOC *see* Blaye AOC (*pronounced* kót də bláy)

Côte de Brouilly AOC
France a small appellation in the Beaujolais region of France in the hills above the Brouilly AOC. It grows Gamay grapes to produce good-quality fruity red wine. (*pronounced* kót də broo yeé)

Côte de Nuits
France a famous wine-producing district in the north of the Côte d'Or area of the Burgundy region of France, containing many of the grand cru and premier cru vineyards of Burgundy. The area grows mostly Pinot Noir grapes for its world-famous red wines. (*pronounced* kõt də nweé)

Côte des Blancs
France the area of the Champagne region of France near Épernay, which is especially suited to Chardonnay grapes (*pronounced* kõt day blaáN)

Côte d'Or
France a famous wine-producing area that dominates the high-quality wine produced in the Burgundy area of France. It is divided into two sections: Côte de Beaune in the south and Côte de Nuits in the north. (*pronounced* kōt dáwr)

Côte Rôtie AOC
France an appellation in the very north of the Rhône region of France, producing very good-quality red wine from Syrah grapes, sometimes with a percentage of Viognier. The wines are full-bodied, age well and have a deep colour and rich flavour. (*pronounced* kõt rō teé)

Côtes d'Auvergne VDQS
France a VDQS area in the Loire region of France producing light red wines made with Gamay and some Pinot Noir grapes. It also produces some rosé wines and grows the Chardonnay grape variety for white wines. (*pronounced* kõt dō váirn)

Côtes d'Auxerre
France a district of the Burgundy region of France producing good white wines from Chardonnay grapes (*pronounced* kõt dok sáir)

Côtes de Bergerac AOC
France an appellation in the Bergerac region of western France whose wines have a higher minimum alcoholic strength than simple Bergerac AOC wines (*pronounced* kõt də bairzhə rák)

Côtes de Bourg
France an appellation in the Bordeaux region of France on the right bank of the Dordogne river, centred on the town of Bourg. It produces mainly red wines from the Merlot grape variety. (*pronounced* kõt də boór)

Côtes de Castillon AOC
France a large appellation in the Bordeaux region of France that produces mainly red wines with good structure from the Merlot and Cabernet Franc grape varieties (*pronounced* kõt də kass tee yóN)

Côtes de la Malepère AOC
France an appellation in the Aude département in the western Languedoc-Roussillon region of southern France (*pronounced* kõt də la mal páir)

Côtes de Meliton
Greece an appellation in northeastern Greece that grows French and Greek grape varieties to produce red and white wines (*pronounced* kõt də méllee tóN)

Côtes de Millau AOC
France an appellation in the Tarn valley area of southwestern France producing red, white and rosé wines (*pronounced* kõt də mee yõ)

Côtes de Provence AOC
France a vast appellation in the southern coastal Provence region of France, growing Cabernet Sauvignon, Cinsault and Grenache grapes to make mostly rosé wines (*pronounced* kõt də pro vaáNss)

Côtes du Forez
France a wine-producing area in east-central France that produces light red wines from the Gamay grape variety (*pronounced* kõt dŏo fo réz)

Côtes du Lubéron AOC
France an appellation in the mountainous area of the Rhône region of France, growing Syrah and Grenache grape varieties for red wines and Clairette Blanc for white wines (*pronounced* kõt dŏo lŏo bay róN)

Côtes du Rhône AOC
France a large appellation in the Rhône valley in southern France that is second only to the Bordeaux AOC in the quantity of wine it produces within France. Most of the wine produced is red or rosé using mainly the Grenache grape variety. The Côtes du Rhône-Villages AOC produces higher-quality red wines with a slightly higher level of alcohol than those from the bigger Côtes du Rhône AOC. (*pronounced* kõt dŏo rõn)

Côtes du Roussillon AOC

France an appellation in the Languedoc-Roussillon region of southern France that produces mostly red and rosé wines from Carignan grapes. The Côtes du Roussillon-Villages AOC produces better-quality red wines from the same grapes, but with a slightly higher alcohol content. (*pronounced* kŏt dŏo roossi yóN)

Côtes du Ventoux AOC

France a large appellation in the southern Rhône region of France that produces mainly red wines from a blend of Grenache, Syrah, Cinsault and Carignan grapes (*pronounced* kŏt dŏo vaaN tŏo)

Côtes du Vivarais AOC

France a VDQS area in the Ardèche region of Provence, producing red wines from Grenache and Syrah grape varieties, rosé wines from Grenache, Syrah and Cinsault and white wines from Clairette Blanc and Grenache Blanc (*pronounced* kŏt dŏo vee vaa ráy)

coulure

French the failure of flowers on a vine to develop into a full crop of grapes, normally caused by bad weather during bloom (*pronounced* koo lŏor)

coupe

(*pronounced* koop, *literally* 'cut') *French*

1. the process of blending wines to achieve the correct balance
2. a glass of sparkling wine or Champagne

courtier

French a wine broker who acts between the growers and the négociants (the companies who bottle and sell the finished wines) (*pronounced* koor tyáy)

crackling

USA used to describe wine that is very slightly sparkling. *Compare* **pétillant**

cradle

a device used to hold a bottle of wine horizontal while it is being decanted

♀ cranberry

(*tasting term*) a taste or aroma associated with red wines made from the Sangiovese grape variety

cream *see* **Montilla; sherry**

cream of tartar
a natural chemical component of grape juice and wine, removed during the winemaking process.
Also called **potassium bitartrate**

cream sherry
a very sweet type of sherry

♀ **creamy**
(*tasting term*) used to describe a wine that has a rich taste and a soft mouthfeel, e.g. good Champagne

crémant
French used to describe a wine that is more sparkling than slightly sparkling (or pétillant) wines, but not as sparkling as Champagne or mousseux-style sparkling wines (*pronounced* kray maáN, *literally* 'creaming')

Crémant de Loire AOC
France an appellation for good dry sparkling white wine made by the méthode champenoise in the Anjou, Saumur and Touraine areas of the Loire region of France (*pronounced* kray maáN də lwaár)

criadera
Spanish any of the levels of wine below the final solera in the solera system of making sherry (*pronounced* kreé ə dáirə, *literally* 'nursery')

crianza
Spanish a wine that has been correctly aged according to DO specifications (*pronounced* kree ánthə, *literally* 'breeding')

♥ **Criolla** *another name for* **Mission** (*pronounced* kree ólya)

♀ **crisp**
(*tasting term*) used to describe white wine that is dry and refreshing to taste, normally because the acidity level has been well-judged by the winemaker

Cristal *see* **Louis Roederer**

♥ **Croatina**
a red-wine grape grown mostly in the Lombardy region of Italy to produce round, fruity red wines. Under the name Bonarda it is also now grown in Argentina. (*pronounced* krṍ ə teénə)
Also called **Bonarda**

Croft

one of the oldest port companies, founded in 1678, producing good tawny and ruby ports from its vineyards at Quinta da Roeda. A branch now also produces sherry in Jerez, and pioneered the pale cream style of sherry. Both enterprises are now part of the International Distillers and Vintners group.

Croser, Brian

a famous winemaker from South Australia, best-known for his Petaluma winery producing excellent white wines from Chardonnay and Riesling grapes

cross

1. *see* **hybrid**
2. to use two existing varieties or species to make a new variety with distinctive characteristics

Crouchen

a white-wine grape grown originally in France but now found mostly in Australia and South Africa. (*pronounced* kroo shaán)
Also called **Cape Riesling**; **South African Riesling**

crown cap

a metal cap that is clipped onto the open end of the neck of a bottle of sparkling wine in the bottle-fermentation phase of méthode champenoise. The cap collects the unwanted yeast protein and other sediment that is then removed during disgorgement.

crown graft

a method of grafting in which a branch is cut across at right angles, slits are made in the bark around the edge of the stump, and shoots inserted into the slits

Crozes-Hermitage AOC

France a large appellation in the north of the Rhône region of France, growing Syrah grapes to produce red wines and growing Marsanne grapes for white wine. (*pronounced* krố zair mee taázh)
See also **Hermitage AOC**

cru

French a particular style, source or quality of a wine. In France the term is used with a very specific meaning, particularly to class the quality and source of wine from Bordeaux AOC, Burgundy AOC and Champagne AOC. In these AOCs, the term refers to a particular vineyard or estate that produced the wine; in Beaujolais AOC it refers to a village producing high-quality wine. Other countries use the term 'cru' but with a less strictly controlled meaning, indicating the top-quality wine from a producer. The oldest use of 'cru' is as a historical method of rating wine by the best wine-producing estates in an area, providing five categories of classification for red wines and two for white wines in a system developed as the classification of 1855. Other areas of France, e.g. the Burgundy AOC region, use 'cru' to refer to the actual land on which the vine grows; there are two levels: grand cru (one of the best wines of the area) and premier cru. In the Champagne AOC region 'cru' is used in a way similar to that of Burgundy but refers to the entire village rather than a particular plot of land. (*pronounced* krŏo, *literally* 'growth')

cru bourgeois
French a category of the best wines from estates in the Médoc district of Bordeaux in southwestern France that were excluded from the classification of 1855. It comes just below cru classé. (*pronounced* krŏo boor <u>zh</u>waá, *plural* **crus bourgeois**)

cru classé (*pronounced* krŏo kla sáy, *plural* **crus classés**) *French*
1. a wine placed in one of the five classes of the best French wines used in the classification of 1855
2. any exceptional wine from the Bordeaux region
3. one of the best wines from a particular region of France, selected in schemes similar to the original classification of 1855. *Also called* **classed growth**; **classified growth**

crush
1. to release grape juice from the berries using a mechanical crusher. The stems may also be removed by the same process.
2. *USA* the time in the autumn when grapes are picked and crushed in order to break open the skin to allow the juice to run out

crusher
a mechanical device that uses rollers to break open the skin of grapes to allow the juice to run out when pressed

crusher-stemmer
a mechanical device that removes the stems and leaves from picked bunches of grapes before crushing the berries

crush tank
a tank that holds the crushed grapes

crust
a crystalline sediment that forms inside bottles containing red wine or port during long bottle-ageing

crusted port *see* port

cryoextraction
a process of cooling picked grapes to a very low temperature. The temperature is carefully controlled and is just above the freezing point for the particular grape or ripeness level of the grapes. Any unripe grapes freeze solid before this point because they contain less sugar, leaving grapes of the required ripeness unfrozen and ready to be pressed. The process mimics the natural conditions for the production of ice wine.

crystals
harmless tartrates in crystalline form that are often present in white wine that has not been cold-stabilised, but sometimes also in reds that have been put into a refrigerator on a very hot day

cultured yeast
a pure culture of known strains of yeast that have been selected to ferment wine correctly and completely, without producing off flavours. Wild yeast strains would normally produce unwanted tastes or odours in the wine.

Cune, CVNE
Spain a long-established wine producer (bodega) in the Rioja DOCa region of northern Spain that produces consistently good red and white wines.
Full form **Compañia Vinicola del Norte de España**

♀ **currant leaf**
(*tasting term*) an aroma associated with young white wines made from the Sauvignon Blanc grape variety grown in a cool climate, e.g. in New Zealand, and also with red wines made from Cabernet Franc grapes in the Loire region of France

cut
to blend wine in order to balance it

cutting
a piece cut from a vine that grows into a new vine. These pieces are usually cut from dormant vines in the winter and propagated in the spring.

cuvaison
French a period of time in the making of red wine when the grape juice is kept in contact with the grape skin and seeds (*pronounced* kŏŏ vay zóN)

cuve
French a wine tank or vat (*pronounced* kŏŏv)

cuvée
French a particular blend of different wines to produce a consistent style, as used in making Champagne. (*pronounced* kŏ́ŏ vay)
See also **vin de cuvée**

Cuvée Grand Siècle *see* **Laurent Perrier** (*pronounced* kŏŏ vay graáN syéklə)

cuvée personelle, cuvée réserve, cuvée spéciale
French used on French wine labels to imply a choice wine, but with no official status (*pronounced* kŏ́ŏ vay pair so nél *or* kŏ́ŏ vay ray záirv *or* kŏ́ŏ vay spay syál)

CVNE *see* **Cune**

Cyprus
a wine-producing island in the Mediterranean noted especially for its dessert wine Commandaria and formerly as a producer of cheap sherry-style wines

Czech Republic
a wine-producing country in Central Europe. Production centres on two main regions, Bohemia and Moravia, both of which make mostly white wine.
See map at **Hungary**

D

This wine is too good for toast-drinking, my dear. You don't want to mix emotions up with a wine like that. You lose the taste.

Ernest Hemingway, 1926

Dão DOC
Portugal a DOC region of central Portugal, producing big, full-bodied red wines from a range of grapes, particularly Alfrocheiro Preto. Some dry white wines are also made. (*pronounced* dow)

D'Arenberg *see* **A Winemaker's View**

♀ dark chocolate
(*tasting term*) the chocolate aroma found in some wines, notably red wines made from Cabernet Sauvignon grapes

Darmagi *see* **Gaja, Angelo**

Dashwood
New Zealand a well-respected winery in the Awatere Valley area of New Zealand producing very good white wines from Sauvignon Blanc and fruity red wines from Pinot Noir grape varieties

Daumas Gassac *see* **Mas de Daumas Gassac**

deacidification
the process of reducing acid levels in grape juice or wine by any of a range of methods, e.g. cold stabilisation

decant
to pour wine carefully from a bottle into another container, separating it from any sediment at the bottom of the bottle. Decanting is particularly desirable for old wine and vintage port. Traditionally a candle or other light is placed under the neck of the bottle so that the person pouring can see when the sediment reaches the neck and can stop pouring. Wines without sediment can also be decanted to allow them to 'breathe'.

decanter
a container, usually made from glass, with any of various

shapes, used to hold wine that has been decanted from a bottle
before it is poured into a glass

de Chaunac *see* **Chaunac**

Declared Geographical Origin
Bulgaria an officially defined geographical wine-producing area
in Bulgaria.
Abbreviation **DGO**

deep
(*tasting term*) used to describe a wine with an intense colour or
flavour
See also **depth**

dégorgement
French disgorgement (*pronounced* day gáwr<u>zh</u> maaN)

degree days
a system of measuring the amount of heat received from the
sun during a growing season in a particular region. This is then
used to help identify the suitability of the region for a particular
type of grape and wine production. The units of heat from the
sun are measured in 'degree days' by obtaining the raw monthly
average temperature in degrees C less 10 and multiplying the
result by the number of days in that month, then adding
together the sums for all seven months of the growing season.
On the Fahrenheit scale, 50° is the equivalent starting temperature.

Delaware
a hybrid grape variety grown in the eastern USA and used to
produce still and sparkling wine

delicate
(*tasting term*) used to describe a fine wine that has a light and
well-balanced quality with mild flavour and fragrance

de luxe
used on Champagne labels to indicate the best example of the
house's style

de Malle, Château
France an estate within the Sauternes AOC in Bordeaux, southwestern France, graded deuxième cru (second growth) in the

classification of 1855. It produces sweet Sauternes wines from Sémillon and Sauvignon Blanc grapes. (*pronounced* də mál)

demijohn
a large glass bottle or jug, sometimes enclosed inside a protective reed or wood wrapper, and usually containing 5 to 10 gallons (about 22 to 44 litres)

demi-sec
French used to describe a slightly or medium sweet sparkling wine, usually from the Champagne district (*pronounced* də mee sék, *literally* 'half dry')

Denmark
Australia a wine-producing area in Western Australia, a sub-region of the Great Southern region

Denominação de Origem Controlada
Portugal a classification system for the best-quality wines in Portugal, similar to the Appellation d'Origine Contrôlée in France. The DOC system covers 14 different regions in Portugal and provides rules for the types of grape grown, methods of production and yield within each area. (*pronounced* de nómminə sów di ori zhéN kontro laádə, *plural* **Denominaçãos de Origem Controlada**)
Abbreviation **DOC**

Denominación de Origen
Spain a classification system for the quality wines in Spain similar to the Appellation d'Origine Contrôlée in France. The DO system covers over 30 different regions in Spain and provides rules for the types of grape grown, methods of production and yield within each area. A higher-quality category, Denominación de Origen Calificada (DOCa), has been introduced to discriminate among the very large number of wines that fall into the Denominación de Origen system. (*pronounced* de nómmi nath yón də o reéhen, *plural* **Denominaciones de Origen**)
Abbreviation **DO**

Denominación de Origen Calificada
Spain a classification system for the best-quality wines in Spain, above Denominación de Origen (DO), that currently only has one region, Rioja, that meets its high standards. (*pronounced* de nómmi nath yón də o reéhen kaa lee fee kaádə, *plural* **Denominaciones de Origen Calificada**)
Abbreviation **DOCa**

Denominazione di Origine Controllata

Italy a classification system for the quality wines in Italy, similar to the Appellation d'Origine Contrôlée in France. The DOC system covers over 250 different regions in Italy and provides rules for the types of grape grown, methods of production and yield, alcohol levels and ageing to be used. Further regulations cover the look and taste of the wine, including its colour and flavour within each area. A higher-quality category, Denominazione di Origine Controllata e Garantita (DOCG), helps define the very best wines in Italy. (*pronounced* de nómmi naa tsyáw nay di o reéji nay kontro laátə, *plural* **Denominazioni di Origine Controllata**)
Abbreviation **DOC**

Denominazione di Origine Controllata e Garantita

Italy a classification system for the best-quality wines in Italy that uses rules similar to but more rigorous than those of the Denominazione di Origine Controllata (DOC) system. Fewer than a dozen regions meet these rules and can use a special seal on the capsule on the neck of the bottle. (*pronounced* de nómmi naa tsyố nay di o reéji nay kontro laátə e gaáraan teétə, *plural* **Denominazioni di Origine Controllata e Garantita**)
Abbreviation **DOCG**

♀ **dense**
(*tasting term*) used to describe a young wine that has concentrated aromas on the nose and palate

densimeter
a measuring device used to measure the specific gravity (density) of a liquid, comparing it to the density of pure water. This provides a measure of the sugar content of grape juice in the fermentation container. The instrument has a hollow cylindrical bulb with a lead weight in the bottom to make it float vertically and a number scale on the long stem that can be read as it floats in the liquid.
Also called **hydrometer**

département
French one of the 95 local administrations that make up France. Each has a number and influences the way local cooperatives market and sell their wines. (*pronounced* day paárt maaN)

deposit
sediment that accumulates at the bottom of bottles of aged red and port wines. It does not mean the wine is spoiled, but that it should be decanted.

♀ **depth**
1. (*tasting term*) the quality of a wine that is full-bodied and releases a whole range of intense, complex flavours when tasted
2. (*tasting term*) the intensity of the colour of a wine. For red wines, the more intense the colour, the more body the wine has.
See also **deep**

dessert wine
a sweet wine, sometimes fortified to higher alcohol content with brandy, traditionally served with dessert or as an after-dinner drink. Well-known dessert wines are port, sherry, sweet Riesling, Muscat, Madeira and Tokay.

destemming
a mechanical process before fermentation to remove the stems from the crushed must of grape skins, seeds and juice. The stems of bunches of grapes are very bitter and would change the taste of the wine if included.

Deutscher Tafelwein
German German table wine, the lowest class in the German wine classification system. (*pronounced* dóytchə taáf'l vīn)
Abbreviation **DTW**

deuxième cru
French the second-best level of wines rated in the classification of 1855 that listed 15 estates from the Médoc district of Bordeaux in southwestern France. (*pronounced* dőzyem króo, *literally* 'second growth', *plural* **deuxièmes crus**)
See also **classification of 1855**

deuxième taille *see* **taille** (*pronounced* dőzyem tī)

♀ **developed**
(*tasting term*) used to describe the maturity of a wine, indicating how close it is to being ready to drink. Underdeveloped wine needs to be aged longer before it is ready to drink; overdeveloped wine has aged for too long and is no longer at its prime; well-developed wines are perfectly matured and ready to drink.

Dézaley
Switzerland a well-known wine-producing region in the Vaud canton of Switzerland, growing mostly Chasselas grapes to produce steely white wines (*pronounced* day zaa láy)

DGO *abbreviation Bulgaria* Declared Geographical Origin

♡ **Diamond**
a hybrid grape variety grown in the USA and used to produce white wine

♡ **Diana**
a hybrid grape variety grown in the eastern USA and used to produce white wine

Die *see* **Clairette de Die AOC**

♀ **diesel**
(*tasting term*) an aroma associated with white wines made from the Riesling grape variety

digestif
French an alcoholic drink such as a Cognac or liqueur drunk after a meal, supposedly to aid digestion (*pronounced* dée jess téef)

dinky
South Africa a small bottle of wine, usually containing 250 ml

Dionysus
the Greek god of wine and fertility.
Compare **Bacchus**

♀ **direct**
(*tasting term*) used to describe a wine that has no hidden flavours and is defined immediately by its first taste

♀ **dirty**
(*tasting term*) used to describe an unpleasant smell that can occur in a wine, including one caused by a bad barrel or cork, and normally a sign of poor winemaking

disgorgement
a step in the traditional méthode champenoise of making sparkling wine in which the liquid and sediment in the neck of the bottle are frozen and the ice 'plug' is removed. Extra wine is then added, in a process called dosage, to make up for the liquid lost in the ice removed, before the bottle is finally corked.
Also called **dégorgement**

distillate
a product of distillation, e.g. a spirit

distillation
the process of boiling wine to turn the alcohol and volatile flavour-carrying substances into a steam vapour, which is then channelled and cooled along a tube to condense the steam into a

liquid that has high alcohol levels and the essential flavours of the wine. The resulting liquid is called a brandy and what is left of the original wine is thrown away.

♀ **distinguished**
(*tasting term*) used to describe a wine of a very good character or quality

DO *abbreviation Spain* Denominación de Origen

DOC *abbreviation*
1. *Italy* Denominazione di Origine Controllata
2. *Portugal* Denominação de Origem Controlada

DOCa *abbreviation Spain* Denominación de Origen Calificada

doce
Portuguese sweet (*pronounced* dó say)

DOCG *abbreviation Italy* Denominazione di Origine Controllata e Garantita

dolce
Italian sweet (*pronounced* dól chay)

◊ **Dolcetto**
an early-ripening red-wine grape variety widely grown in the Piedmont region of northwestern Italy to produce a soft, fruity wine that is normally a deep purple colour and is intended to be drunk when young. Producers of slow-maturing wines such as those made from the Nebbiolo grape often also grow Dolcetto to get a quicker financial return. (*pronounced* dol chéttō)

Dolcetto d'Alba DOC
Italy a DOC zone in the Piedmont region of northwestern Italy growing mostly the Dolcetto grape (*pronounced* dol chéttō dálbə)

domaine
French a wine-growing estate, which can have either adjacent or scattered vineyards. The term is mostly used in the Burgundy region of France. (*pronounced* dō mén, *literally* 'estate')

Domaine B. Chave
France an estate in the Rhône valley region of France, producing good-quality Crozes-Hermitage and Hermitage wines (*pronounced* do mén bay shaáv)

Domaine Clape
France a well-respected vineyard based in Cornas in the Rhône region of France, producing very good red wines from Syrah grapes (*pronounced* do mén kláp)

Domaine de Chevalier
France a leading château in the Graves district of the Bordeaux region of France, producing good red and white wines (*pronounced* do mén də shə val yáy)

Domaine du Vieux Télégraphe
France a vineyard in the Châteauneuf-du-Pape AOC area of the southern Rhône valley in France, producing very good red wines with intense flavours and the ability to age well (*pronounced* dō mén dŏo vyố taylay graáf)

Domaine Étienne Guigal
France one of the leading winemaking companies in the Rhône valley region of France, producing high quality Côte-Rôtie, Crozes-Hermitage and Hermitage wines from its various vineyards (*pronounced* dō mén ay tyén gee gál)

Domaine Leroy
France a wine-producing estate in the Côte d'Or area of the Burgundy region of France, producing good-quality red and white wines (*pronounced* dō mén lə rwaá)

Domäne
German a wine-producing estate, usually one owned either by the state or by a member of the former nobility (*pronounced* do máynə, *plural* **Domänen**)

Domecq
a famous sherry producer with vineyards in the Jerez Superior area of southern Spain. It also produces brandy. The firm was family owned until the mid-1990s when it became part of the global Allied Domecq business. (*pronounced* do mék)

Dom Pérignon
(*pronounced* dom pérri nyoN)
1. a Benedictine monk, called the 'father of Champagne', who was a cellar-master at the Benedictine Abbey of Hautvillers in France in the late 1600s. Dom Pérignon is said to have been the first to accidentally trap the carbon dioxide created in the secondary fermentation of still table wine to create sparkling wine, though there is little historical evidence to confirm this.

2. a famous premium Champagne brand produced by Moët et Chandon

☼ Doradillo
a grape variety, originally Spanish, that was once widely grown in Australia for distillation and dessert wines but is now very much rarer (*pronounced* dorə deélyo)

dorado
Spanish gold
See also **Rueda DOC**

☼ Dornfelder
a hybrid red grape bred in Germany in the 1950s and grown there for simple red wines (*pronounced* dáwrn feldər)

dosage
I. a mixture of sugar, water or wine, and yeast added to still white wine just before bottling to start secondary fermentation and produce sparkling wine. Dosage is used as a means of controlling the sweetness of the finished wine and is often the way of producing different styles of sparkling wine from brut (very dry, with no added sugar in the dosage) to doux (sweet, with added sugar in the dosage).
Also called **dosage de tirage**; **liqueur de tirage**; **liqueur d'expédition**
2. the process of adding a small quantity of extra wine to each bottle of Champagne after disgorgement to make up for the liquid lost, before the bottles are closed

dosage de tirage
French same as **dosage I** (*pronounced* dō saázh də tee raázh, *plural* **dosages de tirage**)

dose
an additional ingredient such as syrup added to wine to fortify it

double magnum
a bottle that can hold three litres, equivalent to four standard 750 ml bottles

Douro DOC
Portugal a wine- and port-producing region of central and northern Portugal that produces some of Portugal's best wines from a wide range of grape varieties (*pronounced* doórō)

doux
French sweet. On a label, usually of sparkling wine, this indicates very sweet wine. (*pronounced* doo)
See also **vin doux naturel**

Dow
one of the top port-producing companies, producing very good vintage port as well as a good single-quinta port and white, ruby and tawny ports. The company is owned by the Symington family, which also owns Warre, Graham and Smith Woodhouse port producers.

downy mildew
a disease caused by the fungus *Plasmopara viticola* that affects vines and rots their leaves and stems.
See also **powdery mildew**

drain hopper
a special crush tank fitted with a filter and valve that can be opened to allow juice from the freshly crushed grape must to drain out. When producing white wine the winemaker does not want the juice to be in contact with the seeds and other solids, so the juice is drained off. When making red wine the valve is closed to allow the juice to macerate and take on the colour and flavour of seeds and skins.

dregs
small solid particles found in wine that sink to the bottom of a container

dried out
(*tasting term*) used to describe a wine that is no longer balanced and has lost its original fruity taste, normally giving way to dominant tastes of acid and tannin

Drouhin, Joseph
a famous négociant of Beaune in the Burgundy region of France, producing a range of excellent Chablis white wines (*pronounced* droo aN)

Drumborg
Australia a cool winemaking area within the Henty wine region of southwestern Victoria

dry
(*tasting term*) used to describe a wine in which the sugars have been almost totally fermented, producing a wine that has no

noticeable sweetness. A dry wine is commonly defined as one containing less than about 0.5% residual sugar.
See also **bone dry**; **medium dry**

Dry Creek Valley
USA a wine-growing area in the Sonoma Valley, California that is noted especially for its red wines made from the Zinfandel grape variety. It also grows Cabernet Sauvignon grapes for red wines and Sauvignon Blanc for white wines.

dry-grown
used to describe vines watered only by natural rainfall in an area where irrigation is usual. It is commonly believed that irrigation reduces quality, but lack of water can also stress the vines.

♀ dryness
(*tasting term*) the absence of any sugar that could ferment, as in a dry wine

DTW *abbreviation German* Deutscher Tafelwein

Duboeuf, Georges
a prominent maker of Beaujolais and Mâconnais wine in France (*pronounced* dŏo böf)

dulce
Spanish sweet (*pronounced* dŏol thay)

♀ dull
(*tasting term*) used to describe a wine that is drinkable but uninteresting

♀ dumb
(*tasting term*) used to describe a wine that is too young or possibly served too cold to show any flavour or bouquet. The term is normally used for red wine that could improve with ageing.
Compare **closed**

♡ Duras
a minor grape variety grown in the Gaillac AOC in south-western France to produce full-bodied red wines (*pronounced* dŏo raâ)

Durbanville
South Africa a wine-producing region northeast of Cape Town, South Africa, growing especially Sauvignon Blanc grapes to produce white wines

Durif

a red-wine grape variety, bred in the 1880s and originally, but now rarely, grown in southern France. It is also found in northeastern Victoria, Australia and in California, USA. It is sometimes identified with the Petite Syrah grape. (*pronounced* dŏŏ reéf)

dusty

(*tasting term*) used to describe a wine that gives the impression of containing sediment or grit or that has a smell of a dusty room

du Tertre, Château

France a château in the Margaux AOC in the Médoc area of Bordeaux in southwestern France, graded cinquième cru (fifth growth) in the classification of 1855 and producing good quality red wine from Cabernet Sauvignon and Merlot grape varieties (*pronounced* dŏŏ táirtrə)

duty *see* excise duty

d'Yquem, Château

France a famous estate in the Sauternes region of Bordeaux, southwestern France, producing some of the best sweet white wines in the world. In the classification of 1855 this estate was considered so good that it was placed in a class of its own, premier grand cru classé. (*pronounced* dee kém)

E

early harvest
wine produced in a cooler-than-usual year when the grapes have not reached their expected ripeness. The wines produced are light and have high levels of acidity but do not age well. In Germany, these wines are labelled trocken or halbtrocken.

earthy
1. (*tasting term*) used to describe a simple, country wine that reminds the drinker of a rustic, country setting
2. (*tasting term*) used to describe a wine evocative of the pleasant smell of damp soil. If too pronounced, it turns unpleasant. In French it is termed 'goût de terroir' and is noticeable on red wines from Graves made from Cabernet Sauvignon grapes on the gravel-rich soil of the region.

East India sherry *same as* **amoroso**

eau de vie
French any colourless alcoholic drink made from distilled fruit juice, e.g. brandy (*pronounced* ṓ də veé, *literally* 'water of life', *plural* **eaux de vie**)

ebulliometer
a piece of equipment used in the laboratory to measure the alcohol content of a wine. It measures the exact boiling point of the wine, which can be compared with the boiling point of pure alcohol and water to determine the alcohol content of the wine.

Echézeaux AOC
France an important wine village in the Côte de Nuits district of the Burgundy region of France that produces famous red wines from the Pinot Noir grape variety (*pronounced* áy shay zṓ)

Edelfäule
German noble rot caused by the fungus *Botrytis cinerea* (*pronounced* áyd'l foylə)

◊ **Edelzwicker**

an ordinary blended white wine from the Alsace region of France (*pronounced* áyd'l tsvíkə)

Eden Valley

Australia a cool-climate wine-producing region in South Australia, adjoining the Barossa Valley, that is famous for its white wines made from the Riesling grape variety. It also grows Chardonnay, Syrah (Shiraz) and Cabernet Sauvignon grapes.

Edna Valley AVA

USA a wine-producing area in San Luis Obispo County, California, known in particular for its white wines made from Chardonnay grapes

Eger

Hungary a wine-producing region in northeastern Hungary known especially for its robust red wine Egri Bikavér (Bull's Blood) (*pronounced* éggər)

♀ **eggs** *see* **rotten eggs**

egg white

albumin from an egg that is used in fining to clarify red wines after barrel-ageing to help remove excessive tannins

égrappage

French the removal of stems from bunches of grapes (*pronounced* áy gra paázh)

◊ **Egri Bikavér**

Hungarian the Hungarian name for Bull's Blood (*pronounced* éggri bíkə vair, *literally* 'Eger Bull's Blood')

♢ **Ehrenfelser**

a white-wine grape variety, a hybrid of Riesling and Sylvaner, developed in Germany and mostly grown in Germany to produce wine similar to Riesling (*pronounced* áirən felzə)

Einzellage

German the smallest officially recognised unit in the German wine classification system, a vineyard that covers more than five hectares. The definition resulted in thousands of tiny vineyards combining to form a single Einzellage when this system was introduced in the 1970s. The next largest area in this system is a Grosslage, containing many Einzellagen, then a Bereich (a wine-producing area), then an Anbaugebiet (general region). (*pronounced* ínz'l laagə, *literally* 'single vineyard')

Eiswein

a sweet wine made from grapes that are still frozen. The grapes are pressed before they are allowed to thaw, ensuring that any juice extracted is very concentrated with sugar and acid. Eiswein is the second-highest of the QmP categories of German wine classification and one of the categories of Prädikatswein in Austria. (*pronounced* íss vīn, *plural* **Eisweine**)
Also called **ice wine**

Elba DOC

Italy a DOC zone on the small island of Elba off the coast of Italy that grows Trebbiano grapes to produce white wine and Sangiovese to produce red wine

○ Elbling

a white-wine grape variety that is mostly grown in the Mosel region of Germany where it is often used to produce sparkling white wine. (*pronounced* élb ling)
Also called **Burger**

♀ elderflower

(*tasting term*) a taste or aroma associated with white wines made from the Sauvignon Blanc grape variety

♀ elegant

(*tasting term*) used to describe a well-balanced wine of very high quality

élevage

French the time, care and attention given to good wine during its maturation (*pronounced* áy lə vaázh, *literally* 'bringing up')

élevé en futs de chêne

French aged in oak barrels (*pronounced* áy lə vay aaN fŏŏ də shén)

éleveur

French a person who buys new wine that has just been fermented and blends it and then bottles the wine to produce a finished wine (*pronounced* áylə vúr)

embotellado de origen

Spanish produced and bottled at a winery from grapes grown in

the winery's own vineyards. (*pronounced* em bote lyaádo day o reé hen)
Compare **estate bottled**

☼ Emerald Riesling
a white-wine grape variety developed in the USA and grown in California, USA to produce white wine

Emilia-Romagna
Italy a wine-producing region of north-central Italy, with Bologna as its capital city. This region is a gastronomic centre and produces both red and white wines from Sangiovese, Lambrusco and Albana grapes. (*pronounced* ay meélyə rō mánnyə)

♀ empty
(*tasting term*) used to describe a wine without character.
Compare **hollow**

encapsulated yeast
yeast absorbed into beads of calcium alginate, now sometimes used to eliminate the need for riddling in making sparkling wine according to the méthode champenoise. The beads roll into the neck of the bottle and are easily removed during disgorgement, while not interfering with the secondary fermentation.

☼ Encruzado
a Portuguese white grape variety grown especially in the Dão region to produce good white wine (*pronounced* én kro̎o zaádō)

♀ end-palate *see* palate

England
The English climate is not well-suited to viticulture. However, even at these high latitudes, some very successful still and sparkling wine is being made. The country has several hundred vineyards, predominantly in the southern counties of Essex, Hampshire, Hereford, Kent, Somerset, Suffolk and Sussex. Müller-Thurgau is the predominant grape variety, and Seyval Blanc performs well. Other German varieties such as Huxelrebe and Schönburger are also used. The best wines are crisply acidic.

enologist, enology, enophile
US spelling of **oenologist**; **oenology**; **oenophile**

en primeur
French used to describe wine for sale before bottling, usually in the year following the vintage (*pronounced* aaN pree múr)

en tirage
French used to refer to the period of time a sparkling wine has rested in the bottle in contact with the yeast sediment from the secondary fermentation. (*pronounced* aaN tee raázh)
See also **tirage**

Entre-Deux-Mers AOC
France a large appellation within the Bordeaux region of France that grows Muscadelle and Sauvignon Blanc grapes to produce crisp, dry white wine (*pronounced* aáNtrə dö máir, *literally* 'between two seas')

enzyme
a protein produced by yeast during fermentation that acts as a catalyst to start and control the chemical reactions to convert the sugar in the grape juice into alcohol. Enzymes are also responsible for reactions in almost all plant and animal tissue during metabolism.

Épernay
France a town considered to be the centre of the Champagne region of northeastern France. The city of Reims is much bigger, but Épernay is close to the vineyards. Moët et Chandon, Mercier, Perrier Jouet, Pol Roger and a number of lesser-known companies are based there. (*pronounced* áy pair náy)

Epitrapezios Oenos
Greek an official category for basic-quality Greek wine, below the category of Topikos Oenos (*pronounced* éppi tra páy zi oss eénoss)

⟡ Erbaluce
a white-wine grape variety mostly grown in the Piedmont region of Italy to make dry white wines or, when the grapes are dried, to make sweet white wines (*pronounced* áir baa loó chay)

Errázuriz
Chile an internationally respected estate near Santiago, Chile, growing mostly Sauvignon Blanc and Cabernet Sauvignon grapes. Founded in 1870, Errázuriz was once the largest privately owned vineyard in the world and is now overseen by Eduardo Chadwick, the fifth generation of his family to be involved in the wine business. (*pronounced* er rá soo réez)

Erstes Gewächs
German a new category of top-quality dry white wine from

narrowly demarcated areas in the Rheingau region of Germany. (*pronounced* áirstəss gə véks, *literally* 'first growth')
Compare **Grosses Gewächs**

Erzeugerabfüllung
German bottled by the producer. The term is similar to 'estate bottled', but it can also be used by cooperatives. (*pronounced* air tsóygə áb fŏol lŏong)
Compare **Gutsabfüllung**; **Originalabfüllung**

♥ **Espagne** *another name for* **Cinsault** (*pronounced* es pánnyə)

espalier
a way of training vines so that only shoots and branches on two opposite sides of the trunk are kept – any on the other sides of the trunk are cut off – and those remaining are tied horizontally to supporting wires. The vine appears two-dimensional, wide but with no depth. Maximum exposure of grape bunches to the sun is ensured and picking is easier. (*pronounced* e spállyur)

♥ **Esparte** *another name for* **Mourvèdre** (*pronounced* e spaárt)

espumante
Portuguese sparkling (*pronounced* éspŏo mán tay)

espumoso
Spanish sparkling (*pronounced* éspoo mŏssō)

estate bottled
used on a wine label to indicate that the wine was produced and bottled at the winery from grapes grown in the winery's own vineyards. It generally refers to good-quality wine and its use is carefully monitored in Europe.

ester
an aromatic chemical compound produced by the chemical reaction between the acids and alcohol in wine that give the wine a fruity bouquet

esterification
the process of chemical reactions occurring between the acids and alcohol in wine to form esters, which give the wine a fruity bouquet

Est! Est! Est! di Montefiascone DOC
Italy an oddly named but famous DOC zone in the Latium region of Italy that grows mostly the Trebbiano grape to

produce light white wine. The story behind the name is that a bishop on his travels sent his servant ahead to taste the local wines on the route and write 'Est' ('it is') when he found good wines; when the servant reached a tavern in this region he found the wine so good that he wrote 'Est! Est! Est!' on the wall. (*pronounced* ést ést ést dee món tay fya skố nay)

Estremadura

Portugal a large wine-producing region north of Lisbon (*pronounced* é stray ma doőrə)

estufagem

Portuguese the distinctive method of making Madeira, in which wine is placed in a heated tank for at least three months. Fine Madeira wine is placed in wooden casks and stored in a heated room for years at a time. This gives the wine its distinctive burnt, caramelly flavour. (*pronounced* ésh toŏ faázhaN)
Also called **baking**

ethanol

alcohol produced by the fermentation of sugar by a yeast catalyst. It is one of the main by-products of fermentation and is the main type of alcohol in wine.
Also called **ethyl alcohol**

ethyl acetate

an aromatic chemical compound (an ester) that is present in all wine but if present in excessive quantities gives a fruity vinegar smell that spoils the wine

ethyl alcohol *same as* **ethanol**

♀ eucalyptus

(*tasting term*) a spicy bouquet of red wine, particularly those made from Cabernet Sauvignon grapes or from Central Victorian Shiraz

evaporation

loss of moisture from wine into the atmosphere, necessitating the regular topping up of barrels while the wine is maturing unless the wine is on ullage for a purpose, e.g. in sherry-making

ex cellar, ex cellars

awaiting the payment of necessary taxes before release.
Compare **bonded cellar**

excise duty
a tax levied by a government on some items sold in a country. For example, in the UK there is excise duty on wine, beer and spirits. Excise duty on wine is payable once it is sold to a consumer, but if people buy wine to store and age, they can store the wine in a bonded cellar licensed by the government and only pay excise duty when the wine is removed from the cellar.

extended maceration
a period of time after primary fermentation when the new wine stays in contact with the grape skins and seeds. It only applies when making red wine, which takes colour and tannin from the skin and seeds during maceration.

extra *see* **Cognac**

extract
the minerals and trace elements that are part of any wine and give the impression of richness or density of colour and texture. If you remove the basic elements of water, sugar, acid and alcohol what is left is the 'extract'.

extra dry
1. used on the labels of sparkling wines to indicate that the wine is slightly sweet, sweeter than wine labelled brut, and has around 1–2% residual sugar. In French, the term is 'extra sec'.
2. used on sherry labels to indicate that the sherry is very dry

extra sec
French extra dry

Extremadura
Spain a large wine-producing region in western Spain, between Castilla-La Mancha and Portugal (*pronounced* é stray ma dóorə)

♀ exuberant
(*tasting term*) used to describe a wine that is lively and full of fruity tastes

F

Give me books, fruit, French wine and fine weather and a little music out of doors, played by somebody I do not know.

John Keats, August 28, 1819

○ Faber
a hybrid white-wine grape variety, similar in style to Riesling, that is grown mostly in Germany (*pronounced* faábər)

♀ faded
(*tasting term*) used to describe a wine that has lost its character, colour or flavour as a result of old age

Fahrenheit
a scale of temperature in which the freezing and boiling points of water are 32° and 212°. To convert Fahrenheit temperatures to Celsius, subtract 32, multiply by 5 and divide by 9; so 68°F equals 20°C. As a quick rough estimate, subtract 30 and divide by two.
Compare **Celsius**

Falerno del Massico DOC
Italy a DOC area in Campania, southwestern Italy, that produces especially red wine from a blend of Aglianico, Piedirosso and Primitivo or Barbera grape varieties or from all Primitivo grapes. It also produces some white wine. (*pronounced* fa láirnō del mássikō)

fan leaf
a major virus disease of grapevines. Its main symptom is that part of the vine's leaf becomes distorted and has the appearance of a fan.

♀ farmyard
(*tasting term*) used to describe a pleasant aroma of straw and farms associated with some fine red and white wines from the Burgundy region of France.
Also called USA **barnyard**

Far South West *Australia see* **Henty**

♀ **fat**
(*tasting term*) used to describe a wine that has a favourably high alcohol content, is low in acidity and offers a full-bodied, bold and rich flavour. When a wine has not enough acidity to balance the body, it is referred to as flabby, and if a wine does not quite reach the quality of a fat wine, it is termed plump.
Compare **flabby**; **plump**

Faugères AOC
France an appellation in the Languedoc region of southern France that grows mostly Carignan, Cinsault and Grenache grapes to produce full-bodied red wines. Like a number of areas of the Languedoc, however, use of the Carignan grape is in decline, being replaced by Syrah, Mourvèdre and Grenache, and more up-to-date winemaking technology is being introduced. (*pronounced* fō zháir)

♀ **fault**
(*tasting term*) a flaw in a wine that causes it to be atypical of the style of wine and impairs enjoyment

Faustino Martínez
a wine producer (bodega) in the Rioja DOCa region of Spain, best-known for its range of reserva and gran reserva red wines (under the Faustino label), together with a range of white and sparkling wines (*pronounced* fow steénō maar teé neth)

♀ **feeble**
(*tasting term*) used to describe wine that lacks any notable qualities of aroma, body or flavour

fehér
Hungarian white (*pronounced* fé hair)

♀ **feminine**
(*tasting term*) used to describe a wine that is soft and delicate, especially in comparison with other wines from the same region or grape

♢ **Fendant** *another name for* **Chasselas** (*pronounced* faáN daaN)

♢ **Fer**
a red-wine grape variety grown in small quantities in parts of southwestern France and in Argentina where it is used to enhance the colour and aroma of red-wine blends. (*pronounced* fair)
Also called **Fer Servadou**

ferment
a product of fermentation

fermentation
the chemical process during which the juice from grapes is turned into alcoholic wine. There are two stages of fermentation that can occur. The first stage, called primary or alcoholic fermentation, is the process in which the sugars within the grape juice are converted into alcohol by a catalytic reaction started and controlled by the enzymes in yeast. This first stage of fermentation stops either when the sugar has all been converted or when the alcoholic content is strong enough to kill off the enzymes in the yeast (over 15% alcohol per unit volume). The second stage, called malolactic fermentation, occurs when the malic acid in the wine is converted into a less astringent lactic acid with a by-product of carbon dioxide gas. Almost all red wines see both stages of fermentation, but producers of white wine often prevent malolactic fermentation to ensure that the wine tastes crisp and sharp. This second-stage fermentation is also avoided when the grapes are overripe and too sweet.

fermentation container
a container that holds grape juice during fermentation. Fermentation containers were originally wooden barrels and casks but are now usually stainless steel tanks that allow the temperature to be carefully controlled.
Also called **fermentor**

fermentation in bottle *see* **bottle fermentation**

fermentation lock, fermentation trap
a one-way valve in a fermentation container that allows carbon dioxide produced as a by-product of fermentation to escape, without allowing air, and so oxygen, to enter the container

fermentation yeast
pure strains of yeast that are used to start and control the fermentation process. Wild yeasts tend not to be as predictable and have largely been replaced with cultivated yeast strains.

fermentazione
Italian fermentation (*pronounced* fúr men tátsi ő nay)

fermentazione naturale
Italian the Charmat or bulk process (*pronounced* fúr men tátsi ő nay náttoo raá lay)

fermented on the skins

used to describe wine that has been fermented with the grape juice, grape skins and seeds in the same container. The solid matter is removed after fermentation.

fermentor *same as* **fermentation container**

◊ **Fernão Pires**

a Portuguese white-wine grape variety, grown throughout Portugal. (*pronounced* fáir now píresh)
Also called **Maria Gomes**

◊ **Fer Servadou** *another name for* **Fer** (*pronounced* fáir sair va doó)

Fetzer

USA an estate in Mendocino County, California, producing a wide range of good-quality wines from Cabernet Sauvignon, Sauvignon Blanc, Riesling, Zinfandel and Chardonnay grape varieties (*pronounced* fétsər)

feuillette

French a small wooden barrel of a type traditionally used in the Chablis region of France (*pronounced* fö yét)

◊ **Fiano**

a Campanian grape variety used to make Fiano di Avellino white wine (*pronounced* fi aánō)

Fiano di Avellino DOC

Italy a DOC zone in the Campania region of Italy, growing the local Fiano grape variety to produce a good white wine (*pronounced* fi aánō dee avə leénō)

field blend

a wine produced from the grapes of a vineyard that has been planted with several different grape varieties that are harvested together

field budding, field grafting

a method of grafting grapevines in which the rootstock is planted and allowed to grow for a season. The graft is then made by fixing a small piece of the fruiting variety, which has just a single dormant bud on it, in a cut in the rootstock just above ground level. The graft is held in place with a rubber patch and earth is piled up over the graft to keep the bud dormant. The following season the original rootstock is cut off just above the graft, ensuring that the dormant bud is the only bud available from which a shoot can grow.

field selection *same as* **mass selection**

fifth growth *see* **cinquième cru**

♀ **fig**
(*tasting term*) an aroma associated with wines made from the Sémillon grape variety or, in Australia, with Chardonnay

fill level
the level of wine in a bottle

film yeast *same as* **flor**

filter
to strain out any solids in a wine and clarify it just before it is bottled. The solids are mostly yeast cells and sediment that could spoil the wine.

filtration
the process of removing solid matter or impurities from a wine by pouring the liquid through a very fine filter. It is quicker but more expensive than letting the wine settle naturally. Filtration, like fining, improves the colour of a wine and provides a clarity to the liquid; it is used particularly with white wines. The process also removes any unwanted bacteria and yeasts still present in the wine that might continue to ferment once the wine has been bottled. The drawback is that filtering can remove some of the taste and character of a wine and so it is avoided in fine wines.
See also **centrifuge filtration**
Compare **fining**

fine¹
to remove any solid particles left in wine after fermentation.
See **fining**

fine²
Italian the youngest of the categories of Marsala wine (*pronounced* féenay, *literally* 'fine')
See also **Marsala DOC**

fine Champagne
French a term printed on labels of Cognac brandy that indicates that the original wine, before it was distilled, was made from grapes grown in the Champagne region of France (*pronounced* feén shom pánnyə)

♀ **finesse**
(*tasting term*) the well-balanced quality and elegant, subtle flavour and bouquet of very good wine

fine wine
high-quality wine, especially classic wine of classed growth or similar quality. The term has no official status.

Finger Lakes AVA
USA a wine region of New York State, eastern USA, that grows mostly native American grape varieties such as Catawba and Concord

fining
a method of removing solid matter or impurities from a wine by adding a substance to the top of the bottle or barrel and allowing it to sink down through the liquid, gathering the impurities as it sinks. The original substance used for this purpose was egg white, but fine clay called bentonite is now used as a more effective agent. Fining, like filtration, improves the colour of a wine and provides a clarity to the liquid. It also removes any unwanted bacteria and yeasts still present in the wine that might continue to ferment once the wine has been bottled. Fining is now avoided by most producers of fine wine. *Compare* **filtration**

fining agent
a substance used to clarify and purify wine, e.g. bentonite or egg white

♀ **finish**
(*tasting term*) the taste that lingers in your mouth after the wine has been swallowed. It is often the best indicator of the quality of a wine. The length of time the taste lingers can vary from a short to a long finish.

finishing
the final steps in wine production before bottling, including fining, blending and filtering

fino
a light-bodied dry sherry, normally the lightest and driest from an estate, that is very pale yellow in colour and often served cold as an apéritif. Fino is one of the two main types of sherry, the other being oloroso. (*pronounced* feénō)
See **sherry**

fino amontillado *see* **sherry** (*pronounced* feénō ə monti laádō)

♀ **firm**
(*tasting term*) used to describe a wine in which the tannin or acid content is noticeable, but in a good way

first growth *see* **premier cru**

Fitou AOC
France an appellation in the Languedoc region of southern France that grows mostly Carignan, Grenache and Mourvèdre grapes to produce some of the best red wines in the region (*pronounced* feétoo)

fixed acid
a naturally occurring acid such as malic acid or tartaric acid within fruit. These acids help balance the wine, reacting with alcohol to produce aromatic esters and giving the wine its bouquet.

fizz
(*informal*)
1. sparkle or effervescence in a wine
2. sparkling wine

♀ **flabby**
(*tasting term*) used to describe a wine that has too little acidity and so does not have a well-defined taste.
Compare **fat**; **plump**

Flasche
German a bottle (*pronounced* fláshə, *plural* **Flaschen**)

♀ **flat**
1. (*tasting term*) used to describe a wine that has very low acid levels, so is out of balance and lacks any crispness or liveliness and flavour
2. (*tasting term*) used to describe a sparkling wine that has lost its effervescence

flavescence dorée
a disease that causes yellowing and then kills grapevines which is transmitted by an insect and by grafting (*pronounced* flá ve saaNss do ráy)

♀ **flavour**
(*tasting term*) the way a wine tastes, or one of the ways in which a wine tastes, a complex interaction between grapes, soil, viti-cultural techniques and chemical processes

♀ **flavoursome**

(*tasting term*) used to describe a red or white wine with a pleasant, full flavour

♀ **fleshy**

(*tasting term*) used to describe a wine with a high alcohol content and a low tannin content, giving it a full but smooth body and smooth texture.

Compare **lean**

Fleurie AOC

France a small cru (village and surrounding area) in the Beaujolais area of the Burgundy region of France that grows Gamay grapes to produce fruity red wine which should be drunk young (*pronounced* flúree)

flier

a tiny particle that sometimes appears in wine that is stored in a very cold environment. These particles disappear when the wine warms up.

flight

a group of wines considered together in a tasting

♀ **flinty**

(*tasting term*) used to describe a wine that has a dry, mineral character. It is often used to describe white wines from the Chablis region of France.

Compare **stony**

Floc de Gascogne

a blend of Armagnac and white wine served chilled as an apéritif rather in the manner of Pineau des Charentes (*pronounced* flók də gas kónyə)

flor

Spanish yeast that is sometimes seen floating and growing on the surface of wine during fermentation. It is most commonly associated with sherry production or with other wines fermented in barrels. The barrels are not filled, leaving enough air for the yeast to grow. (*pronounced* flawr, *literally* 'flower')

Also called **film yeast**

floraison

the flowering period of grapevines (*pronounced* flaw ray zóN)

♀ **floral, flowery**
(*tasting term*) used to describe white wines that have an aroma of fresh flowers, e.g. white Mosel wines

floral abortion
a disorder of some varieties of vine that causes many of the flowers to fail to develop properly, leading to a very reduced crop

flowering
the period when a grapevine flowers

♀ **flowery** *see* **floral**

flute
1. a tall, thin glass with a long stem, usually used to serve Champagne
2. a tall, thin bottle used in different countries and regions, e.g. in parts of Germany and France

flying winemakers
Australian winemakers, usually young and technically trained, who take their expertise to Europe and South America to help modernise winemaking practices there

foil
a thin metal capsule covering the cork and top of the neck of a wine bottle

♢ **Folle Blanche**
a white grape variety originally grown in the Cognac region of western France to make Cognac and Armagnac. It was affected by phylloxera and rot and is no longer much grown in these areas, although it is still grown in the Loire region. (*pronounced* fol blaáNsh)
Also called **Gros Plant**

♢ **Folle Noire**
a red-wine grape variety grown in Provence and adjoining regions of France (*pronounced* fol nwaár)

◊ **Fondillon**
a high-alcohol sweet white wine made from the Monastrell grape variety using a solera system in the Alicante DO in southeastern Spain (*pronounced* fon deé lyōn)

Fonseca, Fonseca Guimarãens
a famous producer of port (*pronounced* fon sékə)

♀ **food-friendly**
(*tasting term*) used to describe a wine that goes very well with food

♀ **foodie**
(*tasting term*) a wine that goes very well with food

♀ **fore-palate** *see* **palate**

Forez *see* **Côtes du Forez**

fortified wine
a wine that has had extra alcohol added to prevent further fermentation and to increase the alcohol content. Dessert wines with high levels of alcohol such as port, Madeira and sweet sherry are fortified with brandy during fermentation to stop the fermentation process while there is still sugar in the wine to give it sweetness.

fortify
to add alcohol, usually brandy, to wine to stop further fermentation and increase the alcohol content

♀ **forward**
(*tasting term*) used to describe a wine that gives an immediate impression of fruitiness, often because it has matured too early

fourth growth *see* **quatrième cru**

♀ **fox grape**
a wild grape, *Vitis labrusca*, native to the eastern USA that has purplish fruit and is the source of many cultivated grape varieties

♀ **foxiness**
(*tasting term*) the degree to which a taster can notice the foxy taste in a wine

♀ **foxy**
(*tasting term*) used to describe the character of a wine, normally one made from a variety of the American fox grape, *Vitis labrusca*

♀ **fragrant**
(*tasting term*) used to describe a wine that is aromatic and flowery

frais
French used on wine labels to indicate the wine should be served chilled (*pronounced* fray, *literally* 'cool')

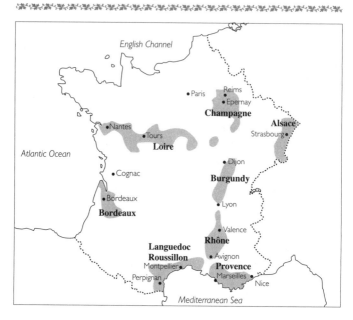

Wine regions of France

France

the most important wine-producing country in the world. France leads the field both in wine production and in consumption of wine per capita. Consumption is, however, falling, although the French are drinking better-quality wines. France introduced the admittedly controversial method of classifying wines as crus classés in the classification of 1855 and developed a strictly controlled national Appellation d'Origine Contrôlée system to help define and regulate wine production in different areas of the country. The country makes a very diverse range of wine: very light rosé wines in Provence in the south, an area which also produces full-bodied reds; predominantly white wines in the Loire and Alsace; and strong, classic red wines in the Bordeaux region that can age for tens of years. The classic wines of Bordeaux, Burgundy, the Rhône and Champagne have exerted influence on every winemaker and producer in the world and have set the standards to which all aspire. However, in return, the success of the wines of New World producers in Australia and the USA has encouraged the more basic levels of the French wine industry to greatly improve vineyard and winemaking practices and the results can be seen in the vastly improved wines emerging from regions such as the Languedoc.

Franciacorta DOC
Italy a DOC area in the Lombardy region of Italy producing a well-known sparkling (spumante) white wine from Pinot Blanc (Pinot Bianco) and Chardonnay grapes using the méthode champenoise. The area also produces good still white wines and some red. (*pronounced* fráonchə káwrtə)

Franconia
the English name for the Franken region of Germany (*pronounced* frang kőni ə)

Franken
Germany an Anbaugebiet (quality wine-producing region) in the north of the Bavaria region of Germany that grows mostly white grape varieties such as Sylvaner, Riesling and Müller-Thurgau to produce dry white wines (*pronounced* fróngkən)

ⓞ Franken Riesling *another name for* Sylvaner (*pronounced* fróngkən reéssling)

Frankland River
Australia a wine-producing area in Western Australia, a sub-region of the Great Southern region

Frascati DOC
Italy a DOC area in the Latium region of Italy near Rome that grows mostly Malvasia, Trebbiano and Greco grapes to produce fruity white wine that ranges from dry to sweet (*pronounced* fra skáati)

free-run
used to describe red wine that has just fermented and is drawn off before it is pressed

free-run juice
juice that has come out of crushed grapes (the must) without any pressing

ⓞ Freisa
a red-wine grape variety grown in the Piedmont region of northwestern Italy that produces a fruity light red wine with high acid content (*pronounced* fráyzə)
Also called Fresa; Fresia

Freixenet
one of the biggest sparkling wine producers in the world, based near Barcelona, Catalonia, Spain, with a range of good ordinary and vintage sparkling Cava wine (*pronounced* fráy shen ét)

French Colombard *another name for* Colombard (*pronounced* frénch kólləm baar, *used in* the USA)

French oak
a type of oak traditionally used when making wine barrels. It imparts a flavour of vanilla and cedar to wine and is used to age white and red wines.

French vermouth
unsweetened vermouth

Fresa *another name for* Freisa (*pronounced* fráyzə)

Frescobaldi
Italy one of the oldest and most important winemaking companies in Italy with major vineyards around Florence in the Tuscany region and producing a wide range of very good wines (*pronounced* fréskō báldi)

fresh
(*tasting term*) used to describe a young white wine, or light red wine, that has a level of acidity that provides a pleasant, clean palate

Fresia *another name for* Freisa (*pronounced* fráyzə)

Friuli
Italy a wine-producing area of northern Italy that includes the Grave del Friuli DOC (*pronounced* fri óoli)

frizzante
Italian lightly sparkling. The word is equivalent to 'pétillant' in French and is used to describe sparkling wines made at a lower pressure than Champagne or spumante. (*pronounced* fri tsán tay)

Fronsac AOC
France a small appellation on the right bank of the Dordogne river in the Bordeaux region of western France that produces only red wines, mostly from Cabernet Franc grapes (*pronounced* fróN sak)

Frontignan
(*pronounced* frónti nyaaN)
I. *another name for* **Muscat à Petits Grains**
2. *see* **Muscat de Frontignan AOC**

♀ **front palate** *see* **palate**

fructose
one of the two main naturally occurring sugars in fruit, including grapes. It reacts during fermentation to form alcohol and esters that provide most of the body and flavour of wine.
Compare **glucose**

♀ **fruit**
(*tasting term*) a fruity taste in wine

♀ **fruit-driven**
(*tasting term*) used to describe the predominant taste of fruit in a red or white wine

♀ **fruity**
(*tasting term*) used to describe a wine with a pleasant bouquet, smell and taste of fruit. This bouquet is produced by the aromatic esters developed in a wine by chemical reactions between the acids and alcohol.

Füder
German a large wine cask (*pronounced* fóodər, *plural* **Füder**)

♀ **full**
(*tasting term*) used to describe a wine with a round, rich flavour, normally as a good point, but sometimes implying that the wine is not elegant. When describing red wines, it normally refers to wine with higher levels of tannin and alcohol, e.g. Barolo or Châteauneuf-du-Pape wines. When describing white wines it normally refers to wines with high levels of alcohol or glycerol.
Compare **big**

♀ **full-bodied** *see* **body**

♀ **fulsome**
(*tasting term*) used to describe a wine that is full-bodied and fruity, sometimes a bit too much so

♀ **Fumé Blanc** *another name for* **Sauvignon Blanc** (*pronounced* fóo may blaáN)

fumigation
the process used to sterilise barrels by burning sulphur in a closed barrel. The burning sulphur forms sulphur dioxide, which kills any yeast or bacteria left in the barrel.

fungus
a microorganism such as a yeast, mushroom or mould. Some fungi cause plant diseases such as mildew. Yeasts react with sugar to form alcohol during fermentation.

♢ **Furmint**
a white-wine grape variety grown in the Tokay region in north-eastern Hungary and used to make the well-known sweet dessert wine Tokay (*pronounced* főor mint)

fusel oil
a mixture of higher alcohols and esters that are created during distillation of wine and provide most of the flavour of brandy

fût
French a barrel (*pronounced* főo)

fût neuf
French a new barrel, which adds to the flavour of the wine (*pronounced* főo nőf, *plural* **fûts neufs**)

G

Come, come; good wine is a good familiar creature if it be well used; exclaim no more against it.

William Shakespeare, 1602–1604

Gaglioppo
a red grape variety with high sugar content and medium acidity best-known as the grape of the red wines produced in the Cirò DOC in the Calabria region of Italy (*pronounced* ga lyóppō)

Gaia
Greece a Greek wine producer with vineyards in the Nemea region of the northeastern Peloponnese in southern Greece and also on the island of Santorini (*pronounced* gī ə)

Gaillac AOC
France an appellation in southwestern France growing a wide range of grape varieties including Duras, Fer and Gamay for red and rosé wines and Mauzac for white wines (*pronounced* gī yak)

Gaillac Mousseux
a slightly sweet sparkling white wine made in the Gaillac AOC in France using the méthode champenoise (*pronounced* gī yak moo só)

Gaillac Perlé
a slightly sparkling (pétillant) white wine produced in the Gaillac AOC in France (*pronounced* gī yak pair láy)

Gaja, Angelo
Piedmont's most famous, innovative and respected wine producer and an Italian who has travelled the world for decades promoting the wines of Barbaresco and Barolo with almost missionary zeal. He pioneered the method of maturing Italian wines in small oak barrels and has even planted Chardonnay and Cabernet Sauvignon in his vineyards. His wines are opulent, intense, powerful and expensive. When Gaja introduced Cabernet Sauvignon to Piedmont he named it Darmagi, local dialect for 'What a pity', which is what his father said every

time he walked past the Cabernet Sauvignon vines that had replaced the native Nebbiolo.

Gallo
a large wine company based in Modesto, California, USA. It was developed by the brothers Ernest and Julio Gallo. (*pronounced* gállō)

gallon
1. a measure of capacity equivalent to 8 pints, or 4.55 litres, used both for liquids and for measuring dry goods.
Also called **imperial gallon**
2. *USA* a measure of capacity equal to 3.78 litres, used only for liquids

gallo nero
Italian a black cockerel logo embossed onto the bottles of Chianti DOCG wines (*pronounced* gállō náirō)

۞ Gamay, Gamay Noir à Jus Blanc
a black grape variety grown in the Beaujolais region of Burgundy, France, and used, particularly, as the sole source for Beaujolais AOC wines. It is also used in other regions in France and in South Africa and California, USA to produce fruity red wines. (*pronounced* ga máy *or* ga máy nwaár a <u>zh</u>oó blaáN)

۞ Gamay Beaujolais
a black grape variety grown in California, USA. It is not related to the Gamay grape variety but to the Pinot Noir grape, and is now often labelled as such. (*pronounced* ga máy bó<u>zh</u>ə láy)

Gambellara DOC
Italy a DOC area in the Veneto region of Italy, near Venice that uses the Garganega grape to produce light, dry white wines similar in style to the white wines from the neighbouring Soave DOC (*pronounced* gámbə laárə)

☿ gamey
(*tasting term*) used to describe a bouquet of old wines that is similar to the smell of slightly decaying game birds

۞ Garganega, Gargana
a white-wine grape variety widely grown in the Soave and Gambellara DOC areas of the Veneto region of Italy to produce

light, crisp dry white wines (*pronounced* gaárgə náygə *or* gaar gaánə)

◊ **Garnaccia** *another name for* **Grenache** (*pronounced* gaar náchə, *used in* Italy)

◊ **Garnacha** *another name for* **Grenache** (*pronounced* gaar náchə, *used in* Spain)

◊ **Garnacha Blanca** *another name for* **Grenache Blanc** (*pronounced* gaar náchə blángkə, *used in* Spain)

◊ **Garnacha Tinta** *another name for* **Grenache** (*pronounced* gaar náchə teéntə, *used in* Spain)

garrafada na origem
Portuguese produced and bottled at a winery from grapes grown in the winery's own vineyards. (*pronounced* garə faádə na ori zhéN)
Compare **estate bottled**

garrafeira
Portuguese a word used on wine labels to indicate a red wine that has been aged for at least three years or a white wine that has been aged for at least one year (*pronounced* gárrə fáyrə)

Gascony
France a wine-producing region of southwestern France known especially as the home of Armagnac

♀ **gassy**
(*tasting term*) used to describe a wine that has suffered from unexpected secondary fermentation in the bottle, producing unwanted carbon dioxide. Though not unpleasant in white wines, gassiness produces bitter red wines.

Gattinara DOCG
Italy a DOCG area in the Piedmont region of northwestern Italy that grows the Nebbiolo grape variety to produce good full-bodied red wines that are aged for at least four years (*pronounced* gátti naárə)

Gavi DOC
Italy a DOC area in the Piedmont region of northwestern Italy that grows the Cortese grape variety to produce a good dry white wine as well as a sparkling (spumante) version (*pronounced* gaávi)

gazéifié
French carbonated (*pronounced* gá zay yee fyáy)

Geelong
Australia a cool winemaking region immediately to the west of Melbourne, Victoria, that grows the Chardonnay grape variety for white wines and Pinot Noir for red wines

Geisenheim
Germany a town in the Rheingau of Germany known for its world-famous college of viticulture as well as its vineyards growing very good Riesling wine. One of the most significant members of the college was Professor Müller-Thurgau who in 1882 crossed Riesling and Sylvaner vines to produce the Müller-Thurgau grape variety. (*pronounced* gíz'n hīm)

generic wine
words printed on labels in the USA for marketing blended wine produced in the USA of ordinary quality and labelled as if from a well-known wine-producing region of Europe, e.g. Burgundy, Chablis or Chianti

generoso
Spanish used to describe a wine with a higher-than-normal level of alcohol that is normally served as an apéritif or dessert wine (*pronounced* hénnə róssō)

♀ generous
(*tasting term*) used to describe a wine that is full-bodied, rich in flavour and bouquet and has high levels of alcohol

genetic modification, genetic engineering
the insertion of DNA from another variety or a different organism into the genetic material of a grape variety to produce higher yields, improve disease resistance or combine characteristics of two or more varieties, e.g. flavour with early ripening for cooler northern climates

Geographic Indication
in the Australian system of specifying a wine's origin, a zone, region or subregion from which at least 85% of the grapes used in the wine's production must derive. The structure of Geographic Indication was introduced in December 1993 to meet export requirements for the European Union and the USA. It is administered by the Australian Wine and Brandy Corporation (AWBC).

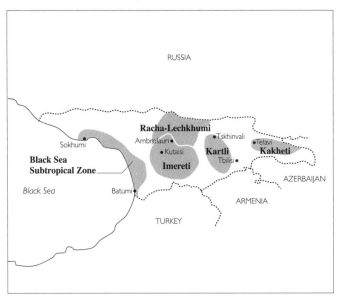

Wine regions of Georgia

Georgia

a wine-producing country, a former member of the USSR, to the north of Turkey and south of Russia with a coast bordering the Black Sea. Although not well-known, the quality and quantity of wine exports are growing. The main regions are Kakheti, Kartli, Imereti and Racha-Lechkhumi, growing a range of local grape varieties.

♀ geranium

(*tasting term*) a smell that is reminiscent of crushed geranium leaves and is a fault caused by sorbic acid reacting with lactic bacteria

Germany

a European country, the seventh-largest wine-producing nation in the world, that mainly produces, and is best-known for, white wines because of its cool climate. It grows mostly the Müller-Thurgau, Riesling and Sylvaner grape varieties. Germany has 13 general growing regions over the country, called Anbaugebiete, which are divided into smaller Bereiche (districts), Grosslagen (general areas) and the highly specific Einzellagen (vineyards). The German wine classification system, set up in the 1970s, has

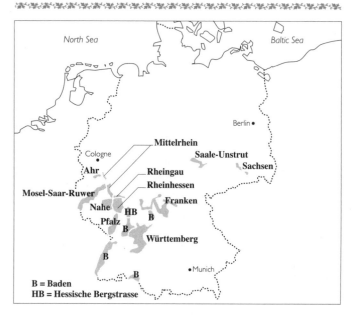

Wine regions of Germany

three broad categories: Qualitätswein mit Prädikat (QmP) for top-quality wine, Qualitätswein bestimmtes Anbaugebiet (QbA) for middle-quality wines and Deutscher Tafelwein (DTW) for table wines. Within the top QmP classification there are six levels, ranging from top to bottom as: Trockenbeerenauslese, Eiswein, Beerenauslese, Auslese, Spätlese and Kabinett. Under the classification system adding sugar to wine (chaptalisation) is allowed for DTW- and QbA-quality wines but not for QmP higher-quality wines. In addition to these levels of wine classification, a further laboratory test on the finished wine is carried out, and to confirm that the wine meets levels of sugar and alcohol the wine is assigned an Amtliche Prüfungsnummer (A.P.Nr), which is printed on the label. Germany has long been synonymous with cheap, semisweet wines stacked in huge quantities on supermarket shelves. This has left a lasting impression on wine consumers, one that the German wine industry is finding it hard to shake off. But Liebfraumilch and Piesporter Michelsberg are waning in popularity and the future for German wine must lie in the drier, fuller single estate wines that are being increasingly produced and especially in those using the Riesling grape.

germinate
(*of a plant seed*) to start to grow by breaking out of the seed casing and forming the first roots and a shoot

geropiga *see* **jeropiga**

Gerovassiliou
Greece a Greek wine producer with vineyards around Epanomi near Thessaloniki in northeastern Greece (*pronounced* yérrō va seélyoo)

Gevrey-Chambertin AOC
France a famous appellation around the small town of Gevrey-Chambertin in the Côte de Nuits district of the Burgundy region of France that grows Pinot Noir grapes to produce high quality red wines in various grand cru vineyards. (*pronounced* zhévvree shómbər táN)
See **Chambertin AOC**; **Chambertin Clos de Bèze AOC**; **Charmes-Chambertin AOC**; **Mazis-Chambertin AOC**; **Ruchottes-Chambertin AOC**

Gewürztraminer
a white grape variety grown in the Alsace region of France and in Australia, Germany, New Zealand, the USA and Chile. It produces highly flavoured, perfumed, spicy medium sweet or dry white wines. (*pronounced* gə voórts tra meenər)
Also called **Traminer; Tramini**

Ghemme DOC
Italy a DOC wine-producing zone in the north of the Piedmont region of northwestern Italy that produces good red wine primarily from the Nebbiolo grape variety (*pronounced* gémmay)

Gigondas AOC
France an appellation in the Rhône region of southern France that produces mostly full-bodied red wines from Grenache and Cinsault grapes (*pronounced* zhée goN daá)

Gironde
(*pronounced* zhee rónd) *France*
1. a tidal estuary in the Bordeaux region of France into which the Garonne and Dordogne rivers flow. Most of the finest vineyards of the Médoc are on the right bank of this estuary.
2. one of the 95 départements of southwestern France that covers roughly the same area as the Bordeaux region

Gisborne
New Zealand a wine-producing region in New Zealand, in the east of the North Island, producing mainly white wines from the Müller-Thurgau, Chardonnay and Sauvignon Blanc grape varieties

Givry AOC
France a village appellation in the Côte Chalonnaise area of the Burgundy region of France that produces mostly fruity, light red wine from Pinot Noir grapes (*pronounced* zheévree)

glass
an object that holds wine so that it can be tasted, enjoyed and drunk. The shape of the glass is very important, particularly when tasting at a professional level: the glass should be clear to show the true colour of the wine and the shape of the bowl should taper in slightly at the top to allow the scents from the wine to concentrate there when the taster smells the wine. There is an ISO (International Organization for Standardization) standard shape and size of glass that is recommended for tasting wine. The only glass not in this shape is a flute-style tall, thin glass for drinking Champagne, since the older-style wide, shallow glasses for Champagne allow the bubbles to disperse too quickly.

Glenrowan
Australia a wine-producing region in northeastern Victoria

glogg
a hot punch consisting of brandy, red wine and sherry, flavoured with sugar, spices, fruit pieces and blanched almonds. It was originally served in Scandinavia at Christmas.

glucose
one of the two main naturally occurring sugars in fruit, including grapes. It reacts during fermentation to form alcohol and esters that provide most of the body and flavour of wine. *Compare* **fructose**

glühwein
warmed red wine flavoured with spices and added sugar (*pronounced* glyoó vīn)

glycerol, glycerine
a colourless liquid formed during fermentation that adds a little to the sweetness and smoothness of a wine

gnarly
1. used to describe an old, knobbly or twisted vine
2. used to describe a rough red wine that has extracted too much taste from the grape skins

◊ **Godello**
a white grape variety native to the Valdeorras area of the Galicia region of northwestern Spain that produces good crisp white wines (*pronounced* go dáy lyo)

Gonzáles Byass
one of the best-known sherry houses in Jerez de la Frontera, Spain, that produces a best-selling fino sherry together with a range of other styles and a range of brandies (*pronounced* gon zaá less bí əss)

♀ **gooseberry**
(*tasting term*) used to describe a white wine, especially one made from the Sauvignon Blanc grape variety, with a slightly but pleasantly acidic taste or an aroma reminiscent of goose-berries

Goulburn Valley
Australia a large wine region north of Melbourne, Victoria, that produces red wines from the Syrah (Shiraz) and Cabernet Sauvignon grape varieties and white wines from Marsanne

Goumenissa
Greece an appellation in northern Greece that produces red and white wines and a good rosé from the Xinomavro grape variety (*pronounced* goo ménni sa)

goût
French taste (*pronounced* goo)

♀ **goût de bouchon**
French (*tasting term*) the quality of a wine that is corked (*pronounced* goó də boo shóN, *literally* 'taste of cork')

♀ **goût de terroir**
French (*tasting term*) the combined characteristics of the region, climate and soil (the 'terroir') that can be tasted in a wine. For example, the tasting term 'flinty' refers to the goût de terroir of Chablis. (*pronounced* goó də ter rwaár, *literally* 'taste of earth')

◌ **Gouveio** *another name for* **Verdelho** (*pronounced* goo váyō, *used in* Portugal)

governo, governo alla toscana
Italian a former traditional winemaking technique in Italy, especially Tuscany, in which semi-dried must from a previous batch of winemaking was added to newly fermented wine to start the secondary fermentation process. This was useful in old, cold cellars but also produced softer wines with more alcohol and a richer colour, and sometimes with slight effervescence. (*pronounced* go vúrno *or* go vúrno ala toss kaána)

♀ **graceful**
(*tasting term*) used to describe a wine that is subtle, well-balanced and generally pleasing to drink

◌ **Graciano**
a red-wine grape variety grown mostly in the Rioja and Navarra regions of Spain that produces a fragrant, richly coloured red wine. It has low yields, so has largely been replaced in the Rioja region, but is being planted again in Navarre. (*pronounced* gráthi aánō)
Also called **Morastel**

graft
a piece of plant tissue inserted into another plant and growing from it

grafting
a method of propagating vines that is the only sure way of producing plants resistant to phylloxera or other diseases. A phylloxera-resistant rootstock is used and a piece of a fruiting variety, which has a single bud, is inserted into a hole in the rootstock so that the inserted stem (the scion) can draw nutrients from the rootstock and grow. The join heals with time and the new fruiting stem produces grapes, while the rootstock remains resistant to disease.
See **green grafting**; **T-bud grafting**

graft union
the place where the scion joins the rootstock

Graham, W. & J.
one of the top port companies producing very good vintage port as well as a good second-label port, Malvedos. It is owned by the Symington family who also own Dow, Warre and Smith Woodhouse.

Graillot, Alain
a well-known wine producer based in the Crozes-Hermitage AOC in the northern Rhône region of southern France (*pronounced* grī ṓ)

Grampians
Australia a winemaking region in west-central Victoria, northeast of Henty

grand cru
French a term with different meanings in different parts of France. In Bordeaux, the title is given to some estates, but apart from indicating good wine, has no real legal significance and is not related to grand cru classé. In Burgundy, it is used to denote one of the 30 or so vineyards judged to be the best in the region, though it does not always guarantee the best wine, since one vineyard in Burgundy is often split between different producers; it is above the premier cru classification. In the Champagne region, it is the top rating for a village that produces the best wines, although in Champagne the estate or Champagne house is often more important. In Alsace, it is the top classification for the best vineyards and wines of the region. (*pronounced* graaN krṏ, *literally* 'great growth', *plural* **grands crus**)

grand cru classé
French a term with different meanings in different parts of France. In the Médoc area of Bordeaux, estates listed as deuxième cru, troisième cru, quatrième cru or cinquième cru (second, third, fourth or fifth growth) in the classification of 1855 can use the term grand cru classé on their labels. In the much later classification of the Saint-Émilion region, this was awarded to the second-best wines of the area, though these are still not as good as those of the Médoc deuxième cru rating that can use a similar wording. (*pronounced* graáN krṏ kla sáy, *literally* 'great classed growth', *plural* **grands crus classés**)

Grande Champagne
France a small area in the Cognac region of western France having vineyards that grow some of the best grapes for distilling into Cognac (*pronounced* graáNd shom pánnyə)

grande cuvée
French used on French wine labels to imply a top-quality wine, but with no official status (*pronounced* graaNd kṏ váy)

Grande Cuvée *see* Krug

grande marque
French any one of the best estates of the Champagne region of France (*pronounced* graaNd maárk, *plural* **grandes marques**)

Grand Roussillon AOC
France an appellation in the Roussillon area of southern France that produces sweet wines (*pronounced* graáN roo see yóN)

grand vin
French used on labels to describe good wine, but with no official status (*pronounced* graaN váN, *literally* 'great wine', *plural* **grands vins**)

Grange
an excellent red wine usually made wholly from the Syrah (Shiraz) grape that was developed for Penfolds in South Australia by Max Schubert

gran reserva
Spanish a very good wine that has been aged for at least five years (*pronounced* gran rə záirvə)

grape
a fruit, technically a berry, from a vine that is used to produce wine. Although many other types of fruit can also be used to produce wine, grapes dominate the world market. When making wine the grapes are usually crushed to break open the skin, then pressed to release the juice from inside the grape, then fermented to convert the natural sugars in the grape juice into alcohol.

grape concentrate
concentrated grape juice, in which the water content has been reduced so that the concentration of soluble solids is increased to around 70 degrees on the Brix scale. It is very sweet and is used to add sugar to a wine during a process called chaptalisation, which is illegal in some countries such as Italy, to increase the alcohol content or sweetness of the wine.
Also called **concentrate**

grapefruit, grapefruity
(*tasting term*) a taste or aroma found in some white wines

grape skin
the tough skin protecting and enveloping the pulp of grape berries. The skin provides the colour of red wine, together with a lot of its flavour, acidity and tannins.

grapevine
a plant of the genus *Vitis* that produces grapes

♀ grapey
(*tasting term*) used to describe a wine that smells and tastes like grapes

grappa
Italian an Italian spirit distilled from the residue ('pomace') left over from fermentation of grapes, not from wine like Cognac, producing a dry highly alcoholic drink. In France spirit made in this way is called marc. (*pronounced* gráppə)

♀ grassy
(*tasting term*) used to describe the pleasant aromas and flavours in a wine that are reminiscent of newly cut grass or hay. It is often used of wines made from the Sauvignon Blanc grape.

♢ Grauburgunder
another name for **Pinot Gris** (*pronounced* grów boŏr gúndər, *used in* Germany)

Grave del Friuli DOC
Italy a DOC area in northeastern Italy that grows a range of Cabernet Franc, Cabernet Sauvignon and other local grape varieties for red wines, Chardonnay, Pinot Blanc and Pinot Gris for white wines and Merlot for its rosé wines (*pronounced* graávay del fri oóli)

♀ gravelly
(*tasting term*) used to describe a wine that has the clean smell of dry soil, as opposed to damp compost or clay. It is most often used to describe wines from the Graves region of France.

graves
French a region where the soil is stony (*pronounced* graav, *literally* 'gravel')

Graves
France a wine-producing area in the Bordeaux region of south-western France, named after its stony, gravelly soil. It produces a wide range of very good wines and contains a number of appellations, with the best in the north of the area called Pessac-Léognan AOC. In the classification of 1855 only the wines from neighbouring Médoc area were considered good enough: the only non-Médoc exception in the list was Château Haut-Brion in the north of the Graves area, which was given a premier cru ranking. (*pronounced* graav)

Graves AOC
France an appellation in the south of the Graves area of the Bordeaux region of France producing red wines from Cabernet Sauvignon, Cabernet Franc and Merlot grapes and dry white wines from Sauvignon Blanc, Sémillon and Muscadelle grapes (*pronounced* graav)

Graves de Vayres AOC
France a small appellation in the Bordeaux region of France that gets its name from its stony soil and produces dry white wines and red wines. It is not part of the Graves region. (*pronounced* graáv də váir)

Graves Supérieures AOC
France a small appellation producing a small quantity of dry and sweet white wines in the south of the Graves area of the Bordeaux region of France from Sauvignon Blanc, Sémillon and Muscadelle grapes (*pronounced* graáv sŏŏ páyr yúr)

Great Southern
Australia a large and important wine region in the southwest of Western Australia, having five subregions: Albany, Frankland River, Mount Barker, Porongurup and Denmark. It produces good red wines from Cabernet Sauvignon, Syrah (Shiraz) and Pinot Noir grapes and white wines from Chardonnay and Riesling.

Grecanico
a white-wine grape variety grown in Sicily and parts of Greece (*pronounced* grékə neékō)

Grechetto
a white-wine grape variety grown in Italy that produces a rich white wine (*pronounced* gre kétto)

Greco
(*pronounced* grékō)
1. a white-wine grape variety grown in the south of Italy to produce rich white wines either in a dry or sweet style
2. *another name for* **Albana** (no relation of Greco proper)

Greco di Ancona *another name for* **Albana** (*pronounced* grékō dee an kónə)

Greco di Tufo DOC
Italy a DOC area near Naples in Italy, growing mostly the Greco grape variety to produce dry white and sparkling (spumante) wines (*pronounced* grékkō dee toófō)

Wine regions of Greece

Greece

the world's 14th-largest wine-producing country and generally considered to be the birthplace of wine. It is uncertain how winemaking arrived in Greece. It may have been brought to Crete by Phoenician traders, or it may have arrived from the north, by land, from Asia Minor. There is evidence of winemaking on Crete during the Minoan civilisation in the middle of the third millennium BC. Evidence also suggests that winemaking was common in Greece and around the Aegean a few centuries later. It is known that sweet wines were popular and the Greeks were not afraid to mix wine with water, honey, spices and even sea water. Greek wines often bore the flavour of the pine resin with which they coated the amphorae and jars used to store wine. Retsina – pine-resin-flavoured wine – enjoys immense popularity in modern Greece. Ancient Greece may fairly be said to have invented wine as a social and cultural phenomenon, to have technically mastered the art of winemaking and, trading wine wherever Greek ships sailed, to have been responsible for the spread of viticulture throughout the western world. However the Ottoman Empire inhibited the industry until the late 20th century. A wide array of different growing conditions, offering an extraordinary palette of styles and varieties, encouraged producers and winemakers to move away from cheap bulk wines and invest in modern wine-making methods and technology. New stainless steel wineries, new oak barrels and increased awareness of terroir and microclimates have all contributed to a substantial improvement in Greek wine. Consequently, numerous producers of quality wines have emerged, such as Gaia, Gerovassiliou, Boutari, Tsantali and Antonopoulos. Many of the top Greek winemakers have learnt their trade in more traditional winemaking regions such as Burgundy, Bordeaux and parts of Australia. Legally, three categories of Greek wine may be made. Appellation of Origin of Superior Quality (OPAP) and Controlled Appellation of Origin (OPE) are used to describe wines, sweet and dry, from defined areas, made in prescribed ways, using particular grape varieties. Some 28 wines enjoy appellation status. Epitrapezios Oenos (vins de table) include the Topikos Oenos (vins de pays) and the Onomasia kata Paradosi (Traditional Appellation). Topikos Oenos wines bear the name of the region, county or town, from which they come. The vast majority of Greek wines are made from unique indigenous varieties such as Xinomavro, Aghiorghitiko and Limnio.

♀ green
1. (*tasting term*) used to describe a wine that is still too acidic or too young to drink and enjoy
2. (*tasting term*) used to describe a wine with high acidity and grassy flavours

green grafting
a grafting technique that is used to introduce a new fruit-bearing grape variety onto an existing rootstock. A T-shaped notch is made at the top of the rootstock and the new variety grafted into this notch.
Also called **T-bud grafting**

♀ green pepper
(*tasting term*) an aroma associated with red wines made from the Cabernet Franc grape variety and also from Cabernet Sauvignon grapes grown in a cool climate

Green Valley-Solano AVA
USA a small AVA region of California, between San Francisco and Sacramento that sells its products mainly locally

Green Valley-Sonoma
USA a subregion of the Russian River Valley AVA in California that has a cooler climate than the Green Valley-Solano area and grows Chardonnay and Pinot Noir grapes to produce still and sparkling white and red wines

green wine
a literal translation of Vinho Verde, a wine of Portugal

♀ Grenache
a red-wine grape variety widely planted around the world, particularly in hot and dry regions, and producing big, peppery wines. It is very popular in southern France and also in Spain, where it is known as Garnacha. (*pronounced* grə násh)
Also called **Carignan Rosos**; **Garnaccia**; **Garnacha**; **Garnacha Tinta**; **Grenache Noir**

♀ Grenache Blanc
a white-wine grape variety, widely grown in southern France and Spain, producing white wines with low acid levels and high alcohol content. (*pronounced* grə násh blaáN)
Also called **Garnacha Blanca**

♀ Grenache Noir *another name for* **Grenache** (*pronounced* grə násh nwaár)

♀ Grey Riesling *another name for* **Trousseau Gris** (*used in* New Zealand)

grey rot
a disease caused by the fungus *Botrytis cinerea* that can destroy grape berries. If the rot is carefully controlled on white grapes, its effect of shrivelling the grapes concentrates the sugars and produces a very sweet wine.
See also **noble rot**

♀ Grignolino
a red-wine grape variety that was originally from the Piedmont region of northwestern Italy but is now grown in other countries and used to produce light-bodied red wines (*pronounced* grínnyə leénō)

Grillet *see* **Château-Grillet**

♀ Grillo
a Sicilian white-wine grape variety used especially in the making of Marsala (*pronounced* greél lō)

♀ **Gringet** *another name for* **Savagnin** (*pronounced* graN <u>zh</u>áy)

♀ **grip**
(*tasting term*) a firm texture of a wine, usually with high levels of tannin and good definition

gris
French pale rosé. (*pronounced* gree, *literally* 'grey')
See also **vin gris**

♀ **Grolleau** *another name for* **Groslot** (*pronounced* gro lṓ)

Groot Constantia
South Africa a wine-producing estate in Constantia in Cape Province, South Africa, producing good Sauvignon Blanc and Sémillon wines (*pronounced* hrṓot kon staántyə)

♀ **Groppello**
a red-wine grape variety grown mostly in the Lombardy region of Italy to produce red and rosé wines (*pronounced* gro péllō)

♀ **Groslot**
a red-wine grape variety mostly grown in the Loire region of France to produce ordinary medium sweet Rosé d'Anjou wines. (*pronounced* grō lṓt)
Also called **Grolleau**

♀ **Gros Manseng** *see* **Manseng** (*pronounced* grṓ maaN sáN)

♀ **Gros Plant** *another name for* **Folle Blanche** (*pronounced* grṓ plaáN)

Gros Plant VDQS
France a VDQS wine-producing area in the Loire region of France producing dry white wine from Folle Blanche (Gros Plant) grapes (*pronounced* grṓ plaáN)

Grosses Gewächs
German a new category of top-quality dry white wines from narrowly demarcated areas of Germany other than in the Rheingau region. (*pronounced* grṓssəss gə véks, *literally* 'great growth')
Compare **Erstes Gewächs**

♀ **Grosse Syrah** *another name for* **Mondeuse** (*pronounced* grṓssə sírrə, *used in* Germany)

Grosslage
German a group of separate vineyards that are individually called Einzellagen. Grosslagen are then grouped into regional

Bereiche and these districts are grouped into the general Bereich wine-producing regions of Germany. (*pronounced* grṓss laagə, *literally* 'large vineyard', *plural* **Grosslagen**)

grower *see* **winegrower**

Gruaud-Larose, Château
France a château in the Saint-Julien AOC in the Médoc district of Bordeaux in southwestern France, graded deuxième cru (second growth) in the classification of 1855. It produces consistently excellent red wines. (*pronounced* grṓo ō la rṓz)

Grüner Veltliner, Grünmuskateller
a white grape variety widely planted in Austria and used to produce light, crisp dry white wines (*pronounced* grónər félt leenər *or* grōon mooskə téllə)

Guenoc Valley AVA
USA an AVA area in the Napa Valley region of California that has one winery

Guigal
an important wine producer based in Côte Rôtie in the northern Rhône region of France (*pronounced* gee gaál)

gunflint
(*tasting term*) an aroma or flavour associated with Riesling wines from the Alsace region of France

Gutedel *another name for* **Chasselas** (*pronounced* góotə dell, *used in* Germany)

Gutenborner
a German-bred white-wine grape variety grown in England (*pronounced* góotən báwrnər)

Gutsabfüllung
German estate bottled. (*pronounced* góots ap fŏol lŏong)
Compare **Erzeugerabfüllung**; **Originalabfüllung**

guyot
French a method of pruning and training (trellising) a vine so that branches are only allowed to grow from one side of the vine. It is mostly used in the Médoc district of Bordeaux in southwestern France. (*pronounced* geé ō)

gyropallet
an automatic riddling machine

H

Strategy is buying a bottle of fine wine when you take a lady out for dinner. Tactics is getting her to drink it. Frank Muir

ha *abbreviation* hectare

Halbstück
German a wooden barrel used by some winemakers in Germany, especially in the Rheingau (*pronounced* hálp shtŏok, *plural* **Halbstücke**)

halbtrocken
German used to describe a wine that is sweeter than a trocken wine, with a little residual sugar (*pronounced* hálp trókən, *literally* 'half dry')

half-bottle
a bottle of wine containing 375 ml, half the 750 ml capacity of a standard bottle

Hanepoot *another name for* **Muscat** (*pronounced* haánə póoərt, *used in* South Africa)

hard
(*tasting term*) used to describe a wine that has a high level of acid or tannin and is astringent, making your mouth pucker in reaction. It is often used to describe young red wines that need to be aged.

Hardys *see* **BRL Hardy**

harmonious
(*tasting term*) used to describe a wine in which all the elements of the wine are in balance

harsh
(*tasting term*) used to describe a very astringent wine that has a high level of alcohol and excessive tannin. This type of wine will probably not improve with age.

Hárslevelü
a white-wine grape variety grown mostly in Hungary and used for its range of Tokay wines (*pronounced* haár shlevelŏo)

Harveys of Bristol
a Bristol-based sherry company, now part of the Allied-Lyons group, that created the cream style of sherry and is most famous for Harveys Bristol Cream

haut
French geographically high (*pronounced* ō)

Haut Armagnac
France one of the three subregions of Armagnac in southwestern France, wrapping around the east and south of the region (*pronounced* ŏt aarma nyák)

Haut-Brion, Château
France a famous vineyard in the Graves district of Bordeaux, southwestern France, producing a very good red wine rated premier cru (first growth) in the classification of 1855 (*pronounced* ō bree óN)

Hautes-Côtes de Beaune AOC
France an appellation in the upper hills of the Côtes de Beaune area of Burgundy in France that grows Pinot Noir grapes to make red wine and Chardonnay for white wine (*pronounced* ŏt kŏt də bŏn)

Haut-Médoc AOC
France an appellation covering the southern part of the Médoc area of the Bordeaux region of southwestern France. It is considered to be one of the best areas of the Médoc, and produces fine wines from Cabernet Franc, Cabernet Sauvignon and Merlot grape varieties. (*pronounced* ŏ may dók)

Hawkes Bay
New Zealand one of the oldest wine-producing regions in New Zealand, in the North Island, producing white wines from the Chardonnay, Müller-Thurgau and Sauvignon Blanc grape varieties and red wines especially from Cabernet Sauvignon and Merlot grapes

♀ hay
(*tasting term*) an unpleasant aroma found in some wines

♀ hazelnut
(*tasting term*) a taste or aroma associated with Champagne and oak-aged white wines made from the Chardonnay grape variety

♀ **hazy**
(*tasting term*) used to describe a wine that is not crystal clear and has a cloudy appearance, normally because of tiny particles. It may simply indicate a wine that is unfiltered or not fined, but it can also indicate a cloudy wine that is likely to be spoiled.

♀ **heady**
(*tasting term*) used to describe a wine that is very alcoholic and likely to be full-bodied

heartwood
the inner part of dead woody tissue (xylem cells) making up the trunk of a woody plant such as a vine and giving the plant strength

♀ **hearty**
(*tasting term*) used to describe a full-bodied red wine with lots of fruit

heat summation
a measure of the climate of a region obtained by measuring the average temperature each day, over a season.
See **climatic regions**

♀ **heavy**
(*tasting term*) used to describe an unsubtle wine that has an obviously high alcohol content

hectare
a unit of measure for land equal to 10,000 square metres, or 2.47 acres.
Abbreviation **ha**

hectolitre
a unit of measure for liquid capacity equal to 100 litres.
Abbreviation **hl**

Heidsieck *see* **Charles Heidsieck; Piper Heidsieck**

Hennessy
an old-established Cognac producer that merged with Moët et Chandon and then became part of the giant LVMH company

Henty
Australia a winemaking region in southwestern Victoria, west of Grampians and stretching to the coast. It was formerly known as Far South West.

Hérault, l'Hérault
France a département in southern France, part of the Langue-doc-Roussillon region, with many vineyards producing especially ordinary red wine using the Carignan grape variety (*pronounced* ay rố *or* l'ayrố)

herbaceous
(*tasting term*) used to describe a wine that has a green, grassy, plant-like taste or aroma. It is usually associated with grape variety rather than climate or soil, particularly Merlot for red wines and Sauvignon Blanc or Sémillon for white.

Hermitage
1. *another name for* **Cinsault** (*used in* South Africa)
2. *another name for* **Syrah** (*formerly used in* the Hunter Valley, Australia)

Hermitage AOC
France an appellation in the northern part of the Rhône region of southern France that produces some of the best red and white wines in France. The wines are capable of many years of ageing before being at their best, and are grown in vineyards perched dramatically on the steep hillside above the town of Tain-l'Hermitage. The red wines are made from Syrah grapes and the white wines from Marsanne and Rousanne. (*pronounced* áir mee taázh)
See also **Crozes-Hermitage AOC**

Hessische Bergstrasse
Germany a small Anbaugebiet (quality wine-producing region) in Germany that grows mostly the Riesling grape variety to produce white wine (*pronounced* héssishə báirg shtraassə)

Heurige
German in Austria, wine from the latest vintage (*pronounced* hóyrigə, *literally* 'new wine', *plural* **Heurigen**)

high-toned
(*tasting term*) used to describe a wine that has been made with a slight level of volatile acidity to help improve its smell and taste

hind palate *see* palate

hl *abbreviation* hectolitre

Hochgewächs
German a higher-quality wine in the QbA class of German wines, made only from the Riesling grape variety (*pronounced* hókh gə veks, *plural* **Hochgewächse**)

◊ **hock**
a German white wine produced in the Rhine region. The term originates from the town of Hochheim in the Rhine Valley, and is used only in British English.

hogshead
a wooden barrel used to store wine and spirits, containing about 250 litres

♀ **hollow**
(*tasting term*) used to describe a wine that lacks depth of flavour, with no body and a very short finish.
Compare **empty**

♀ **honest**
(*tasting term*) used to describe a wine that is simple, straightforward and typical of its type of wine, but nothing special

♀ **honeyed**
(*tasting term*) used to describe a white wine, usually a botrytised one, that has a rich, sweet flavour and aroma

♀ **honeysuckle**
(*tasting term*) an aroma associated with white wines made from the Muscat grape variety

horizontal tasting
a wine tasting that has a selection of wines from the same vintage but from different estates or vineyards.
Compare **vertical tasting**

Hospices de Beaune
France a famous charity hospital in the town of Beaune, in the heart of the Burgundy region of France that owns some of the best vineyards in the region. Its wines are auctioned before being bottled each year in what is often the biggest wine event in Burgundy. (*pronounced* os peéss də bőn)

♀ **hot**
(*tasting term*) used to describe a wine that has high levels of alcohol, giving a burning sensation in the mouth

hotte
French a basket carried on a worker's back and used to transport the freshly picked grapes to a lorry (*pronounced* ót)

house
an estate that produces Champagne

house wine
a relatively cheap, but sometimes good, wine in a restaurant or café that is chosen by the proprietor for continued use and is often served by the glass, carafe or bottle

Howell Mountain AVA
USA a small wine-producing region within the Napa Valley AVA that grows a range of grape varieties, particularly Cabernet Sauvignon and Zinfandel

Hudson River Valley AVA
USA a viticultural area in New York State with wineries on both sides of the Hudson River

Hugel
one of the best-known and most influential families of the Alsace region of France. Wine producers since the 17th century, the Hugels are based in the picturesque village of Riquewihr. They have long spearheaded the drive for quality in the region and were influential in creating the strict regulations governing the local Alsace Vendange Tardive and Sélection de Grains Nobles styles of wine made from sweet, overripe grapes infected with *Botrytis cinerea*. (*pronounced* hóog'l)

Hungary
a country in eastern Europe that produces a wide range of wines in different styles and grows a wide range of grape varieties. The two best-known exported wines are Tokay, one of the world's great dessert wines, and Egri Bikavér (Bull's Blood), a full-bodied red wine made in the Eger region. In the 1600s, some 200 years before France, the Tokaj-Hegyalja region around Tokay introduced the very first classification system for wine, based on quality. During the Communist era Hungarian wine was wholly state-controlled. In the ten years since the fall of the Eastern bloc, Hungary has successfully modernised its wine industry and winemakers are starting to re-establish Hungarian wine styles. Foreign winemakers and foreign investment have arrived to support these developments. Hungarian wines are labelled

according to the variety. Indigenous Hungarian varietals mix with imported grape varieties. Among the whites, Furmint, Királyleányka, Hárslevelü, Irsai Olivér and Welschriesling (Olaszrizling) are capable of good and even fine wine, along with Sauvignon Blanc, Chardonnay and Gewürztraminer (Tramini). Quality home-grown reds include Kékfrankos and Kadarka, while Cabernet Sauvignon, Merlot and Pinot Noir have been successfully introduced. The great success of the imported varieties would suggest a very rosy future for Hungary's wine.

Wine regions of Hungary, Czech Republic,
Croatia and Slovenia

Hunter Valley

Australia a well-known wine-producing zone in the state of New South Wales, not far from Sydney, that produces some of the best wines in Australia. A warm wine-growing region, it grows mostly Sémillon and Chardonnay grapes to produce white wines and Syrah (Shiraz) and Cabernet Sauvignon to produce red wines.

⟡ **Huxelrebe**
a white-wine grape with good acid levels and high sugar content that is grown in Germany and in parts of England (*pronounced* hŏoks'l raybə)

⟡ **hybrid**
a grape variety produced either by crossing one species of grape vine with another, e.g. crossing the main species *Vitis vinifera* with *Vitis labrusca* or *Vitis riparia* (an interspecific cross), or by crossing two varieties of the same species (an intraspecific cross), to obtain a variety with improved characteristics such as disease resistance or winemaking quality

hybridisation
the production of hybrid vines by cross-pollination between different species or between varieties in the same species

hybrid vigour
an increase in size, rate of growth, fertility or resistance to disease found in offspring of a cross between parent vines with different characteristics

hydrogen sulphide
an unwanted chemical produced by yeast combining with sulphur that gives a wine a smell of rotten eggs

hydrogen tartrate
a salt or ester of tartaric acid, e.g. potassium hydrogen tartrate, that forms deposits in wine vats

hydrometer
a measuring device used to measure the specific gravity of a liquid, comparing it to the density of pure water. This provides a measure of the sugar content of grape juice in the fermentation container. The instrument has a hollow cylindrical bulb with a lead weight in the bottom to make it float vertically and a number scale on the long stem that can be read as it floats in the liquid.
Also called **densimeter**

I

Once wine has been drawn it should be drunk, even if it's good.
Marcel Pagnol, 1936

ice wine *same as* **Eiswein**

IGT *abbreviation Italian* Indicazione Geografica Tipica

imbottigliato all'origine
Italian produced and bottled at the winery from grapes grown in
the winery's own vineyards. (*pronounced* im bótti lyaáto al o
ríggi nay)
Compare **estate bottled**

Imereti
Georgia a wine-producing region in western Georgia that uses a
local method of wine production and a local grape variety

imperial
an oversize wine bottle with the shape traditionally used for
Bordeaux wines that can contain 6 litres, equivalent to eight
standard 750 ml bottles.
Compare **methuselah**

imperial gallon *same as* **gallon l**

INAO *abbreviation French* Institut National des Appellations
d'Origine

♀ **incisive**
(*tasting term*) used to describe a wine with 'bite', because of its
noticeable levels of acid and tannin

Indicação de Proveniencia Regulamentada
the second class of wines in the classification system used in
Portugal. The best wines are called Denominação de Origem
Controlada (DOC). (*pronounced* índikə sów də provə nyénsi ə
réggŏola men taádə)
Abbreviation **IPR**

Indicazione Geografica Tipica
Italy a classification of Italian wines outside the DOC system

but considered excellent Vini da Tavola. (*pronounced* indi ká tsyő nay jay o graáfikə típpikə)
Abbreviation **IGT**

INDO *abbreviation Spanish* Instituto Nacional de Denominaciones de Origen

Inferno
Italy an Italian wine-producing region in Valtellina province near Milan that produces red wines from the Nebbiolo grape variety (*pronounced* in fáirnō)

infiltration
the action of rainwater as it soaks downwards into the soil. As the surface layers become waterlogged the water seeps down into lower dry layers.

ingredient
one of the components of a mixture. For example, grape juice is an ingredient of wine.

♀ **inky**
1. (*tasting term*) used to describe the unpleasant, slightly metallic flavour that is present in some red wines
2. (*tasting term*) used to describe the deep red colour of some red wines

inner staves
oak barrel staves suspended in wine, as a cheap way of adding oak flavour

inorganic
used to describe a substance that does not come from animal or vegetable sources and does not contain carbon. Inorganic chemicals are widely used, e.g. copper is in Bordeaux mixture for use against blight, and sulphur is used against mildew.

inorganic fertiliser
an artificial synthesised fertiliser, as opposed to manure, compost and other organic fertilisers that are produced from bones, blood and other parts of formerly living matter

inorganic pesticide, inorganic fungicide, inorganic herbicide
a pesticide, fungicide or herbicide made from inorganic substances such as copper or sulphur

insecticide
a natural or synthetic substance that kills insects. In agriculture most pesticides are either chlorinated hydrocarbons, organophosphorous compounds or carbamate compounds, although some are produced from plant extracts. Insecticides are used in a number of ways, including spraying and dusting, or in granular forms as seed dressings. In the form of a gas, insecticides are used to fumigate greenhouses and granaries.

♀ insipid
(*tasting term*) used to describe a wine that has no particularly good characteristics and lacks body and flavour

Institute of Masters of Wine *see* Master of Wine

Institut National des Appellations d'Origine
France the regulating body responsible for the rules that apply to the Appellations d'Origine Contrôlées in France. (*pronounced* áNstee tǒo nassyə naál dayz appə lássyoN dori zheén)
Abbreviation **INAO**

Instituto Nacional de Denominaciones de Origen
Spain the regulating body responsible for the rules that apply to the Denominaciones de Origen in Spain (*pronounced* insti tǒotō nathyo naál day de nómmi nath yónness day o reé hen)
Abbreviation **INDO**

♀ integration
(*tasting term*) the way in which the structure and other characteristics of a wine combine to form a harmonious whole

♀ intense
(*tasting term*) used to describe a wine with a powerful, concentrated flavour or aroma

internodal
situated between the nodes on a plant's stem

interspecific cross *see* hybrid

interveinal
situated between the veins of a leaf

interveinal chlorosis, interveinal yellowing
a condition of plants caused by magnesium deficiency, in which the surface of the leaves turns yellow and the veins stay green

intraspecific cross *see* hybrid

♀ **intricate**
(*tasting term*) used to describe a wine with a complex bouquet or flavour

invecchiato
Italian aged (*pronounced* in véki aátō)

◊ **Inzolia**
a Sicilian white-wine grape that is grown for use in Marsala and to produce a light fragrant table wine. (*pronounced* ínzō leé a)
Also called **Ansonica**

◊ **Iona**
a white-wine grape variety developed as a hybrid in New York, USA, and often used for sparkling wines produced in the eastern USA

IPR *abbreviation Portuguese* Indicação de Proveniencia Regulamentada

iron deficiency
a lack of iron in the growing medium, resulting in yellowing leaves. Iron deficiency occurs in chalky soils, or in soil that has been limed too much; it can be corrected by applying iron chelate solution. The role of iron in the physiology of plants appears to be associated with specific enzymatic reactions and the production of chlorophyll. Iron deficiency occurs always in soils with a pH of over 7.5. It affects young leaves, which appear scorched. It should be dealt with by reducing the pH level by adding peat. Aluminium sulphate or ferrous sulphate can be used, but they may have the effect of making the phosphate in the soil unavailable to plants, resulting in phosphorus deficiency.

Irouléguy AOC
France a small appellation in the Basque region of France, near the western Pyrénées, that produces red, rosé and white wines from local grape varieties, including Tannat (*pronounced* ee roó lay geé)

irrigation
the artificial supplying and application of water to land with growing crops. Irrigation can be carried out using powered rotary sprinklers, rain guns or spray lines or by channelling water along underground pipes or small irrigation canals from reservoirs or rivers.

☼ Irsai Olivér, Irsay Oliver
an eastern European hybrid white grape variety that produces an aromatic white wine rather like a Muscat. 'Irsai Olivér' is the Hungarian form of the name and 'Irsay Oliver' the Slovakian. (*pronounced* éershī ólivair)

☼ Isabella
a red-wine hybrid grape variety grown decreasingly in parts of Georgia, Brazil, Switzerland and Uruguay.
Also called **Americano**

Ischia DOC
Italy a DOC area on the island of Ischia in the bay of Naples in Italy that produces small quantities of red and white wines. The reds are often made with the Piedirosso grape variety. (*pronounced* íski ə)

isinglass
a type of gelatin obtained from freshwater sturgeon fish and once used in fining red wines. It is now replaced mostly by gelatin made from cattle bones.

ISO glass
a standard shape and size of the ideal glass for use when tasting wine, established by the International Organization for Standardization.
See also **glass**

Isonzo DOC
Italy a DOC area in northeastern Italy growing a wide range of grape varieties but producing particularly good red wine from Cabernet Sauvignon and Cabernet Franc grapes and white wine from Chardonnay and Sauvignon Blanc (*pronounced* ee zóntsō)

Italian vermouth
a dark-coloured sweet vermouth made in Italy

Italy
the second-largest wine-producing country in the world. Italy has a wide range of climatic regions, from cool mountain ranges in the north to hot regions in the south, and grows an equally wide range of grape varieties. Within Italy there are 20 large grape-growing regions, which have smaller areas and vineyards within them. There are 900,000 registered vineyards. The Italian wines are classified in a system similar to the French Appellation

d'Origine Contrôlée: the highest-quality wines are listed as DOCG (Denominazione di Origine Controllata e Garantita), which so far only applies to fifteen areas; DOC (Denominazione di Origine Controllata) includes a wide range of medium-quality wines; Vino Tipico refers to a lower-quality local wine; the lowest quality of wine is classed as Vino da Tavola (table wine). Italy is a mixture of fierce tradition and sophisticated modern methods, and vines are grown everywhere from north to south. In Piedmont, in the northwest, the Nebbiolo grape produces the fine wines of Barolo and Barbaresco, and the Dolcetto and Barbera varieties are also found. On the other side of the country, in Friuli-Venezia, Alto Adige and the Veneto, indigenous white grapes such as Garganega, Tocai and Ribolla Gialla vie with the imported varieties, Sauvignon Blanc, Pinot Gris (Pinot Grigio) and Chardonnay. The popular light, sparkling red wine Lambrusco comes from central Italy, and Tuscany provides the world with Chianti. Of note also are the wines from this area known as Supertuscans.

See also **Sicily**

Wine regions of Italy

J

Wine is the most healthful / and most hygienic / of beverages.
Louis Pasteur, 1873

Jaboulet-Aîné, Paul
a well-known négociant and grower in the Rhône region of France, producing good quality red and white wines (*pronounced* zhábboo lay ay náy)

Jacob's Creek
Australia a well-respected winery in the Barossa Valley region of South Australia, producing good red and white still wines from Riesling, Sémillon, Chardonnay, Merlot, Cabernet Sauvignon and Syrah (Shiraz) grape varieties. Britons drink more than 30 million bottles of Jacob's Creek a year.

☌ Jacquère
a white-wine grape variety grown mostly in the Savoie region of eastern France to produce dry, light white wines (*pronounced* zha káir)

Jadot, Louis *see* Maison Louis Jadot

Jaffelin
an old-established négociant in Beaune in the Burgundy region of France (*pronounced* zhaf láN)

Jahrgang
German year, or vintage year (*pronounced* yaár gang, *plural* Jahrgänge)

James Herrick Wines
an Australian-owned wine-producing company in the Languedoc-Roussillon region of southern France best-known for producing white wines from Chardonnay and full red wines from Syrah grapes

♀ jammy
(*tasting term*) used to describe a wine with a strong, sweet, fruity taste of berries

jaune
French yellow. (*pronounced* zhōn)
See also **vin jaune**

Jerez-Xérès-Sherry DO
Spain a DO area in southwestern Spain, with Jerez de la Frontera as its main city, where sherry is made, particularly centred on a smaller subregion called Jerez Superior that has soil better suited to the grapes required to make sherry. (*pronounced* hé reth hé ress shérri)
See also **sherry**

Jerez-Xérès-Sherry Manzanilla
Spain a sherry-producing area of southwestern Spain comprising the Jerez-Xérès-Sherry and Manzanilla Sanlúcar de Barrameda DOs (*pronounced* hé reth hé ress shérri manthə neélyə)

jeroboam
an oversize wine bottle that can hold the equivalent of four standard bottles of sparkling wine in the Champagne region (3 litres) or six standard bottles of wine in the Bordeaux region (4 litres)

jeropiga, geropiga
Portuguese partially fermented sweet grape juice that is used to blend with port wines to sweeten the blend (*pronounced* zhair róppigə)

🕏 **Johannisberg Riesling** *another name for* **Riesling**

joven
Spanish used to describe a wine from the previous year's harvest and with little or no oak ageing (*pronounced* khóven, *literally* 'young')

jug wine
a cheap wine sold in large bottles or plastic containers. Originally jug wines were those sold to customers who brought and filled their own containers in the shop or cellar.

♀ **juicy**
(*tasting term*) used to describe a wine with a lot of sweet fruit

Juliénas AOC
France a cru (village and surrounding area) in the Beaujolais region of France growing Gamay grapes to produce relatively full-bodied red wines (*pronounced* zhóol yay naá)

Jumilla DO
Spain a DO area in eastern Spain growing the Monastrell grape to produce hearty red wines with high alcohol levels and the Merseguera grape to produce ordinary white wines (*pronounced* hoo meélyə)

Jura
France a wine region named after the Jura Mountains of eastern France near the Swiss border that produces a wide range of wines but is best-known for a vin jaune ('yellow wine') that is similar to a pale sherry (*pronounced* zhŏo rá)

Jurançon AOC
France an appellation in the Pyrénées region of southwestern France that produces dry, aromatic white wines from local varieties of grape (*pronounced* zhóor aaN sóN)

K

Truth comes out in wine.   Pliny the Elder, 77

Kabinett
German the lowest of the six categories in the German classification for its highest-quality wines (Qualitätswein mit Prädikat, QmP). These wines tend also to be the driest. Kabinett is
also the first subcategory of Qualitätswein in Austria. (*pronounced* kábbi nét)

Kadarka
a red-wine grape variety grown widely in Hungary and many
other eastern European countries where it is used to produce
full-bodied, spicy red wines with high levels of tannin (*pronounced* kúdurkə)

Kaiserstuhl-Tuniberg
Germany one of the 43 Bereich regions of Germany, neighbouring the French Alsace region and growing Müller-Thurgau,
Pinot Gris and Pinot Noir grape varieties (*pronounced* kīzər
shtool toóni bairg)

Kakheti
Georgia a wine-producing region in the southeast of Georgia
that grows 70% of the country's wine grapes

Kartli
Georgia a large wine-producing region in Georgia that grows
grapes mainly for sparkling wines

Kasel
Germany a wine-producing area in the Mosel-Saar-Ruwer region of Germany with many individual Einzellagen (vineyards)
producing good white wines from Riesling grapes (*pronounced*
kaáz'l)

Katnook Estate
Australia one of the most respected estates in the Coonawarra
region of South Australia, near Adelaide, producing a range
of red wines from Cabernet Sauvignon and Merlot grape
varieties, white wines from Sauvignon Blanc and Chardonnay,

a sparkling white wine from Chardonnay and a sweet wine from botrytised Riesling

keg
a small barrel used to age or store wine

Kékfrankos *another name for* **Blaufränkisch** (*pronounced* káyk frunkosh, *used in* Hungary)

Kéknyelü
a white-wine grape variety that was once widely grown in Hungary but is now grown in few vineyards. It produces slightly sweet white wines. (*pronounced* káyk nyellŏ)

Keller
German a cellar, especially in an estate or vineyard (*pronounced* kéllər, *plural* **Keller**)

Kellerei
German a wine cellar, especially at a wine merchant (*pronounced* kéllə rī, *plural* **Kellereien**)

Kendall-Jackson
a large wine-producing company based in California, USA, but with interests also in Chile and Argentina

Kent Rasmussen Winery *see* **A Winemaker's View**

Keppoch *see* **Padthaway**

Kerner
a white hybrid grape variety grown mostly in Germany to produce wine similar to Riesling (*pronounced* káirnər)

kick-up, kick *same as* **punt**

King Valley
Australia a wine-producing region in northeastern Victoria

kir
a popular apéritif invented in the Burgundy region of France, in which a tiny spoonful of crème de cassis (a blackcurrant liqueur) is added to a glass of dry white wine to give it a pale pink colour. If it is dark pink, it has too much cassis and will be too sweet to drink. (*pronounced* keer)

Királyleányka
a native Hungarian white grape variety producing an aromatic, grapey white wine (*pronounced* kí raa le aa nyəkə)

kir royale
a popular variation on the traditional kir in which sparkling white wine or Champagne is used instead of still dry white wine. (*pronounced* kéer roy aál)
See also **kir**

Klein Constantia
South Africa a wine-producing estate in Constantia in Cape Province, South Africa, producing superb Sauvignon Blanc and Sémillon wines but also a sweet dessert wine made from Muscat à Petits Grains grapes (*pronounced* kláyn kon staántya)

☿ **Klevner** *another name for* **Pinot Blanc** (*pronounced* kléfnər, *used in* Alsace, France)

Kloster Eberbach
Germany an ancient former Cistercian monastery, now state-owned, in the Rheingau region of Germany that produces Steinberg, a famous Riesling (*pronounced* klőstər áybər baakh)

Knappstein, Tim
a well-respected winemaker based in the Adelaide Hills region of South Australia, producing a range of good wines based on Chardonnay, Pinot Noir and Sauvignon Blanc grape varieties (*pronounced* náp stīn)

Knights Valley AVA
USA a small appellation in Sonoma County, California, between Napa Valley AVA and Alexander Valley AVA, that grows mainly Cabernet Sauvignon grapes for red wines

kokineli
Greek on retsina labels, rosé.
See **retsina**

kosher wine
a wine made according to strict Jewish law, subject to inspection by a rabbi and with each step of the process handled only by Orthodox Jews

Krug
a famous Champagne house in the Champagne region of France, producing high-quality non-vintage wine (called Grande Cuvée) and a small quantity of vintage and rosé (*pronounced* kroog)

KWV
S African the South African Cooperative Wine-growers Association, a leading exporter of wine and spirits from South Africa.
Full form **Ko-operatiewe Wijnbowers Vereniging**

*The Wine of Life keeps oozing drop by drop, / The Leaves of Life keep
falling one by one.*   Edward FitzGerald, 1859

label
a piece of printed paper that is stuck around a bottle of wine
giving the name of the wine and other details about the wine and
its origins

labelling information
information printed on the label of a wine bottle. Some of the
information is required by law, some is provided by the producer. The alcoholic content by volume and the volume of the
wine contained in the bottle must be shown, and still wines
usually include the year the grapes were picked, the name of the
vineyard or estate and the name of the importer or négociant.
Wines from some countries also include the name of the village
or appellation, the standard to which the wine was made or the
grading supplied for the wine by the country's quality standard
and the name of the predominant grape used in making the
wine. Lastly, the label also includes the name of the importer.
Some countries such as the USA also require the sulphite levels
to be noted together with a government health warning.

labrusca *see* Vitis labrusca

La Côte
Switzerland a wine-producing area in Switzerland growing
mostly Chasselas grapes for white wine (*pronounced* la kőt)

lactic acid
a natural acid that occurs in wine, as well as in many other foods
and drinks, and is only noticeable if the wine has undergone
malolactic fermentation

Lafite-Rothschild, Château
France a famous vineyard in the Pauillac AOC in the Médoc
district of Bordeaux in southwestern France, producing a red
wine graded premier cru (first growth) in the classification of
1855 (*pronounced* la feet rot sheeld)

lagar

a large stone trough traditionally used to tread and ferment grapes when making port or sherry. It has now largely been replaced by crushing machines and stainless steel vats. (*pronounced* la gaár, *plural* **lagares**)

La Grande Dame *see* **Veuve Clicquot**

♢ **Lagrein**

a red-wine grape variety grown mostly in the Trentino-Alto Adige region of Italy and used to make big red wines and good rosé wines (*pronounced* laag rín)

LAI *abbreviation* leaf area index

Lake County

USA a large county in California that covers part of the North Coast AVA but also includes three smaller AVAs within its boundaries, Benmore Valley, Clear Lake and Guenoc Valley. It grows mostly Chardonnay, Cabernet Sauvignon, Sauvignon Blanc and Zinfandel grape varieties.

Lake Erie AVA

USA a viticultural area that takes in parts of the states of Pennsylvania, Ohio and New York. It produces wine from classic vines, hybrids and native American varieties.

Lalande-de-Pomerol AOC

France an appellation in the Pomerol district of the Bordeaux region of southwestern France, growing mostly Merlot grapes to produce good red wines (*pronounced* la laáNd də pommə ról)

La Mancha DO

Spain the largest wine-producing DO region in Spain in the central Castilla-la Mancha region, producing good everyday red, white and rosé wines (*pronounced* la máncha)

♢ **Lambrusco**

a red-wine grape variety that is widely grown across Italy, especially in the Emilia-Romagna region (*pronounced* lam broóskō, *plural* **Lambruscos**)

Lambrusco di Sorbara DOC

Italy a DOC area in the Emilia-Romagna region of northern Italy that grows Lambrusco grapes to produce a well-known slightly sparkling (frizzante), medium sweet, pale red wine (*pronounced* lam broóskō di sawr baárə)

la Mejanelle *see* **Coteaux de la Mejanelle**

La Mission Haut-Brion, Château
France a cru classé château in the Pessac-Léognan AOC in the Graves district of the Bordeaux region of France. Its top-quality red wine is made from Cabernet Sauvignon, Merlot and Cabernet Franc grapes. (*pronounced* la meéss yoN ō bree yóN)

◊ **Lancers**
a brand of medium sweet, slightly sparkling rosé Portuguese wine that is especially sold in the USA

Landwein
German a category within the German wine classification that relates to its table wine, Deutscher Tafelwein, and describes a better class of table wine. These wines have low levels of sugar, so are dry (trocken) or slightly sweet (halbtrocken) and are roughly equivalent to the French vins de pays. (*pronounced* lánd vīn, *plural* **Landweine**)

Languedoc
France a wine-producing area of southern France, the eastern part of the Languedoc-Roussillon region. (*pronounced* laáNgə dok)
See also **Coteaux du Languedoc AOC**

Languedoc-Roussillon
France a large and rapidly improving wine-producing area in southern France stretching along the Mediterranean coast and producing over a third of all the wine produced in France. It includes 4 of the 95 administrative départements (Aude, Gard, Hérault and Pyrénées-Orientales). Most of the wine is red, from Carignan, Cinsault and Grenache grape varieties. There are four areas of AOC status: Fitou, Corbières, Minervois and Coteaux du Languedoc. In its more than 500 cooperatives Languedoc-Roussillon also makes more wine of vin ordinaire quality than any other part of France, as well as a huge quantity of vin de pays, labelled as Vin de Pays d'Oc. Merlot, Cabernet Sauvignon, Chardonnay and Sauvignon Blanc are used in vins de pays (they are not permitted in the AOC wines) and are most often sold as varietals. (*pronounced* laáNgə dok roóssi yoN)
Also called **Midi**

♀ **lanolin**
(*tasting term*) a creamy flavour and aroma associated with wines made from Sémillon and Chenin Blanc grapes

Lanson
a well-known Champagne house in the Champagne region of France, best-known for its non-vintage Black Label Champagne but also producing a good vintage Champagne (*pronounced* laáN soN)

Lardot *another name for* **Macabeo**

La Rioja Alavesa, La Rioja Alta, La Rioja Baja *see* **Rioja DOCa**

La Romanée AOC
France a very small vineyard appellation in the village of Vosne-Romanée in the Burgundy region of France classed as a grand cru and producing some of the very best red wine in the region. It grows Pinot Noir grapes to produce some of the best red wines of Burgundy. (*pronounced* la rō ma náy)

La Tâche AOC
France a vineyard appellation in the Burgundy region of France producing some of the very best red wine in the region. Rated grand cru, like its neighbouring vineyard, Romanée-Conti, it grows Pinot Noir grapes on the small vineyard to produce rich, intense red wines. (*pronounced* la taásh)

late bottled vintage *abbreviation* **LBV**
See **port**

late disgorged
used to describe a sparkling wine that has been aged on the lees longer than normal, providing more flavour, before it goes through the process of disgorgement, when the sediment is removed

late harvest
used on wine labels to refer to a wine made from grapes left on the vine to ripen, often till almost dry and raisin-like, then picked. This gives the grapes much higher than normal levels of sugar and can also include grapes affected with *Botrytis cinerea* rot, further concentrating sugar levels. The result is a very rich, sweet dessert wine.

lateral
1. a bud or shoot that branches off from the main branch of a vine
2. a root that branches off a main root

latitude
the geographical location of a vineyard described using the
parallel rings around the Earth running east-west. Vineyards
in different countries on the same latitude can have similar
climates and growing conditions.

Latium *see* **Lazio** (*pronounced* látti əm)

Latour, Château
France a château in the Pauillac district of the Haut-Médoc in
the Bordeaux region of southwestern France, graded premier
cru (first growth) in the classification of 1855. It grows Cabernet
Sauvignon grapes to produce red wine that ages well. The
second-label wine is labelled Les Forts de Latour. (*pronounced*
la toór)

Latour, Louis
a vineyard-owner and négociant in the Côte d'Or region of
Burgundy, best-known for his good-quality white wines and
range of red wines (*pronounced* la toór)

La Tour Blanche, Château
France a château in the Sauternes area of Bordeaux, graded
premier cru (first growth, below only Château d'Yquem) in the
classification of 1855. The estate was given to the French
government at the start of the 20th century and is now a college
of viticulture. (*pronounced* la toór blaáNsh)

La Tour-Carnet, Château
France a château in the Haut-Médoc area of Bordeaux graded
quatrième cru (fourth growth) in the classification of 1855. It
produces good red wines from Cabernet Sauvignon, Merlot,
Cabernet Franc and Petit Verdot grape varieties. (*pronounced* la
toór kaar náy)

l'Aubance *see* **Coteaux de l'Aubance AOC**

Laurent Perrier
a Champagne house in Tours-sur-Marne in the Champagne
region of France, producing a large quantity of non-vintage
Champagne, a premium Cuvée Grand Siècle and its vintage
Champagne Millésime Rare (*pronounced* law raáN pérree ay)

Lavaux
Switzerland a wine-growing region in the Vaud canton in
Switzerland, producing some of the country's best white wines
from Chasselas grapes (*pronounced* la võ)

laying down
the act of storing wine in the correct environment to age and improve it.
See also **temperature; wine cellar**

Layon *see* **Coteaux de Layon AOC**

Lazio
Italy a wine-producing region around Rome that includes 16 DOC areas and produces predominantly white wines from Trebbiano and Malvasia grapes. (*pronounced* látsi ō)
Also called **Latium**

LBV *abbreviation* late bottled vintage (port)

lead
The lead content of modern wines is generally extremely low. Lead in wine is caused mainly by two things, lead wrappers around the top of a bottle (now almost totally replaced with aluminium foil or plastic wrappers) and the possible leaching of lead from crystal decanters if used to store wines for an extended period.

leaf
While leaves are needed for photosynthesis to occur, which provides some of the energy for a plant, if a vine produces too many leaves, it could produce too little fruit; leaf, or canopy, control is therefore important in viticulture. The leaves can also shade the grape berries from the sun, which would prevent them ripening well, and the different vine training and canopy management techniques are designed to avoid this.

leaf area index
the area of green leaf exposed to sunlight per unit area of ground.
Abbreviation **LAI**

leaf axil
the angle above a leaf stem at the point where it is attached to a plant shoot where buds develop

leaf burn
damage done to leaves by severe weather conditions or herbicides

leafroll virus
a disease affecting vines that leads to reduced yields and quality. The leaves curl and the grapes ripen slowly.

leaf to fruit ratio
a measurement of the ability of a vine to provide enough energy through photosynthesis for development while maintaining the yield and quality of the crop. The ratio is affected by the way in which the vine has been trained.

♀ **leafy**
(*tasting term*) used to describe a wine that has a flavour or aroma reminiscent of green leaves

leaker
a bottle of wine in which wine is slowly oozing from the cork

♀ **lean**
(*tasting term*) used to describe a wine that is low on fruit with noticeable acidity. Leanness is not necessarily a bad quality.
Compare **fleshy**

♫ **Leányka**
a white-wine grape variety grown in Hungary and Romania that produces soft white wines that are often medium sweet (*pronounced* láy annyəkə)

♀ **leathery**
(*tasting term*) used to describe a wine with a definite smell and taste of new leather, normally a big red wine with a lot of tannin

Lebanon
a country whose wine exports are dominated by the Château Musar vineyard, which has endured the wars to produce a range of high quality red wines and a range of white wines.
See also **Musar, Château**

Le Cigare Volant *see* **Bonny Doon Vineyard** (*pronounced* lə seegaár vo laáN)

lees
solid waste matter such as bits of grape skin, pips and pulp, that gradually sinks to the bottom of a cask or barrel. Some wines, especially white wines, are stored with this waste matter (called being 'kept on its lees') for a period of time to improve the complexity and structure of the wine. If a wine is to be stored on its lees in this way, the winemaker does not need to add as much sulphur to prevent oxidation during the ageing process in the cellar, although this calls for careful winemaking to prevent excess influence on the wine's taste from the lees. In a sparkling wine the lees consists of dead yeast cells that are removed during disgorgement.
Compare **sediment**

lees contact

the process of leaving a wine in contact with the lees to try and encourage the development of more flavour in the wine.
See also **sur lie**

lees stirring

the process of stirring the lees in the bottoms of barrels containing white wines, usually Chardonnays, to increase their complexity.
Also called **batonnage**

Leeuwin Estate

Australia a wine-producing estate in the Margaret River area of Western Australia, producing excellent-quality red wine from Cabernet Sauvignon grapes and white wine from Chardonnay

♀ **legs**

(*tasting term*) long lines of wine that run down the inside of the glass after the wine has been swirled around the glass. Higher alcohol content in the wine produces thicker legs that move slowly down the inside of the glass.

Lehmann *see* **Peter Lehmann**

Lemnos

an island appellation in eastern Greece that grows especially Muscat and the native Limnio grapes

♀ **lemony**

(*tasting term*) used to describe a white wine that is slightly acidic and reminiscent of fresh lemons

♀ **length**

(*tasting term*) the amount of time a wine's flavour and aroma will stay on the palate after the wine is swallowed.
See also **finish**

Lenz Moser

Austria a well-respected winemaking company based near Krems in Austria, producing very-good-quality red wines from Cabernet Sauvignon and Zweigelt grape varieties as well as premium white wines (*pronounced* lénts mózər)

Léoville-Barton, Château

France a château in the Saint-Julien AOC in the Médoc district of Bordeaux in southwestern France, graded troisième cru (third growth) in the classification of 1855. It produces very good red wines. (*pronounced* láy ō veel baar tóN)

Léoville Las-Cases, Château

France a château in the Saint-Julien AOC in the Médoc district of Bordeaux in southwestern France, graded deuxième cru (second growth) in the classification of 1855. This large estate produces powerful red wines of very good quality. (*pronounced* láy ō veel laass kaáz)

Le Pin, Château

France a famous château in the Pomerol district of Bordeaux, southwestern France, producing tiny quantities of superb-quality red wines which are possibly the most expensive and most sought-after red wines in the world. Le Pin is the original microchâteau and a mere 500–600 cases of its cult wines are produced in the garage under a small house on the property. (*pronounced* le páN)

Les Forts de Latour *see* Latour, Château (*pronounced* lay fáwr də la toór)

l'Hérault *see* Hérault

◊ Liebfraumilch

a style of sweet, often cheap, white wine exported in vast quantity from Germany. It originates in the Rheinhessen region and is made from Müller-Thurgau, Sylvaner, Kerner or Riesling grapes. It is in the QbA category of wine quality classification used in Germany. (*pronounced* leéb frow milkh)

♀ lifted

(*tasting term*) used to describe a bouquet of full-bodied red wines produced by volatile acidity

♀ light

1. (*tasting term*) used to describe a wine that is low in alcohol, a wine that has a light texture or light body, or a wine that is young and fruity and ready to drink young
2. *USA* used, almost exclusively in California, to describe wine that has fewer calories than normal wine.
See also light wine

♀ light-bodied *see* body

light soil

soil consisting mainly of large particles that are loosely held together because of the relatively large pore space. Light soil is usually easier to cultivate than heavy soil, but may dry out too quickly.

light wine
USA a wine with less than 14% alcohol per unit volume. This is an official categorisation.

Liguria
Italy a region on the northwestern coast of Italy, next to the French border, that has few DOC areas and produces red, white and rosé wines (*pronounced* li goóri ə)

♡ **Limburger** *another name for* **Blaufränkisch** (*pronounced* lím boŏrgər)

lime¹
calcium compounds used to spread on soil to increase the pH level and correct acidity. Lime is usually applied as simple chalk or limestone. It takes time to affect the soil's pH level.

♀ **lime²**
(*tasting term*) a taste or aroma associated with Australian white wines made from the Riesling grape variety

limited bottling
a marketing term used to describe wine that is supposedly produced in small quantities

♡ **Limnio**
a dark grape variety grown on the island of Lemnos, northeastern Greece, and in parts of the northeastern mainland

Limousin
France a region in the south of France, near the town of Limoges, that grows the oak used in many wine barrels. This oak has a more open grain than other oak woods which may allow the oak flavour to be extracted quickly. (*pronounced* lee moo záN)

♀ **limpid**
(*tasting term*) used to describe wine that is brilliant and bright

Lindauer
New Zealand a well-known winery producing good-quality sparkling wines from Pinot Noir and Chardonnay grape varieties (*pronounced* lín dow ər)

Lindemans
Australia a wine-producing estate in the Hunter Valley area of New South Wales, Australia producing good-quality red wine from Syrah (Shiraz) grapes and white wines from Chardonnay and Sémillon (*pronounced* líndəmənz)

Lingenfelder *see* Weingut Lingenfelder

♀ lingering
(*tasting term*) used to describe a wine whose flavour persists on the palate for a long time after tasting.
Compare long

liqueur
a strong, sweet alcoholic drink, often made from wine, usually taken after a meal. Most liqueurs are sold under trade names.

liqueur de tirage
French same as dosage 1 (*pronounced* lee kúr də tee ra<u>azh</u>, *plural* liqueurs de tirage)

liqueur d'expédition
French same as dosage 1 (*pronounced* lee kúr dek spə díssyoN, *plural* liqueurs d'expédition)

◊ Liqueur Muscat
an Australian dessert wine made from Muscat grapes

liquoureux
French (*tasting term*) used to describe a sweet dessert wine (*pronounced* lee koo rố)

♀ liquorice
(*tasting term*) a taste or aroma associated with young tannic red wines, e.g. from the Rhône region of France, and also with red or white wines made from grapes that have been partially dried in the sun

liquoroso
Italian a sweet, fortified wine with a high alcohol content, e.g. Marsala (*pronounced* líkə rốssō, *plural* liquorosi)

Lirac AOC
France a large appellation in the southern Rhône region of France that grows mostly Grenache, Cinsault and Mourvèdre grape varieties to make full-bodied red wines and some rosé wines (*pronounced* lee rák)

Lison-Pramaggiore DOC
Italy a DOC area in the Veneto region of northeastern Italy, growing a range of red and white grapes (*pronounced* leézon pramə jáw ray)

Listrac AOC
France an appellation in the Haut-Médoc district of the Bordeaux region of France producing red wines from Cabernet Franc, Cabernet Sauvignon and Merlot grape varieties (*pronounced* lee strák)

litre
the standard metric unit of volume measurement

♀ **lively**
(*tasting term*) used to describe a wine that is crisp, fresh and fruity

Livermore Valley AVA
USA a small wine-producing area in Almeda County that was one of the first regions to grow vines in California. It now produces a range of wines from Sauvignon Blanc, Cabernet Sauvignon and Chardonnay grape varieties.

lodge
a warehouse where port is stored and aged

Lodi AVA
USA a wine-producing area in the Central Valley region of California that grows Sauvignon Blanc and Zinfandel grape varieties as well as having smaller vineyards growing Chardonnay and Chenin Blanc

Loir *see* **Coteaux du Loir AOC**

Loire
France a famous, large wine-producing region in northeastern France, running along the Loire river and containing a range of famous appellations that produce fine white and red wines and, in Anjou, also rosés (*pronounced* lwaar)

Lombardy
Italy a wine-producing region in northern Italy growing mostly Nebbiolo grapes for red wine and Trebbiano grapes for white wine (*pronounced* lómbərdi)

♀ **long**
(*tasting term*) used to describe a desirable lingering flavour on the palate after the wine has been swallowed

Long Island
USA a wine-producing island in New York State that has two AVAs growing a wide variety of vines: native American, American hybrids, European hybrids and especially classic Bordeaux

Loosen, Dr
a famous winemaker from the Mosel region of Germany, running the family winery and producing a range of very good white wines based on the Riesling grape variety (*pronounced* lōs'n)

Los Carneros *see* Carneros AVA

Louis Roederer
a famous though small grande marque Champagne house in the Champagne region of France producing some of the best Champagnes in the world, including those under its prestige label, Cristal (*pronounced* loó ee rõdərər)

Loupiac AOC
France an appellation in the Bordeaux region of France, growing Sémillon, Sauvignon Blanc and Muscadelle grapes to make a light, sweet white wine similar to Sauternes (*pronounced* loo pee yák)

☿ Loureiro
a white-wine grape variety grown especially in northwestern Portugal to produce Vinho Verde (*pronounced* loo ráyrō)

Lower Great Southern Region
Australia a large region that is part of the state of Western Australia in Australia, growing Cabernet Sauvignon, Syrah (Shiraz) and Merlot grapes to make red wine and growing Riesling, Chardonnay and Sauvignon Blanc to make white wine

Lubéron *see* Côtes du Lubéron AOC

Lunel *see* Muscat de Lunel AOC

Lungarotti
Italy an influential winemaker with vineyards in the Torgiano DOCG in the Umbria region of Italy

Lurton
a family of wine-estate owners and growers in the Bordeaux region of France, some of whose younger members have become viticultural consultants throughout the world (*pronounced* loór toN)

♀ **luscious, lush**
(*tasting term*) used to describe a rich, smooth wine with lots of residual sugar content, e.g. a sweet white wine from Sauternes

Lussac-Saint-Émilion AOC
France an appellation on the outskirts of the Saint-Émilion district of Bordeaux, southwestern France, growing mostly Merlot grapes to produce good red wine (*pronounced* lŏŏ sak sant ay méelyoN)

◊ **Lutomer**
a brand of medium dry white wine produced in Slovenia from Riesling grapes (*pronounced* loo tŏmər)

Luxembourg
a tiny country between Germany and Belgium that produces small quantities of light, fruity white wine from grapes growing along the Mosel (Moselle) river, which forms the border with Germany to the east. It grows mostly Auxerrois Blanc, Elbling, Riesling and Gewürztraminer grape varieties.

LVMH
a giant French company that owns a wide range of luxury brands including Moët-Hennessy (the MH of its name) producing Moët et Chandon Champagne and Hennessy Cognac

♀ **lychee**
(*tasting term*) a taste or aroma associated with white wines made from the Gewürztraminer grape variety

Lynch-Bages, Château
France a château in the Pauillac AOC in the Médoc district of Bordeaux in southwestern France, graded cinquième cru (fifth growth) in the classification of 1855. It produces a fragrant red wine that has always been highly regarded in the UK. (*pronounced* láNsh baáazh)

Lyonnais
(*pronounced* lee o náy)
◊ **1.** a white-wine grape variety grown in small quantities in the Bordeaux region of France
2. *see* **Coteaux du Lyonnais AOC**

lyre
a trellis structure developed in Bordeaux to help train and support vines to improve the yield and quality of the grapes

It's a naive domestic Burgundy, without any breeding. But I think you'll be amused by its presumption.   James Thurber, 1943

☙ **Macabeo**
a white grape variety, now grown widely in Spain, particularly in the Rioja region (where it is often called Viura), that produces high yields of grapes that make light, fruity white wines that are high in acid. The wine does not oxidise easily in the same way as wine from some of the more traditional white Rioja grapes that it has largely displaced. This grape variety is also blended to make sparkling white wines in Spain and is grown in southern France, where it is used to produce Côtes du Roussillon white wine. (*pronounced* mákə báy ō)
Also called **Alcanol**; **Lardot**; **Maccabéo**; **Maccabeu**; **Viura**

☙ **Maccabéo, Maccabeu** *same as* **Macabeo** (*pronounced* mákə báy ō *or* mákə báy oo, *used in* France))

maceration
the period of time during which the grape juice is left in contact with the grape skins, seeds and fragments of stem, and the processes that take place during this time. This period of contact allows the grape juice to take on colour, flavour and acids. In red wines maceration lasts at least as long as primary fermentation, but may be prolonged, in extended maceration, for up to several weeks to increase the colour and flavour. Before primary fermentation some winemakers undertake cold maceration, in which the grape juice is stored with the skins and seeds at a temperature too cold to allow fermentation to start. Carbonic maceration, used particularly in the Loire region of France, involves fermenting the whole bunches of grapes, with their stalks, in a closed container; it produces wine that is full-flavoured with a deep red colour and lots of fruit flavour but low in tannin.

macération carbonique
French carbonic maceration (*pronounced* mássay rássyoN káárbo neék)
See **maceration**

Mâcon AOC
France an appellation that covers a large area of southern Burgundy growing Chardonnay and Gamay grape varieties to produce red, white and rosé wine (*pronounced* má koN)

◊ Mâconnais
(*pronounced* má ko náy)
1. *France* a large wine-producing region in southern Burgundy, just to the north of the Beaujolais region, with the town of Mâcon on the Saône river as its centre. Two-thirds of this region's production is white wine from the Chardonnay grape. Gamay is grown for sale under the Mâcon Rouge label, along with a smaller but increasing quantity of Pinot Noir grapes for wine that can be labelled Bourgogne and sold at a higher price. The region includes a number of its own appellations, including the three regional Mâcon AOCs of Mâcon, Mâcon Supérieur and Mâcon-Villages, as well as a number of villages that have their own appellations, the most famous of which is Pouilly-Fuissé.
2. *another name for* **Altesse**

Mâcon Supérieur AOC
France an appellation that indicates wines produced within the Mâcon AOC but with at least 1% more alcohol per unit volume than the standard red or white wine (*pronounced* má koN sŏo payree úr)

Mâcon-Villages AOC
France an appellation that produces the best-quality white wine of the three Mâconnais appellations. The wines can either be named Mâcon-Villages or Mâcon followed by the name of one of the 43 qualifying local villages, e.g. Mâcon-Viré is a Mâcon-Villages AOC wine. (*pronounced* má koN vee laázh)

macroclimate
the climate over a large area such as the Côte de Nuits
Compare **mesoclimate**; **microclimate**

Madeira DOC
Portugal an island in the Atlantic Ocean about 1,000 kilometres, or 625 miles, off the coast of Portugal. It is a DOC wine-producing area renowned for the famous fortified wine of the same name. It can be one of the longest-living wines in the world. Most Madeira is produced in an unusual way through heat and oxidation, which would usually spoil a wine. This

process is called estufagem, or baking, and in effect accelerates the ageing of the wine. The more ordinary wine is placed in a lined concrete tank containing a stainless steel coil through which hot water circulates for at least three months; finer Madeira is placed in wooden casks and stored in a heated room for a longer time. The finest wine is not heated artificially at all, but is exposed only to the sun. The wine develops a slightly bitter, tangy taste and can vary in colour from pale gold to dark tawny. There are four different styles of Madeira: Sercial is light, dry and pale gold in colour; Verdelho is sweeter and stronger; Boal is sweeter, stronger and darker in colour; finally Malmsey is the sweetest and darkest. Sercial and Verdelho are normally served as an apéritif, Boal and Malmsey as a dessert wine. A historic medium dry style called rainwater is still also sometimes found.

Madera AVA
USA a large wine-producing area of California that covers much of Madera County and part of Fresno County. It grows mostly Colombard and Chenin Blanc grape varieties for white wines and Zinfandel and Grenache for red wines.

♀ maderised
(*tasting term*) used to describe spoiled table wine that has been badly stored and has oxidised, resulting in a wine with a brown colour and flat, oxidised taste

Madiran AOC
France an appellation in southwestern France around the base of the Pyrenean mountains that grows the Tannat grape variety to produce red wines (*pronounced* máddee raaN)

madre
Italian a reduced sweet liquid produced from the previous year's wine, added in the production of vin santo (*literally* 'mother')

Madrid *see* Vinos de Madrid DO

maduro
Portuguese mature or aged (*pronounced* ma doórō)

Magdelaine, Château
France an estate within the Saint-Émilion AOC of Bordeaux in southwestern France, classed as a premier grand cru classé and producing good-quality red wine from Merlot and a small proportion of Cabernet Franc grapes (*pronounced* magdə láyn)

magnum

a bottle that can contain 1.5 litres, twice the size of a standard 750 ml bottle.

See also **double magnum**

Maipo

Chile the smallest and most famous of the wine-producing regions of Chile producing roughly equal quantities of red and white wines, mainly from Cabernet Sauvignon and Sémillon grapes

Maison Louis Jadot

France an influential grower and négociant in Beaune in the Burgundy region of France that owns a range of vineyards in the area producing excellent white wines and very good red wines (*pronounced* máy zoN loʹo ee zha dő)

maître de chai

French a cellar-master who is in charge of the ageing of wines (*pronounced* máytrə də sháy, *plural* **maîtres de chai**)

🍇 **Malaga** *another name for* **Cinsault** (*pronounced* mállagə)

Málaga DO

Spain a small DO region in southern Spain, centred on the city port of Málaga, that, historically, was the dominant area for sweet, fortified wine production in Spain until it was devastated by phylloxera in the late 1870s. The wine was much drunk in the UK and USA under the name 'Mountain'. Now sherry from the neighbouring Jerez area is the best-known sweet, fortified wine of Spain. The Málaga region still produces sweet, fortified wines from Moscatel or Pedro Ximénez grapes in a range of styles, some using the solera system. To qualify for DO status, wines must be aged within the city of Málaga. The sweetness can result from stopping fermentation by adding grape spirit, by adding concentrated unfermented grape must before or after fermentation, or, less commonly now, by the traditional method of drying the grapes in the sun. (*pronounced* mállagə)

🍇 **Malbec**

a red-wine grape grown in the Bordeaux, Loire and Cahors regions of France, in parts of California, USA, and widely in Argentina and Chile. This grape produces wines with an intense deep red colour with a berry flavour. Malbec is used alone to produce good fruity reds in Chile and Argentina but is blended with other varieties when it is used in France. (*pronounced* mál bek)

Malepère *see* **Côtes de la Malepère AOC**

Malescot-Saint Exupéry, Château
France an estate within the Margaux AOC in the Médoc district of Bordeaux in southwestern France, graded troisième cru (third growth) in the classification of 1855. The red wines are made from a blend of Cabernet Sauvignon, Merlot, Cabernet Franc and Petit Verdot grape varieties. (*pronounced* maálə skō saNt ekzoo pereé)

malic acid
an acid present within grapes that is converted to the milder lactic acid during the malolactic fermentation process in wine-making

Malmsey
(*pronounced* maámzi)
1. *another name for* **Malvasia** (*used in* Madeira)
2. the sweetest and darkest of the fortified wines from the Madeira DOC on the island of Madeira

Malmsey-style
used to describe sweet, dark fortified wine that is produced with grape varieties that are good but not classic or historically correct for Malmsey Madeira. True Malmsey Madeira should be made with at least 85% of the Malvasia grape variety.

malolactic fermentation, malolactic secondary fermentation
a bacterial secondary fermentation that converts the malic acid present in grapes into the milder lactic acid, with a by-product of carbon dioxide gas. Almost all red wines include this second stage of fermentation, but producers of white wine often prevent this stage to ensure that the wine tastes crisp and sharp. It is also avoided when the grapes are overripe and too sweet.
Also called **secondary fermentation**
Compare **primary fermentation**
Abbreviation **M-L**

✿ **Malvasia**
a grape variety that has both black and lighter-skinned forms and is used in many different styles of wine, white or light red. Malvasia is one of the most widely planted grapes in Italy. In Madeira it is the main constituent of its classic fortified wines. (*pronounced* mal váyziə)
Also called **Malmsey**; **Malvoisie**

◊ **Malvasia Bianco**
a white-skinned form of the Malvasia grape variety, grown in
the Tuscany, Umbria and Lazio regions of Italy to produce
flavoursome white wine that is often used to give character to
blends (*pronounced* mal váyziə byángkō)

◊ **Malvasia Nera, Malvasia Rossa**
a dark-skinned form of the Malvasia grape variety, grown in the
Apulia, Tuscany and Piedmont regions of Italy to produce
flavoursome red wine that is usually used in blends (*pronounced*
mal váyziə náyrrə *or* mal váyziə ráwssə)

Malvedos *see* **Graham, W. & J.**

◊ **Malvoisie** *another name for* **Malvasia** (*pronounced* mál vwaa
zeé, *used in* France)

Mancha *see* **La Mancha DO**

manhole
a large opening in the side of a wine tank through which the
pomace and lees can be removed after the wine is drained off

◊ **Manseng**
a grape variety that is used for sweet white wines, particularly in
the southwestern region of France. It has two clones: Gros
Manseng and Petit Manseng. Gros Manseng is often used for
drier sweet wines; Petit Manseng has smaller berries than Gros
Manseng and a thicker skin, giving the wines a stronger flavour.
Neither type is widely grown. (*pronounced* maaN saN)

manzanilla
a dry, tangy style of fortified fino sherry produced in the Manzanilla Sanlúcar de Barrameda DO in the Jerez region of southwestern Spain (*pronounced* mánzə neélyə *or* mántha neélyə)
See **sherry**

manzanilla pasada *see* **sherry** (*pronounced* mánzə neélyə pə
saádə *or* mántha neélyə)

Manzanilla Sanlúcar de Barrameda DO
Spain a sherry-producing DO in the Jerez region of southwestern Spain centred on the coastal town of Sanlúcar de
Barrameda and producing manzanilla (*pronounced* mánzə
neélyə san loókə day barə máydə *or* mántha neélyə)

marc
(*pronounced* maar)
1. *French* the residue (pomace) of grape skins, seeds and fragments of stalks left after grapes have been pressed

2. a distilled spirit (eau de vie) made in many parts of the world by distilling pomace. In Italy it is called grappa.

Marcobrunn
Germany a small, but famous, Einzellage (vineyard) in the Rheingau region of Germany producing full-bodied, aromatic white wines (*pronounced* maárkō broŏn)

♀ Maréchal Foch
a red hybrid grape variety grown in the eastern USA and Canada to produce light red wines (*pronounced* má ray shal fósh)

Margaret River
Australia a well-known wine-producing area in Western Australia successfully growing Chardonnay, Sémillon, Cabernet Sauvignon, Merlot and other grape varieties

Margaux, Château
France a château in the Médoc district of Bordeaux in south-western France graded premier cru (first growth) in the classification of 1855. It produces deep, full-bodied red wines mainly from Cabernet Sauvignon and Merlot grapes, and also produces a little white wine from Sauvignon Blanc grapes. (*pronounced* maar gō̃)

Margaux AOC
France a famous appellation in the Médoc district of Bordeaux in southwestern France that includes vineyards around the village of Margaux. It has 21 cru classé châteaux topped by Château Margaux. The AOC grows Cabernet Sauvignon, Cabernet Franc, Merlot and some Petit Verdot grapes for its red wines. (*pronounced* maar gō̃)

♀ Maria Gomes *another name for* **Fernão Pires** (*used in* the Bairrada region of Portugal) (*pronounced* ma reéa go mésh)

Marino DOC
Italy a wine-producing area in the Latium region of Italy, southeast of Rome, that grows Malvasia, Trebbiano and Bonvino grape varieties to produce dry, still white wines that are similar in style to Frascati (*pronounced* mə reénō)

maritime climate
the climate of growing regions near the coast that normally enjoy a temperate climate warmed during the day and cooled by sea breezes at night. New Zealand is one example of a region

with a maritime climate that benefits growing and ripening.
Compare **continental climate**

Markgräflerland
Germany a large wine-producing Bereich (subregion) in the
Baden region of Germany, growing mostly Chasselas (Gutedel),
Müller-Thurgau and Pinot Noir (Spätburgunder) grape vari-
eties (*pronounced* maark gráyfflər land)

Marlborough
New Zealand the largest wine-producing region in the country,
in the South Island, with close to 40% of all the vineyards.
Pioneered in 1973 by New Zealand's biggest producer, Montana
Wines, Marlborough is especially known for wines made from
the Sauvignon Blanc white-wine grape variety. Marlborough
established its international reputation in the 1980s through one
wine, the renowned Cloudy Bay.

Marqués de Cáceres
Spain a large wine-producing estate (bodega) in the Rioja DOCa
a region of northern Spain producing mostly red wine from
Tempranillo, Grenache (Garnacha) and Carignan (Cariñena)
grapes and smaller quantities of fruity white wines from Macabeo (Viura) grapes (*pronounced* maar késs day káthə ress)

Marqués de Murrieta
Spain a wine-producing estate (bodega) with vineyards in the
Rioja DOCa region of northern Spain that produces good red
wine and a traditional white Rioja that is considered to be one of
the best in Spain (*pronounced* maar késs day moori áytə)

Marqués de Riscal
Spain a wine-producing estate (bodega) with vineyards in the
Rioja DOCa region of northern Spain whose red wine is allowed
to contain more Cabernet Sauvignon and Merlot grapes than
other Riojas (*pronounced* maar késs day reess kaál)

Marsala DOC
Italy the DOC area on the western edge of the island of Sicily that
produces the famous sweet, fortified wine of the same name in
vineyards around the town of Marsala. Marsala is produced in a
similar way to sherry and Madeira, with oxidation during ageing.
Marsala wine can be made from white grapes (Catarratto and
Inzolia are popular) to produce wines of amber (ambra) or gold
(oro) colour. Wine made from red grapes (Sangiovese, Nerello or

Perricone grapes are widely used) is called rubino (ruby) Marsala. The wines are graded in quality, depending upon ageing and type of alcohol used in fortifying the wine, as fine, superiore, superiore riserva, vergine and vergine stravecchio, with all but fine made using a solera method. The finest quality of Marsala is vergine stravecchio, which must be aged in wood for a minimum of ten years. (*pronounced* maar saálə)

☿ **Marsanne**
a white-wine grape variety most often used in the northern Rhône region of France, but also grown in Australia and the USA. It is widely used in white wines produced in the Crozes-Hermitage and Hermitage areas of France. (*pronounced* maar sán)

☿ **Marsanne Noir** *another name for* **Syrah** (*pronounced* maar sán nwaár)

Marsannay AOC
France an appellation in the Côte d'Or area of the Burgundy region of France that produces red, white and rosé wines (*pronounced* maar sa neé)

Martell
an old-established Cognac firm, now belonging to the Canadian company Seagram

Martha's Vineyard AVA
USA a wine-producing area on the island of Martha's Vineyard in the state of Massachusetts. The single vineyard in this area grows mostly Cabernet Sauvignon, Chardonnay and Chenin Blanc grape varieties.

Martinborough and Wairarapa
New Zealand a wine-producing region in the south of the North Island of New Zealand growing the Cabernet Sauvignon and Pinot Noir grape varieties

♀ **marzipan**
(*tasting term*) a sweet, almond taste or aroma associated with white wines made from the Chenin Blanc grape variety and with young Champagne

mas
French an estate house or farmhouse, especially in the south of France (*pronounced* maa, *plural* **mas**)

♀ **masculine**
(*tasting term*) used to describe a wine that is big and full, especially in comparison with other wines from the same region or grape

Mas de Daumas Gassac
France an estate near Montpellier in the Languedoc region founded in 1970 and once called 'Lafite of Languedoc'. It produces some of the best vins de pays in France, red wine from the Cabernet Sauvignon grape variety and white still and sparkling wines from Chardonnay. (*pronounced* maá də dō maá ga sák)

Masi
Italy a famous Italian winery based near Verona producing a range of very good Valpolicella and Soave wines (*pronounced* maázi)

Masson *see* **Paul Masson**

mass selection
a method of taking vine cuttings with buds, sometimes called bud wood, from all the vines in a vineyard to graft onto rootstocks rather than taking cuttings from a single plant.
Also called **field selection**
Compare **clonal selection**

Master of Wine
a qualification and title granted by the Institute of Masters of Wine (founded in 1955 in the UK) to students who have passed intensive study and a rigorous three-day exam that includes blind-tasting over 30 wines.
Abbreviation **MW**

♡ **Mataro** *another name for* **Mourvèdre** (*pronounced* ma taárō, *used in* Spain)

♀ **matchstick**
(*tasting term*) an odour caused by excess sulphur dioxide gas, similar to the smell of burnt matches and very occasionally found in negligible amounts trapped in bottled white wine. It will normally dissipate.

◊ **Mateus Rosé**
a popular medium sweet, slightly effervescent rosé wine produced from a range of grapes grown in northern Portugal and

produced by the country's largest wine producer, Sogrape (*pronounced* mátti əss rố zay)

Matino
Italy a DOC wine-producing area in the Apulia region of southern Italy, producing dry red and rosé wines from Negro-amaro grapes (*pronounced* ma téénō)

maturation
the process of maturing, or the period of time taken for a wine to mature, normally in a barrel

mature
1. to allow a wine time to develop the characteristics that make it ready to drink, or to develop these characteristics.
See ageing
♀ **2.** (*tasting term*) used to describe a wine that is fully developed and correctly aged and ready to drink

Maury AOC
France an appellation in the Languedoc-Roussillon region of southwestern France that grows mostly Grenache grapes to produce red and rosé wines (*pronounced* mō reé)

♢ Mauzac, Mauzac Blanc
a white-wine grape grown in southwestern France, especially in the Gaillac AOC. It is usually blended with other wine. (*pronounced* mō zák, mō zák blaáN)
Also called **Blanquette**

♢ Mavrodaphne
a red-wine grape variety grown mostly in Greece to produce sweet, full-bodied red wines that are often drunk as dessert wines (*pronounced* mávro dáfni)

♢ Mavrud
a low-yielding red grape variety native to Bulgaria with grapes that produce a tannic, long-lasting red wine (*pronounced* máv rŏod)

Mazis-Chambertin AOC
France a grand cru vineyard in Gevrey-Chambertin in the Côte de Nuits district of the Burgundy region of France that grows Pinot Noir grapes to produce high quality red wines (*pronounced* mázzee shom bair táN)

Mazouna *see* **Algeria**

Mazuelo *another name for* **Carignan** (*pronounced* ma thwáylō, *used in* Spain)

McLaren Vale
Australia a wine-producing region of South Australia, south of Adelaide, with many small wineries. Its reds, made from Cabernet Sauvignon and Syrah (Shiraz) grapes, are much prized, but the diverse soil types and topography allow for many varieties: Malbec, Merlot, Chardonnay, Sémillon, Grenache, Sauvignon Blanc, Riesling and Verdelho, to name just a few.

meagre
(*tasting term*) used to describe a wine that is insipid and lacks body and depth

mealy bug
a grey insect of the genus *Pseudococcus* that attacks vines

meaty
(*tasting term*) used to describe a red wine that is rich, full-bodied and chewy

mechanical harvesting
the process of using a machine to automate picking the ripe grapes from the vine. Traditionally harvesting was, and in many vineyards is still, done by hand, cutting off the bunches of grapes, but this is slow, hard work. If the vines are trained so that the fruit hangs freely below the canopy, a machine can be used to cut off the bunches.

mechanical pruning
the process of using a machine to automate pruning the unwanted young shoots on a vine. The traditional method of pruning is to cut off the shoots by hand, but this is very slow work. Mechanical pruning works well if the method of training the vines suits the machinery; cordon training is perhaps the best suited to this.

mechanisation
the introduction of machines in what were traditionally jobs done by hand, e.g. pruning the shoots and picking the grapes

medal
an award presented to wines in the numerous competitions and tastings sponsored by magazines, countries and wine

associations. Medals are normally gold, silver and bronze for the top three positions.

Mediterranean climate
a climate in which there are very warm summers with little or no rainfall and mild wet winters

♀ **medium-bodied** *see* **body**

♀ **medium dry**
(*tasting term*) used to describe a wine that is partially or moderately dry.
See also **semidry**

♀ **medium sweet**
(*tasting term*) used to describe a wine that is partially or moderately sweet.
See also **semisweet**

Médoc
France the largest wine-producing district within the Bordeaux region of southwestern France. The district has two main area appellations: Médoc AOC and Haut-Médoc AOC. Both appellations produce high-quality red wines, but the wines of Haut-Médoc AOC are generally of slightly better quality because of better-quality soil. The Haut-Médoc AOC covers the entire southern area of the district except for six villages that have their own appellations (Listrac, Margaux, Moulis, Pauillac, Saint-Estèphe and Saint-Julien). The main red-wine grape varieties grown are Cabernet Sauvignon, Merlot and Cabernet Franc. White wines produced in either area are normally sold under the more generic Bordeaux AOC label. In 1855 the classification of wines in France was limited to the Médoc district, except for one wine from Graves, since this was considered at the time to be the only place producing high-quality wine. It still produces some of the best wines in the world. (*pronounced* may dók)

Médoc AOC
France an appellation for red wines grown in the Bas-Médoc, the northern area of the Médoc district of the Bordeaux region of France (*pronounced* may dók)

◊ **Médoc Noir** *another name for* **Merlot** (*pronounced* máy dok nwaár)

♀ **mellow**
(*tasting term*) used to describe a wine that is soft, smooth, correctly aged and pleasant to drink

♀ **melon**
(*tasting term*) a taste or aroma associated with white wines made from the Chardonnay grape variety in parts of the New World

Melon de Bourgogne *another name for* **Muscadet** (*pronounced* me lóN də boor gónnyə)

Melton, Charles
a famous winemaker who owns an eponymous winery in the Barossa Valley, South Australia, and produces high-quality classic Barossa red wines from Syrah (Shiraz), Grenache and Mourvèdre grape varieties as well as a rosé from Grenache grapes

Mendocino AVA
USA a viticultural area in the south of Mendocino County, California, that includes Anderson Valley and two other AVAs and is the location of the Fetzer estate (*pronounced* ménd ə seénō)

Mendocino County
USA a county in the north of California that is best-known for growing Zinfandel, Cabernet Sauvignon and Merlot grape varieties. It includes the Mendocino AVA. (*pronounced* méndə seénō)

Mendoza
Argentina a city in northwestern Argentina that is the centre for the surrounding wine region of the same name. This region produces the majority of Argentina's wine. (*pronounced* men dŏzə)

Menetou-Salon AOC
France an appellation in the Loire valley region of western France that produces white wines from Sauvignon Blanc grapes that are similar to the wines from the neighbouring Sancerre AOC, together with good-quality red and rosé wines from Pinot Noir grapes (*pronounced* ménnə too sa lóN)

meniscus
the very edge of the surface of wine in a glass, where the liquid touches the glass and is slightly curved up, accurately showing the colour of the wine

Méntrida DO
Spain a large DO wine-producing region in the central-south-west of Spain that grows mostly Grenache (Garnacha) grapes to produce red and rosé wines that are normally sold in bulk or blended with other wines (*pronounced* mén treedə)

mercaptan
a chemical compound of a group that form in wines, usually white wines, after yeast fermentation, creating an unpleasant, sulphur-like smell similar to rubber that is a signal that the wine has been badly made or is deteriorating

Mercurey AOC
France a well-known village appellation in the Côte Chalonnaise area of the Burgundy region of France, producing almost entirely red wine from Pinot Noir grapes (*pronounced* mair kŏŏ ráy)

meritage
a marketing term used by a number of US wineries on labels to describe good-quality blended wines that do not have a single particular grape variety. The term is the result of a competition to find a suitable descriptive term and combines 'merit' with 'heritage'.

◊ Merlot
a popular black grape variety used to produce red wines in many different regions around the world. The wines are rich, fruity, and often with blackcurrant flavours. The grape is used as the foundation for some of the great red wines of the Bordeaux region of southwestern France such as Saint-Émilion and Pomerol, and in Bordeaux-style wines around the world. Merlot grapes have a thinner skin and more sugar than Cabernet Sauvignon and so produce softer red wine with a higher alcohol content. The grape is unrelated to Merlot Blanc. (*pronounced* máirlō)
Also called **Bigney**; **Médoc Noir**; **Merlot Noir**

◊ Merlot Blanc
a white-wine grape variety, unrelated to the black grape variety Merlot, grown in small quantities in parts of France and often producing uninteresting white wines (*pronounced* máirlō blaáN)

◊ Merlot Noir *another name for* **Merlot** (*pronounced* máirlō nwaár)

◊ **Merseguera**
a relatively undistinguished Spanish white-wine grape variety
grown especially in the Alicante, Jumilla and Valencia DOs
(*pronounced* máirssə gáirə)

mesa
Spanish table. (*pronounced* máyssə)
See also **Vino de Mesa**

mesoclimate
a climate within a small area such as a hillside or valley that
could include one or more vineyards
Compare **macroclimate**; **microclimate**

♀ **metallic**
(*tasting term*) used to describe a wine that has a taste of metal or
tin, often caused by excess time in contact with a metal container

méthode champenoise
French a traditional method of producing sparkling wine,
originally especially Champagne but now used to produce almost all good sparkling wines. The process includes a second
stage of fermentation (malolactic fermentation) that takes place
in the bottle and produces carbon dioxide gas as a by-product,
which dissolves into the wine to create the sparkling style.
(*pronounced* may tód shompə nwaáz, *literally* 'Champagne
method')
Also called **Champagne method**; **méthode classique**; **méthode
traditionelle**; **metodo classico**; **metodo tradizionale**

méthode classique
French same as **méthode champenoise** (*pronounced* may tód kla
seék, *literally* 'classic method')

méthode dioise
French a local term in the Clairette de Die AOC in the Rhône
region of France for a method of making sparkling wine that is
similar to the méthode rurale. The wine is fermented slowly at
low temperatures for several months, then filtered and bottled.
Once bottled, the wine starts to warm up and the fermentation
process starts again naturally, creating carbon dioxide gas as a
by-product, which creates bubbles in the wine. The sediment at
the bottom of the bottles is removed by decanting and filtering
the wine in a pressurised container to retain the effervescence,
and the wine is bottled again in fresh bottles. Wine made by this

method must have it stated on the label. (*pronounced* may tód dee waáz, *literally* 'Die method')

méthode gaillacoise *same as* **méthode rurale** (*pronounced* may tód gī yak waáz, *literally* 'Gaillac method', *used in* the Gaillac AOC in France)

méthode rurale
French a traditional method of producing sparkling wine, now generally replaced by the méthode champenoise or the Charmat process, in which the fermenting wine is cooled to almost stop fermentation. The wine is then bottled and warmed slightly to restart the fermentation in the bottle, creating sparkling wine from the carbon dioxide released during this secondary fermentation. (*pronounced* may tód roŏr raál, *literally* 'rural method')

méthode traditionnelle *same as* **méthode champenoise** (*pronounced* may tód tra deéssyo nél, *literally* 'traditional method')

methuselah
an oversize wine bottle of the shape traditionally used for Burgundy and Champagne wines that can hold 6 litres, equivalent to eight standard 750 ml bottles.
Compare **imperial**

metodo classico, metodo tradizionale
Italian same as **méthode champenoise** (*pronounced* méttōdō klássikō, méttōdō tra ditsyo naá lay, *literally* 'classic method' *or* 'traditional method')

♡ **Meunier**
a red-wine grape variety in the Pinot family that is widely grown in the Champagne region of France where it is blended with Pinot Noir and Chardonnay grapes to produce sparkling wine. (*pronounced* mŏnyay)
Also called **Pinot Meunier**

Meursault AOC
France an appellation that includes the vineyards around the large village of Meursault in the Côte de Beaune area of the Burgundy region in France. It is known mostly for its white wines, which are produced entirely from Chardonnay grapes. Meursault white wines are soft and rich. (*pronounced* mur só)

Mexico
a country bordering the south of the USA that has a history of growing vines going back to the 16th century but a climate that

is not ideally suited to growing vines. The wine that is produced, especially in the north of the country, is often fortified or distilled to produce brandy. Nevertheless Mexico is now being influenced by nearby California and growing a wide range of grapes and producing and even exporting some reasonably good table wine.

Michel, Louis
a well-respected winemaker based in the Chablis area of the Burgundy region of France, renowned for his classic unoaked Chablis (*pronounced* mee shél)

micro-appellation
in the USA, a winery with only a small amount of land planted with vines but producing its own unique wines

microchâteau
a château with only a small amount of land planted with vines but producing its own unique wines. The best example is Château Le Pin in the Pomerol district of France: it has fewer than two hectares of vineyards, but produces some of the best wines in the country. These wines are sold at prices rivalling the best traditional large estates of Bordeaux though all the wine-making takes place in the garage under the house. (*pronounced* mīkrō shattō, *plural* **microchâteaux**)

microclimate
a climate found in a very small area, e.g. a few square metres or two or three vines
Compare **macroclimate**; **mesoclimate**

middle palate, mid-palate *see* palate

Midi
France same as **Languedoc-Roussillon** (*pronounced* meé dee)

mildew
one of two diseases caused by fungi that affect grapevines.
See **downy mildew**; **powdery mildew**

Millau *see* Côtes de Millau AOC

millerandage
poor fruit setting, giving rise to berries of different sizes in a bunch and no seeds in varieties that usually have them. It usually results in yield reductions.

millésime
French a year or vintage year (*pronounced* meé lay seém)

Millésime Rare *see* **Laurent Perrier** (*pronounced* meé lay seem raár)

♀ **mineral, minerally**
(*tasting term*) a taste of dissolved nonorganic salts in a wine, deriving from the soil in which the vine was grown

Minervois AOC
France an appellation in the Languedoc-Roussillon region in the south of France that produces good, inexpensive red wines from Carignan, Cinsault, Grenache, Mourvèdre and Syrah grapes. As with other wine-growing areas of southern France, a great deal of effort and investment is being put into improving quality with the planting of better grape varieties and the upgrading of equipment and techniques. (*pronounced* meé nair vwaá)

Minho
Portugal a wine-producing region around the Minho river in northern, near the border with Spain. Part of the **Vinho Verde DOC** (*pronounced* mínyō)

♀ **minty, mint**
(*tasting term*) used to describe a wine made from Cabernet Sauvignon or Zinfandel grapes, especially one from California, USA

Mireval *see* **Muscat de Mireval AOC**

mis en bouteille
French bottled (*pronounced* meéz aaN boo tī)

mis en bouteille á la propriété
French same as **mis en bouteille au domaine** (*pronounced* meéz aaN boo tī alla própree ay táy)

mis en bouteille au château
French used to describe a wine produced and bottled at the château where the grapes are grown (*pronounced* meéz aaN boo tī ō sha tō)

mis en bouteille au domaine
French used to describe a wine produced and bottled at the estate where the grapes are grown (*pronounced* meéz aaN boo tī ō dō mén)

mis en bouteille dans nos caves
French used to describe a wine made from grapes grown else-where and often of lower quality than estate-bottled or château-bottled wine (*pronounced* meéz aaN boo tí daaN nō kaáv, *literally* 'bottled in our cellars')

○ **Mission**
the first red-wine grape variety introduced into California, on the western coast of the USA, by Spanish Catholic missionaries travelling up from Mexico in the 1700s. Little is grown today and the wines are normally of poor quality and only used for blending.
Also called **Criolla; Pais**

Mission Haut-Brion *see* **La Mission Haut-Brion, Château**

mistelle
French partly fermented grape juice that has had alcohol added to stop the fermentation process. Since only a little of the natural sugars in the grape juice has been fermented, this juice is very sweet. (*pronounced* mee stél)
Compare **surdo**

Mittelmosel
Germany a wine-producing region in the centre of the Mosel-Saar-Ruwer region of Germany, producing some of the coun-try's best wines and known particularly for its Riesling white wines (*pronounced* mítt'l mōz'l)

Mittelrhein
Germany one of the 13 Anbaugebiete (quality wine-producing regions) of Germany that follows the Rhine river and mostly grows the Riesling grape variety. Production is small and mostly for local consumption. (*pronounced* mítt'l rīn)

M-L *abbreviation* malolactic fermentation

Mocadelo di Montalcino DOC
Italy a wine-producing DOC zone in the Tuscany region of Italy that grows mostly Muscat grapes (locally called Moscato Bian-co) to produce sweet white wines that are either still or slightly sparkling (*pronounced* móka déllo dee món tal cheénō)

♀ **moelleux**
French (*tasting term*) used to describe a white wine that still has a little residual sugar and is soft and mellow (*pronounced* mwaa lő)

Moët et Chandon
the biggest Champagne house in France, producing almost 20 million bottles of Champagne per year under a range of different vintage and non-vintage labels including the prestige Dom Pérignon label. After merger with the Cognac firm Hennessy it later became part of the giant LVMH. (*pronounced* mő ay ay shaáN doN)

Moldova
a country and former Soviet republic that now offers one of the most diverse and interesting range of vineyards from the Central European region
See map at **Bulgaria**

⟡ Molette Noire, Molette *another name for* Mondeuse (*pronounced* mo lét nwaár)

⟡ Monastrell
a red-wine grape variety widely planted in Spain, especially in the Rioja and Alicante regions, that produces moderately heavy, dark wines that are high in alcohol and low in acid. (*pronounced* mónna strél)
Also called **Alcayata**; **Morastel**; **Morrastel**; **Valcarcelia**

Monbazillac AOC
France an appellation in the Bergerac region of southwestern France that grows mostly Sémillon, Muscadelle and Sauvignon Blanc grape varieties that are infected with *Botrytis cinerea* to produce medium sweet and sweet wines. Lower-quality wines from this region are often labelled with the more generic Côtes de Bergerac AOC. (*pronounced* moN bázzee yák)

Mondavi, Robert
an influential winemaker in California, USA, who emphasised the use of traditional European grape varieties. He set up the Opus One winery with Baron Philippe de Rothschild, and worked with Peter Newton to develop the Sauvignon Blanc grape in California.

⟡ Mondeuse, Mondeuse Noir
a red-wine grape variety that is grown in small areas of France, Italy, Argentina, Australia and the USA. The grapes produce good-quality wine with a rich, deep colour. (*pronounced* moN dőz *or* moN dőz nwaár)
Also called **Grosse Syrah**; **Molette**; **Molette Noire**; **Refosco**; **Savoyance**

⟡ Monestel *another name for* **Carignan** (*pronounced* món e stél)

Monopole
French a term used on labels on some French wines to indicate that there is one single owner of the wine's name or that it is a trademark. It has no bearing on the wine's quality, which tends to be uniform each year. (*pronounced* mónnō pól)

Montagne de Reims
France one of the four main regions within the Champagne region. (*pronounced* mon tánnyə də ráNss)
See also **Champagne AOC**

Montagne-Saint-Émilion AOC
France an appellation on the outskirts of the Saint-Émilion district of the Bordeaux region in southwestern France that grows mostly Merlot grapes to produce good-quality red wines (*pronounced* mon tánnyə sant ay meél yoN)

Montagny AOC
France a village appellation in the Côte Chalonnaise area of the Burgundy region of France that only produces white wine from the Chardonnay grape variety (*pronounced* móN ta nyeé)

Montalbano *see* **Chianti DOCG** (*pronounced* mónt al baánō)

Montalcino *see* **Brunello di Montalcino DOCG**; **Mocadelo di Montalcino DOC**; **Rosso di Montalcino DOC**

Montana Wines
New Zealand a wine-producing estate in the North Island, New Zealand, that is one of the country's largest estates producing high-quality red, white and sparkling wines

Montecarlo DOC
Italy a small DOC zone in the northwest of the Tuscany region of Italy that produces red wines from Sangiovese, Canaiolo Nero and Syrah grapes and white wines from Trebbiano and a mix of other local grape varieties

Montecompatri-Colonna DOC
Italy a wine-producing DOC zone south of Rome in the Lazio region of Italy that produces a dry white wine from Malvasia and Trebbiano grapes similar in style to Frascati (*pronounced* món tay kom páttri ko lónnə)

Montefalco DOC
Italy a wine-producing DOC zone in the Umbria region of Italy that produces good red wine from the Sangiovese, Sagrantino

and Trebbiano grapes. There is the Sagrantino di Montefalco high-quality DOCG zone within this area that is known for its rich red wines made from Sagrantino grapes. (*pronounced* món tay fálkō)

☌ Montepulciano

a red-wine grape variety grown widely throughout Italy and particularly in the southeast of the country. It is used to produce spicy medium- to full-bodied red wines with good structure. It is the grape used in Rosso Conero. (*pronounced* món tay pŏol chaánō)
See also **Rosso di Montepulciano DOC**; **Vino Nobile di Montepulciano DOCG**

Montepulciano d'Abruzzo DOC

Italy a DOC region in the Abruzzo region of Italy that produces red wines from Montepulciano and some Sangiovese grapes (*pronounced* món tay pŏol chaánō da brŏotsō)

Monterey AVA

USA a viticultural area that includes most of the vineyards of Monterey County, California

Monterey County

USA a large wine-producing area in California, just south of the San Francisco Bay area. The most-used grape varieties include Chardonnay, Riesling and Pinot Blanc as well as the more common Cabernet Sauvignon, Merlot and Pinot Noir. This county includes several AVAs including Arroyo Seco, Chalone, Carmel Valley and Monterey.

Montes

Chile a wine-producing firm based in the Curicó and Colchagua Valley regions of Chile growing Cabernet Sauvignon and Merlot grape varieties for premium-quality red wines and Sauvignon Blanc and Chardonnay for white wines. Respected winemaker Aurelio Montes is a founding partner. (*pronounced* mónt ess)
See also **A Winemaker's View**

Monthélie AOC

France a small appellation in the Côte de Beaune area of the Burgundy region of France that produces mostly red wines made from Pinot Noir grapes (*pronounced* móN tay leé)

◊ Montilla

a sherry-style wine produced using the solera system in the

Montilla-Morilés DO in southern Spain. The types of Montilla are similar to the types of sherry, but the names (amontillado, fino etc.) are not allowed on labels outside Spain: they are usually given a description such as pale dry, medium dry, pale cream or cream. Montilla wines are often not fortified but have naturally high levels of alcohol. (*pronounced* mon teélya)

Montilla-Morilés DO
Spain a wine-producing Denominación de Origen region in southern Spain growing mostly Pedro Ximénez grapes to produce the sherry-like sweet wine Montilla (*pronounced* mon teélya mo ree léss)

Montlouis AOC
France an appellation in the Loire region of France that grows Chenin Blanc grapes to produce a range of styles of white wine (*pronounced* móN loo eé)

Montrachet AOC
France a small vineyard appellation in the Côte de Beaune area of the Burgundy region of France, famous for its white wine, which is considered to be amongst the best in the world, and is one of the most expensive. This small 8 hectare grand cru vineyard straddles two villages, and both villages, Puligny and Chassagne, as well as several surrounding villages, include the name Montrachet in their labels. (*pronounced* móN ra sháy)

Montravel AOC
France an appellation in the Bergerac region of France, bordering the Bordeaux region, that grows mostly Sémillon, Sauvignon Blanc and Muscadelle grape varieties to produce dry or medium sweet white wines of modest quality (*pronounced* móN ra vél)

Montrose, Château
France a château in the Médoc district of the Bordeaux region of southwestern France, graded deuxième cru (second growth) in the classification of 1855. It grows Cabernet Sauvignon, Merlot and a little Cabernet Franc to produce good-quality red wines. (*pronounced* moN rőz)

ᗑ Morastel
(*pronounced* mórrə stél)
1. *another name for* **Monastrell**
2. *another name for* **Graciano**

Moravia
Czech Republic a wine-producing region in the Czech Republic producing a wide range of red, white and sparkling wines. The other region in the country is Bohemia.

Morellino di Scansano DOC
Italy a wine-producing DOC zone in the Tuscany region of Italy that grows primarily Sangiovese grapes to produce good-quality red wine (*pronounced* mórrə leénō dee skan saánō)

Morey-Saint-Denis
France a commune in the Côte de Nuits area in the Côte d'Or district of Burgundy in France. The vineyards in this area include 5 grand cru vineyards and 20 premier cru vineyards. The great growths of Morey-Saint-Denis are Bonnes Mares, Clos de la Roche, Clos Saint Denis and Clos de Tart. The vineyards produce red wines from Pinot Noir grapes. (*pronounced* mo ráy saN də neé)

Morgon AOC
France an appellation in the Beaujolais region of France that grows Gamay grapes to produce intensely coloured and full-bodied wines (*pronounced* mawr góN)

۞ Morio-Muskat
a white-wine grape hybrid that is a cross between Sylvaner and Pinot Blanc and is grown mostly in Germany to produce flowery wines that are often used in blending (*pronounced* mórri ō moóss kat)

۞ Moristel
a red-wine grape variety grown mostly in northern Spain in the Somontano region of the Pyrenean mountains (*pronounced* mórri stél)

Mornington Peninsula
Australia a cool-climate wine region in the state of Victoria, south of Melbourne, growing some of Australia's best Pinot Noir grapes for red wine and Chardonnay of equal quality grapes for white

۞ Morrastel *another name for* Monastrell (*pronounced* mórrə stél)

Moscatel de Setúbal *see* Setúbal DOC

۞ Moscatello *another name for* Aleatico (*pronounced* móskə téllō)

○ **Moscato, Moscato Bianco** *another name for* **Muscat** (*pronounced* mos kaátō *or* mos kaátō byángko, *used in* Italy)

◊ **Moscato d'Asti**
a slightly sparkling (frizzante) white wine produced in the same DOCG as Asti. The main difference is that when making Moscato d'Asti the fermentation is stopped sooner, producing a wine that is sweeter and has less carbon dioxide so is less fizzy. It is sold in normal wine bottles with a normal cork rather than a Champagne cork. (*pronounced* mos kaátō dásti)

◊ **Moscato di Canelli** *same as* **Moscato d'Asti**

Mosel, Moselle
France, Germany a river that starts in eastern France and passes through Luxembourg then through Germany. 'Mosel' is the German form and 'Moselle' the French. (*pronounced* mōz'l *or* mō zél)
See also **Vins de Moselle VDQS**

Mosel-Saar-Ruwer
Germany one of the Anbaugebiete (quality wine-producing regions) in northern Germany that borders the Mosel river and its two tributaries the Saar and the Ruwer. This region grows Riesling grapes to produce white wines, low in alcohol, that are some of the best Riesling wines in the country. (*pronounced* mōz'l zaár roóvər)

Moseltaler
German a category of wines produced in the Mosel-Saar-Ruwer region that must be made from Riesling, Elbling, Kerner or Müller-Thurgau grapes and reach the national QbA quality level (*pronounced* mōz'l taalər)

Mossel Bay
South Africa an area in the southern Cape region of South Africa with a cool climate and a number of small vineyards such as Ruiterbosch, growing grape varieties from northern Europe

mosto
Italian must (grape juice) (*pronounced* móstō)

Moueix
France a well-known négociant in the Pomerol and Saint-Émilion areas of the Bordeaux region of France, producing good-quality wines from its range of AOC vineyards and châteaux (*pronounced* moo áyks)

♀ **mouldy**
(*tasting term*) used to describe a wine that smells or tastes of damp mould, indicating that the wine was made from mouldy grapes or that it has been badly stored or produced in dirty barrels or tanks

Moulin-à-Vent AOC
France an appellation in the Beaujolais region of France, generally considered to be the best of the Beaujolais appellations, producing good, full-bodied red wines from the Gamay grape. These are unlike the lighter style of young red wines normally associated with Beaujolais and should be allowed to acquire some age. (*pronounced* moó laN aa vaáN)

Moulis AOC
France a small village appellation in the Haut-Médoc district of France producing some very good red wines (*pronounced* moo leé)

Mountain
a former name for Málaga sweet fortified wine

Mount Barker
Australia a wine-producing area in Western Australia, a subregion of the Great Southern region

Mount Veeder AVA
USA a viticultural area in California growing Cabernet Sauvignon and Chardonnay grape varieties

♢ **Mourvèdre**
a black grape variety grown in southern France, Australia and California, USA, that produces red wine with strong colour, body and the flavour of pine. It requires an environment with a lot of sunshine to ripen the grapes. It is used in French Mediterranean red wines from regions such as Châteauneuf-du-Pape as well as in full-bodied red wines from Australia and California. (*pronounced* moor véddrə)
Also called **Mataro**

♀ **mousey**
(*tasting term*) used to describe a sharp, slightly vinegary smell and flavour of a wine, caused by bacterial contamination during production

mousse
French the foam on the top of a glass of sparkling wine when it is poured (*pronounced* mooss)

mousseux
French used to describe sparkling wine. The term is not used on Champagne labels. (*pronounced* moo số)

♀ **mouthfeel**
(*tasting term*) the sum of the various sensations a wine can create in your mouth, covering a range of tastes and textures including richness, crispness, ripe, oaked, sweet, spicy and acidity

♀ **mouth-filling**
(*tasting term*) used to describe a wine that is soft, full-bodied and complex

Mouton d'Armailhacq, Château
France a château in the Bordeaux region of France, graded cinquième cru (fifth growth) in the classification of 1855, owned by Baron Philippe de Rothschild and next door to the better-known Château Mouton-Rothschild. It grows Cabernet Sauvignon and Merlot grapes to produce good-quality red wine. (*pronounced* moó toN daar mī yák)

Mouton-Rothschild, Château
France a château in the Bordeaux region of France that was originally graded deuxième cru (second growth) in the classification of 1855 but was then upgraded to premier cru (first growth) in 1973, the only change ever to the original classification. It produces very good red wines from Cabernet Sauvignon, Merlot and Cabernet Franc grapes. Over the years, the work of many famous artists has adorned the labels of Château Mouton-Rothschild, including Salvador Dalí, Francis Bacon, Georges Braque and Jean Cocteau. (*pronounced* moó toN rōt sheéld)

Mudgee
Australia a wine-producing region in New South Wales producing flavoursome red wines from the Syrah (Shiraz) and Cabernet Sauvignon grape varieties

muffa nobile
Italian noble rot produced by the fungus *Botrytis cinerea* (*pronounced* moóffə nõbi lay)

Muga
Spain a wine producer (bodega) in the Rioja DOCa region of
northern Spain producing high-quality red and rosé wines
(*pronounced* moóga)

mulled wine
red wine mixed with any combination of sugar, fresh orange or
lemon and spices, usually including cinnamon, cloves and
nutmeg, and served hot

Müller-Thurgau
a white-wine grape hybrid, originally produced by crossing the
Riesling variety with Sylvaner, that is widely grown in Germany, Austria, Switzerland and New Zealand and is also grown
in the UK. It has high yields and produces a light white wine
(*pronounced* moóllər toór gow)

Mumm
a large Champagne house in Reims in the Champagne region of
France producing mostly the non-vintage Cordon Rouge
Champagne and small quantities of its premium René Lalou
wine

murky
(*tasting term*) used to describe a red wine that lacks brightness
and clarity of colour

Murray-Darling
Australia a wine-producing region in Victoria and New South
Wales growing the majority of the grapes in Victoria and
producing mostly everyday-quality white wines

Murrumbidgee
Australia see **Riverina**

Musar, Château
Lebanon a famous vineyard producing good-quality red and
white wine (*pronounced* moŏ saár)

Muscadel
(*pronounced* múskə dél)
1. *another name for* **Muscat** (*used especially in South Africa*)
2. *see* **Muscadelle**

Muscadelle, Muscadel
a white-wine grape grown mainly in the Bordeaux region of

France where it produces highly perfumed white wines that are used to add sweetness and flavour to other white wines. It is also grown in Australia (where it is called Tokay) to produce sweet dessert wines. (*pronounced* mǒoska dél *or* múskə dél)
Also called **Muscadet Doux**; **Sauvignon Vert**; **Tokay**

Muscadet
a white-wine grape variety grown mostly in the Loire valley of France to produce light, crisp, dry white wines. (*pronounced* mǒoss ka dáy)
Also called **Melon de Bourgogne**

Muscadet AOC
France an appellation in the Loire valley of France that is named, unusually for France, after a grape variety rather than a town or village. The region produces light, crisp, dry white wine made from grapes of the same name (elsewhere called Melon de Bourgogne). The wines from Muscadet AOC are the lowest quality. The best are from the Muscadet de Sèvre-et-Maine AOC. (*pronounced* múskə day, mǒoss ka dáy)

Muscadet de Sèvre-et-Maine AOC
France by far the largest and the best of the appellations in the Muscadet AOC. Its fresh white wines are bottled 'sur lie', giving a yeasty flavour and a slight sparkle. (*pronounced* mǒoss ka day də sévr ay mén)

Muscadet Doux *another name for* **Muscadelle** (*pronounced* mǒoskə day doó)

Muscadine
a native American grape, found originally in the southeast of the USA. It is unusual in that the grapes tend to grow not in distinct bunches but as individual berries everywhere and anywhere on the vine. The most common variety of this class is Scuppernong. They are normally grown for eating fresh but some wine is made from these intensely flavoured grapes.

Muscat
a family of grapes that has hundreds of varieties that range from white- to black-skinned grapes and produces fruity, softly perfumed wines. The grapes are grown in temperate climates including in Australia Austria, France, Greece, Italy, Spain and the USA to produce a wide range of styles of wine including sparkling wines and sweet dessert wines. (*pronounced* mús kat, mǒoss kaá)
Also called **Hanepoot**; **Moscato**; **Muscatel**

○ **Muscat à Petits Grains, Muscat Blanc à Petits Grains**
one of the Muscat grape varieties that is generally considered the
best. It has small round berries with a concentrated flavour due
to the low yield. It is used notably in Muscat de Beaumes-de-
Venise wines. (*pronounced* mŏoss kaá (blaáN) aa pətee graN)
Also called **Brown Muscat**; **Frontignan**; **Muscat d'Alsace**

○ **Muscat d'Alsace** *another name for* **Muscat à Petits Grains**
(*pronounced* mŏoss kaá dal zaáss)

Muscat de Beaumes-de-Venise AOC
France an appellation in the Rhône valley region of France that
grows mostly the Muscat à Petits Grains variety of the Muscat
grape to produce a very good, sweet, fortified white wine
(*pronounced* mŏoss kaá də bŏm də və neéz)

Muscat de Frontignan AOC
France an appellation on the Mediterranean coast in the Languedoc-Roussillon region of southern France that is best-
known for its sweet, fortified white wines made from the Muscat
à Petits Grains variety of the Muscat grape (*pronounced* mŏoss
kaá də frŏN tee nyaáN)

Muscat de Lunel AOC
France an appellation near Montpellier in the south of France
producing fortified wines from Muscat grapes grown locally
(*pronounced* mŏoss kaá də lŏo nél)

Muscat de Mireval AOC
France an appellation on the Mediterranean coast in the
Languedoc-Roussillon region of southern France that is
best-known for its sweet, fortified white wines made from the
Muscat à Petits Grains variety of the Muscat grape (*pronounced*
mŏoss kaá də meer vaál)

Muscat de Rivesaltes AOC
France an appellation in the Languedoc-Roussillon region of
southern France that is best-known for its sweet, fortified white
wines made from the Muscat à Petits Grains variety of the
Muscat grape (*pronounced* mŏoss kaá də reev zaált)

Muscatel
(*pronounced* múskə tél)
○ **1.** a sweet white wine made from Muscat grapes
○ **2.** *another name for* **Muscat**

♀ **Muscateller** *another name for* **Aleatico** (*pronounced* moͦoͦskə
téller, *used in* Germany and Austria)

♀ **Muscat Hamburg**
a white-wine Muscat grape variety grown primarily in eastern
Europe to produce dark-coloured wine.
Also called **Black Muscat**

♀ **Muscat Ottonel**
a variety of the Muscat grape producing a much lighter flavour
of wine. It grows in cool climates and is used to make dry,
perfumed white wines or rich dessert wines. (*pronounced* moͦoͦs
kaͦa ottə nél)

♀ **muscular**
(*tasting term*) used to describe a red wine that is big and full-
bodied

Musella *see* **A Winemaker's View**

♀ **mushrooms**
(*tasting term*) a bouquet of fresh-picked mushrooms sometimes
found in old red wines

Musigny AOC
France a vineyard appellation with grand cru status in the
Burgundy region of France that grows Pinot Noir grapes to
produce very good light, elegant red wines (*pronounced* myoo
seͤenyi)

♀ **musky**
(*tasting term*) used to describe a wine with a sweetish earthy
smell and flavour

must
grape juice, often including skin, seeds, fragments of stalk and
pulp, that is produced when the bunches of grapes have had
their stems removed and are then crushed, but that has not yet
been fermented

must weight
a method used in Germany to determine the likely alcohol level
of the final wine by comparing the liquid from the fermenting
wine with the specific gravity of water in degrees on the Oechsle
scale

♀ **musty**
(*tasting term*) used to describe faulty wine that has a stale, mouldy smell due to a faulty cork in the bottle, production from mouldy grapes or dirty tanks and barrels

mutage
French the process of stopping fermentation by using sulphur dioxide or by adding alcohol to the fermenting liquid (*pronounced* mŏŏ taázh)

muté
(*pronounced* mŏŏ táy) *French*
1. partially fermented grape juice that has had its fermentation stopped
2. a sweetening agent for winemaking produced by fortifying fresh juice or by chilling the juice and adding high amounts of sulphur dioxide

MW *abbreviation* Master of Wine

mycoderma
bacteria that give wine a vinegary taste and smell by converting alcohol into acetic acid and ethyl acetate

Wine comes in at the mouth / And love comes in at the eye; / That's all we shall know for truth / Before we grow old and die.

W. B. Yeats, 1910

Nahe
Germany an Anbaugebiet (quality wine-producing region) in Germany. The Nahe river is a tributary of the Rhine and the vineyards are arranged along the banks of this smaller river where Müller-Thurgau and Riesling grape varieties are planted to produce good-quality wines. (*pronounced* naá ə)

nailpolish
(*tasting term*) an aroma like that of the solvent used in nail varnish or nail varnish-remover, arising from ethyl acetate or amyl acetate and found especially in young wines

Nairac, Château
France a château in the Sauternes AOC region in southern Bordeaux, graded deuxième cru (second growth) in the classification of 1855. This estate grows mostly Sémillon grapes to produce high-quality sweet white wines. (*pronounced* nay rák)

Naoussa
Greece an appellation in northern Greece that grows especially the Xinomavro grape to produce good red wines

Napa Valley AVA
USA the best-known of the USA's wine-producing regions, situated in northern California and containing over 250 wineries. Around 65% of the white grapes planted are Chardonnay, but Sauvignon Blanc, Riesling, Chenin Blanc and Sémillon are also present. Red varieties are dominated by Cabernet Sauvignon, but Merlot, Zinfandel, Cabernet Franc and Petite Sirah are also found. As well as the main Napa Valley AVA, there are 13 other AVAs within the main area. Amongst these are Rutherford, producing some of the very finest Napa Cabernet, Oakville, Mount Veeder, Howell Mountain and Stags Leap District.

naturel

(*pronounced* náttŏŏ rél) *French*

1. used to describe a wine that has had neither sugar nor alcohol added

2. used on labels of Champagne and sparkling wines to describe a wine that has not had a dosage added

3. used to describe a sparkling wine that is very dry, or the driest style from a particular producer.

See also **vin doux naturel**

Navarra DO

Spain a wine-producing DO region in north-central Spain that mostly grows the Grenache (Garnacha) grape variety to produce red and rosé wines (*pronounced* na vaárə)

○ Nebbiolo

a red-wine grape variety that is grown in the Piedmont region of northwestern Italy to produce rich, full-bodied red wines that often need ageing to soften the tannins. The wines called Barolo, Barbaresco and Spanna are made from the Nebbiolo grape. (*pronounced* nébbi ólō)

Also called **Spanna**

Nebbiolo d'Alba DOC

Italy a wine-producing DOC area in the south of the Piedmont region of northwestern Italy that grows the Nebbiolo grape. The wine is only aged for one year to produce a lighter red than many other Nebbiolo-based wines. (*pronounced* nébbi ólō dálbə)

Nebbiolo delle Langhe DOC

Italy a wine-producing DOC area in the Piedmont region of northwestern Italy producing ruby-red wines with blackberry flavours (*pronounced* nébbi ólō dellə lángay)

nebuchadnezzar

an oversize wine bottle that can hold 15 litres, equivalent to 20 standard 750 ml bottles

négociant

French a wine dealer or merchant who buys and sells grapes to produce wine or who buys wines wholesale and blends them and bottles the blend to sell under the house's own label (*pronounced* nay gō syaáN)

○ **Negra Mole**
a red-wine grape that is most commonly grown on the island of Madeira and in the Algarve region of Portugal. It is used to produce fortified wines in Madeira. (*pronounced* néggrə mố lay)
Also called **Tinta Negra Mole**

○ **Négrette**
a red-wine grape variety grown in southwestern France and in parts of California, USA, where it is called Pinot Saint George. It produces smooth red wines with strong berry flavours. (*pronounced* nay grét)
Also called **Petit Noir**; **Pinot Saint George**

○ **Negroamaro**
a dark-skinned southern Italian grape grown especially in Apulia for use in blends and to produce powerful red wines and some rosés (*pronounced* náygrō ə maárō)

negus
a hot drink made of port or sherry with water, sugar, lemon juice and spices

Nelson
New Zealand a wine-producing region in the northeast of the South Island of New Zealand growing especially the Chardonnay, Sauvignon Blanc, Riesling and Pinot Noir grape varieties

Nemea
Greece an appellation in the northeastern Peloponnese in southern Greece that grows especially the Aghiorghitiko grape to produce intense red wines

○ **Nerello**
a Sicilian red grape variety that produces red wine that is high in alcohol (*pronounced* ne réllō)

○ **Nero d'Avola**
a red-wine grape variety grown in Sicily that produces deep-coloured full-bodied wines and ages well (*pronounced* naírō davốla)

♀ **nerveux**
French (*tasting term*) nervous (*pronounced* nair vố)

♀ **nervous**
(*tasting term*) used to describe a wine that is lively and full-bodied but well-balanced

♀ **nettles**
(*tasting term*) an aroma associated with white wines made from
the Sauvignon Blanc grape variety

♀ **Neuburger**
a white grape variety, a cross between Sylvaner and Pinot Blanc,
that is grown in Austria to make perfumed white wines (*pronounced* nóy boorgər)

Neusiedlersee
Austria a wine zone in Burgenland, Austria, centred on the lake
of the same name, producing a good proportion of the entire
grape harvest of Austria including a large harvest of (normally)
Botrytis cinerea-infected white grapes for variable-quality white
wines and Pinot Noir (Blauburgunder) and Cabernet Sauvignon
for red wines (*pronounced* noy zeédlər zay)

♀ **neutral**
(*tasting term*) used to describe a wine that is drinkable but has
no special qualities

nevers
French a type of French oak used to make wine barrels (*pronounced* ne váir)

New South Wales
Australia a state in Australia, the first to cultivate grapevines,
including 17 regions. Hunter Valley is probably the best-known,
producing red wines from Syrah (Shiraz) grapes and white wines
from Sémillon grapes.

Newton, Peter
a well-known winemaker in the Napa Valley region of California,
USA, who introduced the Merlot grape to the area and developed
Sauvignon Blanc with Robert Mondavi. His current vineyard
produces a small range of very good red and white wines from
Merlot, Sauvignon Blanc and Pinot Noir grape varieties.

New World
New Zealand and Australia, California in the USA, South
Africa or South America, or these regions collectively, often
associated with an innovative approach to winemaking

New York State
USA a wine-producing state on the eastern coast of the USA

that is unusual in that most of the vines planted are not traditional *Vitis vinifera* varieties but are native American breeds or hybrids. New York State has four main areas: Lake Erie, Long Island, the Hudson River Valley and the Finger Lakes. New York State has around 140 mostly small wineries, growing 50 different grape varieties. Chardonnay, Riesling, Cabernet Sauvignon and Merlot are the most successful. Sparkling wine is also made, as well as some superb dessert wines, namely late-harvest Rieslings and even Riesling ice wines.

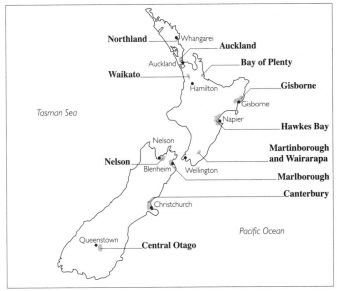

Wine regions of New Zealand

New Zealand

a country that has been growing vines and producing wine since the early 1800s but has only recently become an important producer in the world market. Winemakers have imported European vines and hybrids to test in the local cool climate, and now vineyards are widely planted with the Müller-Thurgau, Chardonnay, Riesling and Sauvignon Blanc white-wine grape varieties, although Sauvignon Blanc is the variety with which New Zealand has been most successful. The country's best wines are its white wines produced from this range of grape varieties, including sweet dessert wines made from Riesling grapes infected with the fungus *Botrytis cinerea*. Its red wines are produced from other European grape varieties including Cabernet Sauvignon, Pinot Noir and Merlot, and also the South African Pinotage. The regions on the North Island are: Auckland, which includes some of the country's oldest established vineyards and wineries and is best-known for its Bordeaux-style wines, especially its mouth-filling Cabernet Sauvignons and its complex, fruity Chardonnays; Gisborne, producing distinctive Chardonnays; Hawkes Bay, where Chardonnay is the most widely planted grape variety, but the long sunshine hours are conducive to later-ripening red grape varieties such as Cabernet Sauvignon, Merlot, Cabernet Franc and Syrah; and Martinborough and Wairarapa, populated by small producers making good Cabernets and Pinot Noirs. The South Island is dominated by Marlborough, New Zealand's best-known area. Two hours' drive from Marlborough lies Nelson, whose vineyards concentrate on cooler climate varieties: Chardonnay, Sauvignon Blanc, Riesling and Pinot Noir account for over 80% of the grapes grown. Canterbury's first vineyard was only planted in 1977 but it is becoming well-known and appreciated for its Chardonnay, Riesling and Pinot Noir wines. Central Otago is the world's southernmost wine-producing region. The conditions are ideal for producing high-quality Pinot Noir and Riesling wines.

Niagara
a white hybrid American grape that is grown primarily in the eastern USA and Canada to produce sweet and medium sweet white wines

noble
1. (*tasting term*) used to describe high-quality wine that has character
2. used to describe grape varieties traditionally used in making high-quality wine

noble rot, noble mould
the fungus *Botrytis cinerea* growing on white grapes, which, if carefully controlled, enhances the sweetness and flavour of sweet white wines made from them.
Also called **Edelfäule**; **muffa nobile**; **pourriture noble**

non-filtré
French unfiltered (*pronounced* noN feél tray)

non-vintage
used to describe a wine produced with a blend of wines from more than one year (vintage). Such blending is often used to provide a consistent product for Champagne. In the case of port, a vintage year is declared by the producer if the wine is exceptional, otherwise it is classed as non-vintage.
Abbreviation **NV**

North Coast AVA
USA a viticultural area in California, USA that comprises the major wine-producing areas of Napa, Sonoma, Mendocino, Solano, Lake and Marin counties

North East Victoria
Australia a wine-producing zone in Victoria encompassing five regions: King Valley, Glenrowan, Rutherglen, Beechworth and Alpine Valleys

North Yuba AVA
USA a small viticultural area in California, USA, within the larger Sierra Foothills AVA. It has just one winery.

Norton
an American hybrid grape variety that is not strongly flavoured and not suitable for ageing

nose
1. (*tasting term*) the smell of a wine
2. (*tasting term*) to smell a wine. The best way to smell a wine is to use a glass in which the body is wider than the top to help trap the smell. A small portion of wine should be poured into the glass and the wine gently twirled inside the glass to release the smell into the glass before you finally smell the wine.

note
(*tasting term*) a distinct element in the taste or aroma of a wine

nouveau
French used to indicate a young wine that has just been made and has a light, fruity style and that should be drunk immediately. The term is most often applied to Beaujolais red wines. (*pronounced* noo võ, *literally* 'new', *plural* **nouveaux**)

novello
Italian used to indicate a young wine that has just been made

and has a light, fruity style and that should be drunk immediately. (*pronounced* nə véllō, *literally* 'new', *plural* **novelli**)
See also **vino novello**

Nuits-Saint-Georges AOC
France an appellation in the Côte de Nuits area of the Burgundy region of France that has over 30 premier cru vineyards mostly producing very good red wines from Pinot Noir grapes (*pronounced* nweé saN zháwrzh)

♀ numb
(*tasting term*) used to describe a wine has lost its taste or smell, e.g. if it is served too cold

☼ Nuragus
a white-wine grape variety grown mainly on the island of Sardinia (*pronounced* noor aágəss)

Nuragus di Cagliari DOC
Italy a wine-producing DOC zone on the island of Sardinia, growing mostly Nuragus grapes to produce dry, light white wines (*pronounced* noor aágəss dee ka lyaári)

♀ nutty
(*tasting term*) used to describe a wine with a flavour reminiscent of nuts, particularly hazelnuts. The term is mostly used to describe sherry or port wines.

NV *abbreviation* non-vintage

O

oak

a type of hardwood commonly used for making wine barrels that are used to store and age wine and give it distinctive flavours and tannins. The barrels start losing their ability to provide flavours and tastes after around five years, but the major vineyards producing high-quality wine replace the barrels each year.

oak ageing

the process of ageing wine in oak barrels. Oak is the preferred wood for ageing because it gives the wine flavour and some tannins.

oak chips

shavings of oak used as a low-cost alternative to storing wine in oak barrels, which are expensive. They are added to a vat of fermenting wine to provide some of the oak flavour to the wine. The wine will not have been aged in an oak barrel, so will not have the added complexity of flavour of this ageing process.

oaked

flavoured with oak from the wine having been aged in an oak barrel, or from oak chips immersed in it

oak essences

a flavoured liquid added to a fermenting wine to add some flavour similar to that produced by ageing the wine in an oak barrel. This is the cheapest way of adding an oak flavour, but the least satisfactory for the end user.

Oakville AVA

USA a wine-producing region that covers part of the Napa Valley region of California, western USA

oaky

1. (*tasting term*) used to describe a smell or taste of vanilla and oak in a wine that has been aged in an oak barrel

2. (*tasting term*) used to describe excessive oak flavours that spoil the balance of a wine

Oechsle scale

a density scale used in Germany to measure the specific gravity of a liquid. In winemaking it is used to check the sugar levels in grape juice and so estimate the ripeness of grapes and predict the eventual alcohol content of a wine produced from those grapes, establishing the quality levels of wine for QbA and QmP. (*pronounced* ŏkslə)

oeil-de-perdrix

(*pronounced* ŏ ee də pair dreé, *literally* 'partridge's eye')
1. (*tasting term*) a brownish colour tinge to light red wines
2. a white wine made from a black-skinned grape and having a pinkish tinge

oenologist

a person who studies or practises the science of winemaking (*The US spelling is* **enologist**.)

oenology

the science of wine and winemaking (*The US spelling is* **enology**.)

oenophile

a person who enjoys wine (*The US spelling is* **enophile**.)

off

(*tasting term*) used to describe a wine that is spoiled

off-dry

used to describe a wine that is not quite a dry wine and is very slightly sweet, where the residual sugar is only just perceptible

off-flavour

(*tasting term*) a flavour that is not consistent with or typical of the type or style of the wine

Office International de la Vigne et du Vin

an international organisation that provides standards for the production of wine, based in Paris, France. (*pronounced* ofeéss aN tair nassyə naál dəla veényə ay dŏo váN)
Abbreviation **OIV**

off-smell

(*tasting term*) an odour of rotten eggs or some other smell indicating that the wine is spoiled

oidium
French the fungal disease powdery mildew of grapevines (*pronounced* ō eédee əm)

♀ **oily**
(*tasting term*) used to describe a wine that has the texture of oil and has a fat sensation on the palate caused by a combination of high glycerol and low acid levels. Oiliness is sometimes found in good-quality wines or sweet wines.

OIV *abbreviation* Office International de la Vigne et du Vin

♻ **Olaszrizling** *another name for* **Welschriesling** (*pronounced* ő ́ləs reézling, *used in* Hungary)

Old World
Europe and the areas around the Mediterranean, as opposed to the New World

♀ **olive**
(*tasting term*) a taste or aroma associated with red wines made wholly or partly from the Cabernet Sauvignon grape variety

oloroso
one of the two main categories of Spanish sherry that is bigger, darker and sweeter and has a fuller body than the fino style of sherry (*pronounced* óllə ŕóssō, *plural* **olorosos**)

Oltrepò Pavese DOC
Italy a wine-producing DOC zone in the Lombardy region of Italy that produces a wide range of red and white wines in a range of styles from dry to sweet. It is best known for two styles of full-bodied red wine made from Barbera, Croatina and Pinot Noir grapes, normally in a slightly sparkling style. (*pronounced* oltrə pố pa váy zay)

Onomasia kata Paradosi
Greek Traditional Appellation, an official category of Greek wines, especially for retsina

OPAP *abbreviation Greek* Appellation of Origin of Superior Quality

OPE *abbreviation Greek* Controlled Appellation of Origin

♀ **open**
(*tasting term*) used to describe a wine that is full-flavoured and ready to drink

opening
(*tasting term*) the first smells and flavours encountered when tasting a wine

open-top tank
a winemaking tank that has no permanent cover, used to ferment red wine. This is the traditional design for tanks, but it has mostly been replaced with closed-top tanks that are easier to clean and manage.

Opitz, Willi
a famous winemaker in the Neusiedlersee area of Austria, best-known for a range of excellent sweet wines (*pronounced* ṓpits)

Oporto
(*pronounced* ə páwrtō)
1. *Portugal another name for* **Porto**
2. *Hungary another name for* **Portugieser**

Optima
an early-ripening German white-wine grape variety that was created as a cross between Müller-Thurgau and a hybrid of the Riesling and Sylvaner grape varieties. This grape is very sweet and is used primarily in blends. (*pronounced* óptimə)

opulent
(*tasting term*) used to describe a wine that is smooth and full-flavoured

Opus One
USA a winery based in the Napa Valley, California, that was set up by Robert Mondavi and Baron Philippe de Rothschild. The winery makes a very well-regarded red wine from predominantly Cabernet Sauvignon grapes.

orange
(*tasting term*) a taste or aroma associated with sweet and fortified white wines

Orange Muscat
a variety of the Muscat grape that is highly perfumed and is popular in California, USA

ordinaire
French an inexpensive, basic wine (*pronounced* áwrdi náir, *literally* 'ordinary', *derived from* vin ordinaire 'ordinary wine')

Oregon
USA a wine-producing state in the northwest of the USA with a cool climate that allows the vineyard owners to grow Pinot Noir for red wines and Chardonnay and Riesling for white wines. Oregon's Pinot Noir flourishes in the state's wet, cool conditions and is especially treasured by wine-lovers. There are 138 wineries and five AVAs, Willamette Valley being the most important.

organic
1. used to describe the growing of vines using only a restricted number of permitted chemical pesticides and fertilisers
2. used to describe a method of making wine without the use of some chemicals and additives such as sulphites (sulphur dioxide) during production

organically grown
grown using only the fertilisers and pesticides permitted by organic growers

organic fertiliser
a plant nutrient that is returned to the soil from dead or decaying plant matter and animal wastes, e.g. compost, farm-yard manure or bone meal

organic viticulture
the philosophy and practice of growing vines without the use of many chemicals, either as fertilisers or pesticides. Grasses and other plants may be grown between the vines to help improve the soil and also compete with the vines for water and nutrients in the soil, leading to less vigorous growth of the shoots and leaves, which allows more sunlight onto the berries ensuring that they ripen well.

organic wine
wine that has been produced from organically grown and processed grapes. In the USA, this term is not allowed to be used on labels and instead a phrase such as 'made from grapes organically grown' is used.

organoleptic
used to describe a method of evaluating a wine by taste, smell and sight rather than through chemical analysis

Originalabfüllung
German bottled by the producer (*pronounced* ə ríggi naál áp fŏol lŏong)
Compare **Erzeugerabfüllung; Gutsabfüllung**

oro

Italian gold (*pronounced* áwrō)
See also **Marsala DOC**

Ortega

a white-wine grape variety that is popular in Germany and used to produce wines with a floral character (*pronounced* awr táygə)

Orvieto DOC

Italy a wine-producing DOC zone in the south of the Umbria region of Italy, best-known for producing a dry, white wine (*pronounced* awr vyáytō)

Osborne

a producer of sherry and Spanish brandy whose silhouetted black bull advertisements are a familiar feature of the Spanish landscape

ouillage

French the topping-up of wine barrels to make up for liquid lost through evaporation (*pronounced* wee yaázh)
See **ullage**

overcropped

used to describe a vine that carries more crop than it should so that not all the crop will ripen, normally caused by poor pruning

overdeveloped *see* **developed**

overripe

used to describe grapes that have been left on the vine too long before being picked, having extra sugar that can produce wines that are unbalanced

oxidation

an unwanted change in the flavour or colour of a wine caused by exposure to air that causes a chemical reaction in the wine or grape juice as it reacts with oxygen

oxidise

to react with oxygen and convert a substance into an oxide

oxidised

(*tasting term*) used to describe wine that has suffered oxidation, giving it a stale smell or flavour and often changing the colour of the wine so that it takes on a brownish tint. Fortified wines such as sherry and Madeira gain their characteristics by controlled oxidation.

oxygen
a chemical element (formula O) that is a common colourless gas present in the air and essential to biological life. In winemaking it is important to exclude oxygen from most processes because of the risk of oxidation. Exposure to the air before drinking is sometimes thought to improve some red wines.

P

Paarl
South Africa a wine-producing region northeast of Cape Town in South Africa (*pronounced* paal *or* pérəl)

Padthaway
Australia a wine-producing region in South Australia previously called Keppoch, producing wines of consistent quality and style. Chardonnay reigns supreme, but fine examples of Cabernet Sauvignon and Syrah (Shiraz) made from old vine material can also be found.

paille
French straw. (*pronounced* pī)
See also **vin de paille**

Pais *another name for* **Mission** (*pronounced* pī yeéss, *used in* Chile)

palate
(*tasting term*) the way wine tastes in the mouth. It is normally divided into three sections: front or fore-palate (the initial sensation of the wine), middle or mid-palate (the taste of the wine in the mouth) and hind or end-palate (the sensation on swallowing).

pale
(*tasting term*) used to describe a light-coloured fortified wine or brandy

pale cream
used to describe a fino sherry or a dry Montilla that has been sweetened

Palette AOC
France a small appellation in the west of the Provence region of France producing red and rosé wines (*pronounced* pa lét)

pálido
Spanish pale. (*pronounced* paálidō)
See also **Rueda DOC**

Palmer, Château
France a well-regarded château in the Margaux AOC area of the
Bordeaux region of southwestern France, graded troisième cru
(third growth) in the classification of 1855. It produces very
good wines from a blend of Cabernet Sauvignon and Merlot
grapes. (*pronounced* paal máir)

palo cortado
a style of sherry that is midway between a pale fino and a dark-
brown, sweeter oloroso, though this varies between producers.
(*pronounced* paálō kawr taádō, *plural* **palos cortados**)
See also **sherry**

Palomino
a grape variety used to make some table wines, but normally
used to make sherry in the Jerez de la Frontera region of Spain.
(*pronounced* pállə meénō)
Also called **Ablan**

Pansá Blanca *another name for* **Xarel-lo** (*pronounced* pan sá
blángka, *used especially in* the Alella DO)

paraffin
(*tasting term*) the pleasant slight smell and sensation of paraffin,
particularly on Riesling white wines

Parellada
a white-wine grape variety, widely grown in the Catalonia region
of northeastern Spain that produces good-quality light and fruity
white wines and sparkling wines (*pronounced* párrə lyaádə)

Parker, Robert M., Jr.
a famous American wine-taster and critic whose tasting notes
and ratings (out of 100) – in his books and in his magazine *The
Wine Advocate* – are widely read and respected throughout the
USA and the rest of the world. A good (or bad) rating can
transform the fortunes of a vineyard.

Passe-Tout-Grains *see* **Bourgogne Passe-Tout-Grains AOC**

passing the port
the tradition of passing a decanter or bottle of port clockwise

around a table. After serving yourself, you pass it to the person on your left.

passito
(*pronounced* pa seétō, *plural* **passiti**)
1. *Italian* an Italian winemaking process in which harvested grapes are dried before being pressed to help increase and concentrate the sugar levels prior to fermentation
2. a strong sweet wine made using the passito process

Pasteur, Louis
a famous scientist who identified the yeasts that caused fermentation and so developed pasteurisation, a process of heating a liquid then rapidly cooling it to kill off any yeasts, to stabilise liquids such as milk and wine and prevent spoilage. This process is not used for fine wines, which rely on these bacteria to help age and improve the wine.

pasto
Italian meal (*pronounced* pástō)
See also **vino da pasto**

Patras
Greece an appellation in the northern Peloponnese in southern Greece that grows especially white-wine grapes

Pauillac AOC
France a famous appellation in the Haut-Médoc area of the Bordeaux region in southwestern France producing some of the best red wines in France. The area contains three of the five premier cru estates: Latour, Lafite-Rothschild and Mouton-Rothschild. The area is mostly laid to Cabernet Sauvignon grapes together with some Merlot and Cabernet Franc. (*pronounced* paw yák)

Paul Masson
USA a winery that was established in Santa Clara County in California and was one of the first to produce sparkling wine in the state. The winery closed and concentrated on musical concerts but is now planning to replant vines.

pays
French see **vin de pays; vin du pays**

pazo
Spain a wine-producing estate in the Galicia region of northwestern Spain (*pronounced* paáthō)

♀ **peach**
(*tasting term*) the flavour of sweet peaches in some sweet, late-picked wines affected by the fungus *Botrytis cinerea*, or in wines made from Muscat grapes

♀ **peak**
(*tasting term*) the point at which a wine has aged correctly and is at its best in terms of flavour and taste. This is very subjective.

♀ **pear**
(*tasting term*) a taste or aroma associated with young light white wines and also with Beaujolais Nouveau

♀ **peardrops**
(*tasting term*) an aroma arising from ethyl acetate or amyl acetate, found especially in young wines

Pécharmant AOC
France an appellation in the Bergerac region of southwest France that is best-known for its good-quality red wines made from Cabernet Sauvignon, Cabernet Franc and Merlot grape varieties (*pronounced* páy shaar maáN)

◊ **Pederanão** *another name for* **Arinto** (*pronounced* pe dair nów)

Pedesclaux, Château
France a château in the Pauillac AOC region in central Bordeaux that was graded cinquième cru (fifth growth) in the classification of 1855. It produces mostly red wine from Cabernet Sauvignon and Merlot grape varieties. (*pronounced* péddə sklṓ)

◊ **Pedro Ximénez, Pedro Jiménez**
a white-wine grape variety grown in Argentina, Australia and, mainly, in southern Spain. Originally used as the main sherry grape, it has now been replaced by the Palomino grape variety and is used in smaller quantities to add sweetness to a sherry blend. In other regions it is used to produce sweet white wines or light, dry table wines. (*pronounced* péddrō hi máy ness)
Abbreviation **PX**

♀ **pencil shavings**
(*tasting term*) an aroma associated with red wines made wholly or partly from the Cabernet Franc grape variety

Penedès DO
Spain a wine-producing DO zone near Barcelona in Catalonia, Spain, that produces good-quality red and white wines. Its wine production has been revolutionised by Miguel Torres. The area's important sparkling wines bear the Cava DO label. (*pronounced* pénnə déss)

♀ **penetrating**
(*tasting term*) used to describe a wine that has an intense aroma, often because of high levels of alcohol

Penfolds
a famous estate in Barossa, South Australia, producing a wide range of very good red and white wines including the excellent Syrah-(Shiraz-)based Penfolds Grange wine, acknowledged as the greatest wine produced in Australia

Penfolds Grange *see* **Grange; Penfolds; Southcorp**

♀ **peppery**
(*tasting term*) used to describe a wine with a spicy flavour, which is often found in port and some red wines from the Rhône region of France

♀ **perfumed**
(*tasting term*) used to describe the sweet and floral aromas of some white wines

♡ **Periquita**
a red-wine grape variety grown in southern Portugal that produces full-bodied red wines that need ageing to soften the tannins (*pronounced* pérri kéétə)

perlant
French used to describe a wine that is very slightly sparkling in a way that is only just noticeable (*pronounced* pair laâN)

Perlwein
a slightly sparkling German wine, usually of low quality, that has been artificially carbonated (*pronounced* páirl vīn, *plural* **Perlweine**)

Pernand-Vergelesses AOC
France an appellation near Corton in the Côte de Beaune district of the Burgundy region of France (*pronounced* pair naáN vairzhə léss)

Perricone
a Sicilian red grape variety grown especially for use in blends

Perrier *see* **Laurent Perrier**

Perrier-Jouet
a Champagne house based in Épernay, in the Champagne region of France. This medium-sized producer is best-known for its premium Champagne, Belle Epoque, in a bottle with flowers painted directly onto the glass. The company is owned by Mumm. (*pronounced* pérree ay zhoó ay)

persistence
(*tasting term*) the length of the flavour and aroma of a wine on the palate

Pessac-Léognan AOC
France an appellation in the Graves district of the Bordeaux region of southwestern France. This appellation was formed in 1987 and includes the famous Château Haut-Brion, which was graded premier cru (first growth) in the classification of 1855. (*pronounced* péss ak láy o nyaaN)

Peter Lehmann
Australia a well-respected winery in the Barossa Valley region of South Australia, producing a range of good-quality red and white wines

pétillance
French a slight sparkle in a wine. (*pronounced* páy tee yaáNss) *Compare* **spritz**

pétillant
French slightly sparkling (*pronounced* páy tee yaáN)

petit
French used to describe a style of wine that is of lower quality or has less alcohol or body than the original (*pronounced* pə teé)

Petit Chablis AOC *see* **Chablis** (*pronounced* pə teé sha bleé)

◊ **Petite Sirah, Petite Syrah**
a red-wine grape variety that is grown mainly in California, USA, to produce full-bodied red wines with a peppery taste. It has no relation to the Syrah grape.

◊ **Petit Manseng** *see* **Manseng** (*pronounced* pə teé maaN saáN)

◊ **Petit Noir** *another name for* **Négrette** (*pronounced* pə teé nwaár)

◊ **Petit Verdot, Petit Verdau**
a red-wine grape variety grown mainly in the Bordeaux region of France to produce good-quality red wines with a deep colour and high levels of tannin and alcohol. The grapes are often used for blending with Cabernet Sauvignon grapes. (*pronounced* pə teé vair dó)
Also called **Verdot Rouge**

Pétrus, Château
France a very famous estate in the Pomerol area of Bordeaux in southwestern France growing old Merlot vines on its clay soil to produce some of the best red wines in the world. The Pomerol area has never been classified, but Pétrus is widely recognised as being of premier cru status and it generally sells for higher prices than any other red wine of Bordeaux. (*pronounced* pay troóss)

Pfalz
Germany a large Anbaugebiet (quality wine-producing region) in southern Germany that runs parallel to the Rhine river north of Alsace in France. The region produces large quantities of cheap Liebfraumilch white wines, with a few vineyards producing good-quality white wines from Riesling and Müller-Thurgau grapes. (*pronounced* falts)
Also called **Rheinpfalz**

pH
a measure of the concentration of hydrogen ions in a solution, which shows how acid or alkaline it is: pH is shown as a number. A value of 7 is neutral. Lower values indicate increasing acidity and higher values indicate increasing alkalinity, so 0 is most acid and 14 is most alkaline. This system is used to measure the acidity of wine and the type of soil in an area. Plants vary in their

tolerance of soil pH: some grow well on alkaline soils, some on acid soils only and some can tolerate a wide range of pH values.

phenolic compound *same as* **polyphenolic compound**

photosynthesis
the process by which green plants convert carbon dioxide and water into sugar, starch and oxygen using light as energy. Several factors are required for photosynthesis to take place: carbon dioxide, light, heat and water.

phylloxera
the root aphid *Daktulosphaira vitifoliae* (formerly *Viteus vitifolii*) that attacks vines. It threatened to destroy the vineyards of Europe in the 19th century, but the vines were saved by grafting susceptible varieties onto resistant American rootstock.

physiological ripeness
full ripeness of a grape determined using not only the sugar levels in the grape but also by taking into account the balance of sugars, acids and tannins that will yield the optimum flavour

Piane del Sole *see* **A Winemaker's View**

Pichon-Longueville Comtesse de Lalande, Château
France a château in the Pauillac AOC area of the Médoc district of Bordeaux in southwestern France graded deuxième cru (second growth) in the classification of 1855. It produces top-quality red wines from Cabernet Sauvignon, Merlot and Cabernet Franc grapes. (*pronounced* peé shoN lóngə veel koN téss də la laánd)
Also called **Pichon-Lalande, Château**

Picolit
an ancient white-wine grape variety that is grown only in the Friuli region of northeastern Italy. It has a very low yield and is used to produce limited quantities of sweet white wine with a floral aroma. (*pronounced* peékō lít)

Picpoul, Picpoul Blanc
a white-wine grape variety native to the Languedoc region of southern France where it produces crisp dry white wines, the best-known of which is Picpoul de Pinet (*pronounced* peek poól *or* peek poól blaáN)

pièce
French a barrel. The term is used in the Burgundy region for barrels of a size similar to that of the oak barrels used in the Bordeaux region (called barriques and of 225 litre capacity). (*pronounced* pyess)

○ **Piedirosso**
a red-wine grape variety grown in Campania, southwestern Italy, especially on the islands of Ischia and Capri (*pronounced* pyáydee ráwssō)

Piedmont, Piemonte
Italy a major wine-producing region of northwestern Italy that includes 4 DOCGs and over 30 DOC areas. The region is best-known for its red wines produced from the Nebbiolo and Barbera grape varieties. (*pronounced* peéd mont *or* pye món tay)

○ **Piesporter Michelsberg**
an ordinary white wine from the Mosel region of Germany (*pronounced* peéss pawrtər míkhəlzbaírg)

○ **Pigato**
a white-wine grape variety grown mainly in the Liguria region of Italy that is used to produce good-quality, full-bodied, aromatic dry white wines (*pronounced* pi gaátō)

Pin *see* **Le Pin, Château**

○ **Pineau d'Aunis**
a black grape variety grown in the Loire valley region of France to produce red and rosé wines (*pronounced* peénō dō neéss)

○ **Pineau des Charentes**
a sweet apéritif wine that is essentially a mixture of grape juice and brandy matured together in casks and is normally drunk cold or with ice. It is made in the Cognac region of western France by adding Cognac to grape juice to prevent the fermentation process. (*pronounced* peénō day sha raáNt)

○ **Pinot**
a family of French grape varieties including Pinot Blanc, Pinot Gris, Pinot Noir and Meunier. Unrelated grapes have often also been given the name, which is believed to refer to the shape of the grape bunches, resembling pine cones. (*pronounced* peénō)

○ **Pinotage**
a red-wine grape variety that is a cross between Pinot Noir and

Cinsault, developed in South Africa and grown widely in South Africa, New Zealand and California, USA, to produce medium-bodied red wines. The name is a blend of Pinot and Hermitage, a South African name for Cinsault. (*pronounced* pínnō taa<u>zh</u>)

◊ **Pinot Bianco** *another name for* **Pinot Blanc¹** (*pronounced* péenō byángkō, *used in* Italy)

◊ **Pinot Blanc**
(*pronounced* péenō blaáN)
I. a white-wine grape variety in the Pinot family that is grown around the world including a concentration in the Alsace region of France. This grape produces a pleasant dry, medium-bodied white wine that is similar to Chardonnay but without its depth or ability to age.
Also called **Beli Pinot; Pinot Bianco**

◊ **Pinot Chardonnay** *another name for* **Chardonnay**

◊ **Pinot Grigio** *another name for* **Pinot Gris** (*pronounced* péenō gréejō, *used in* Italy)

◊ **Pinot Gris**
a grape variety in the Pinot family with a greyish-to-pinkish skin colour that is used to produce a range of white and pale rosé wines. It produces particularly good, rich white wines in the Alsace region of France, but is also popular in Italy, Germany and eastern Europe. (*pronounced* péenō grée)
Also called **Auxerrois Gris**; **Grauburgunder**; **Pinot Grigio**; **Pinto Gris**; **Rulander**; **Tokay d'Alsace**

◊ **Pinot Liebault**
a little-known red-wine grape variety, a clonal variant of Pinot Noir, grown and used mostly in the Burgundy region of France (*pronounced* péenō lee bố)

◊ **Pinot Meunier** *another name for* **Meunier** (*pronounced* péenō mốn yay)

◊ **Pinot Nero** *another name for* **Pinot Noir** (*pronounced* péenō náiro, *used in* Italy)

◊ **Pinot Noir**
a highly regarded red grape variety in the Pinot family that dominates the vineyards of the Burgundy region of France, where it is used to produce some of the best red wines in the country. It is one of the oldest grape varieties cultivated and is best suited

to cool climates, such as that of Burgundy; it is difficult to grow in other areas and countries. It is one of the three varieties of grape used to produce sparkling white wine in the Champagne region of France and is grown in parts of Australia, New Zealand, USA and in Germany. (*pronounced* péenō nwaár)
Also called **Blauburgunder**; **Savagnin Noir**; **Spätburgunder**

♢ **Pinot Saint George** *another name for* **Négrette** (*used in* California, USA)

♢ **Pinto Gris** *another name for* **Pinot Gris** (*pronounced* péentō greé)

pip
a seed inside a grape. If the seeds are crushed when pressing the grapes, they can give a bitter taste to the wines.

pipe
1. a unit of liquid measure for wine, equal to four barrels, two hogsheads, or 105 gallons (about 478 litres)
2. a large container for wine

Piper Heidsieck
a Champagne house based in Reims in the Champagne region of France, producing a range of Champagne styles. It is owned by Rémy Martin. (*pronounced* pípər hīd sek)

♢ **Plant Gris** *another name for* **Aligoté** (*pronounced* plaáN greé)

plastering
a process, now outdated, of adding plaster of Paris to grape juice to increase its acid levels

plonk
simple, ordinary wine (*informal*)

♀ **plummy, plum**
(*tasting term*) used to describe a fruity taste or aroma in red wines made from the Syrah (Shiraz), Cabernet Sauvignon and Grenache grape varieties

♀ **plump**
(*tasting term*) used to describe a wine that does not quite reach the quality of a fat wine.
Compare **fat**; **flabby**

podere
Italian a wine-producing estate (*pronounced* pṓdə ray, *plural* **poderi**)

points
a method of rating a wine, used by tasters and magazines, assigning points according to a range of indicators

Poitou VDQS
France a VDQS wine-producing area in the Loire region of France, producing red and rosé wines from Gamay and Cabernet Franc grapes. Some white wines are made from Sauvignon Blanc and Chardonnay grapes. (*pronounced* pwaa toó)

Pol Roger
a small but high-quality Champagne house based in Épernay in the Champagne region of France (*pronounced* pol ro z̲háy)

polyphenolic compound
a naturally occurring chemical compound found in grapes and wine that contributes to the colour, taste and tannins of a wine and its ageing characteristics.
Also called **phenolic compound**

pomace
the residue of skins, seeds, pulp and fragments of stems left in the fermenting vat or cask after winemaking. Pomace is the basic ingredient used in the distillation of the brandy called marc in France and grappa in Italy. (*pronounced* púmmiss)

Pomerol AOC
France an appellation on the right bank of the Dordogne river in the Bordeaux region of southwestern France that grows mostly Merlot grapes and produces good-quality red wines that are a little softer and less tannic that the better-known wines of the Médoc AOC region of Bordeaux, which grows mostly Cabernet Sauvignon. The Pomerol area has never been classified, but its Château Pétrus is widely recognised as being of premier cru status. (*pronounced* pómmə ról)

Pomino DOC
Italy a wine-producing DOC area in the Tuscany region of Italy that produces a range of red wines mainly from Sangiovese grapes and white wines from a mix of Pinot Blanc (Pinot Bianco) and Chardonnay. The area also produces sweet white or red vin santo wine styles. (*pronounced* po méenō)

Pommard AOC
France an appellation in the Côte de Beaune area of the Burgundy region of France that produces good-quality red wines from the Pinot Noir grape (*pronounced* pom maár)

♀ **ponderous**
(*tasting term*) used to describe a heavy, strong, unsubtle taste or aroma in a wine that masks any desirable acidity or tannins

Pontet-Canet, Château
France a château in the Pauillac AOC area of the Bordeaux region of France graded cinquième cru (fifth growth) in the classification of 1855. It produces good-quality red wine mainly from Cabernet Sauvignon grapes. (*pronounced* póN tay ka náy)

Porongurup
Australia a wine-producing area in Western Australia, a sub-region of the Great Southern region

port
a sweet fortified wine produced by adding grape alcohol to a fermenting wine to stop the fermentation process and retain a high level of natural sugar, producing a sweet wine with high levels of alcohol (usually around 20% per unit volume). Port originated in the Douro valley region of northern Portugal and European Union law restricts use of the term to a defined area there, though port-style wines are made elsewhere in the world. Port was traditionally shipped from the city of Porto (Oporto). Port is produced as a red wine and a white wine, with two effective methods of ageing, either in wooden casks (or in cheaper versions sometimes cement tanks) or in bottle. Port aged in wood is ready to drink immediately after filtration and bottling; port intended to age in bottle spends some time in wood then is bottled without filtration. The wine has four basic styles: white, tawny, ruby and vintage port. White port is produced using white grapes such as Malvasia and Verdelho and can be in a dry or sweet style. Dry white port is produced by increasing the fermentation period, so reducing the residual sugar levels. The three red-wine ports are made using a range of different grapes including Tinta Barroca and Tempranillo (Tinta Roriz). Tawny port is made from a blend of grapes produced in different years and can be aged in barrels for between 10 and 40 years. Vintage port is made from the best grapes from the best areas of a vineyard harvested in a single

year and bottled within two years – not all years are considered worthy of turning into vintage port, but if the producer considers it a good year, he or she will 'declare' this a vintage year. Ruby port is made from lower-quality grapes from the vineyard and is aged for two years before bottling. Ruby ports have the most fruit in their flavour and tend to be a brighter red colour; tawny ports are a dark reddish-brown colour and can age well; vintage ports can age for 50 years or longer. Within these basic styles of port, there are four categories of quality: single-quinta port is produced from a single estate in a non-vintage year; second-label vintage port is produced from a single estate when the producer thinks the grapes are very good but not quite of a quality for a declared vintage; late bottled vintage (LBV) port is produced from grapes grown in one year and then aged in barrels for between four and seven years; crusted ports are blended from wines produced in different years and then allowed to age in the bottle for three or four years, where a sediment, or crust, develops; vintage character ports are blended from several different vintages and retain the character and style of a ruby port. Bottle-aged ports (vintage, crusted and some late bottled vintage wines) need to be decanted before drinking.

Porto
Portugal a major sea port in northern Portugal that is the mandatory point from which all port wines must be shipped. (*pronounced* páwrtō)
Also called **Oporto**

○ **Portugais Bleu** *another name for* **Portugieser** (*pronounced* páwr tŏo gay blŏ, *used in* France)

Portugal
the fifth-largest European wine-producing country, after France, Italy, Spain and Germany. Of the top five, Portugal dedicates the highest percentage of its agricultural land to viticulture. It is most famous for the port produced around the city of Porto (Oporto) in the north of the country and Madeira, from the Atlantic island of the same name. Portugal is responsible for the medium sweet, rosé wines Mateus and Lancers, which enjoyed huge international success during the 1960s and 1970s. However, since Portugal joined the European Union in 1986, the Portuguese wine industry has undergone a revolution, with investment and innovation, including the use of stainless steel

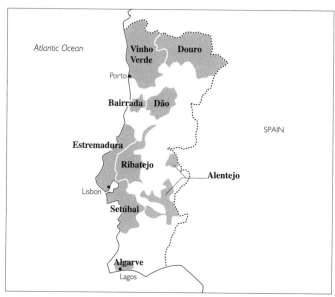

Wine regions of Portugal

fermentation tanks and small, new oak barrels. The old days of anonymous wines have been replaced by wines whose region of production is stated on every bottle. Estate bottling is on the increase and only the best grape varieties are being grown. The 10 demarcated wine regions of 1985 have risen to 55. Its wine-growing is characterised by a huge number of smallholdings, and in 1996 it had 367,000 farming estates primarily producing wine, about half of these occupying less than 2 hectares. Portugal is a treasure trove of indigenous grape varieties, and one of the most interesting and exciting aspects of contemporary Portuguese winemaking is the trend amongst the new generation of wine-makers to produce wines with all that modern technology can offer, but using these native varieties. White varieties include Alvarinho and Trajadura, used in the making of Vinho Verde; Arinto; Encruzado, grown in the Dão region; Loureiro; Fernão Pires (Maria Gomes), the predominant white grape in the Bair-rada region; and Muscat. Red varieties grown include Baga, grown in the Bairrada region; Tinta Roriz, the name used in the Douro and Dão regions for Tempranillo and called Aragonez in

Alentejo, where it is the most widely planted red variety; Touriga Nacional, considered the noblest Portuguese variety; and Trincadeira Preta, the red-wine grape that is the same as the port variety Tinta Amarela. Portugal was responsible for one of the earliest demarcations of a wine area when, in 1756, the Marquis of Pombal ordered that the borders of the Douro valley – the home of port – be delimited by 335 stone markers, and in the first 30 years of the 20th century, the status of Região Demarcada was awarded to a number of regions – Bucelas, Colares, Carcavelos (three small regions near Lisbon), Dão, Madeira and Setúbal. This mark of quality has now been replaced by Denominação de Origem Controlada (DOC). Other classifications are Vinho Regional, the most basic level, similar to French vin de pays, and Indicação de Proveniencia Regulamentada (IPR). Wines in this category are termed VQPRD (Vinhos de Qualidade Produzidos em Região Determinada). Portuguese wine regions are, from north to south: the Minho, part of the Vinho Verde DOC and best known for its slightly sparkling wine; the Douro, land of port and some good red wines; Beiras, incorporating the Dão, with its distinctive reds, and Bairrada, producing solid, tannic reds, made almost exclusively from the Baga grape; Estremadura, home to light, quaffable and affordable wines; and Ribatejo, currently one of the country's most exciting regions, with fruity, reasonably priced wines and the increasing presence of international grape varieties such as Cabernet Sauvignon and Syrah. Peninsula de Setúbal produces the fortified, sweet wine Setúbal (formerly Moscatel de Setúbal) and good red and white wines. South of Lisbon, Alentejo provides the world with cork and is beginning to make exciting red and white wines, using modern technology.

◊ Portugieser
a red-wine grape variety widely grown in Austria, France and Hungary and used to produce slightly sweet, light red and rosé wines. (*pronounced* páwrtoo géezər)
Also called **Oporto**; **Portugais Bleu**

potassium bitartrate
a natural chemical component of grape juice and wine, removed during the winemaking process.
Also called **cream of tartar**

potassium metabisulphite, potassium metabisulfite
a chemical compound that is added to wine or must (grape juice), where it reacts with acids to produce sulphur dioxide

which protects the wine against oxidation and some types of bacteria

♀ **potent**
(*tasting term*) used to describe a wine that has a strong, powerful or intense flavour

potential alcohol
a calculation of what the alcoholic strength of a fermenting wine or must would be if the all the sugar was fully fermented

Pouget, Château
France a château in the Margaux AOC area of the Médoc district of Bordeaux in southwestern France, graded quatrième cru (fourth growth) in the classification of 1855. It produces good red wine from Cabernet Sauvignon, Cabernet Franc and Merlot grapes. (*pronounced* poo <u>zh</u>áy)

Pouilly-Fuissé AOC
France an appellation in the Mâconnais area in the Burgundy region of France that produces dry white wines from five villages within the area that grow Chardonnay grapes (*pronounced* poó yee fwee sáy)

Pouilly-Fumé AOC
France an appellation in the Loire region of France that shares its centre, the town of Pouilly-sur-Loire, with the Pouilly-sur-Loire AOC. It produces white wines from the Sauvignon Blanc grape that are crisp and dry with a distinctive smoky flavour, hence the 'fumé' ('smoked') name. (*pronounced* poó yee foó máy)

Pouilly-Loché AOC
France an appellation in the Burgundy region of France, neighbouring the Pouilly-Fuissé AOC, that produces white wines from the Chardonnay grape, similar in style to, though usually considered not so good as, wines from Pouilly-Fuissé AOC (*pronounced* poó yee lo sháy)

Pouilly-sur-Loire AOC
France an appellation in the Loire region of France that shares its centre, the town of Pouilly-sur-Loire, with the Pouilly-Fumé AOC. It produces white wines from Sauvignon Blanc grapes and in some vineyards from the Chasselas grape traditionally grown in the area. (*pronounced* poó yee soór lwaár)

Pouilly-Vinzelles AOC
France an appellation in the Macônnais area in the Burgundy region of France that grows mostly Chardonnay grapes to produce a white wine that is similar to but lighter in style than that from the neighbouring Pouilly-Fuissé AOC (*pronounced* poó yee vaN zél)

◌ Poulsard
an unusual and rarely grown grape variety producing perfumed red wine that is often blended with other wines. It is particularly grown in the Arbois AOC region of Jura, eastern France. (*pronounced* poŏl saár)

pourriture
French rot (*pronounced* pooree toŏr)

pourriture noble
French noble rot caused by the fungus *Botrytis cinerea* (*pronounced* poóree toŏr nóbblə)

powdery mildew
a disease caused by the fungus *Podosphaera necator* that occurs in hot dry weather on the upper surface of leaves of vines. Powdery mildew has two forms: primary mildew, which forms on young leaves in spring, and the more serious secondary mildew, which makes leaves dry and fall off in summer.

♀ powerful
(*tasting term*) used to describe a wine that has a high alcohol content or is full-bodied

Prädikat
German a distinction accorded under German wine laws to wines made with grapes of a particular degree of ripeness or must of a particular weight. (*pronounced* práydi kaát)
See also **QmP**

Prädikatswein
German the highest general category of wine in Austria, referring to the use of late-picked grapes infected with noble rot and including Spätlese, Auslese, Strohwein, Eiswein, Beerenauslese, Ausbruch and Trockenbeerenauslese (*pronounced* práydi kaats vín, *plural* **Prädikatsweine**)

♀ precocious
(*tasting term*) used to describe a young wine that has the characteristics of a mature wine of its type

premier cru
French any one of the best wines in a particular region of

France. In the Bordeaux region, particularly the Médoc and
Sauternes areas, it refers to estates graded as the best producers
of wine in France in the great classification of 1855, when just
four red-wine estates – Château Lafite-Rothschild, Château
Haut-Brion, Château Latour and Château Margaux – were
awarded this status (a fifth estate, Château Mouton-Rothschild,
was upgraded in 1973). These five estates can label their red
wines premier cru. In the Sauternes area of Bordeaux there are
11 white-wine-producing estates judged to be premier cru and
one of even higher quality (Château d'Yquem) judged as premier grand cru. In the Burgundy region of France the premier
cru description confusingly refers to the second-best wines – the
best are labelled grand cru. (*pronounced* prəm yáy kroó, *literally*
'first growth', *plural* **premiers crus**)

Premières Côtes de Blaye AOC *see* **Blaye AOC** (*pronounced* prəm yáir kōt də bláy)

Premières Côtes de Bordeaux AOC
France an appellation in the Bordeaux region of southwestern
France that produces good red, white and rosé wines from
Sauvignon Blanc, Sémillon and Muscadelle grapes for white
wines and Cabernet Franc, Cabernet Sauvignon and Merlot for
red wines (*pronounced* prəm yáir kōt də bawr dó̄)

première taille *see* **taille** (*pronounced* prəm yáir tī)

premier grand cru
French the best white-wine-producing estate in the Sauternes area
of the Bordeaux region of France, Château d'Yquem, according
to the classification of 1855 (*pronounced* prəm yáy graaN kroó,
literally 'first great growth', *plural* **premiers grands crus**)

premier grand cru classé
French any one of the best wines of the Médoc and Sauternes
areas of Bordeaux and in the Saint-Émilion AOC wine-producing area (*pronounced* prəm yáy graaN kroó kla sáy, *plural*
premiers grands crus classés)

premium
used to describe a wine of high quality and usually commanding
a very high price, or the vines or grapes from which such a wine
is made

press
I. a mechanical device used to squeeze the juice from grapes.
There are three main types of press: the basket press, the bladder

press and the screw press. The grapes are normally first crushed to break open their skins and make it easier to press them. When making red wine the crushed grapes are first fermented in contact with the skins to provide the red colour of the wine before they are pressed; when making white wine the grapes are first crushed, then pressed, then the fermentation takes place without contact with the grape skins.

2. to squeeze juice from grapes

pressing
I. the process of extracting the juice from grapes
2. the juice extracted in a single pressing operation

press juice
grape juice that runs out of a press when squeezing grapes

press wine
a juice extracted from grapes after pressing (in the case of white wines) or after fermenting (for red wines). It has more flavour and aroma, deeper colour and often more tannins than free-run juice. It is normally either blended with the free-run juice or processed separately as a second-label wine.

prestige cuvée
the best wine from an estate

♀ pricked
(*tasting term*) used to describe a spoiled wine that has a fault with its acid levels

primary fermentation
the chemical process in which the yeasts and sugars in wine react to produce alcohol and carbon dioxide. The fermentation process stops when the sugar has all been converted or when the alcohol content reaches a high enough level (normally over 15%) to kill off the yeast.
Also called **alcoholic fermentation**
Compare **secondary fermentation; malolactic fermentation**

♀ primary fruit
(*tasting term*) the fruity aroma and flavour of a young wine that has berry or cherry tastes

primary mildew *see* **powdery mildew**

primeur
French wine made to be drunk young. The term normally refers to the light, fruity red wines marketed between 21 November of

the year of harvest and 31 January of the following year, of which the best-known is Beaujolais Nouveau. (*pronounced* pree múr)
See also **en primeur**

☼ Primitivo
a red-wine grape variety grown mostly in the Apulia region of southern Italy, producing robust red wines (*pronounced* primmi teévō)

Primitivo di Manduria DOC
Italy a wine-producing DOC area in the Apulia region of southern Italy that primarily grows the Primitivo grape variety to produce a dry red wine, and also produces a range of white and sweet wines (*pronounced* prímmi teévō dee man doória)

Priorat DO, Priorato DO
Spain a wine-producing DO area in the Catalonia region of northeastern Spain that produces mostly full-bodied red wines from Grenache (Garnacha) and Carignan (Cariñena) grapes (*pronounced* preé aw raát *or* preé aw raátō)

Private Reserve
USA a term that denotes quality and originally was used to refer to the best wines a winery produced, though this is no longer always true

produced and bottled by
a term on a wine label that indicates that the winery crushed, fermented and bottled at least 75% of the wine in the bottle

propriétaire
French the owner of a particular estate (*pronounced* prố pree ay táir)

☼ Prosecco
a white-wine grape mostly grown in Italy and most commonly used to produce crisp, dry sparkling white wines. (*pronounced* pro sékō)
Also called **Balbi**

Prosecco di Conegliano-Valdobbiadene DOC
Italy a wine-producing DOC area in the Veneto region of northeastern Italy that is best-known for its sparkling crisp, dry or slightly sweet white wines made from Prosecco grapes (*pronounced* pro sékō dee kone lyaánō vál dóbbyə dáy nay)

protective juice-handling

the protecting of freshly pressed juice from contact with oxygen by using antioxidants such as sulphur dioxide or by preventing the juice from reacting with oxygen by chilling it. Both methods ensure that the juice retains its fresh, primary fruit flavours and does not lose its bright green colour (the juice would slowly yellow in contact with oxygen).

protective winemaking

the procedures implemented throughout the process of making (normally white) wine to protect it from contact with oxygen, which would discolour the wine and reduce the original fresh fruit flavours. This involves careful handling of the grapes so that the berries do not split and storing the freshly pressed juice either chilled or in a container with an antioxidant.

Provence

France a wine-producing region of southeastern France that borders the Mediterranean Sea and has a year-long warm climate. It is well-known for dry rosés and fruity red wines. (*pronounced* pro vaáNss)
See also **Côtes de Provence AOC**

◊ **Prugnolo** *another name for* **Sangiovese** (*pronounced* proó-nyōlō, *used in* Tuscany, Italy)

◊ **Prunella** *another name for* **Cinsault**

♀ **pruney**
(*tasting term*) used to describe an often undesirable flavour of overripe grapes similar to the taste of dried prunes

pruning

the action of cutting off parts of a plant to make it healthier, to encourage new growth or to make it more convenient for harvesting. Vines that are pruned tend to be healthier and have improved yield and improved quality of grapes. Pruning also makes it easier to pick the grapes.

Puisseguin-Saint-Émilion AOC

France an appellation on the northeastern outskirts of the Saint-Émilion district in the Bordeaux region of France producing good-quality red wines (*pronounced* pweéss gaN saNt ay meél yoN)

Puligny-Montrachet AOC

France an appellation centred on the small village of Puligny-Montrachet in the Côte de Beaune district of the Burgundy

region of France that produces some of the world's best white wines from Chardonnay grapes. (*pronounced* poŏ lee nyee moN ra sháy)
See also **Montrachet AOC**

pulp
the soft part of a grape, inside the skin, that contains the juice

pumping over
the process of passing wine over the cap (the mass of skins, pips and fragments of stalks) floating on the surface of red wine during fermentation to ensure that the cap does not dry out, which could allow bacteria to develop, and to allow the wine to extract the maximum colour and flavour from the cap

punch
a drink made with a mixture of fruit juice, spices and wine or spirits, usually served hot

puncheon
a large oak barrel

punching down
the process of pushing the cap (the mass of skins, pips and fragments of stalks) floating on the surface of red wine during fermentation down into the liquid to ensure that the cap does not dry out, which could allow bacteria to develop, and to allow the wine to extract the maximum colour and flavour from the cap

♀ **pungent**
(*tasting term*) used to describe a wine with a powerful aroma, normally due to high acid levels

punt
the indentation in the bottom of a bottle.
Also called **kick-up**

puttony
a measure of the sweetness of Tokay dessert wines from Hungary. The word derives from the tubs used to collect the late-picked grapes – three puttonyos is equal to three tubs of grapes – and ranges between three and six puttonyos. (*pronounced* púttonyə, *plural* **puttonyos** *or* **puttonys**, a term approved by the European Union)

putts *abbreviation Hungarian* puttonyos

PX *abbreviation* Pedro Ximénez

This bread I break was once the oat, / This wine upon a foreign tree / Plunged in its fruit; / Man / in the day or wind at night / Laid the crops low, broke the grape's joy.   Dylan Thomas, 1936

QbA
German the set of German laws, enacted in 1971, that define the levels of quality of wine.
Full form **Qualitätswein Bestimmtes Anbaugebiet** *see* **Germany**

QmP
German the highest quality of wines within the QbA quality levels defined in Germany.
Full form **Qualitätswein mit Prädikat** *see* **Germany**

♀ quaffable
(*tasting term*) used to describe a wine that is pleasant to drink but not deserving of careful tasting attention

♀ quaffing wine
(*tasting term*) an everyday wine that is pleasant but not deserving of careful tasting attention

Qualitätschaumwein
German the highest official quality of sparkling German wine, which is usually produced using the Charmat process and often using the Riesling grape variety. (*pronounced* kválli tayts shówm vīn, *plural* **Qualitätschaumweine**)
Also called **Sekt**

Qualitätswein
German in Germany and Austria, wine of a particular defined quality. In Austria it is both a category including Kabinett and a subcategory of wine. (*pronounced* kválli táyts vīn, *plural* **Qualitätsweine**)

Qualitätswein bestimmtes Anbaugebiet
German full form of **QbA** (*pronounced* kválli táyts vīn bə shtímtəs án bow gə beet)

Qualitätswein mit Prädikat
German full form of **QmP** (*pronounced* kválli táyts vīn mit práydi kaát)

Quarts de Chaume AOC
France an appellation in the Loire region of France, producing sweet white wines from Chenin Blanc grapes (*pronounced* kaár də shốm)

quatrième cru
French the fourth-highest quality of wine in the classification of 1855 within the Médoc area of Bordeaux (*pronounced* káttri em krốo, *literally* 'fourth growth', *plural* **quatrièmes crus**)

Queensland
Australia a state and wine zone in northeastern Australia producing wine from the Syrah (Shiraz), Cabernet Sauvignon, Sémillon and Chardonnay grape varieties. It now has two wine regions: Granite Belt and South Burnett.

♀ quince
(*tasting term*) a taste or aroma associated with white wines made from the Chenin Blanc grape variety in the Loire region of France

Quincy AOC
France an appellation in the Loire region of France, growing Sauvignon Blanc grapes to produce a dry white wine (*pronounced* kaN seé)

quinta
Portuguese a wine-producing estate or vineyard (*pronounced* kíntə)

Here among flowers / one glass of wine, / with no close friends, I pour it alone. / I lift cup to bright moon, beg its company, / then facing my shadow, we become three.   Li Bai, 8th century

Rabaud-Promis, Château
France a château in the Sauternes AOC of the Bordeaux region of southwestern France graded premier cru (first growth) in the classification of 1855. It produces good white wines from mostly Sémillon and Sauvignon Blanc grapes. (*pronounced* rábbō pro meé)

Raboso
a red-wine grape variety that is mostly grown in the Veneto region of northeastern Italy to produce red wines that are high in acid and tannin levels and have a deep red colour. It is often used in blends. (*pronounced* ra bṓzō)

Raboso Veronese
a variety of the Raboso red-wine grape that provides higher yields and as a result is more widely grown than the original Raboso vine. It is grown mostly in the Veneto region of north-eastern Italy. (*pronounced* ra bṓzō verə náy zay)

race
(*tasting term*) the distinctive taste of a wine, by which its grape variety or region of origin can be identified

racemic acid
a form of tartaric acid found in grape juice

Racha-Lechkhumi
Georgia a wine-producing region in Georgia, north of Imereti, that grows grapes with a high sugar content

racking
the process of transferring wine from one cask or barrel to another to separate it from its lees

racy
(*tasting term*) used to describe a light wine with a lively quality from well-balanced acid levels

Radford Dale *see* **A Winemaker's View**

Raimat
Spain a wine-producing estate in Catalonia, Spain that occupies about a third of the Costers del Segre area and grows French as well as indigenous Spanish grape varieties (*pronounced* ray maát)

rainwater
a historic medium dry style of Madeira fortified wine, still made in small quantities

♀ **raisiny**
(*tasting term*) used to describe a wine with a rich, concentrated taste of grapes. A raisiny quality is considered an asset in sweet fortified or late-harvest wines but a fault in dry white table wines. It is normally caused by the grapes drying out while still on the vine.

raki
an aniseed-flavoured alcoholic drink from the eastern Mediterranean, especially Turkey and the Balkans, made from grapes or sometimes other fruits (*pronounced* raáki)

rancio
a wine with a sweet, nutty flavour like that of an old sherry or port, produced by leaving a barrel of wine in a hot room, or, traditionally, in the sun, to oxidise the wine. The process is rather like that used to produce Madeira wines. This style of wine is found in Spain and France, e.g. in the Banyuls AOC. (*pronounced* rán thee ō *or* raán syō, *plural* **rancios**)

rape
the skins and stalks of grapes after their juice has been extracted for use in winemaking

Rapel
Chile a wine-producing region of Chile noted especially for its red wines made from Cabernet Sauvignon grapes but also growing Sémillon grapes for white wine

♀ **raspberry**
(*tasting term*) a taste or aroma associated with red wines made from the Pinot Noir grape variety, e.g. in the Burgundy region of France, and with some red wines from the Rhône

Rasteau
France one of the villages entitled to the Côtes du Rhône-Villages AOC growing mostly Grenache grapes for a sweet dessert wine (vin doux naturel), sweet white wines and strong red wines (*pronounced* ra stố)

ratafia
a style of apéritif wine produced in France by mixing grape juice with brandy to prevent the fermentation process (*pronounced* rắttə feé ə)

Rausan-Ségla, Château
France a château in the Margaux AOC of the Bordeaux region of southwestern France graded deuxième cru (second growth) in the classification of 1855. It produces good-quality full-bodied red wine from mostly Cabernet Sauvignon and Merlot grapes. (*pronounced* rō zaáN sáy glaa)

Rauzan-Gassies, Château
France a château in the Margaux AOC of the Bordeaux region of southwestern France graded deuxième cru (second growth) in the classification of 1855. It produces red wine from mostly Cabernet Sauvignon, Cabernet Franc and Merlot grapes. (*pronounced* rō zaáN ga seé)

♢ Ravat 51
a hybrid white-wine grape variety developed in France by J. F. Ravat, who bred a range of hybrid varieties. It is grown in the east of the USA to produce dry or sweet table wines. (*pronounced* ra vaá)
Also called **Vignoles**

♢ Ravat 262, Ravat Noir
a hybrid red-wine grape variety developed in France by J. F. Ravat, who bred a range of hybrid varieties. It produces light, fruity red wines but is not often grown. (*pronounced* ra vaá *or* ra vaá nwaár)

♀ raw
(*tasting term*) used to describe an undeveloped, young wine, often high in alcohol and acidity and therefore harsh

rayas
lower-quality oloroso sherry used in blending medium dry sherry (*pronounced* rí ass)

Rayne-Vigneau, Château
France a château in the Sauternes AOC of the Bordeaux region of southwestern France graded premier cru (first growth) in the classification of 1855. It produces good dry and sweet white wines from mostly Sémillon and Sauvignon Blanc grapes. (*pronounced* ráyn vee nyő)

Rebula *another name for* **Ribolla Gialla** (*pronounced* re boólə, *used in* Slovenia)

recioto
a style of wine produced in the Veneto region of northeastern Italy, made using the passito method in which the grapes are left to dry out in the sun to increase the natural sugar levels and produce good-quality dry (recioto amarone) or sweet (recioto) wines. The method is used in the Valpolicella, Gambellara and Soave DOC regions. (*pronounced* re chőtō)

Recioto della Valpolicella Amarone *same as* **Amarone della Valpolicella** (*pronounced* re chőtō delə vál poli chéllə amə rő nay)

Recioto di Soave
a sweet white wine made in the Soave DOC area of the Veneto region of northeastern Italy using the passito method in which the grapes are left to dry out in the sun (*pronounced* re chőtō dee swaávay)

récolte
French a grape harvest (*pronounced* ray kólt)

red spider mite
a red mite in the *Tetranychus* genus of which several species infest vines in warm dry conditions

reduced
(*tasting term*) used to describe a wine, typically one made from the Syrah grape variety in a hot climate, that has a smell of mercaptan, because of a shortage of oxygen

red wine
a style of wine made by crushing red- or black-skinned grapes and leaving the juice in contact with the skins during fermentation to allow the colour and tannins from the skins to transfer to the wine. Rosé wines are made in the same way, but the skins are not kept in contact with the fermenting wine for as long. *Compare* **white wine**

♀ **refined**
(*tasting term*) used to describe a high-quality, well-balanced wine

◊ **Refosco** *another name for* **Mondeuse** (*pronounced* re fŏskō)

refractometer
a device used to measure the sugar content of grape juice or must. The device relies on the characteristic of a liquid to bend, or refract, light at different angles according to the levels of sugar dissolved in the liquid. The light strikes a scale that is calibrated to show the sugar content and the possible alcohol level of the finished wine using the Baumé, Brix or Oechsle scale.

Região Demarcada
Portuguese an old term for the highest-quality wine produced in Portugal, now replaced by Denominação de Origem Controlada (DOC) (*pronounced* re zhów dáy maar kaáədə)

region
1. in general use, a relatively large wine-producing area that is geographically or administratively distinct
2. in the Australian system of Geographic Indications, a single tract of land containing at least five independently owned vineyards of at least 5 hectares each and usually producing at least 500 tons of wine grapes per year. A region must be distinct from other regions and, according to the AWBC Act that established the system, have 'measurable homogeneity in grape-growing attributes over its area'. It may contain one or more subregions.

regionality
Australia, New Zealand, USA the local conditions in which grapes are grown and that influence the final wine. The term is similar to French 'terroir', which describes everything from the climate to the soil surrounding a vine.

regional wine
a wine blended from wines produced in different parts of a region, e.g. 'Bordeaux regional wine' is blended from wines produced anywhere within the large region of Bordeaux in southwestern France rather than from a specific estate or vineyard

Region I, II, III, IV, V *see* **climatic regions**

regions *see* **climatic regions**

Régnié AOC
France an appellation in the Beaujolais region of France that was originally a part of the Beaujolais-Villages AOC until upgraded. It grows mostly the Gamay grape variety to produce a range of styles of red wine. (*pronounced* ray nyáy)

rehoboam
an oversize bottle, no longer made, that could hold 4.5 litres, equivalent to six standard 750 ml bottles

Reid
German a vineyard in Austria (*pronounced* rīt, *plural* **Reide**)

Reims, Rheims
France the larger of the two towns at the centre of Champagne production in the Champagne region of northeastern France. Épernay is closer to the vineyards. (*pronounced* raNss)

remuage
French a process used in making Champagne in which the sediment is removed after secondary fermentation has occurred in the bottle (*pronounced* rə mwaázh)

Rémy Martin
a long-established Cognac house making a range of good brandies

René Lalou *see* **Mumm**

reserva
Spanish used to describe good-quality wine produced from a good vintage that meets various regulatory specifications on ageing. Red wines should have been aged for at least three years, including at least one year in a wooden barrel; white and rosé wines should have been aged for at least two years, including at least six months in a wooden barrel. (*pronounced* re záirva, *literally* 'reserve')
See also **gran reserva**

reserve
a term used on wine labels to imply a choice wine, but with no official status.
See also **Cognac**

réserve
French reserve (*pronounced* ray záirv)

residual sugar

natural sugar that remains in a wine after the fermentation process or that is added to a sparkling wine as a dosage to cause secondary fermentation in the bottle. The natural sugars remain in a wine either because the original grape juice had so much natural sugar to start with that it is not all used up in fermentation, e.g. when producing sweet wines; because the fermentation process was stopped by adding alcohol (raising the alcohol level to one that prevents the yeast from working), e.g. when producing fortified sweet wine such as port; or because they are of the small proportion of the types of sugar that do not easily ferment. Residual sugar is usually measured by percentage, weight or volume.

residuo

Italian residual sugar (*pronounced* rə zíddoo ō)

♀ resinous

(*tasting term*) used to describe a wine with a pungent smell and taste of pinewood. A resinous quality is normally found in Greek wine such as retsina, which has been processed with pine resin.

resistant

used to describe a microorganism that is not affected by specific pesticides or a plant that is not susceptible to specific diseases or unfavourable climatic conditions

Restzucker

German residual sugar (*pronounced* rést tsŏokər)

resveratrol

a phenolic compound found in red wine as well as other foods that is believed to provide anti-inflammatory and anti-carcinogenic effects

retsina

a style of wine made according to a traditional process used in Greece for several thousand years, in which pieces of resin from pine trees are added to the grape juice and left in it until racking, giving the resulting wine a pungent smell and taste of pinewood. White wine produced in this way is called simply 'retsina' and rosé wine is called 'kokineli'. (*pronounced* ret seénə)

Reuilly AOC

France a small appellation in the Loire region of France

neighbouring the Sancerre and Pouilly-Fumé AOCs and using Sauvignon Blanc grapes to produce dry, crisp white wines and Pinot Noir grapes to produce light red wines (*pronounced* rố yee)

Rheims *see* Reims

Rheingau
Germany an Anbaugebiet (quality wine-producing region) that runs along the right bank of the Rhine and along the Main river, growing Riesling grapes on the steep vineyard slopes to produce good-quality rich, fruity white wines (*pronounced* rĭn gow)

Rheinhessen
Germany the largest Anbaugebiet (quality wine-producing region) in Germany that runs along the Rhine river between the other Rhine regions of Rheingau and Pfalz. It mostly produces cheap Liebfraumilch white wines, with a few vineyards producing good-quality white wines from Müller-Thurgau grapes. (*pronounced* rĭn hess'n)

Rheinpfalz
Germany same as **Pfalz** (*pronounced* rĭn falts)

Rhine Riesling *another name for* Riesling

Rhine wine
USA medium sweet white wine. The term does not refer to wines from Germany.

Rhône
France, Switzerland a river that starts in Switzerland then runs through France, with vineyards either side of it, forming one of the major wine-producing regions of France and including many well-known appellations. In the north Syrah is the only red grape allowed and it produces the region's rarest and most expensive red wine. Marsanne and Viognier are grown for white wines. Côte Rôtie and Hermitage are the best-known red wines of the northern Rhône. Other appellations are Condrieu, Château-Grillet, Crozes-Hermitage and Saint-Joseph. Some of the world's greatest producers work here: Chave, Guigal, Graillot and Colombo to name but a few. In the southern stretch of the river mostly Grenache grapes are grown for red wine, but 12 grapes in total are permitted, and a range of grapes are allowed for white wines. Châteauneuf-du-Pape is the most famous wine of the southern Rhône, but there are other well-known areas:

Vacqueyras, Gigondas and Tavel, home of rosé wines. (*pronounced* rōn)

Rhône Rangers
a group of winemakers based in California, USA, who are dedicated to growing the grape varieties from the Rhône region of France (Grenache, Mourvèdre and Syrah). Their base includes an area of Los Carneros County that, due to its climate, provides good conditions for growing these grape varieties, as well as those required for sparkling wine.

Rias Baixas DO
Spain the main DO area in the Galicia region of northwestern Spain producing dry white wines from the Albariño grape variety (*pronounced* reé əss bay shaáss)

Ribatejo
Portugal a large wine-producing region of Portugal, divided by the River Tagus (*pronounced* reébə táy<u>zh</u>ō)

Ribeiro DO
Spain a wine-producing DO area in the Galicia region of northwestern Spain that grows mostly the Palomino grape to produce predominantly white wines, although Grenache (Garnacha) is also grown for red wines (*pronounced* ri báyrō)

Ribera del Duero DO
Spain a wine-producing DO area in Castilla-León, northern Spain, running along the Duero river and best-known for its good red wines produced from Tempranillo grapes (*pronounced* ri báirə del dwáirō)

♢ Ribolla Gialla, Ribolla
a white-wine grape variety grown in some European countries, notably Italy, Greece and Slovenia, and used to produce dry, crisp medium-bodied white wines. Ribolla is the Italian form; in Greece it is Robola and in Slovenia Rebula. (*pronounced* ri bóllə jaálə)

♢ Ribolla Nera *another name for* Schioppettino (*pronounced* ri bóllə náirə)

♀ rich
(*tasting term*) used to describe a wine with good body and full flavour and bouquet

Richebourg AOC
France an estate appellation in the Côte de Nuits district of Burgundy growing Pinot Noir grapes to produce one of the great red wines of Burgundy (*pronounced* reésh boor)

riddling
the process of removing sediment formed during secondary fermentation when producing Champagne. Once the still white wine is bottled, a dosage (a mix of sugar, water or wine, and yeast) is added to each bottle to start secondary fermentation in the bottle. This secondary fermentation produces some sediment inside the bottle, which needs to be removed. The bottles are arranged at an angle with the neck pointing down; once all the sediment has collected in the neck, it is removed in the disgorgement process.

♢ Riesling
one of the world's great white-wine grape varieties producing good-quality, fruity white wines that can range in style from dry to sweet. Grown around the world, it is best-known as the source of the best-quality wines from Germany. There is a wide range of different names and clones of the Riesling grape: Rhine Riesling and Weisser Riesling are names for true Riesling, whereas Cape Riesling is a Crouchen grape variety and Sylvaner Riesling is a clone of the original Riesling grape variety. (*pronounced* reéssling)

♢ Riesling Italico *another name for* Welschriesling (*pronounced* reéssling i tálli kō)

Rieussec, Château
France a château in the Sauternes AOC of Bordeaux in southwestern France graded premier cru (first growth) in the classification of 1855. It grows Sémillon grapes to produce good-quality sweet white wine. (*pronounced* ree yő sek)

Rioja DOCa
Spain the only DOCa region of Spain, in the north of the country, that produces some of the country's best red wines, as well as some whites and rosés (rosados). The region is divided into the three areas of La Rioja Alavesa, La Rioja Alta and La Rioja Baja, of which La Rioja Alta generally produces the best-quality wines. The region grows mostly Tempranillo and some Grenache (Garnacha) grapes to produce the red and rosé wines and Macabeo (Viura) grapes to produce the white wines. (*pronounced* ri óhə)

ripasso
Italian a winemaking process used in the Veneto region of northeastern Italy in which a batch of newly fermented wine is put into a vat that contains the lees (skins and pips) from a previous batch of recioto-style wine, in which the grapes were sun-dried to increase the concentration of the sugars and flavours. It is used by some producers to create red wines with additional flavour and body. (*pronounced* ri pássō)

♀ **ripe**
(*tasting term*) used to describe a wine that is rich, fruity and characteristic of correctly ripened grapes

ripeness *see* **physiological ripeness**

riserva
Italian used to describe wine produced in a DOC or DOCG region and aged for three or more years (*pronounced* ri záirvə, *literally* 'reserve')

Riverina
Australia a wine region centred on Griffith, 600 km southwest of Sydney, providing the majority of New South Wales wines, mostly of average quality, but renowned for its botrytised Sémillon styles, which rival even Sauternes in lusciousness

riserva speciale
Italian used to describe riserva wine that has been aged for an additional year or more (*pronounced* ri záirvə spe cháa lay, *literally* 'special reserve')

Rivesaltes AOC
France a small appellation in the Languedoc region of southern France that produces red, white and rosé wines but is perhaps best-known for its sweet, fortified wines (vins doux naturels), the best of which is produced from Muscat grapes. (*pronounced* reév zaált)
See also **Muscat de Rivesaltes AOC**

♡ **Rkatsiteli**
a white-wine grape variety used for table wines, fortified wines and brandy in Russia, Georgia, Bulgaria and other countries of eastern Europe and the former Soviet Union (*pronounced* rə kát si téllee)

♀ **roast chestnut**
(*tasting term*) an aroma associated with full-bodied southern Italian red wines

Robert Mondavi
USA an influential estate in the Napa Valley region of California, originally set up by Robert Mondavi, that produces white wines (including its well-known Fumé Blanc) from oak-aged Sauvignon Blanc grapes and red wines from Cabernet Sauvignon grapes

Robertson
South Africa a hot dry wine-growing region east of Paarl that grows white-wine grapes, including Chardonnay, but that is also now looking to produce good red wines, especially from Syrah (Shiraz) grapes

♡ **Robola** *another name for* **Ribolla Gialla** (*pronounced* rə bółə, *used in* Greece)

♀ **robust**
(*tasting term*) used to describe a wine that is full-bodied with intense fruit aroma, normally red wine

Roederer *see* **Louis Roederer**

Roero DOC
Italy a wine-producing DOC area in the Piedmont region of northwestern Italy that produces red wine from Nebbiolo grapes and some white wine. A style of white wine made from Arneis grapes in this area is called Arneis di Roero. (*pronounced* rō áirō)

Rogue River Valley AVA
USA a wine-producing region in Oregon, western USA, that grows mostly Chardonnay grapes for white wine and Cabernet Sauvignon grapes for red wine

Rolland, Michel
a well-known oenologist travelling and advising over 100 vineyards around the world on good winemaking and the style of winemaking from Bordeaux. With his wife he also runs their own vineyards in a number of regions of France, including Pomerol and Saint-Émilion. (*pronounced* ro laáN)

Romanée, La AOC *see* **La Romanée AOC**

Romanée-Conti AOC
France a very small, yet hugely famous grand cru vineyard in the village of Vosne-Romanée in the Burgundy region of France.

It grows Pinot Noir grapes to produce excellent and expensive spicy red wines. (*pronounced* rō ma nay kóntee)

Romanée-Saint-Vivant AOC
France a small grand cru vineyard in the village of Vosne-Romanée in the Burgundy region of France. It grows Pinot Noir grapes to produce some of the best red wines in Burgundy, though it is less famous than neighbouring vineyards in the village. (*pronounced* rō ma nay saN vee vaáN)

Romania, Rumania
a country in eastern Europe with a long history of wine production. It grows a wide range of grape varieties, classic as well as local. *See* map at **Bulgaria**

Rondel *see* **Codorníu**

Rondinella
a red grape variety grown in the Veneto region of northeastern Italy to produce light, fruity red and rosé wines (*pronounced* rondi néllə)

Rondo
a red-wine grape variety developed in the Czech Republic and producing full-bodied ruby-red wines

room temperature
the ideal serving temperature of red wines, which should be around 15–16°C, or 60°F, though this can be cooler than the often very warm temperature of rooms, and wine should not really be served at a temperature warmer than 18°C (around 65°F). Cellars where wine is stored are usually cooler, around 10–13°C, or 50–55°F, so red wines need time to warm slightly to ensure that the aroma and flavours of the wine are realised. Some red wines can be served cool, e.g. some of the reds from the Loire valley in France and those made in Australia from the Tarrango grape variety.

rootstock
the part of a vine that includes the roots and the first few centimetres of the stem above ground. Most vines consist of two different varieties: a disease-tolerant rootstock that can resist the phylloxera root aphid and a fruiting variety grafted on to it to produce the variety of grapes required.

Roriz *another name for* **Tempranillo** (*pronounced* rō reéz, *used in* Portugal)

rosado
1. *Spanish* rosé (*pronounced* rō saádō)
2. *Portuguese* rosé (*pronounced* ro zaádō)

rosato
Italian rosé (*pronounced* rō zaátō)

♀ **rose**
(*tasting term*) a taste or aroma associated with white wines from Alsace or made from the Muscat grape variety, but also with some red Burgundies and Barolos

Rosé d'Anjou AOC
France an appellation in the Anjou area of the Loire valley in France that produces moderate-quality slightly sweet rosé wine from a range of grape varieties including Malbec and Gamay (*pronounced* rṓ zay daaN zhoŏ)

Rosé de Loire AOC
France an appellation in the Loire valley of France that covers a wide area and produces dry rosé wines from a blend of Cabernet Franc and Gamay grapes (*pronounced* rṓ zay də lwaár)

Rose des Riceys AOC
France a small appellation in the Champagne region of France producing an unusual and rare still rosé wine made from Pinot Noir grapes (*pronounced* rōz day ree seé)

Rosemount Estate
Australia an estate in the Hunter Valley region of New South Wales producing consistently good-quality white Chardonnay-based wines and good red wines

rosé wine
French a pink-coloured wine that is usually made from red-skinned grapes in a similar way to red wine, except that the grape skins are only left in contact with the fermenting wine for a very short time – only a few days – ensuring that the wine has only a light tinge of colour from the skins, but also reducing the flavour, tannins and structure that the skins impart to a red wine during fermentation. Rosé still wine is normally light, fresh and slightly sweet and best drunk cool rather than at room temperature. Rosé Champagne is made by adding a little red wine to a normal white Champagne just before the secondary bottle fermentation.
See also **vin rosé**

◊ Rossese
a red grape variety grown in the Liguria region of northwestern Italy to produce fruity red wine (*pronounced* rō sáy zay)

Rossese di Dolceacqua DOC
Italy a small wine-producing DOC area in the Liguria region of northwestern Italy producing fruity red wines from the Rossese grape (*pronounced* rō sáy zay dee dól chay ákwa)

rosso
Italian used to describe red wine, especially in a dry style (*pronounced* róssō)
See also **vino rosso**

Rosso Conero DOC
Italy a wine-producing DOC area in the Marche region of central Italy that produces red wine from Montepulciano and Sangiovese grape varieties (*pronounced* róssō ko náirō)

Rosso di Montalcino DOC
Italy a wine-producing DOC area in the Tuscany region of Italy that grows the Sangiovese grape (called Brunello locally) to produce a light red wine (*pronounced* róssō dee mónt al cheénō)

Rosso di Montepulciano DOC
Italy a wine-producing DOC area in the Tuscany region of Italy that grows a mix of Sangiovese (called Prugnolo locally) and Canaiolo Nero grapes to produce a flowery, light red wine (*pronounced* róssō dee món tay poöl chaánō)

Rosso Piceno DOC
Italy a wine-producing DOC area in the Marche region of central Italy that produces a dry style of red wine from Montepulciano, Sangiovese and Trebbiano grape varieties. If aged for a year, the better wines with a little more alcohol are given the label 'superiore'. (*pronounced* róssō pi cháynō)

Rothschild
France the name of a European family whose members have been influential vineyard owners. The French branch of the family acquired Château Lafite (now Lafite-Rothschild) in 1868 and subsequently other top Bordeaux properties, as well as interests in Chile, Portugal and the USA. The English branch of the family bought and developed Château Mouton-Rothschild. (*pronounced* rōt sheéld)
See **Lafite-Rothschild, Château; Mouton-Rothschild, Château**

Rothschild, Baron Philippe de

the member of the Rothschild family who successfully campaigned to have Château Mouton-Rothschild promoted in 1973 from deuxième cru (second growth) to premier cru (first growth) status. He advocated château-bottling and introduced designer wine labels. With Robert Mondavi he also set up Opus One, a winery based in the Napa Valley, California, USA.

Rotling

pink-coloured wine produced in small quantities in parts of Germany from a mixture of red-skinned and white-skinned grapes, rather than from just red-skinned grapes, as with French rosé wines (*pronounced* rőtling)
See also **Schillerwein**

♀ rotten eggs

(*tasting term*) the smell of sulphur from spoiled wine

Rotwein

German red wine (*pronounced* rőt vīn, *plural* **Rotweine**)

rouge

French red. (*pronounced* roo<u>zh</u>)
See also **vin rouge**

♀ rough

(*tasting term*) used to describe a wine that has a harsh texture or flavour due to an excess of tannin or acid. In some wines this character can dissipate with ageing.

♀ round

(*tasting term*) used to describe a smooth, full-bodied and well-balanced wine

♦ Roupeiro

a Portuguese white-wine grape variety grown especially in the Alentejo region of southern Portugal (*pronounced* roo páyrō)

♦ Roussanne

a white-skinned grape variety grown mostly in the northern Rhône valley region of France, and in limited quantity in parts of Italy and in Australia. It produces a delicate white wine and is used in many Rhône estates for blending, but is also the main grape of the well-known white wines from the Châteauneuf-du-Pape and Crozes-Hermitage AOCs. (*pronounced* roo sán)

Roussette *another name for* **Altesse** (*pronounced* roo sét, *used in* the Savoie region)

Roussette de Savoie AOC *see* **Savoie** (*pronounced* roo sét də sa vwaá)

Roussillon

a wine-producing area of southern France, the western part of the Languedoc-Roussillon region. (*pronounced* roo see yóN)
See **Côtes du Roussillon AOC**; **Grand Roussillon AOC**; **Languedoc-Roussillon**

Royalty

an unusual red-skinned grape that produces red-coloured juice rather than the more usual white juice when the grapes are pressed. It is grown in small quantities in parts of California, USA, and is mainly used in blends.

rubbery

(*tasting term*) used to describe the unpleasant smell of rubber on a wine, caused by the chemical compound mercaptan and normally the result of poor winemaking

rubino

Italian ruby (*pronounced* roo bée̱nō)
See also **Marsala DOC**

Rubired

a red-skinned grape variety with red flesh that produces red juice rather than the more usual white juice when the grapes are pressed. It is grown in small quantities in parts of California, USA, and is mainly used in blends. (*pronounced* roóbi red)

Ruby Cabernet

a red-wine grape variety produced as a cross between Cabernet Sauvignon and Carignan varieties, grown in small quantities in parts of California, USA. It provides high yields but without the structure and flavours of the original grape varieties.

ruby port *see* **port**

ruby-red

(*tasting term*) used to describe a wine with a deep purplish red colour

Ruchè

a little-used red grape variety grown in the Ruchè DOC of

Piedmont in Italy to produce a red wine high in tannins and with a bitterish aftertaste (*pronounced* roó kay)

Ruchè DOC

Italy an ancient DOC area in the Piedmont region of north-western Italy that uses the local Ruchè grape variety to produce red wines (*pronounced* roó kay)

Ruchottes-Chambertin AOC

France a grand cru vineyard in Gevrey-Chambertin in the Côte de Nuits district of the Burgundy region of France that grows Pinot Noir grapes to produce high-quality red wines (*pronounced* rŏo shót shóm bair táN)

Rueda DOC

Spain a wine-producing DO region in the Castilla-León region northeast of Madrid, best-known for its good-quality white wines produced from Verdejo and Macabeo (Viura) grapes. It also produces a sweet wine similar to sherry, called pálido for the pale, fino style and dorado for the darker, nuttier style. (*pronounced* roo áydə)

Rufina *see* Chianti DOCG (*pronounced* roo feénə)

Ruiterbosch

South Africa a vineyard near Mossel Bay in the southern Cape region of South Africa with a very cool climate, allowing the cultivation of Chardonnay, Pinot Noir, Rhine Riesling and Sauvignon Blanc grape varieties (*pronounced* rítər bosh)

◊ Rulander *another name for* Pinot Gris (*pronounced* roó landər, *used in* Germany)

Rully AOC

France a village appellation in the Côte Chalonnaise area of the Burgundy region of France that grows Chardonnay grapes to produce crisp, dry white wine and grows Pinot Noir grapes to produce light red wines (*pronounced* roó yee)

Rumania *see* Romania

rural method *same as* méthode rurale

Russia

a country that produces red wines from Cabernet Sauvignon grapes grown in the south and east of the country and white wines from a variety of grapes including Muscat, Riesling and especially the native Rkatsiteli

Russian River Valley AVA
USA a high-quality viticultural area in Sonoma County, California, that grows Pinot Noir grapes for red wines and Chardonnay, Riesling and Gewürztraminer for white wines

rustic
(*tasting term*) used to describe a wine that is either made using an old-fashioned, traditional process or a wine tasting as if it had been made using an old-fashioned method

Rutherford AVA
USA a wine-producing region in the Napa Valley of California that includes a large number of wineries

Rutherglen
Australia a wine-producing zone in North East Victoria, known especially for its sweet dessert wines made from Muscat grapes

Ruwer
Germany an area around a small tributary of the Mosel river in the Mosel-Saar-Ruwer region of Germany with some of the best vineyards in Germany (*pronounced* roóvər)

S

Saale-Unstrut
Germany a small Anbaugebiet (quality wine-producing region) in eastern Germany that grows mostly the Müller-Thurgau and Sylvaner grape varieties to produce white wines (*pronounced* zaálə oŏn stroot)

Saar
Germany an area around a small tributary of the Mosel river in the Mosel-Saar-Ruwer region of Germany that can produce some of the country's best wines (*pronounced* zaar)

Sachsen
Germany a very small Anbaugebiet (quality wine-producing region) in eastern Germany around the Elbe river that grows mostly the Müller-Thurgau and Gewürztraminer grape varieties to produce white wines (*pronounced* záks'n)

sack
an old name for white wine from Spain, Portugal or the Canary Islands

Sacramento Valley
USA the northern half of the Central Valley area of California. The Central Valley accounts for three-quarters of all grapes grown in California because of the good climate and high yields.

Sagrantino
a red grape variety grown especially in the Umbria region of Italy to produce a rich red wine that is high in tannins (*pronounced* sa gran teénō)

Sagrantino di Montefalco DOCG *see* Montefalco DOC

saignée
(*pronounced* sayn yáy) *French*
1. used to describe a rosé wine that has a dark pink colour

2. used to describe the process of pressing grapes lightly and not using this lightest-coloured juice, allowing it to run off, and then pressing the fruit again and collecting the darker-coloured juice. The higher skin-to-grape juice ratio results in a darker and more full-flavoured wine. This is sometimes used to produce darker-coloured red wines from grape varieties that normally produce lighter-coloured red wines, e.g. Pinot Noir.

Saint-Amour AOC

France a small appellation in the north of the Beaujolais region of France that produces light, fruity red wines from the Gamay grape variety (*pronounced* sánt a moór)

Saint-Aubin AOC

France an appellation in the Côte de Beaune area of Burgundy in France that produces red wines from Pinot Noir grapes and very good white wines from Chardonnay grapes (*pronounced* sánt ō báN)

Saint Bris *see* Sauvignon de Saint Bris VDQS

Saint-Chinian AOC

France an appellation in the Languedoc region of southern France that produces good-quality full-bodied, spicy red wines from Carignan, Cinsault and Grenache grapes (*pronounced* saN shee nyaáN)

Sainte-Croix-du-Mont AOC

France an appellation in the Bordeaux region of France, on the northern bank of the Garonne river, opposite Sauternes, that produces sweet white wines (*pronounced* sant krwaá doo móN)

Saint-Émilion *another name for* **Trebbiano** (*pronounced* sant ay meél yoN, *used in* France)

Saint-Émilion AOC

France a famous appellation centred on the village of Saint-Émilion in the Bordeaux region of southwestern France. Located on the eastern side (the right bank) of the Dordogne river, it grows Merlot grapes, along with some Cabernet Franc, Cabernet Sauvignon and Malbec, to produce very good red wines. The classification of 1855 did not cover Saint-Émilion, and it was not until a hundred years later, 1955, that it began its own listings, grading the hundreds of estates into premiers crus, grands crus classés or grands crus; below this, wines that do not reach the grand cru level can be graded as Saint-Émilion AOC, and below this level as Bordeaux Supérieur AOC or plain Bordeaux AOC. (*pronounced* sant ay meél yoN)

Saint-Estèphe AOC
France an appellation in the Haut-Médoc area in the Bordeaux region of southwestern France that produces good-quality red wines and includes five grand cru classé châteaux, including the well-known Cos d'Estournel. The appellation grows Cabernet Sauvignon, Merlot and Cabernet Franc grapes to produce tannic, full-bodied red wines. (*pronounced* sánt e stéf)

Saint-George d'Orques
France a wine-producing area near the town of Montpellier in the Coteaux du Languedoc AOC of southern France (*pronounced* saN zháwrzh dáwrk)

Saint-Georges-Saint-Émilion AOC
France a small appellation on the outskirts of the Saint-Émilion district of the Bordeaux region of southwestern France that grows the Merlot grape to produce good-quality red wine (*pronounced* saN zháwrzh sant ay meél yoN)

Saint-Jean-de-Minervois AOC
France an appellation in the Midi region of France producing a vin doux naturel from Muscat à Petits Grains grapes (*pronounced* saN zhaáN də mee nair vwaá)

Saint-Joseph AOC
France an appellation in the northern Rhône valley region of France that produces good-quality, full-bodied red wine mostly from Syrah grapes and good-quality white wine mainly from Marsanne and Rousanne grapes (*pronounced* saN zhō zéf)

Saint-Julien AOC
France a famous appellation in the Haut-Médoc area of Bordeaux in southwestern France that includes 11 cru classé châteaux. It grows mostly Cabernet Sauvignon grapes to produce very good red wine. (*pronounced* saN zhool yáN)

◊ Saint-Laurent
an unusual and rarely grown red-wine grape, originally from Austria, producing high-quality full-bodied wine (*pronounced* saN law raáN)

Saint-Nicolas-de-Bourgueil AOC
France a village appellation in the Loire valley of France, that produces light, fruity red wine from Cabernet Franc grapes. This red wine can be served cool. (*pronounced* saN nikō laá də boor gố ee)

Saint-Péray AOC
France an appellation in the north of the Rhône valley region of France producing white wine using the Marsanne grape. The area also produces a sparkling white wine under the Saint-Péray Mousseux AOC. (*pronounced* saN pay ráy)

Saint-Pierre, Château
France a small château in the Saint-Julien AOC of the Haut-Médoc area of Bordeaux in southwestern France graded qua-trième cru (fourth growth) in the classification of 1855. It produces good-quality, full-bodied red wines from Cabernet Sauvignon and Merlot grapes. (*pronounced* saN pyáir)

Saint-Romain AOC
France an appellation in the Côte de Beaune area of the Burgundy region of France that grows Pinot Noir grapes for red wines and Chardonnay grapes for white wines (*pronounced* saN rō máN)

Saint-Véran AOC
France an appellation in the Mâconnais area of the Burgundy region of France that grows Chardonnay grapes to produce good-quality white wines (*pronounced* saN vay raáN)

Salice Salentino DOC
Italy a DOC area in the Apulia region of southeastern Italy that grows mainly Negroamaro grapes to produce robust red wines (*pronounced* sa leéchay salen teénō)

salmanazar
an oversize bottle that can hold 9 litres, equivalent to 12 standard 750 ml bottles

♀ **salty, salt**
(*tasting term*) used to describe the taste of manzanilla sherry

Samos
Greece an island appellation in eastern Greece that grows especially Muscat grapes to produce dry and sweet white wines

Sancerre AOC
France a well-known appellation in the Loire region of France that grows Sauvignon Blanc grapes to produce crisp white wines and also produces small quantities of light red and rosé wines from Pinot Noir grapes (*pronounced* saaN sáir)

Sandeman
a large producer of port and sherry with a facility in Jerez, Spain, producing fine sherries and a facility in Portugal producing a range of ports. It now belongs to the Canadian company Seagram. (*pronounced* sándi mən)

sangaree
a chilled drink of wine mixed with fruit juice, nutmeg and sometimes other spirits (*pronounced* sáng gə reé)

Sangiovese
one of the most important red-wine grapes used in Italy. It is grown widely, particularly in central and southern Italy, and produces red wine that is high in acid and tannin and can be used to make a range of different styles of wine, from fresh, light, young wines to full-bodied reds. It is best-known as the main grape used in the Chianti red wines (where it is called Sangioveto). Some Sangiovese is now also grown in California, USA. (*pronounced* sán jō váyzi)
Also called **Brunello**; **Calabrese**; **Sangioveto**

Sangioveto *another name for* **Sangiovese** (*pronounced* sán jō váytō, *used in* the Chianti DOCG area of Tuscany)

sangria
a chilled drink, originating in Spain, of red wine, fruit juice, lemonade or soda water and brandy or another spirit, usually served in a jug with pieces of fruit (*pronounced* sang greé ə)

Santa Maddalena DOC
Italy a wine-producing DOC area in the Alto Adige area of the Trentino-Alto Adige region of Italy that produces good-quality fruity red wines from mostly Schiava grapes, which should be drunk young (*pronounced* sántə madə láynə)

Santa Rita
Chile a wine-producing company based in Chile noted as the main exporter from the country. It has vineyards in a variety of regions including the Casablanca region of Chile, producing red and white wines.

Santenay AOC
France a small village appellation in the Côte d'Or area of Burgundy that includes a number of premier cru estates that produce good-quality red wine from Pinot Noir grapes (*pronounced* saaNtə náy)

Santorini
Greece a wine-producing region that encompasses many islands in the Cyclades where the Assyrtiko grape is grown to produce a dry and sweet white wine

Sardinia, Sardegna
Italy an island in the Mediterranean off the west coast of Italy, growing mostly traditional grape varieties and producing red wines especially from Grenache (Cannonau) grapes and white wine from Nuragus and Torbato grapes

Sassicaia DOC
Italy a wine-producing DOC that is unusual in being a single private estate, in the Tuscany region of Italy. It grows Cabernet Sauvignon grapes to produce very good red wines in a Bordeaux style. (*pronounced* sássi kī ə)

Saumur AOC
France a large appellation, centred on the town of Saumur, in the Loire valley region of France that produces red and rosé wines using Cabernet Sauvignon and Pineau d'Aunis grapes and white wines using Chenin Blanc grapes. The better-quality rosé wines are often sold under the Cabernet de Saumur label. The area contains several smaller AOCs. (*pronounced* sō móor)

Saumur-Champigny AOC
France an appellation within the Saumur AOC in the Loire valley region of France that produces fruity red wines from the same Cabernet Sauvignon and Pineau d'Aunis grapes as the Saumur AOC but of better quality, These red wines can be served cool (*pronounced* sō móor shom pee nyeé)

Saumur Mousseux AOC
France an appellation within the Saumur AOC in the Loire valley region of France that produces sparkling white wine from Chenin Blanc, Chardonnay and Sauvignon Blanc grape varieties. The same region also has the better-quality Crémant de Loire AOC sparkling wine appellation. (*pronounced* sō móor moo só)

Sauternes AOC

France a famous appellation in the Graves district of the Bordeaux region of southwestern France that produces some of the best sweet white wines in the world. It grows mostly Sémillon grapes and a little Sauvignon Blanc. Its climatic conditions are conducive to infection of the grapes with the *Botrytis cinerea* fungus, which adds more flavour and complexity to the finished wines. This may be late in the season, or not at all, or patchily, and the best wine is produced by the growers who give the greatest attention to the grapes' development and often by those who take the greatest risk in not picking the grapes. If the weather does not allow the grapes to ripen fully, the estates often use them to produce a dry white wine. The châteaux in the region were graded in the classification of 1855, with the best estate, Château d'Yquem, in a class of its own, called premier grand cru, 11 premiers crus (first growths) and 15 deuxièmes crus (second growths). (*pronounced* sō túrn, *plural* **Sauternes**)

♢ Sauvignon

(*pronounced* sô vee nyoN)
1. *another name for* **Sauvignon Blanc**
2. *another name for* **Tocai**

♢ Sauvignon Blanc

a white-wine grape variety grown around the world, particularly in California and in the Loire and Bordeaux regions of France, but also in Italy, Australia, New Zealand and South America. White wine produced from this grape is normally dry, crisp and acidic and with characteristics that are often described in terms such as herbaceous, grassy, gooseberries, elderflower, currant leaf and nettles (but also cat's pee). In the Loire valley region of France, dry white wines are made exclusively from this grape; in the Bordeaux region, it is blended with the Sémillon grape to improve ageing qualities. (*pronounced* sô vee nyoN blaáN)
Also called **Fumé Blanc**; **Sauvignon**; **Sauvignon Jaune**; **Sauvignon Musqué**

Sauvignon de Saint Bris VDQS

France a VDQS area in the Burgundy region of France producing a dry white wine from Sauvignon Blanc grapes (*pronounced* sô vee nyoN də saN breé)

♢ Sauvignon Jaune, Sauvignon Musqué *another name for* **Sauvignon Blanc** (*pronounced* sô vee nyoN zhốn *or* sô vee nyoN moố skay)

♢ **Sauvignon Rouge** *another name for* **Cabernet Sauvignon** (*pronounced* số vee nyoN róozh)

♢ **Sauvignon Vert** *another name for* **Muscadelle** (*pronounced* số vee nyoN váir)

♢ **Savagnin, Savagnin Blanc, Savagnin Jaune**
an unusual white-wine grape variety that is grown mostly in the Jura region of eastern France to produce the local vin jaune, which is made in a similar way to a sherry, producing a light, sweet, nutty wine. (*pronounced* sávvə nyaN *or* sávvə nyaN bláaN *or* sávvə nyaN zhốn)
Also called **Gringet**

Savagnin Noir *another name for* **Pinot Noir** (*pronounced* sávvə nyaN nwaár)

♢ **Sav Blanc** *abbreviation* Sauvignon Blanc (*informal*)

Savennières AOC
France a small appellation in the Anjou area of the Loire valley region of France that produces very-good-quality white wines from the Chenin Blanc grape (*pronounced* sávvə nyáir)

Savigny-lès-Beaune AOC
France an appellation in the Côte de Beaune area of Burgundy that grows Pinot Noir grapes to produce a relatively light red wine and grows Chardonnay grapes for white wine (*pronounced* sá vee nyee lay bốn)

Savoie
France a wine-producing area in eastern France, near the border with Switzerland, that produces dry white, red and rosé wines. It contains several AOCs. The Vin de Savoie AOC produces mostly white wine from Jacquère grapes and red wine from Gamay and Mondeuse grapes. Sparkling white wine is produced in the Vin de Savoie Mousseux AOC and the Roussette de Savoie AOC produces dry white wine from Altesse (Roussette) grapes. (*pronounced* sa vwaá)

♢ **Savoyance** *another name for* **Mondeuse** (*pronounced* sá vwaa yáaNss)

Schaumwein
German the lowest-quality category of sparkling wine in Germany (*pronounced* shówm vīn, *plural* **Schaumweine**)

Scheurebe

a white-wine hybrid grape variety, a cross between Riesling and Sylvaner grapes, that is widely grown in the Rhine region of Germany. It produces good-quality white wine with high alcohol and sugar levels and because it suffers easily from the *Botrytis cinerea* fungus it is generally used to produce sweet, late-harvest wines. (*pronounced* shóy raybə)

Schiava

a red-wine grape grown in the Trentino-Alto Adige region of Italy to produce light, fruity wines that are best drunk young (*pronounced* skyaávə)

Schillerwein

a style of rosé wine produced in the Württemberg region of Germany by fermenting red and white grapes together (*pronounced* shillər vīn, *plural* **Schillerweine**)
See also **Rotling**

Schioppettino

a red-wine grape variety grown in the Giulia region of Italy to produce dry, full-flavoured red wines. (*pronounced* skyóppə teénō)
Also called **Ribolla Nera**

Schloss

German a castle. The term is often used in wine labels to refer to an estate. (*pronounced* shloss, *plural* **Schlösser**)

Schloss Johannisberg

Germany one of the most famous estates in Germany, in the Rheingau, that can trace its history back to the 12th century. Its wines are very good Rieslings with good ageing potential. (*pronounced* shlóss yō hánnis bairg)

Schönburger

a German-bred hybrid pink grape variety grown for wine in England (*pronounced* shúrn boorgər)

Schubert, Max

an influential winemaker in Australia who was the chief winemaker at the Penfolds winery and developed its famous Grange wine as well as developing and promoting the Australian wine industry generally

Sciacarello

a grape variety that is unique to Corsica, where it is grown to produce light-coloured but alcoholic red wines and crisp rosé wines (*pronounced* sha karéllō)

screwcap

a top that screws on the top of a wine bottle, as a substitute for the traditional plug of cork. This is a modern solution to sealing a wine bottle, about which there is a huge debate in the wine industry. The increase in consumption of wine has meant that more corks are required, but the cork oak supply is limited, so corks are not always of perfect quality. They can contain bacteria, or be unsuitable for storing the bottle for a long time on its side, when the cork could dry out and shrink, allowing oxygen into the bottle. A screwcap solves these problems, but is not considered aesthetically pleasing by traditionalists.
See also **Stelvin closure**

screw press

a type of wine press with a screw in a cylindrical housing with perforations. The screw puts increasing pressure on the pomace as it moves along the housing and the juice extracted at the beginning of the process is clearer than that at the end. The method is not suitable for making fine wines.

○ Scuppernong

a white-wine grape variety belonging to the species *Vitis rotundifolia* that is grown in the southeastern USA to produce an unusually flavoured, sweet white wine

Seagram

a very large Canadian firm that owns many spirit brands, including that of Martell brandy, and also the port producer Sandeman

Seaview

Australia a winery near Adelaide in the McLaren Vale region of South Australia best-known for producing good, affordable sparkling wine from a Chardonnay and Pinot Noir mix. It is now part of the Southcorp company.

sec

French used to describe a wine, especially Champagne, that is dry in taste (*pronounced* sek)

secco

Italian dry (*pronounced* sékō)

seco

Spanish dry (*pronounced* sékō)

séco
Portuguese dry (*pronounced* sékō)

secondary fermentation
1. in the méthode champenoise for making sparkling wine, the fermentation that occurs in the bottle once the dosage (a mixture of sugar, water or wine, and yeast) is added. This creates carbon dioxide as a by-product, which – in the sealed bottle – dissolves in the wine creating the sparkling wine.
2. in making still wine, the second stage of the fermentation process that occurs when the bitter malic acid present in grapes is converted into a less astringent lactic acid, with a by-product of carbon dioxide gas. Almost all red wines include this second stage of fermentation, but producers of white wine often prevent this second stage to ensure that the wine tastes crisp and sharp, although it is also avoided when the grapes are overripe and too sweet.
Also called **malolactic fermentation**
Compare **primary fermentation**

secondary mildew *see* **powdery mildew**

second growth *see* **deuxième cru**

second label
a wine produced by a château or estate that does not quite reach the quality level to be sold under the vineyard's main and best-known label and so is sold under a separate name

second-label vintage port *see* **port**

sediment
solids deposited at the bottom of a bottle of wine as it matures. This normally means that the wine has not been overfiltered.
Compare **lees**

◊ **Seibel 9549** *another name for* **Chaunac** (*pronounced* sĩb'l)

◊ **Seibel 10878** *another name for* **Chelois** (*pronounced* sĩb'l)

Sekt
German the best quality of sparkling wine produced in Germany, officially called Qualitätschaumwein, which is usually produced using the Charmat process and often using the Riesling grape variety (*pronounced* zekt, *plural* **Sekte**)

Selak
New Zealand a wine producer in Auckland producing a range of

good-quality wines from Sauvignon Blanc, Chardonnay and Cabernet Sauvignon grapes as well as one of the country's first sparkling wines made by the méthode champenoise

Selection
used on labels of German wine to indicate a dry white wine (unless made from Riesling grapes) from a single vineyard and made with a traditional grape variety of the region.
Compare **Classic**

Sélection de Grains Nobles
a type of wine produced in the Alsace region of France made from late-harvest grapes (Riesling, Gewürztraminer, Pinot Gris or Muscat) infected with the fungus *Botrytis cinerea* to produce very sweet, concentrated white wines (*pronounced* say lék syoN də graN nóblə)

♀ semidry
(*tasting term*) medium dry

♢ Sémillon
a white-wine grape variety that is grown around the world, most notably in the Bordeaux region of France, in Chile, in South Africa and in Australia. It is most often used in blends with Sauvignon Blanc grapes, deriving complexity and depth from the two complementary grapes and providing wines that range in style from the full-bodied dry white wines of the Hunter Valley to sweet white wines from Sauternes. (*pronounced* sáy mee yóN)

semi-seco
Spanish medium dry (*pronounced* semi sékō)

semisweet
medium sweet

Sercial
(*pronounced* sair syaál)
♢ **1.** a white-wine grape variety grown mostly in the Dão region of Portugal, producing highly perfumed but very acidic wines. It was used in the original vineyards of Madeira before being killed off by the phylloxera aphid in the late 1870s, and for many years was neglected, but European Union regulations are fostering a revival.
◊ **2.** the driest, lightest style of sweet Madeira wine.
See also **Madeira DOC**

serre

French in the Champagne region of France, the juice released in the first pressing of the grapes, used to produce the best Champagnes. (*pronounced* sair)
Also called **vin de cuvée**

Setúbal DOC

Portugal a wine-producing DOC region south of Lisbon in Portugal that grows Muscat and other grapes to produce a fortified wine. Until Portugal joined the European Union this wine was known as Moscatel de Setúbal, but local regulations allowed a higher proportion of other grapes than EU practice allows for a grape name to be used for a wine. (*pronounced* se toób'l)

Seyssel AOC

France an appellation in the Savoie region of eastern France producing white wines and best-known for its sparkling white wine Seyssel Mousseux, made by the méthode champenoise from mostly Molette grapes (*pronounced* say sél)

◊ Seyval Blanc, Seyval

a hybrid grape of French origin that is widely used in the USA and in parts of the UK and France to produce crisp white wines (*pronounced* sáy val bláaN)

○ sharp

(*tasting term*) used to describe a wine that is too acidic, with a biting taste

Shenandoah Valley AVA

USA a wine-producing region in the east of California that grows mostly Sauvignon Blanc and Zinfandel grape varieties

sherry

a fortified wine produced in the Andalucía region of southern Spain and officially made in the Jerez-Xérès-Sherry and Manzanilla de Sanlúcar de Barrameda DO areas. Sherry-style wines have been made elsewhere, e.g. in Cyprus, but under European Union regulations only those from the Spanish DOs can label themselves as such. Sherry is normally made from the Palomino grape variety, using the solera system. There is a wide range of styles of sherry, but they can be divided into two main types: fino, which is very dry, light in colour and taste with lower alcohol levels; and oloroso, which has oxidised to a deep brown colour and has a richer taste and higher levels of alcohol. Fino sherry is also produced in different styles with a fino amontillado (aged for five or six years and a darker amber colour with a trace of the nutty flavour of an oloroso), amontillado (aged for longer than a fino amontillado and darker and richer as a result), manzanilla (a very light and tangy fino, made in Sanlúcar de Barrameda), manzanilla pasada (an aged manzanilla that has a darker colour and richer taste) and pale cream sherry (a fino that has been sweetened). Oloroso is also made into other well-known styles of sherry including cream sherry (lower-quality oloroso that has been sweetened) and amoroso or East India sherry (oloroso that has been sweetened); in addition rayas is lower-quality oloroso used in blending medium dry sherry. Lastly, a palo cortado is a fino sherry that has been oxidised further to produce the flavour of an oloroso. During production of fino sherry, a layer of yeast builds up on the surface of the liquid in a cask; this is called the flor, which protects the wine below from oxidising (keeping it a pale colour) and introduces a tangy taste to the sherry.

Shiraz *another name for* **Syrah** (*pronounced* shi ráz)

shoot
a new growth of stems and leaves from an existing stem or branch of a plant

shoot positioning
the process of training young shoots on a vine so that they conform to a particular training system such as the espalier system or the guyot system

shoot thinning
the process of removing unwanted young shoots from a vine so that only one or two remain to be trained in the desired way

short
(*tasting term*) used to describe a wine with very little aftertaste or finish

Sicily
a large Italian island off the toe of the mainland that has a hot climate and a long winemaking tradition. Historically its production was dominated by Marsala fortified wines, but it now produces a range of table wines (often outside the DOC system).

The island has various distinctive grapes, including Nerello, Nero d'Avola and Perricone for red wines and Catarratto, Grillo, Grecanico and Inzolia for white wines.

Sierra Foothills AVA
USA a wine-producing region in California, east of the Napa Valley, with over 30 wineries growing mostly Zinfandel grapes

♀ silky
(*tasting term*) used to describe a wine that has a soft, smooth texture and finish

♀ simple
(*tasting term*) used to describe a wine with a straightforward character that is not complex, but is good

♀ sinewy
(*tasting term*) used to describe a wine that is lean and not very fruity but has a good balance of alcohol and acidity

single-quinta port *see* **port**

skin *see* **grape skin**

skin contact
in making white wines, the leaving of the crushed grape juice in contact with the grape skins for a very short period, often less than a day, to improve flavour and taste. The skins are then removed and the juice fermented.

Slovakia
an eastern European republic that grows some wine-grape varieties similar to those grown in neighbouring Hungary, including Irsai Olivér (Irsay Oliver)

Smith Woodhouse
a port company that produces a range of non-vintage ports including tawny and ruby ports and also a good vintage port and a well-regarded late bottled vintage (LBV) port. It is now owned by the Symington family, who also own Dow, Graham and Warre.

♀ smoky
(*tasting term*) used to describe a wine with an aroma or taste suggestive of smoke, often from the soil in which the vine was grown or if the wine was aged in an oak barrel

♀ **smooth**
(*tasting term*) used to describe a range of characteristics of a well-balanced wine

♀ **soapy**
(*tasting term*) used to describe a wine with an unpleasant taste like soap and water that is a fault except in wines made from the Riesling grape variety that are not yet ready for drinking

Soave DOC
Italy a wine-producing DOC zone in the Veneto region of northeastern Italy that grows the Garganega and Trebbiano grape varieties to make a very popular dry white wine. If it is aged, the wine is labelled 'superiore'. There is also a subzone that produces better-quality 'classico' wines. (*pronounced* swaá vay)

sodium bisulphite, sodium bisulfite
a water-soluble chemical that produces sulphur dioxide when heated and is used for sterilisation in winemaking

♀ **soft**
(*tasting term*) used to describe a wine that is low in tannin or acidity and so is full and gentle on the palate, though this can also result in wine that lacks clarity and definition

softening
a process that happens to a young wine as it ages, reducing the tannin and acid levels and providing a balanced wine

Sogrape
the largest wine producer in Portugal, known especially for its Mateus Rosé

Solano *see* **Green Valley-Solano AVA**

solera
(*pronounced* sō láirə) *Spanish*
1. a cask containing mature wine that has been aged and is ready to bottle
2. a method of producing wine that is a blend of different vintages using a graded series of casks. A proportion of the wine from the cask with the most mature wine is bottled, and replaced with younger wine from the cask containing the wine that is next in maturity, which in turn is refilled with younger wine, and so on. Once a solera is set up, all the casks will contain blended

wine. The system is used especially in Spain for making sherry and also Málaga, Montilla and Alicante's Fondillon, but also in Sicily for Marsala wines.

♀ **solid**
(*tasting term*) used to describe a wine that is full-bodied and well-structured

sommelier
French a waiter in charge of the wine in a restaurant, normally responsible for looking after the cellar in the restaurant and advising on wine with different foods (*pronounced* so mélli ər)

Somontano DO
Spain a wine-producing area in the Pyrenean foothills in north-eastern Spain that grows both local and French grape varieties to produce powerful red and some white wines (*pronounced* so mon taáno)

Sonoma *see* **Green Valley-Sonoma**

Sonoma Coast AVA
USA a large viticultural area in California that has a relatively cool climate and grows a range of different grape varieties

Sonoma County AVA
USA a viticultural area in California that, with the Napa Valley AVA, has helped to bring up the quality and production of wine in California from the 170-plus wineries in the region. The region has a range of climatic conditions and can grow a range of grapes including Cabernet Sauvignon, Chardonnay, Pinot Noir, Sauvignon Blanc and Zinfandel.

Sonoma Valley AVA
USA a viticultural area in western California, northeast of San Francisco, extending northwards from the city of Sonoma and famous for its wineries

♀ **sound**
(*tasting term*) used to describe a wine that has no obvious faults

♀ **sour**
(*tasting term*) used to describe a wine that is starting to turn to vinegar

South Africa
a well-established wine-producing country that first started growing vines in the 17th century and is now the world's

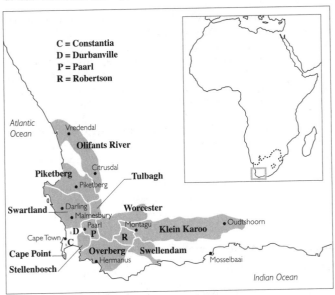

C = Constantia
D = Durbanville
P = Paarl
R = Robertson

Atlantic Ocean

Vredendal

Olifants River

Citrusdal

Piketberg

• Piketberg

Tulbagh

Swartland

• Darling

• Malmesbury

Worcester

Cape Town

• Paarl

Montagu

Klein Karoo

• Oudtshoorn

D   P

R

C

Cape Point

Overberg

Swellendam

Stellenbosch

• Hermanus

Mosselbaai

Indian Ocean

Wine regions of South Africa

ninth-largest wine producer. The major wine-producing regions are in the southwest of the country and are now regulated by an appellation system called Wine of Origin (WO), introduced in 1973 and equivalent to the European model. As in all the other wine-producing countries in search of export markets, new plantings are rapidly being carried out. The country's wine production has historically been dominated by sweet fortified sherry-like wines, but it now produces a wide range of good-quality red, white and sparkling wines. The main white-wine grapes grown are Chenin Blanc (called Steen locally), still the country's most widely planted variety, together with Crouchen, Clairette Blanc, Sémillon, Colombard, Muscat and the ubiquitous Chardonnay. Red-wine grapes include Cinsault (called Hermitage locally), Pinotage, Merlot and Syrah (Shiraz). The South African wine industry suffered greatly during the apartheid years when international trade diminished as sanctions were introduced. The arrival of democracy in 1994 forced change, and the South African Wine Industry Trust was created in 1999 to promote the transformation of the wine industry. White owners still predominate, but change is happening slowly. In 2001 the Vineyard Academy was launched to provide vineyard workers with skills training in various fields. Amongst the most important areas are: Constantia, boasting some of the most famous estate names such as Groot Constantia and Klein Constantia, producing superb Sauvignon Blanc and Sémillon wines; Durbanville, which offers some wonderful Sauvignon Blancs; Paarl, which has cellars both large and small and wine from the ordinary to the sensational – the focus is on Syrah (Shiraz), but some fine Chenin Blancs and Pinotages are also produced; Robertson, which is looking to produce good red wines, especially from Syrah (Shiraz) grapes; and Stellenbosch, considered by many to be South Africa's best wine-growing area, with more than 80 wineries and all the most famous South African wine names and growing Cabernet Sauvignon, Merlot, Pinotage and Chenin Blanc.

South African Riesling *another name for* **Crouchen**

South African Wine Industry Trust *see* **South Africa**

South America *see* **Argentina**; **Brazil**; **Chile**; **Uruguay**

South Australia
Australia a state on the south coast of Australia, of which Adelaide is the capital, that grows close to half of all the grapes harvested in Australia. South Australia produces some of the country's best red, white and sparkling wines and includes the well-known Barossa Valley region (home of the famous Penfolds Grange wine estate), Adelaide Hills, McLaren Vale, Coonawarra and Padthaway regions.

Southcorp
the Australian holding company that includes Penfolds, Lindemans, Killawarra, Seaview and many other famous Australian wine names and brands

South Eastern Australia
Australia a large area that includes the whole of New South Wales, Victoria and Tasmania, and part of Queensland and South Australia. The name was created for use on wine labels, especially for the export market.

Southern Vales
Australia a wine-producing region in the state of South

Australia, growing Cabernet Sauvignon, Syrah (Shiraz) and Grenache grapes for red wines together with Chardonnay and Riesling grapes for white wines

Southwestern France
France an area of France that includes Bergerac, Cahors, Gaillac, Monbazillac and Pacherenc. The term does not normally refer to the Bordeaux region, which stands on its own.

♢ Souzão
a red-wine grape native to Portugal but now grown mostly in the western USA and South Africa. It produces deep-coloured red wines and is often used for producing port-style fortified wines. (*pronounced* soo zów)

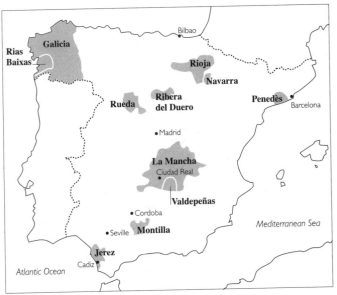

Wine regions of Spain

Spain
one of the largest producers of wine by volume, exceeded only by France and Italy, and with more land devoted to the vine than any other country. Spain is best-known for a diverse selection of regional wines including the fortified wine sherry,

red Rioja wine and its Cava sparkling wines. The Spanish wine industry has been benefiting from huge investment in wine-making technology. Stainless steel, temperature control and the legalisation of irrigation have drastically improved the prospects of Spain's wine regions. Spain's wine-producing regions are classified and recognised by the Denominación de Origen (DO) label, but this is now considered inadequate for high-quality wines, so a higher grade has been introduced, the Denominación de Origen Calificada (DOCa). So far there is just one region that meets these higher standards – Rioja, in the north, Spain's premier wine region, whose wines are predominantly red and aged in oak barrels, lending them earthy, vanilla flavours. Spain has 5 wine-producing regions, classified by the DO system: Penedès, the centre of the Cava industry; Ribera del Duero, on the banks of the River Duero in north-central Spain, rivalling Rioja in producing quality red wines; Rueda, producing white wines, mainly from the Verdejo grape; Valdepeñas, in south-central Spain, producing soft, red wines from Tempranillo (Cencibel) grapes; and Jerez, Spain's sherry-producing region. There are two other legal descriptors for wine. Vino de la Tierra (VdlT) is not unlike France's vin de pays and describes wine from a specific region produced according to certain local strictures. Vino de Mesa (VdM) refers to unclassified or blended wine. As in Italy, there are some very expensive wines that, falling outside the other appellations, use this lowly nomenclature. Spain has literally hundreds of grape varieties. The aromatic Tempranillo, the grape of Rioja and Spain's most widely planted variety, is perhaps its best-known. Grenache (Garnacha) is used to make red wine in northern Spain and the white Airén, planted in La Mancha and Valdepeñas, makes light, dry wines. Palomino, the grape of sherry, is found in Jerez, as well as other parts of Spain, including Rueda. The Pedro Ximénes grape makes sweet wines and is also used in Montilla, while Macabeo (called Viura in Rioja) is used in Penedès in the making of Cava. Needless to say, as elsewhere, international varieties are increasingly to be found.

Spanna *another name for* **Nebbiolo**

sparkle
1. to effervesce
2. effervescence in wine

sparkler
a sparkling wine (*informal*)

sparkling
used to describe wine with bubbles of carbon dioxide, either naturally occurring or created by injecting carbon dioxide gas into the liquid. Wine can be fully sparkling (pétillant in French, frizzante in Italian, spritzig in German, crackling in the USA) or slightly so (mousseux in French, spumante in Italian). In French crémant refers to an intermediate degree of effervescence. Spain describes sparkling wines as espumoso and Portugal as espumante.

sparkling Burgundy
1. a sparkling wine from the Burgundy region of France, red, white or rosé and usually of relatively low quality
2. in the USA and some other non-European countries, a lower-quality sparkling red wine

sparkling wine
wine with bubbles of carbon dioxide. Sparkling wines are produced worldwide. The most famous is Champagne from France; Spain has its Cava wines, Germany its Sekt and Italy its Asti Spumante and Prosecco. In Portugal Sogrape produces Mateus Rosé; in New Zealand Lindauer and Selak are known for their good-quality sparkling wines, and in Australia Seaview and many others including Seppelt, BRL-Hardy, Petaluma and Domaine Chandon (called Green Point in the UK). Among the notable producers in the USA is California's Anderson Valley. There are several different ways of producing sparkling wine, and practice varies according to the quality of wine and the country of origin. These are: the traditional méthode champenoise, in which a dosage (a mixture of sugar, water or wine and yeast) is added to still white wine just before bottling to cause a second fermentation to take place in the bottle, creating carbon dioxide as a by-product; the largely superseded méthode rurale, in which the fermenting wine is cooled to almost stop fermentation before bottling and then warmed slightly to restart the fermentation in the bottle (the méthode dioise and the méthode gaillacoise are local variants of this); the transfer method, which is similar to the traditional méthode champenoise, except that the finished sparkling wine is filtered in a pressurised container to remove the sediment from the second fermentation; the

Charmat or bulk process, which takes place entirely in a pressurised container; finally, the injection of carbon dioxide gas from a canister into the wine under pressure, which is used to produce the cheapest variety of sparkling wine.

Compare **still wine**

Spätburgunder *another name for* **Pinot Noir** (*pronounced* shpáyt boor gŏondər, *used in* Germany)

Spätlese

(*pronounced* shpáyt layzə, *literally* 'late harvest' *or* 'late picked') German

1. a white wine made with sweeter, late-harvest grapes

2. one of the subcategories of the official German classification of quality wines, Qualitätswein mit Prädikat (QmP), and the first category of the Austrian Prädikatswein classification

specific gravity

a scale used to measure the density of a liquid, including wine, and compare it to the density of pure water. It is measured on the Brix, Oechsle or Baumé scales in different parts of the world. Grape juice with natural sugars dissolved in the liquid has a specific gravity higher than pure water, but this drops during fermentation as the sugar is converted into alcohol, which has a specific gravity lower than pure water.

spicy

(*tasting term*) used to describe the complex aroma and taste of a wine that is reminiscent of a spice, e.g. cinnamon or pepper

spitting

the practice of spitting out rather than swallowing a wine after tasting it. Professional wine tasters can taste hundreds of wines in a day, so this is essential to their health.

spittoon

a receptacle into which wine is spat after tasting

Spitzenwein

German good-quality Austrian wine (*pronounced* shpítsən vīn, *plural* **Spitzenweine**)

split

a small bottle size containing 187.5 ml or one quarter of a standard 750 ml bottle, normally used for Champagne or wine served on aeroplanes or trains or in hotels

spritz
a slight sparkle in a wine.
Compare **pétillance**

spritzer
a drink consisting of wine, generally white, diluted with sparkling water or lemonade

spritzig
German slightly sparkling (*pronounced* shprítsig)

♀ **spritzy**
(*tasting term*) used to describe a wine that has a very slight
sensation of effervescence, most common in very young wines
and sometimes considered a minor flaw. The French equivalent
is 'perlant'.

spumante
Italian sparkling. (*pronounced* spoo mán tay, *literally* 'foaming')
Compare **frizzante**

St *abbreviation* Saint

stabilise
to remove any residual particles of yeast or protein or tartaric
acid crystals from a wine that might cause the wine to go cloudy.
Wine can be stabilised at a warm temperature by using a fining
agent that collects the particles as it drifts slowly down through
the wine, collecting as sediment at the bottom of the vat. It can
also be stabilised by cooling the wine to a very low temperature
at which any particles of tartaric acid drift to the bottom and
can be removed.

Stags Leap District AVA
USA a wine-producing region in the Napa Valley region of
California that grows Cabernet Sauvignon and Merlot grape
varieties to produce very good red wines

♀ **stale**
(*tasting term*) used to describe a wine that is lifeless, without any
fresh, lively qualities

♀ **stalky**
(*tasting term*) used to describe a wine that has an often unpleasant taste of grape stems, vines or underripe grapes.
Compare **stemmy**

starter
a yeast culture added to grape juice (must) to initiate the fermentation process. Although fermentation would probably occur naturally because of the yeast spores in the air and on the grape skins, a starter culture gives the winemaker greater control over the process.

Ste *abbreviation French* Sainte

♀ **steely, steel**
(*tasting term*) used to describe a metallic taste to a wine caused by high acid levels or because the vineyard has very mineral-rich soil. This is a notable characteristic of Riesling white wines.

♎ **Steen** *another name for* **Chenin Blanc** (*pronounced* stáy ən *or* stayn, *used in* South Africa)

◊ **Steinberg**
a famous Riesling wine made at Kloster Eberbach in the Rheingau region of Germany (*pronounced* shtín bairg)

Stellenbosch
South Africa an important wine-producing region, classed as a Wine of Origin (WO) in South Africa and producing good red wines from Merlot, Syrah (Shiraz) and Cabernet Sauvignon grapes and good white wines from Chardonnay and Sauvignon Blanc grapes (*pronounced* stéllən bosh)

Stelvin closure
a type of long screwcap

stemmer
a mechanical device that removes the grape stems once the bunches of grapes have been crushed

♀ **stemmy**
(*tasting term*) used to describe a wine that has an often unpleasant taste of grape stems, vines or underripe grapes. *Compare* **stalky**

stem retention
the addition of some grape stems into the must when making red wine to help increase the levels of tannin. Some winemakers do this, but it must be done carefully to avoid making the wine too tannic and bitter.

sterilise
to make something sterile by killing microorganisms

still wine
wine that contains no bubbles from dissolved carbon dioxide gas.
Compare **sparkling wine**

stock *same as* **rootstock**

♀ **stony, stones**
(*tasting term*) used to describe a clean, earthy characteristic in a wine, typically a young white wine.
Compare **flinty**

stravecchio
Italian extra aged. (*pronounced* stra vékkyō)
See also **Marsala DOC**

♀ **strawberry**
(*tasting term*) a taste or aroma associated with red wines from the Beaujolais and Burgundy regions of France or from the Rioja region of northern Spain

straw wine
a sweet wine made from grapes that have been partially dried in the sun, especially on a bed of straw.
Compare **Strohwein; vin de paille**

Strohwein
German a category of Prädikatswein in Austria made from overripe grapes dried on straw or reeds. (*pronounced* shtrő vīn, *literally* 'straw wine', *plural* **Strohweine**)
Compare **straw wine; vin de paille**

♀ **strong**
(*tasting term*) used to describe a powerful and robust wine with a full body

♀ **structure**
(*tasting term*) the way in which a wine is built up from different elements such as acid level, tannin, alcohol, fruitiness and body. All wines have structure, but it is not always well-built, so the term is usually used with another descriptor, as in 'good structure'.

stum
1. *same as* **must**
2. to ferment wine by adding must to it while it is in a cask or vat

♀ **sturdy**
(*tasting term*) used to describe a wine that has an assertive and robust aroma and taste

style
the particular quality of a wine that derives from the grape variety, place of origin or 'terroir', or the manner of production

♀ **stylish**
(*tasting term*) used to describe a wine that has a bold but elegant character

Suau, Château
France a château in the Sauternes area of Bordeaux in south-western France graded deuxième cru (second growth) in the classification of 1855. It produces sweet white wine from Sémillon and Sauvignon Blanc grapes. (*pronounced* syoó ō)

subregion
1. in general use, a wine-producing area that is part of a larger region
2. In the Australian system of Geographic Indications, a sub-region is defined in the same way as a region (a single tract of land containing at least 5 independently owned wineries of at least 5 hectares each and usually producing at least 500 tons of wine grapes per year), but it must have 'substantial' rather than just 'measurable' homogeneity in grape-growing attributes over its area.

♀ **subtle**
(*tasting term*) used to describe a positive characteristic of a delicate wine that has complex layers to its flavour and aroma

Suduiraut, Château
France a château in the Sauternes area of Bordeaux in south-western France graded premier cru (first growth) in the classification of 1855. It produces very fine, sweet white wine from Sémillon and Sauvignon Blanc grapes. (*pronounced* syoó dwee ró)

sugaring
the process of adding sugar to grape must in order to increase the alcoholic strength of a wine. Adding sugar at this fermentation stage of the winemaking does not increase the sweetness of the wine. Although this process is necessary and legal in cold

climates, where the lack of sun does not produce enough sugar in the grape, the process is often illegal and unnecessary in countries with hot climates.
Also called **chaptalisation**

sulphite, sulfite
a chemical compound of sulphur present in tiny quantities in some wines that typically have had sulphur used in them at some stage of the winemaking process – either sprayed onto the grapes on the vine as an insecticide or as sulphur dioxide used as a disinfectant to remove natural yeasts from a barrel, or added to a newly fermented wine to kill off all yeasts and prevent any further, secondary fermentation in the bottle. In some countries such as the USA wine with more than 10 ppm of sulphur compounds must indicate this on the label to warn people allergic to sulphites.

sulphur dioxide, sulfur dioxide
a chemical used to inhibit natural microorganisms from spoiling the wine during the winemaking process

♀ sulphury
(*tasting term*) used to describe an unpleasant smell resulting from excessive use of sulphur dioxide

☼ Sultana
a white grape variety, small and golden in colour, grown for wine production in small quantities in the USA, Australia and parts of South America to produce undistinguished white wines. It is in fact widely planted in California, USA, but for use as a dried fruit and for the table.

supérieur
French better, or of better quality, than the standard. It is normally used to describe a wine with a little more alcohol than usual produced from vineyards with a lower yield and aged for a certain amount of time. (*pronounced* sóo payr yúr)
Compare **superiore**

superiore
Italian better, or of better quality, than the standard. It is normally used to describe a wine with a little more alcohol than usual produced from vineyards with a lower yield and aged for a certain amount of time. (*pronounced* soo páiri áw ray)
Compare **supérieur**

◊ Supertuscan

a premium Tuscan wine with an intense fruit and heavy oak character. The term was coined when the Marchese Incisa della Rochetta of Tuscany worked with Baron Philippe de Rothschild to bring new varieties of Cabernet Sauvignon grapevines into Tuscany. They aimed to concentrate not on the traditional Chianti wines of the region but instead on high-quality, low-yield premium wines that have almost nothing in common with the traditional Chianti DOC requirements. They are labelled Vino da Tavola. Their changes have revolutionised the wine-making of the region.

♀ supple

(*tasting term*) used to describe a red wine that is smooth, well-structured, soft and rounded on the palate

surdo

Portuguese grape juice to which alcohol such as brandy has been added to stop fermentation. The mix is very high in natural sugars and is used to sweeten other wines, notably Madeira fortified wines. (*pronounced* soŏrdō)
Compare **mistelle**

sur lie

French used to describe the technique of storing wine, prior to bottling, in contact with the sediment of dead yeast and grape particles (lees) from the fermentation, which adds complexity and a slight yeasty taste to the wine and can also make the wine very slightly pétillant (*pronounced* soŏr leé, *literally* 'on the lees')

♀ surmaturité

French (*tasting term*) an unpleasant taste in a wine that is reminiscent of port or prunes. Before a wine turns towards this taste, it offers the highly sought-after tastes of dark chocolate or black cherry. (*pronounced* soŏr ma toŏ ree táy)

Süssreserve

German naturally sweet grape juice that has not been fermented is added to a finished dry wine from the same source to provide a required level of sweetness. This means that the fermentation of the wine does not have to be controlled quite so carefully and can be allowed to finish naturally rather than being stopped when the wine reaches a particular level of sweetness. (*pronounced* zoŏss rə zairvə)

sustainable viticulture
land, soil and vine care that ensures that the environment can continue to support vines over a period of years

Swan Valley, Swan District
Australia a very hot winemaking region in Australia, immediately to the north and east of Perth in Western Australia

♀ sweet
(*tasting term*) used to describe a wine that contains a noticeable amount of residual sugar, which occurs when not all of the grape sugar has been converted to alcohol during fermentation or when grape concentrate has been added in the process called chaptalisation. A winemaker can allow fermentation to continue till there is no more natural sugar left in the wine or can stop fermentation early to create a wine with some residual sugars. The fermentation can be stopped by adding sulphur dioxide or by cooling the wine or, for fortified wine, by adding alcohol. Fermentation cannot usually continue when the alcohol level goes above approximately 16%, because yeast cannot live in this environment, and some very sweet grapes contain so much natural sugar that even when the fermentation has finished naturally, when the alcohol level is too high for yeast to live, there is still plenty of residual sugar in the wine, producing sweet unfortified wines such as those from Sauternes, France.
See also **medium sweet**
Compare **dry**

Switzerland
a small, land-locked country in Europe that drinks most of its own wines. The wine-producing regions can be divided in the same way as the administrative districts (called cantons) of Switzerland into French-, German- and Italian-speaking areas, each producing styles of wine reminiscent of these neighbouring countries. Each canton applies its own regulations for wine-making processes and labelling. Most Swiss wine is white and blended, produced from a wide range of grape varieties but especially from Chasselas; some red wine is produced from Pinot Noir and Gamay grapes.

♻ Sylvaner
a white-wine grape variety that was historically widely planted in Germany but has now been replaced in many areas by the Müller-Thurgau grape. It is also grown in small quantities in the

Alsace region of France, in Switzerland and in northern Italy. (*pronounced* sil vaánər)
Also called **Franken Riesling**

◊ **Sylvaner Riesling** *see* **Riesling**

◊ **Syrah**
a classic red-wine grape variety historically grown in the Rhône valley region of France where it produces very good, spicy, aromatic red wines with aromas of berries. This grape variety is widely grown in other countries, including Australia (where it is called Shiraz and is now the most widely planted variety in the country), South Africa and in the western USA. (*pronounced* sírrə)
Also called **Shiraz**; **Hermitage**; **Marsanne Noir**

♀ **syrupy**
(*tasting term*) used to describe a rich, sweet wine that seems thick on the palate

száraz
Hungarian dry (*pronounced* saárəz)

$\mathcal{T}$

Walls have ears, wine bottles have mouths.   Anonymous

table wine
any wine that is not fortified and not sparkling

Tâche *see* **La Tâche AOC**

Tafelwein
German table wine. This is an official category in Germany and Austria. (*pronounced* taáf'l vīn, *plural* **Tafelweine**)

taglio
Italian cut
See also **vino da taglio**

taille
French in the Champagne region of France, the juice from each pressing of the grapes after the first. The juice from the first pressing, also the finest juice, is normally the only juice used for Champagne; the second pressing provides 'première taille', the third 'deuxième taille' and so on. (*pronounced* tī)

Taittinger
an important Champagne house based in Reims, France, established in 1734. The company produces a range of non-vintage Champagne and its premium Champagne, Comtes de Champagne, in both blanc-de-blancs and rosé styles. (*pronounced* tītingər)

Talbot, Château
France a château in the Saint-Julien AOC in the Haut-Médoc district of Bordeaux in southwestern France graded quatrième cru (fourth growth) in the classification of 1855. It grows mostly Cabernet Sauvignon and Merlot grapes to produce good-quality full-bodied red wine, as well as making a little white wine from Sauvignon Blanc grapes. (*pronounced* taal bố)

Tanghrite *see* **Algeria**

♀ **tangy**
(*tasting term*) used to describe a wine with lively citrus or salty tastes

tank method
the making of sparkling wines by the Charmat or bulk process

tank press
a wine press that is fully enclosed to limit contact of its contents with air

♀ **tanky**
(*tasting term*) used to describe a wine that is stale and has a dull character, often from being aged too long in tanks

♢ **Tannat**
a red grape variety, grown mostly in southwestern France, but also in Uruguay and to a lesser extent in Argentina, producing richly coloured red wines with high levels of tannin and alcohol (*pronounced* ta naá)

♀ **tannic**
(*tasting term*) used to describe a wine in which the tannin levels are too high and overpower the fruit and other components, resulting in a wine that is not balanced

tannin
a naturally occurring phenolic compound that is found in grape skins, stalks and pips, and, to a much lesser degree, in wooden barrels, that acts as a preservative of the wine. The taste of tannin in a wine is bitter and gives the impression of drying out your mouth, but these tastes soften as the wine ages or if it comes into contact with air and oxidises, when the tannin compound breaks down. A young wine often has a very strong taste of tannin, but this can be reduced before serving by decanting the bottle or, more simply, by swirling the wine in your glass to oxidise the wine slightly, breaking down the tannin.

tap
to draw off wine from a barrel by means of a tap

Tarragona DO
Spain a large wine-producing DO area in the Catalonia region of northeastern Spain that grows Macabeo and Parellada grapes to produce white wine as well as Grenache (Garnacha) and Carignan (Cariñena) grapes for red wines. Tarragona Clásico is a sweet, often fortified wine. (*pronounced* tárrə gŏnə)

♢ **Tarrango**
an Australian red-wine grape variety that produces light-bodied red wines that can be drunk chilled

♀ **tarry, tar**
(*tasting term*) used to describe a full taste or aroma of red wines such as Barolo made from the Nebbiolo grape variety or of wines from the northern Rhône region of France

♀ **tart**
(*tasting term*) used to describe a wine that is acidic and harsh or sharp to taste

tartar
a substance consisting mostly of potassium bitartrate that is deposited in wine casks during fermentation

tartaric acid
the main natural acid in wine

tartrates
harmless crystals of tartaric acid in a wine. They often form on the bottom of a cork, near the top of the wine, or float in a bottle or cask. They can be removed by stabilising the wine at low temperature.

taste *see* **wine tasting**

taster
1. a small cup for tasting wine
2. a person who engages in wine tasting

tastevin
French a small, shallow cup, usually silver, originally used in the Burgundy region of France by tasters and sommeliers to taste wine and see its colour clearly (*pronounced* tástə vaN)

tasting *see* **wine tasting**

tasting term
a word or expression used to refer to a particular quality or characteristic of a wine, its taste, smell or texture, e.g. blackcurrants, rough or peppery. The characteristic can originate from any of the elements involved in making wine, from the soil to the grape itself to blending, crushing, fermenting or bottling.

Taurasi DOC
Italy a wine-producing DOC area in the Campania region of Italy that grows mostly Aglianico and Barbera grapes to produce good-quality red wines that age well. A higher-quality riserva appellation, Taurasi Riserva DOCG, is used for wine

made from the best grapes and aged for at least four years. (*pronounced* tow raázi)

♀ **taut**
(*tasting term*) used to describe a wine that is not soft and full and may be relatively high in acidity. It can indicate that the wine is still too young for drinking.

Tavel AOC
France an appellation in the southern Rhône region of France that grows Grenache and Cinsault grapes to make very good rosé wines (*pronounced* ta vél)

tavola
Italian table
See also **Vino da Tavola**

tawny port *see* **port**

Taylor Fladgate and Yeatman
one of the best port houses in Portugal producing classic vintage ports and a range of other non-vintage styles including tawny and late bottled vintage (LBV)

TBA *abbreviation German* Trockenbeerenauslese

T-bud grafting
a grafting technique that is used to introduce a new fruit-bearing grape variety onto an existing rootstock. A T-shaped notch is made at the top of the rootstock and the new variety grafted into this notch.
Also called **green grafting**

TCA *abbreviation* trichloranisole

♀ **tears** *same as* **legs**

◊ **Teinturier**
a class of dark-red-skinned grape varieties that is unusual in having red pulp and producing red juice when pressed. It is generally used to blend with other wines to add colour. (*pronounced* táN toŏr yáy)

temperature
A temperature of around 10°C, or 50°F, is ideal for storing wine, though it is more important that the temperature remains constant. When serving wine the temperature varies according to the type of wine; if a wine is served too cold, it impairs the

flavour and aroma and makes the wine seem dull. Sparkling wines and sweet white wine can be served cool at between 4 and 10°C (about 40–50°F); most white wines should be served between 7 and 10°C (about 45–50°F), while rich white wines such as Burgundies should be a little less cold at 10–13°C (about 50–55°F) to help release the complex aromas. Light red wines can be served cool at around 10–13°C, whereas red wines from Pinot Noir grapes, particularly Burgundies, should be around 15–16°C (about 60°F). Full-bodied red wines can be served up to 18°C (about 65°F). Most of these temperatures are below modern 'room temperatures', which are often too warm for a wine.
See also **room temperature**

temperature control
1. the process of ensuring that the temperature in a cellar is correct for storing wine, normally around 10°C
2. the process of ensuring that the temperature of a fermenting wine is correct, allowing fermentation to progress in a steady, controlled way. Wine can be cooled to slow or stop fermentation and warmed to start or speed up fermentation.

♢ Tempranillo
a red-wine grape variety widely grown in northern Spain, Portugal and Argentina, producing good-quality red wines. It is a main ingredient of Rioja wines. (*pronounced* témprə neéllyō)
Also called **Aragonez**; **Cencibel**; **Roriz**; **Tinta Roriz**

Ténarèze
France one of the three subregions of Armagnac in southwestern France, to the north of the region, producing some of the best brandies in the area (*pronounced* táy na réz)

terra rossa
a reddish brown soil found in parts of southern Europe, North Africa and Australia, notably in the Coonawarra region of South Australia

♢ Terret
a red grape variety, grown mostly in southern France, that is one of the 13 varieties allowed in the production of Châteauneuf-du-Pape red wines. Small quantities of a white wine are produced from this grape in some parts of the Languedoc region of southern France. (*pronounced* tay ráy)

♀ **terroir**
French (*tasting term*) the entire physical and environmental characteristics around a particular vineyard that can influence the grapes and so the final wine, including the climate, soil, location, amount of sunshine and altitude. (*pronounced* te rwaár, *literally* 'soil' *or* 'earth')
See also **goût de terroir**

♀ **texture**
(*tasting term*) the quality of a wine that gives a thick, full-bodied sensation on the palate

Thackrey, Sean
a well-known idiosyncratic winemaker running a vineyard in Marin County, California, USA, producing good brawny red wines

☿ **Thalia** *another name for* **Trebbiano** (*pronounced* taáli ə)

♀ **thick**
(*tasting term*) used to describe a wine that is rich, concentrated and often with low acid levels

thief
a syringe-like instrument used to remove a sample of wine from a cask, tank or barrel.
Also called **wine thief**

♀ **thin**
(*tasting term*) used to describe a wine that lacks body, depth and flavour

third growth *see* **troisième cru**

Ticino
Switzerland an Italian-speaking wine-producing canton (district) around the southern Alps in Switzerland that grows mostly Merlot grapes to produce red wines (*pronounced* ti cheénō)

tierra
Spanish country (*pronounced* tyáirə)
See also **Vino de la Tierra**

♀ **tight**
(*tasting term*) used to describe a wine that is still young and underdeveloped without the full body or structure of a mature wine

♀ **tightly knit**
(*tasting term*) used to describe a wine that is well-structured but requires time to develop

♀ **tinny**
(*tasting term*) used to describe a wine that has a slight metallic aftertaste

◊ **Tinta Amarela** *another name for* **Trincadeira Preta** (*pronounced* tintə aməréllə, *used* especially in the north of Portugal)

◊ **Tinta Barroca**
a red-wine grape variety used to make port in Portugal and grown also in South Africa (*pronounced* tintə bərókkə)

Tinta Cão
a red-wine grape variety grown in the Douro and Dão DOCs of Portugal and used to make port (*pronounced* tintə ków)

◊ **Tinta Negra Mole** *another name for* **Negra Mole** (*pronounced* tintə neggrə mólay)

◊ **Tinta Roriz** *another name for* **Tempranillo** (*pronounced* tíntə ro ríz, *used in* Portugal)

tinto
Spanish red (*pronounced* tíntō)

◊ **Tinto de Toro**
a variant of the Tempranillo red-wine grape variety grown especially in the Toro area of Castilla-León, Spain (*pronounced* tíntō day tórrō)

tipico
Italian typical
See also **Vino Tipico**

tirage
French the process of removing wine from a barrel or vat for bottling. (*pronounced* tee ra<u>á</u>zh)
See also **dosage**; **en tirage**

♀ **tired**
(*tasting term*) used to describe a wine that is past its best and rather dull

tireuse
French a bottling machine (*pronounced* tee rőz)

Tischwein
German ordinary table wine that has no regulations governing quality (*pronounced* tísh vīn, *plural* **Tischweine**)

♀ **toasty**
(*tasting term*) used to describe a wine with an aroma and flavour of toast, similar to that of caramel or vanilla. The taste is normally produced by ageing in an oak barrel.

♀ **tobacco, tobacco leaf**
(*tasting term*) an aroma associated with red wines made from the Sangiovese grape variety, e.g. Chianti, and some wines from the Bordeaux region of France

◊ **Tocai, Tocai Friulano**
a white-wine grape variety grown in the Friuli-Venezia Giulia region of northeastern Italy and occasionally in California, USA, to produce an aromatic white wine. (*pronounced* to kī *or* to kī fri oo laánō)
Also called **Sauvignon**; **Tokai**

♀ **toffee**
(*tasting term*) a taste or aroma associated with oak-aged red wines made from the Cabernet Sauvignon grape variety

◊ **Tokai** *another name for* **Tocai**

◊ **Tokay[1], Tokaj, Tokaji**
a renowned sweet white wine produced in Hungary around the town of Tokay, made mostly from Furmint grapes that are sometimes infected by the *Botrytis cinerea* fungus at the end of the summer ripening to produce a very concentrated, sweet grape juice. Sweetness is measured in 'puttonyos' on a scale from three to six. Tokay Essencia is the most rare and finest of the range and is produced from the small amount of juice that escapes from the natural crushing due to the weight of grapes piled on top of each other. Tokay Aszú is made from grapes infected with the *Botrytis cinerea* fungus, whereas Tokay Szamorodni is made from the standard grapes of the area, uninfected with the fungus. (*pronounced* to kī)

◊ **Tokay[2]** *another name for* **Pinot Gris** (*pronounced* to kī, *formerly used in* Alsace, France)

◊ **Tokay Aszú** *see* **Tokay[2]** (*pronounced* tó kī ússə)

Tokay d'Alsace *another name for* **Pinot Gris** (*pronounced* to kī dal záss, *used in* France)

Tokay Essencia, Tokay Szamorodni *see* **Tokay** (*pronounced* tố kī ésenziə *or* tốkī súmorodni)

tonneau
French a measurement of volume used when selling wine, typically in Bordeaux, equal to around 900 litres or four barriques (barrels) (*pronounced* tónnō, *plural* **tonneaux**)

Topikos Oenos
Greek an official category for good-quality Greek wine, bearing the name of the region, county, or town from which it comes

topping up
the process of adding wine to a container to make up for liquid lost through evaporation to ensure that there is no empty space between the top of the wine and the barrel that would allow air to be in contact with the wine and start to oxidise it. The process is known as 'ouillage' in French.

Torbato
a white-wine grape variety grown in Sardinia (*pronounced* tawr báttō)

Torgiano DOCG
Italy a wine-producing DOCG area in the Umbria region of Italy that produces high-quality red wines from mostly Sangiovese, Canaiolo and Trebbiano grapes and white wines mostly from Trebbiano and Malvasia grapes. A riserva wine is also produced from the best grapes and allowed to age for at least three years. (*pronounced* tawr jáánō)

Toro
Spain a wine-producing area in Castilla-León, Spain, producing robust red wines especially from the Tinta de Toro grape variety (*pronounced* tórrō)

Torres
a renowned family-run winemaking company based in Penedès, Catalonia, Spain. Members of the Torres family, especially Miguel Torres Senior and Junior, have transformed the local Catalonian wine production methods producing consistently good red and white wines. (*pronounced* tó ress)

☌ Torrontés
a white-wine grape variety grown extensively in Argentina, and increasingly in Spain, to produce light but assertive white wines with natural acidity (*pronounced* toron táyss)

♀ tough
(*tasting term*) used to describe a full-bodied wine with an astringent taste due to excess tannin. This will often soften with ageing.

Touraine AOC
France a large appellation in the Loire valley region of France that produces good red, white and rosé wines. It grows Cabernet Sauvignon, Cabernet Franc, Gamay and Pinot Noir grapes to produce red wines and uses these grapes and Pineau d'Aunis for its rosé wines. White wines are produced from Chenin Blanc and Sauvignon Blanc grape varieties. (*pronounced* toor rén)

Tour Blanche *see* La Tour Blanche, Château

Tour-Carnet *see* La Tour-Carnet, Château

☌ Touriga Francesca
a red-wine grape variety that is grown and used in Portugal in blending port (*pronounced* too réegǝ fran chéskǝ)

☌ Touriga Nacional
a low-yielding but excellent red-wine grape variety grown in Portugal primarily for use in port but also as a constituent of Dão red wines (*pronounced* too réegǝ nass yō naál)

Traditional Appellation
an official category of Greek wines, especially for retsina. *See also* **Onomasia kata Paradosi**

☌ Trajadura
a Portuguese white grape variety used especially in making Vinho Verde, where it adds body (*pronounced* trázhǝ doórǝ)

☌ Traminer *another name for* Gewürztraminer

☌ Tramini *another name for* Gewürztraminer (*pronounced* trú-minni, *used in* Hungary)

transfer method
a method of making sparkling wine that is similar to the méthode champenoise except that the sediment resulting in the bottle from

the second fermentation is removed by transferring the wine to a pressurised container, where it is filtered before being bottled again

Trebbiano

a famous white-wine grape variety originating in Italy but now very widely planted around the world, including in Italy, eastern Europe, Portugal, France, Australia and South America. It is normally used to produce white wines, but is also blended in small quantities into red Chianti wines and is widely processed to produce Cognac and Armagnac brandies. (*pronounced* tre byaánō)

Also called **Clairette Ronde**; **Clairette Rosé**; **Saint-Émilion**; **Thalia**; **Ugni Blanc**

Trebbiano Abruzzo *another name for* **Bombino Bianco** (*pronounced* tre byaánō ə broótsō, not related to Trebbiano)

trellis

a structure to which a vine is attached for support. A common type of trellising consists of a series of posts with wires between them along which the arms of the vines can be trained.

Trentino-Alto Adige

Italy a large wine-producing region in northeastern Italy that encompasses Trentino in the south, with essentially Italian-style wines, and Alto Adige in the north with affinities to Austria

Trentino DOC

Italy a wine-producing DOC area in the south of the Trentino-Alto Adige region of Italy that produces a wide range of wine from Austrian-style wines near the border with Austria to more Italian-style wines further south in the area. It grows a wide variety of grape types to produce table wine and sweet vin santo. (*pronounced* tren teénō)

trichloranisole, trichloroanisole

a chemical compound that is thought to cause corked wine. It is produced when microorganisms in cork combine with chemicals used in the production process, e.g. the strong chlorine solution in which corks are usually bleached before use. Trichloranisole can be smelt even in minute quantities.

Abbreviation **TCA**

Trimbach

France a well-known winemaker from the Alsace region of France who, with the Hugel family, has tirelessly promoted and developed Alsace wines, including the excellent Riesling-based Clos Sainte-Hune (*pronounced* trím baak)

♢ Trincadeira Preta, Trincadeira
a Portuguese red-wine grape variety producing a rich wine used in making port and also for table wines, especially in the Alentejo region. (*pronounced* trínkə dayrə préttə, *used* especially in the south of Portugal)
Also called **Tinta Amarela**

trocken
German dry (*pronounced* trókkən)

Trockenbeerenauslese
German a top German QmP classification for very-high-quality sweet white wine produced from hand-selected grapes. Trockenbeerenauslese is also the top category of wine in Austria. (*pronounced* trókkən bairən ówss layzə, *literally* 'dry wine from selected berries', *plural* **Trockenbeerenauslesen**)
Abbreviation **TBA**

troisième cru
French the third-highest grade of wines within the classification of 1855 that graded wines in the Médoc area of Bordeaux (*pronounced* twaázyem kroó, *literally* 'third growth', *plural* **troisièmes crus**)

Troncais
a type of French oak from trees grown in the region of the same name, used for wine barrels (*pronounced* troN káy)

♀ tropical fruit, tropical
(*tasting term*) a taste or aroma of fruit such as mango, lychee or papaya associated with some rich white wines, e.g. those made from the Muscat grape variety

♢ Trouchet Noir *another name for* **Cabernet Franc** (*pronounced* troó shay nwaár)

♢ Trousseau Gris, Trousseau
a red-grey coloured grape variety used to make white wines and grown mainly in the Jura region of eastern France, in parts of California, USA, and in parts of New Zealand (*pronounced* troósō greé)
Also called **Chauche Gris**; **Grey Riesling**

Tsantali Vineyards and Wineries *see* **A Winemaker's View**

tsipouro
a Greek spirit distilled from the residue (pomace) left over from
the fermentation of grapes

tun
1. a measure of liquid volume for wine equal to 210 gallons, or
955 litres
2. a large wine cask

Tunisia
a North African country whose wine-producing regions were
originally planted by the French. It produces red, rosé and sweet
white fortified wines.

Turkey
a country with an ancient history of winemaking that was
mostly stopped with the arrival of Islam. The country restarted
its wine production in the 20th century and now grows a range
of European-variety grapes including Cabernet Sauvignon,
Carignan, Chardonnay, Merlot and Pinot Noir. The bulk of
the wine is produced in a government-run winery, but there are
also over 100 private vineyards in the country.

Turkish delight
(*tasting term*) a taste or aroma associated with white wines made
from the Gewürztraminer grape variety

Tuscany
Italy a region of Italy on the northwestern coast of the country
that is one of the leading regions for quality-wine production in
Italy. It is best-known for its Chianti wines.

U

 Ugni Blanc *another name for* **Trebbiano** (*pronounced* óo nyee bláaN, *used in* France)

 Ugni Noir *another name for* **Aramon** (*pronounced* óo nyee nwaár, *used in* France)

UK *see* **United Kingdom**

ullage
the empty space in a wine bottle or barrel between the bottom of the cork or top and the surface of the wine. In a barrel or cask this space must be kept to a minimum by topping up with wine to prevent oxidation, though in some wines such as the vins jaunes of Jura a flor develops and protects the wine. In a bottle, old wine can develop a big space through natural evaporation, but in younger wines it could indicate a faulty cork.

ultra-premium
used to describe a wine of the highest quality and commanding an exceptionally high price, or the vines or grapes from which such a wine is made

Umpqua Valley AVA
USA a wine-producing zone in Oregon that has a cool climate and grows especially Pinot Noir grapes to produce red wines and Chardonnay grapes to make white wines

unbalanced
(*tasting term*) used to describe a wine in which one element such as sweetness, acidity, tannin, alcohol or fruit dominates the others

unctuous
(*tasting term*) used to describe a full-bodied and often sweetish wine

underdeveloped *see* **developed**

unfiltered
used to describe wine that has not been filtered, a process that removes sediment from the wine and clarifies it but can also remove colour and flavour

unfined
used to describe wine that has not been fined, a process that removes sediment from the wine and clarifies it but can also remove flavour and body

unfortified
used to describe wine that has had no extra alcohol added

unit
a measure of alcohol intake used in monitoring the effects of alcohol on the body. One unit is roughly equivalent to the alcohol in one glass of wine or a single measure of spirits.

United Kingdom
a wine-producing country that concentrates its vineyards in the southern regions of England and Wales, which together have over 400 vineyards producing a range of mostly white wines, with some red and sparkling wines of good quality. Because of the climate, similar to that of northern European countries such as Germany, the main grape varieties grown are Müller-Thurgau, Seyval Blanc and Schönburger, though some vineyards grow small quantities of Pinot Noir.
Abbreviation **UK**

United States of America
a wine-producing country that is around the fourth-largest producer of wine in the world. California dominates the wine production in quantity (with over 95% of the country's production) and quality, but wine is made in the majority of the other states, notably in Washington, Oregon and New York. Within the USA there are over 120 wine regions (AVAs) that work in a similar way to the French Appellation d'Origine Contrôlée but with a strictly geographical emphasis and with far less stringent rules, controls and regulations. Most wines in the USA are sold under the name of the winery and then the name of the main grape used to make the wine. *See map overleaf*
Abbreviation **USA**

unoaked
not subjected to oak ageing

Wine regions of the USA

Uruguay

a wine-producing country in South America that began viticulture in the late 19th century with the Tannat grape variety, introduced by Basque immigrants, but that now grows a wide range of classic and hybrid grapes

USA *see* **United States of America**

Utiel-Requena DO

Spain a wine-producing DO area in eastern Spain that produces full-bodied red wines and rosé wines from the Bobal grape variety and white wine from Macabeo grapes (*pronounced* oóti el rə káynə)

uva

Italian a grape (*pronounced* oóvə, *plural* **uve**)

Uva di Troia

a red-wine grape variety that is only grown widely in the Apulia region of Italy, where it is used to produce good-quality red wines (*pronounced* oóvə dee tróy ə)

VA *abbreviation* volatile acidity

Vacqueyras AOC
France a village appellation in the south of the Rhône region of France producing good red wines from Grenache and Syrah grapes and some white wines (*pronounced* vák ay raá)

Valais
Switzerland a wine-producing canton (district) in southwestern Switzerland that produces white wine from Chasselas grapes and red wine from Pinot Noir and Gamay grapes (*pronounced* va láy)

Valcalepio DOC
Italy a wine-producing DOC region in the Lombardy region of Italy that produces white wines from Pinot Blanc and Pinot Gris (Pinot Grigio) grapes and red wines from Cabernet Sauvignon and Merlot grapes (*pronounced* vál ka léppyo)

Valcarcelia *another name for* **Monastrell** (*pronounced* vál kaar cháylyə)

Valdadige DOC
Italy a wine-producing DOC region including parts of the Trentino-Alto Adige and Veneto regions of Italy producing single-grape white wines from Pinot Gris (Pinot Grigio) and Schiava grapes and blended red, white and rosé wines (*pronounced* vál da deé jay)

Valdeorras DO
Spain a wine-producing DO area in the Galicia region of northwestern Spain that produces mostly red wine from the Grenache (Garnacha) grape but also good crisp white wine from the native Godello grape (*pronounced* vál day órrəss)

Valdepeñas DO
Spain a wine-producing DO area in the Castilla-La Mancha

region of Spain that is best-known for its light red wine (called clarete) produced from Tempranillo grapes blended with white Airén grapes (*pronounced* vál day páynyəss)

Valençay VDQS

France a wine-producing VDQS region in the Loire region of France, producing red wines from Cabernet Sauvignon, Cabernet Franc and Gamay grapes and white wines from Arbois, Sauvignon Blanc and Chardonnay grapes (*pronounced* vál aaN sáy)

Valencia DO

Spain a wine-producing DO region on the east coast of Spain that produces white, red and rosé wines from mostly Merseguera grapes for white wine and Bobal and Grenache (Garnacha) for red and rosé wines (*pronounced* və lénssiə)

Valle d'Aosta DOC

Italy a wine-producing DOC region in the northwestern corner of Italy bordering France and Switzerland that produces red, rosé and white wines from a wide range of over 20 approved varieties of grape (*pronounced* vál ay da óstə)

Valpolicella DOC

Italy a wine-producing DOC region in the Veneto region of northeastern Italy that produces more red wine than any other region in Italy except Chianti. It grows mostly Corvina and Rondinella grapes to produce a light, fruity red wine. There is a Valpolicella Classico zone that produces better-quality wines, and 'superiore' on the label means that the wine has been aged for at least one year and will have slightly more alcohol. (*pronounced* vál poli chéllə)
See also **Amarone della Valpolicella**

Valtellina DOC

Italy a wine-producing region in the Lombardy area of northern Italy that produces high-quality red wines mostly from Nebbiolo grapes (*pronounced* vál te leénə)

♀ vanilla

(*tasting term*) an aroma in a wine usually due to ageing the wine in new oak barrels

varietal

1. a wine produced largely from, and named after, a single cultivated grape variety. Proportions of the named grape re-

quired for a varietal vary according to the region or country. Traditionally European wines were identified by the region or estate, but New World, especially Australian, practice has to some extent moved emphasis to the dominant grape variety.
2. referring to a cultivated grape variety

variety
a named type of cultivated grape, e.g. Merlot, Syrah or Pinot Noir

Vaud
Switzerland one of the main wine-producing cantons (districts) in Switzerland, at the top of the Rhône valley, that produces white wine from Chasselas grapes and red wine from Pinot Noir and Gamay grapes (*pronounced* vō)

VC *abbreviation Spanish* Vino Comarcal

VdlT *abbreviation Spanish* Vino de la Tierra

VdM *abbreviation Spanish* Vino de Mesa

VDN *abbreviation French* vin doux naturel

VDQS *abbreviation French* Vin Délimité de Qualité Supérieure

VDT *abbreviation Italian* Vino da Tavola

vecchio
Italian old or aged (*pronounced* vékki ō)

Vega Sicilia
Spain an old-established wine producer in Ribera del Duero, Castilla-León, Spain, established in 1864, whose top red wine is often considered the finest in Spain (*pronounced* váygə si theélyə)

♀ **vegetal**
(*tasting term*) used to describe an aroma or taste on a wine that is similar to that of leafy plants or vegetables

Velletri DOC
Italy a wine-producing DOC region in the Latium region of Italy that produces red wine from Sangiovese grapes and white wine from Malvasia and Trebbiano grapes (*pronounced* ve léttri)

♀ **velouté**
French (*tasting term*) velvety (*pronounced* və loo táy)

♀ **velvety**
(*tasting term*) used to describe a wine with a rich, smooth, silky texture

vendange
French a vintage or harvest (*pronounced* vaaN da͞aNzh)

vendange tardive
French a late harvest. (*pronounced* vaaN da͞aNzh taar de͞ev, *plural* **vendanges tardives**)
See also **Alsace Vendange Tardive**

vendemmia
Italian a vintage or harvest (*pronounced* ven démmyə, *plural* **vendemmie**)

vendimia
Spanish a vintage or harvest (*pronounced* ven de͞emyə)

Veneto
Italy a large wine-producing region in northeastern Italy, surrounding both Venice and Verona, that produces more DOC-graded wine than any other region in Italy. It includes areas such as Bardolino, Soave and Valpolicella. (*pronounced* və náytō)

Ventoux *see* **Côtes du Ventoux AOC**

verde
Portuguese young (*pronounced* váirdə)

☌ **Verdejo**
a white-wine grape variety grown mostly in Spain to produce full-bodied, dry white wines and sherry-style fortified wine (*pronounced* vair dé hō)

Verdelho
(*pronounced* vair déllyō)
☌ **1.** a white-wine grape variety widely grown in Madeira and grown in mainland Portugal for white wine and white port. It is now also grown in Australia to produce a fruity, slightly spicy white wine that can be drunk as an apéritif or with food.
Also called **Gouveio**
2. a light style of Madeira fortified wine (*plural* **Verdelhos**)

☌ **Verdicchio**
a white-wine grape variety originating and grown in central Italy to produce a light, crisp, dry greenish-coloured wine (*pronounced* vair de͞ekyō)

Verdicchio dei Castelli di Jesi DOC
Italy a wine-producing DOC region in the Marche region of Italy that grows predominantly the Verdicchio grape to produce very good crisp, dry white wine. It also includes a small classico area producing better-quality wines that have been aged, and uses the same grapes to produce a sparkling (spumante) white wine. (*pronounced* vair deékyō day ka stélli dee yáyzi)

◊ **Verdot Rouge** *another name for* **Petit Verdot** (*pronounced* váir dō roózh)

◊ **Verduzzo**
a white-wine grape variety originating from and mostly grown in the Venezia region of northeastern Italy that produces rich medium sweet and sweet white wines with a floral aroma (*pronounced* vair doótsō)

vergine, vergine stravecchio (*pronounced* váirjeenay, váir-jeenay straa vekkyō)
Italian see **Marsala DOC**

◊ **Vermentino**
a white-wine grape variety grown mostly in the Piedmont region of northwestern Italy as well as the islands of Corsica and Sardinia that produces fruity, full-bodied white wine but it is often blended with Trebbiano grapes to produce a lighter wine (*pronounced* váir men teénō)

vermouth
a fortified wine that has been flavoured with aromatic herbs or spices and is most often used as an apéritif or in cocktails. Dry white, or French, vermouth can be served by itself or as part of classic dry cocktails such as the martini; sweet vermouth is a dark golden colour and can be served by itself or as part of classic sweet cocktails. Chambéry is a light aromatic vermouth made in the French Alps.

◊ **Vernaccia**
(*pronounced* vair náchə)
1. a white-wine grape variety, primarily grown on the island of Sardinia, off the west coast of Italy, that produces a crisp, dry white wine. It is also used to produce a sherry-like wine.
2. a white-wine grape variety local to the Vernaccia di San Gimignano DOC in Tuscany, Italy, that produces a distinctive dry white wine. It is not the same as the Sardinian Vernaccia.

Vernaccia di San Gimignano DOC
Italy a DOC area in Tuscany, Italy, near Siena, that grows the local Vernaccia grape variety to produce a distinctive dry white wine (*pronounced* vair nácha dee san jimi nyaánō)

vertical tasting
a wine tasting that has a range of wines from different years from one estate or vineyard.
Compare **horizontal tasting**

very superior, very superior old pale, very, very superior old pale *see* **Cognac**

Veuve Clicquot
an important Champagne house in Reims in the Champagne region of France, producing large quantities of non-vintage Champagne as well as its vintage wine, La Grande Dame, named after the original Madame Clicquot, who took over the vineyard when her husband died ('veuve' means 'widow' in French). Madame Clicquot is also known as the person who discovered riddling, a way of removing sediment from Champagne after fermentation. Veuve Clicquot is now owned by the giant French firm LVMH. (*pronounced* vúrv klee kő)

V-graft
a method of grafting vines in which the stem of the stock is trimmed to a point, and the stem of the cutting is split to allow it to be fitted over the point of the stock

Victoria
Australia a state in southeastern Australia, of which the capital is Melbourne, that includes the wine-producing areas of Goulburn Valley, Yarra Valley, Mornington Peninsula, Grampians, Rutherglen and many others. Victoria boasts more than 350 wineries producing a diverse range of wine styles.

Vidal Blanc
a French hybrid white-wine grape variety grown in the eastern USA to produce a wide range of white-wine styles (*pronounced* veé dal blaáN)

vieilles vignes
French old vines. The term is normally used to indicate wine made from grapes grown on old, established vines. (*pronounced* vyáy veényə)

Vieilles Vignes Françaises *see* **Bollinger**

vigna
Italian a vineyard (*pronounced* veényə, *plural* **vigne**)

vigneron
French a winemaker (*pronounced* veényə róN)

vignoble
French a vineyard or wine-growing area (*pronounced* vee nyóbblə)

♢ **Vignoles** *another name for* **Ravat 51** (*pronounced* vee nyól)

♀ **vigorous**
(*tasting term*) used to describe a full-bodied wine with an assertive, lively character

Villages
French used in the names of wine from the better part of an AOC area, e.g. Côtes du Rhône-Villages or Beaujolais-Villages (*pronounced* vee yaázh)

♢ **Villard Blanc**
a white-wine grape hybrid mostly grown in the eastern USA and the Languedoc-Roussillon region of southern France. It is mostly used in blends to produce basic white wines. (*pronounced* veé yaar blaáN)

♢ **Villard Noir**
a red-wine grape hybrid that was popular in the eastern USA and parts of France but is now being replaced by better-quality grapes (*pronounced* veé yaar nwaár)

vin
French wine (*pronounced* vaN)

viña
Spanish a vineyard (*pronounced* veényə)

vin blanc
French white wine (*pronounced* vaN blaáN, *plural* **vins blancs**)

vin bourru
French wine that is siphoned from a barrel immediately after fermentation, giving it a lively, slightly effervescent style (*pronounced* vaN boo roó, *plural* **vins bourrus**)

vin de carafe
French carafe wine (*pronounced* váN də ka ráf, *plural* **vins de carafe**)

vin de cuvée
French in the Champagne region of France, the juice released in the first pressing of the grapes, used to produce the best Champagnes. (*pronounced* váN də kŏo váy, *plural* **vins de cuvée**)
Also called **serre**

vin de garde
French a wine that improves with ageing (*pronounced* váN də gaárd, *plural* **vins de garde**)

vin de l'année
French wine produced from this year's crop of grapes, e.g. Beaujolais Nouveau (*pronounced* váN də la náy, *plural* **vins de l'année**)

Vin Délimité de Qualité Supérieure
French a classification of a second-level quality of French wine between vin de pays and AOC (Appellation d'Origine Contrôlée). (*pronounced* váN day lee mee táy də kálli táy sŏo payr yúr, *plural* **Vins Délimités de Qualité Supérieure**)
Abbreviation **VDQS**

vin de paille
French a sweet wine traditionally produced from grapes that have been dried on straw mats to increase the concentration of natural sugar in the grapes. (*pronounced* váN də pí, *plural* **vins de paille**)
Compare **straw wine; Strohwein**

vin de pays
French a general classification of a third-level quality of French wine below AOC (Appellation d'Origine Contrôlée) and VDQS (Vin Délimité de Qualité Supérieure). (*pronounced* váN də páy ee, *literally* 'wine of the country', *plural* **vins de pays**)
Compare **vin du pays**

Vin de Pays d'Oc
French vin de pays from the Languedoc-Roussillon region of southern France (*pronounced* váN də pay ee dók)

Vin de Qualité Produit en une Région Déterminée
French a European Union labelling term for a quality wine. The

abbreviation is sometimes expanded appropriately in other languages, e.g. Portuguese Vinho de Qualidade Produzido em Região Determinada. (*pronounced* váN də kalli táy prodwée aaN ŏon ray zhóN day táirmee náy, *plural* **Vins de Qualité Produits en une Région Déterminée**)
Abbreviation **VQPRD**

Vin de Savoie AOC, Vin de Savoie Mousseux AOC *see* **Savoie** (*pronounced* váN də sa vwaá (moo sŏ))

vin de table
French same as **vin ordinaire** (*pronounced* váN də taáblə, *plural* **vins de table**)

vin d'honneur
French wine that is served in honour of a guest, e.g. at a celebratory dinner (*pronounced* váN do núr, *plural* **vins d'honneur**)

vin doux naturel
French a sweet fortified wine made from grapes with a naturally high sugar content, e.g. Muscat. Fermentation is stopped by adding alcohol to produce a sweet wine with an alcohol level between 15 and 20%. (*pronounced* váN dóo natŏo rél, *plural* **vins doux naturels**)
Abbreviation **VDN**

Vin du Bugey AOC
France an appellation in the Savoie region of eastern France producing a range of white, red, rosé and sparkling wines (*pronounced* váN dŏo bŏo zháy)

vin du pays
French a local wine. The term is no indicator of quality. (*pronounced* váN dŏo pay eé, *plural* **vins du pays**)
Compare **vin de pays**

vine
a plant of the genus *Vitis* that yields grapes, normally a fruit-bearing variety grafted onto a disease-resistant rootstock

vine age
the age of the vine is significant in that older vines have deeper roots and so reach mineral-rich subsoils that can give grapes extra depth of flavour

vineal
referring to wine, vines or winemaking

♀ vinegary
(*tasting term*) used to describe the strong smell of vinegar from a wine, indicating that it is spoiled through oxidation or other problems during winemaking

vine pull scheme
any of the governmental schemes introduced in the 1980s, notably in the European Union and South Australia, to encourage owners to remove vines from unproductive vineyards. In Australia this unfortunately also resulted in the loss of some well-established old-vine vineyards producing classic wines.

vinery
an area or building, especially a greenhouse, in which grapevines are grown

vine spacing
the distance between vines, determined by the local conditions and method of growing them. In a wet area of France, a vine can survive on a small area of ground; in a dry, arid area of Spain, a vine needs a much larger area for its roots to try and find water. Old vineyards also tend to plant vines in rows close together where a man or horse can pass along the row. In Australia vines are planted with more space between the rows to allow machines to pass along the rows to pick the grapes.

vine weevil
a flightless beetle (*Otiorhynchus sulcatus*) whose larvae are white with brown heads and attack roots of vines in open ground

vineyard
an area of ground planted with vines that are cultivated to produce grapes

Vineyard Academy *see* South Africa

vin gris
a style of very pale rosé wine produced from Pinot Noir, Gamay or Cabernet Sauvignon grapes that have had very little time in contact with the skins after pressing (*pronounced* váN greé, *plural* **vins gris**)

vinha
Portuguese a vineyard (*pronounced* veényə)

vinho
Portuguese wine (*pronounced* veényō, *plural* **vinhos**)

vinho de mesa
Portuguese table wine (*pronounced* veényō de máyzə, *plural* **vinhos de mesa**)

Vinho de Qualidade Produzido em Região Determinada
Portuguese a wine classified Indicação de Proveniencia Regulamentada (IPR), the second class of wines in the classification system used in Portugal. (*pronounced* veényō de kwálli daad prodoo zeédō eN rezhi ów detairmi naádə, *plural* **Vinhos de Qualidade Produzidos em Região Determinada**)
Abbreviation **VQPRD**

Vinho Regional
Portuguese a wine from single a region that does not have DOC status but conforms to particular standards. (*pronounced* veényō rayzhō naál, *plural* **Vinhos Regionales**)
Abbreviation **VR**

Vinho Verde DOC
Portugal a large wine-producing region in northwestern Portugal that is best-known for growing Alvarinho and Loureiro grapes to produce fresh, fruity white wines with a slight sparkle. A slightly sparkling red wine is also produced, but is usually drunk locally. (*pronounced* veényō váirdə)

viniculture
the study and science of growing grapes and making wine

vinifera *see* **Vitis vinifera**

vinification
the processes involved in making wine, especially up to the end of fermentation, before any blending and bottling

vinify
to produce wine from grapes

vin jaune
a style of straw-coloured wine produced in the Jura region of eastern France, often from Savagnin grapes, that is aged for at least six years, in which time, like sherry, it acquires a layer of yeast on its surface that protects against oxidation but colours

and flavours the wine (*pronounced* váN zhṓn, *literally* 'yellow wine', *plural* **vins jaunes**)

vino[1]
Italian wine (*pronounced* veénō, *plural* **vini**)

vino[2]
Spanish wine (*pronounced* veénō, *plural* **vinos**)

vino bianco
Italian white wine (*pronounced* veénō byángkō, *plural* **vini bianci**)

vino blanco
Spanish white wine (*pronounced* veénō blángkō, *plural* **vinos blancos**)

Vino Comarcal
Spanish a wine from a single region that does not have DOC status but conforms to particular standards. (*pronounced* veénō komaar kaál, *plural* **Vinos Comarcales**)
Abbreviation **VC**

vino corriente
Spanish ordinary basic-quality wine (*pronounced* veénō kori én tay, *plural* **vinos corrientes**)

vino da pasto
Italian a wine drunk with a meal rather than before (as an apéritif) or after (as a digestif). (*pronounced* veénō da pástō, *plural* **vini da pasto**)
Compare **vino de pasto**

vino da taglio
Italian a wine with high alcohol levels and a deep, rich colour that is added in tiny quantities to adjust the characteristics of another wine during production (*pronounced* veénō da tályō, *plural* **vini da taglio**)

Vino da Tavola
Italian a wine of the lowest officially recognised quality of ordinary Italian wines that do not fit into DOC regulations. (*pronounced* veénō da távvōlǝ, *plural* **Vini da Tavola**)
Abbreviation **VDT**

Vino de la Tierra
Spanish a basic-quality, local country Spanish wine that

conforms to particular standards. (*pronounced* véenō day la tyáirə, *plural* **Vinos de la Tierra**)
Abbreviation **VdlT**

Vino de Mesa
Spanish a wine of the lowest officially recognised quality of ordinary wine in Spain. (*pronounced* véenō day máyssə, *plural* **Vinos de Mesa**)
Abbreviation **VdM**

vino de pasto
Spanish a wine drunk with a meal rather than before (as an apéritif) or after (as a digestif). (*pronounced* véenō day pástō, *plural* **vinos de pasto**)
Compare **vino da pasto**

vinometer
a device that measures the alcoholic content of low-alcohol dry wines, though not of sweet or fortified wines

Vino Nobile di Montepulciano DOCG
Italy a wine-producing DOCG region, the first DOCG area designated in Italy, in the east of the Tuscany region of Italy that grows mostly Sangiovese grapes to produce a well-known red wine that is then aged for two years, or three years for the riserva variation of the wine (*pronounced* véenō nŏbi lay di món tay pŏol chaánō)

vino novello
Italian light, fruity red wine bottled very soon within the year of harvest and drunk young and cool. It is sold in a similar way to Beaujolais Nouveau. (*pronounced* véenō nə véllō, *plural* **vini novelli**)

vin ordinaire
French basic-quality wine that is below any of the standard classifications such as AOC, VDQS or vin de pays. (*pronounced* váN awrdi náir, *plural* **vins ordinaires**)
Also called **vin de table**

vino rosso
Italian red wine, especially dry red wine (*pronounced* véenō róssō, *plural* **vini rossi**)

Vinos de Madrid DO
Spain a wine-producing DO region centred on Madrid, the

capital of Spain, that grows Tempranillo grapes for full-bodied red wines and Malvar and Airén grapes for good-quality white wines (*pronounced* veénoss day mə dreéd)

♀ **vinosity**
(*tasting term*) the distinctive and essential character of wine, including qualities such as body, colour and taste

vino tinto
Spanish red wine (*pronounced* veénō tíntō, *plural* **vinos tintos**)

Vino Tipico
Italian an official Italian category of wine quality, above Vino da Tavola and below a DOC-graded wine (*pronounced* veénō típpikō, *plural* **Vini Tipici**)

♀ **vinous**
(*tasting term*) used to describe a taste or aroma that is essentially that of a wine

vin rosé
French rosé wine (*pronounced* vaN rō záy, *plural* **vins rosés**)

vin rouge
French red wine (*pronounced* váN roózh, *plural* **vins rouges**)

vin santo
an Italian style of sweet white wine made in several regions of Italy, particularly Tuscany, from grapes that have been dried out to increase the concentration of natural sugar. These grapes are crushed, pressed and fermented in the usual process for making white wine but are stored in small vats or barrels that contain a small amount of 'madre', a reduced sweet liquid produced from the previous year's wine. The wine stays in these barrels for up to five or six years and is allowed to oxidise and vary in temperature, all of which helps the ageing process to produce sweet white wines with a rich golden colour and an alcohol content of below 17% that is relatively low compared to a fortified sweet white wine. (*pronounced* vin sántō, *plural* **vini santi** *or* **vin santos**)

Vins de Moselle VDQS
France a VDQS wine-producing area in eastern France around the Moselle river, producing white wines. (*pronounced* váN də mō zél)
See also **Mosel**

Vins d'Estaing VDQS
France a VDQS area of southwestern France that produces red
and white wines (*pronounced* váN dess táN)

vintage
the year the grapes were harvested and the wine was made. Non-
vintage (NV) wines, when two or more wines from different
years are blended together, are usually only specified as such for
Champagne or other sparkling wines.

vintage chart
a chart that gives information about which vintages are regarded as especially good and when the wine from that year is
suitable for drinking

vintage port, vintage character port *see* port

vintage year
a year in which the wine that is made is of excellent quality

vintner
a person who makes or sells wine

☿ Viognier, Vionnier
a white-wine grape variety that was formerly not widely planted,
but that is now grown in the Rhône valley of France, in parts of
Australia and South America, in South Africa and in California,
USA, to produce very good intense, dry white wines with a very
flowery bouquet. Unusually, this white grape is allowed in
several appellations in France to be added as part of a blend
when producing red wines, particularly in the Côte Rôtie area of
the Rhône region. (*pronounced* vee on yáy)

Viré-Clessé AOC
France an appellation in the Mâcon area of the Burgundy region
of France producing good-quality white wines from Chardonnay grapes (*pronounced* vee ráy kle sáy)

♀ viscous
(*tasting term*) used to describe a wine with a rich texture and
concentrated taste, often with high levels of glycerol in the wine,
producing legs on the glass in which it is drunk

viticulteur
French a person who owns or cultivates a vineyard (*pronounced*
veéttee koͦol túr)

viticultural
relating to the growing of grapes, especially for wine production

Viticultural Area *see* **American Viticultural Area**

viticulture
the study and practice of growing grapes, especially for wine production

Vitis
the genus of the grapevine

Vitis aestivalis
a species of vine native to the USA (*pronounced* vítiss eesti vaáliss)

Vitis labrusca
a species of vine used widely in North America, including the Concord variety (*pronounced* vítiss la brúskə)

Vitis riparia
a species of vine, best-known for its resistance to the root aphid phylloxera, that is often used as a rootstock (*pronounced* vítiss ri páiri ə)

Vitis rotundifolia
a species of vine native to the southeastern USA and Mexico (*pronounced* vítiss rōtundi fõleeə)

Vitis vinifera
the species of vine that is used to produce nearly all of the world's wine grapes. It has thousands of different cultivated varieties ranging in character from Riesling to Merlot. (*pronounced* vítiss vi níffərə)

✑ **Viura** *another name for* **Macabeo** (*pronounced* vee óorə, *used in* the Rioja region of Spain)

Vivarais *see* **Côtes du Vivarais AOC**

volatile
used to describe a wine that is deteriorating and becoming acetic

volatile acidity
the level of acetic acid present in wine. Some volatile acidity helps improve the smell and taste of the wine, but too much causes it to go off or taste of vinegar.
Abbreviation **VA**

Volnay AOC
France a village appellation in the Côte de Beaune district of the
Burgundy region of France that produces a good-quality light
red wine from Pinot Noir grapes (*pronounced* vol náy)

vörös
Hungarian red (*pronounced* vúrur)

Vosne-Romanée AOC
France a village appellation in the Côte de Nuits district of the
Burgundy region of France that produces some of the best red
wines in the region. This appellation includes five famous grand
cru vineyards including Romanée-Conti and La Tâche, growing
Pinot Noir grapes. (*pronounced* vón rō ma náy)

Vougeot *see* **Clos de Vougeot**

Vougeot AOC
France an appellation in the Côte de Nuits district of the
Burgundy region of France that produces red wines from Pinot
Noir grapes and a little white wine from Chardonnay grapes
(*pronounced* voo zhó)

Vouvray AOC
France an appellation in the Loire valley region of France that
grows Chenin Blanc grapes to produce a range of styles of white
wine, from dry to sweet, still and sparkling (*pronounced* voo
vray)

VQPRD *abbreviation*
1. *Portuguese* Vinho de Qualidade Produzido em Região Determinada
2. *French* Vin de Qualité Produit en une Région Déterminée

VR *abbreviation Portuguese* Vinho Regional

VS, VSOP, VVSOP *see* **Cognac**

Walla Walla Valley AVA
USA a viticultural area in eastern Washington State and north-eastern Oregon within the larger Columbia Valley AVA

Walschriesling *see* **Welschriesling**

warm
(*tasting term*) used to describe a soft, immediately pleasing red wine

Warre
the oldest English-owned port company, founded in 1670, now owned by the Symington family who also own Dow, Graham and Smith Woodhouse. Its vintage port is one of the best. It also produces a good single-quinta port.

Washington
USA a wine-producing state in the northwest of the USA that is second only to California in the quantity of wine produced, though its production is still relatively small. It includes over 80 vineyards with the best wineries located in the east of the state, the location of the three main AVAs (Columbia Valley, which includes the Walla Walla Valley and Yakima Valley AVAs).

watery
(*tasting term*) used to describe a wine with not much taste, lacking in an element such as body, flavour or acidity

weedy
(*tasting term*) used to describe a wine with a grassy aroma or taste

weeper
a bottle of wine that is leaking slightly from around the cork, either because of a faulty cork or poor storage allowing the cork to dry and shrink slightly

weeping
used to describe a bottle of wine that is leaking slightly from around the cork, either because of a faulty cork or poor storage allowing the cork to dry and shrink slightly

♀ **weighty**
(*tasting term*) used to describe a wine that is full-bodied with a powerful aroma or taste

Wein
German wine (*pronounced* vīn, *plural* **Weine**)

Weinbaugebiet
German a designated wine region producing the lowest recognised quality of German wine, table wine (Deutscher Tafelwein) (*pronounced* vīn bow gə beet, *plural* **Weinbaugebiete**)

Weinberg
German a vineyard (*pronounced* vīn bairg, *plural* **Weinberge**)

Weingärtnergenossenschaft
German a wine cooperative (*pronounced* vīn gairtnər gə nóss'n shaft, *plural* **Weingärtnergenossenschaften**)

Weingut
German an estate, including the vineyard, cellar and winery (*pronounced* vīn goot, *plural* **Weingüter**)

Weingut Lingenfelder
Germany a winery in the Pfalz region of Germany producing a range of red, white and rosé wines from Riesling, Müller-Thurgau, Pinot Noir and Scheurebe grape varieties (*pronounced* vīn goot língən feldər)

Weinherbst
German a style of rosé wine produced in Germany from a single grape variety and of Qualitätswein grade (*pronounced* vīn hairbst, *plural* **Weinherbste**)

Weinkellerei
German a wine cellar. On a label it can mean that the producer of the wine does not own a vineyard and buys in grape juice to produce wine in his or her own premises. (*pronounced* vīn kelə rī, *plural* **Weinkellereien**)

☼ **Weissburgunder** *another name for* **Pinot Blanc** (*pronounced* vīss boor gŏondər, *used in* Germany)

☿ **Weisser Riesling** *another name for* **Riesling** (*pronounced* víssər reéssling, *used in* Germany)

♀ **well-balanced**
(*tasting term*) used to describe a wine with no one element such as sweetness, acidity, tannin, alcohol or fruit dominating

☿ **Welschriesling, Walschriesling**
a white-wine grape variety that is widely grown in Europe, including in Austria, Hungary, Romania and the Czech Republic. The grape is no relation to Riesling, despite its name, and produces a light still or sparkling white wine. (*pronounced* vélsh reéssling *or* válsh reéssling)
Also called **Riesling Italico**; **Olaszrizling**

Western Australia
Australia a state of Australia and one of its newest wine-producing regions, producing good quality red and white wines. It includes the well-known areas of Margaret River, Mount Barker, Frankland and Swan Valley.

♀ **wet stones**
(*tasting term*) an aroma associated with white wines from the Chablis region of France

white port *see* **port**

☿ **White Riesling** *another name for* **Riesling**

white wine
wine that is made from a light-skinned (pale yellow or green) grape or from a dark-skinned (red or black) grape in which the pressed grape juice is immediately separated from the coloured skins. When making red wine, the skins would normally be left in contact with the grape juice while it fermented, allowing the colour from the skins to transfer to the wine.

white Zinfandel
a style of pale rosé-coloured slightly sweet wine, popular in the USA, that is produced from the red-skinned Zinfandel grape. This style of wine is called 'blanc de noirs' in France, and 'blush' in the USA.

whole-berry fermentation
a variation on the normal red-wine fermentation process in which the winemaker keeps some of the whole grapes separate while the bulk is crushed, pressed and then fermented. The

whole grapes are added during fermentation, extending the fermentation process and reducing the tannin level of the wine and adding more of a berry flavour.

whole-bunch fermentation
a traditional winemaking technique originating in the Burgundy region of France, but adopted around the world (particularly with Pinot Noir grapes) in which an entire bunch of grapes is fermented, rather than individual berries. This reduces handling and improves the flavour and colour of the wine.

whole-bunch pressing
a method of pressing an entire bunch of grapes rather than crushing the individual berries. This ensures that only the juice has the lowest amount of phenolic compounds and is the finest and most delicate juice from the berries. This is considered an essential process in producing high-quality sparkling white wines.

wild-fermented
fermented using a wild rather than a cultivated yeast strain

Willamette Valley AVA
USA a viticultural area in the north of Oregon that grows a wide variety of grapes but especially Chardonnay, Riesling and Pinot Noir

wine
fermented juice from grapes. The term is often extended to include fermented juice from a range of juicy fruit such as the blackberry and other fermented drinks such as rice wine and ginger wine, but these are not the subject of this book. There are four basic styles of wine: still (non-sparkling); sparkling (effervescent due to dissolved carbon dioxide gas); fortified (e.g. port), in which alcohol has been added to stop fermentation, increasing the sweetness, and boost the level of alcohol; and aromatic, flavoured with herbs.

wine bottle
There is a wide range of styles and sizes for containers used to store wine. Some wine bottles are designed with a particular purpose, e.g. Champagne bottles are made of thicker, stronger glass to withstand the extra pressure generated during the second in-bottle fermentation. There is a range of sizes, but the standard size contains 750 ml; the other sizes are variations on this size: split = quarter size, half = half a standard bottle,

magnum = two standard bottles, double-magnum = 4 standard bottles, jeroboam = 6 standard bottles, methuselah = 8 standard bottles of the shape used for Burgundy and Champagne, imperial = 8 standard wine bottles of the shape used for Bordeaux, salmanazar = 12 standard bottles, balthazar = 16 standard bottles, nebuchadnezzar = 20 standard bottles.

wine cellar
a cool, dark storage location that maintains a constant temperature of around 10°C, or 50°F, and a modest humidity level. This provides the ideal way to store wine for decades at a time.

wine cooler
1. a container filled with ice or a refrigerant and used to keep one or more bottles of wine cool
2. a mixture of wine and fruit juice, sometimes with carbonated water, sold in bottles

wine glass
a glass suitable for drinking wine, with a bowl mounted on a stem and usually a rounded base.
See also **glass**

winegrower
a grower of grapes for making wine, especially the owner or manager of a vineyard who also oversees the winemaking

winemaker
a person who produces wine, from the growing of the grapes to the finished product. Specifically, however, a winemaker oversees the vinification processes that take place in the winery up to the end of fermentation, before any blending and bottling. This is a technical task, and has seen many changes and developments in the last few decades.
See also **flying winemakers**

winemaking
the art or business of producing wine, from the growing of the grapes to the finished product

Wine of Origin
a rating scheme used in South Africa to provide a basic quality standard and assurance that the wine has been made from grapes grown in the region.
Abbreviation **WO**

wine press
a piece of winemaking equipment that squeezes the juice from grapes

wine producer
a wine-grower or winemaker

winery
a building and the equipment used to produce wine. This was originally an American term, but is now widely used.

wine tasting
the serious pursuit of judging wines according to a range of criteria to determine their quality. These include the sensation in the mouth, the aroma and the appearance of the wine. A blind wine tasting provides the tasters with a range of wines with no labels – the tasters must use their judgment to source the wines and determine the quality. In a vertical tasting there is a range of wines from different years from one estate or vineyard; in a horizontal tasting there is a range of wines from different vineyards in a region from one year of production.

wine temperature *see* **temperature**

wine thief *see* **thief**

witblits
South Africa illegally distilled alcoholic liquor, usually made from grapes (*pronounced* vít blits)

WO *abbreviation South Africa* Wine of Origin

Wolf Blass
Australia a well-respected winery based in the Barossa Valley region of South Australia and producing a range of very good red and white wines

♀ **wood**
(*tasting term*) the taste of a wine that has been aged in oak barrels

wood-aged *see* **ageing**

♀ **woody**
(*tasting term*) used to describe a wine that has too much aroma and taste of oak, usually caused by ageing for too long in a barrel or cask

woolly vine scale
a brown insect (*Pulvinaria vitis*) that infests vines

Württemberg
Germany one of the 13 Anbaugebiete (quality wine-producing regions) of Germany, situated along the Neckar river and growing equal amounts of red-wine and white-wine grapes (unusual in any German region) and producing especially rosé wine (*pronounced* voˊortəm bairg)

Wynns Coonawarra Estate
Australia a famous estate in the Coonawarra region of South Australia producing very good red and white wines

XYZ

Wine is wont to show the mind of man.
Theognis of Megara, 6th century BC

◊ Xarel-lo
a white-wine grape variety grown widely in Spain, particularly in the Catalonia region in the northeast, where it is normally blended with other grapes to produce sparkling wines. (*pronounced* ha réllō)
Also called **Pansá Blanca**

Xérès *see* **Jerez-Xérès-Sherry DO**

◊ Xinomavro, Xynomavro
an important Greek red-wine grape variety grown especially in the Macedonia region in the northeast of the country (*pronounced* heénō maávrō)

Yakima Valley AVA
USA a wine-producing region in Washington State that has a cool climate and grows a range of grape varieties including Cabernet Sauvignon, Chardonnay and Merlot to produce a wide range of wine styles

Yarra Valley
Australia a wine-producing region near the city of Melbourne in the state of Victoria that is best-known for its wines produced from Chardonnay, Pinot Noir and Cabernet Sauvignon grapes

yeast
a microscopic organism that causes the fermentation process to occur. Wild yeasts are present on the skins of grapes and would start the fermentation process of grape juice naturally, converting natural sugars in the juice into alcohol, but winemakers normally add cultivated yeasts to the grape juice to provide more control over the fermentation process. Yeast cannot exist when the level of alcohol is above around 16% in wine, which is why alcohol such as brandy is added to a wine to stop fermentation and produce a fortified wine.

♀ **yeasty**
(*tasting term*) used to describe a wine, usually Champagne, that has the smell of bread dough or yeast, normally pleasant in small quantities

Yecla DO
Spain a wine-producing DO area in eastern Spain that is best-known for its highly alcoholic red wines (up to 16% alcohol) produced from Monastrell and Grenache (Garnacha) grapes (*pronounced* yáykla)

yield
the amount of grapes that are produced by a vine or by an area of land planted with vines. A yield is normally measured in hectolitres per hectare (though in the USA and Australia it is measured in tons per acre), where one hectolitre of grapes per hectare would fill over 130 standard bottles with wine. Different grape varieties have different yields according to factors such as the size of the grape bunch, and high-yielding vines tend to produce grapes of lower quality. The yield also varies according to the soil and climate of the vineyard. In most regulated wine-producing regions such as those under the AOC system in France there are strict limits on the maximum yield for the appellation to ensure that the finished wine is of good quality.

♀ **young**
(*tasting term*) used to describe a wine that is light, fresh and fruity, or one that may be expected to develop further

Yquem *see* **d'Yquem, Château**

◊ **Yvorne**
Switzerland a good-quality white wine produced in the village of Yvorne in the Vaud canton of Switzerland, made from Chasselas grapes (*pronounced* ee váwrn)

Zentralkellerei
German a central cooperative that gets its wine or must from smaller cellars in the area and blends, produces and bottles the wines (*pronounced* tsen traál kelə rī, *plural* **Zentralkellereien**)

♀ **zesty**
(*tasting term*) used to describe an assertive, especially young wine

◊ **Zin** *abbreviation* Zinfandel (*informal*)

○ **Zinfandel**
a red grape variety that is most commonly grown in California, USA, where it now dominates the planted red-grape vine crops in the state. It is used to produce a wide range of wine styles from slightly pink (called blush) medium sweet white wines to a range of red wines that include light, fruity reds best drunk young and full-bodied reds. Zinfandel is generally considered to derive from the Primitivo grape variety from Apulia, Italy. (*pronounced* zín fand'l)

zone
1. in general use, a wine-producing area that does not usually coincide with any particular geopolitical or administrative boundary
2. in the Australian system of Geographic Indications, a zone is any area of land, not strictly defined in the way that a region or subregion is. Most Australian states are zones.

○ **Zweigelt**
a hybrid red-wine grape variety developed and grown in Austria (*pronounced* tsvī gelt)

VINTAGE CHART

Vintage charts are by their very nature dangerous things. Not only are the judgements fairly subjective, but wine, being a living thing, is constantly evolving and changing in the bottle. There will also be individual wines and producers who buck the trend. Therefore, vintage charts should be treated as no more than a snapshot of a wine or an area or country at a given moment and should be used only as a general guide.

	2001	2000	1999	1998	1997	1996	1995	1994	1993	1992	1991	1990
BORDEAUX												
Red	7	10	7	8	7	9	9	7	6	2	5	10
White Bordeaux	9	7	8	8	9	9	7	6	3	4	4	10
BURGUNDY												
Red Burgundy	7	8	9	7	8	9	8	6	8	5	8	10
White Burgundy	8	8	8	5	8	9	9	6	8	8	6	9
RHONE												
Hermitage	8	9	9	8	8	8	8	7	5	7	7	10
Chateauneuf	8	8	8	9	7	7	8	7	6	6	4	10
LOIRE	7	8	7	7	9	8	8	6	6	6	5	10
CHAMPAGNE-VINTAGE	7	7	8	8	7	9	8	5	6	6	6	10
ITALY												
Chianti etc.	8	8	9	8	10	7	8	6	8	3	6	10
Barolo/Barbaresco	9	9	9	9	9	9	8	6	6	3	6	10
SPAIN	9	8	7	7	6	7	8	9	5	7	8	7
GERMANY	9	7	7	8	9	9	9	9	7	8	6	10
USA	7	8	8	7	9	6	8	8	7	7	9	8
AUSTRALIA	8	8	8	10	8	9	6	8	6	6	9	9

Legend:
- Not ready
- Drink now
- Drink now or keep
- Past its best
- 1 = Not very good
- 10 = Excellent